S0-AWB-002

CRITICAL THINKING

PRENTICE-HALL PHILOSOPHY SERIES
Arthur E. Murphy, Ph.D., Editor

CRITICAL THINKING

Max Black • PROFESSOR OF PHILOSOPHY
CORNELL UNIVERSITY

AN INTRODUCTION TO LOGIC AND SCIENTIFIC METHOD • SECOND EDITION

PRENTICE-HALL, INC.

ENGLEWOOD CLIFFS, N. J.

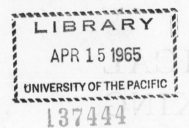

LIBRARY
APR 15 1965
UNIVERSITY OF THE PACIFIC
137444

Copyright, 1946, 1952, by PRENTICE-HALL, INC., *Englewood Cliffs, N. J. All rights reserved. No part of this book may be reproduced in any form, by mimeograph or any other means, without permission in writing from the publishers.*

Printed in the United States of America.

First printing .... *January, 1952*
Second printing .... *July, 1953*
Third printing .... *June, 1954*
Fourth printing .... *June, 1955*
Fifth printing .... *July, 1957*
Sixth printing .... *June, 1959*
Seventh printing .... *May, 1960*
Eighth printing .... *November, 1962*
Ninth printing .... *February, 1965*

19409-C

PREFACE

I have tried to make this book an argument, not a catalogue of dogmas. Its ideal reader will find himself constantly asking questions, for which he will insist on finding his *own* answers. To avoid wasting his time, I have made the fullest use of authentic illustrations from newspapers, books, and other contemporary sources.

One of the wisest things ever said about our subject is that "Logic, like whiskey, loses its beneficial effect when taken in too large doses." While bearing this constantly in mind, I have also aimed at a high level of accuracy and the inclusion of nothing that would have to be unlearnt at a more advanced level of study.

This book could never have been written without the help of the students to whom I have lectured on logic and scientific method. My chief obligations are to them.

Logic ought to be easy, interesting, and enjoyable. This book will have been successful if it helps some readers to find it so.

While the general plan of the book has been left unchanged, minor improvements of wording will be found on almost every page. Many new exercises have been added, and some old ones dropped. The "comprehension tests" have been remodelled, and there are three new appendices. I am most grateful to the many friendly critics who have taken the trouble to send me suggestions; they have helped me considerably in making this revision.

Acknowledgments

The following authors and publishers have kindly allowed the use of quotations from the publications cited.

Allen and Unwin, Ltd.: *Coral Gardens and their Magic,* by B. Malinowski.

D. Appleton-Century Company, Inc.: *Illiteracy of the Literate,* by H. R. Huse.

Arnold and Company: *Some Dogmas of Religion,* by J. McT. E. McTaggart.

Sir Ernest Barker and the *New York Times:* "The Historian Too Must Stand Trial."

Professor C. A. Baylis: an exercise from *Formal Logic* (Prentice-Hall).

The *Chicago Sun:* "Murray Bill Offers Jobs and Freedom."

Collier's Magazine: an editorial.

The Dial Press: *The Flight From Reason,* by Arnold Lunn.

E. P. Dutton & Co., Inc.: *Selected Papers on Philosophy,* by William James, and *Common Sense and its Cultivation,* by H. Hankin.

Fortune Magazine (by special permission of the editors): "The Edge of the Abyss," by Alfred Noyes.

Ginn & Co.: *Social Causation,* by R. M. MacIver.

Mr. Samuel Grafton and the *New York Post:* "Idea of Keeping Hirohito on Throne Affronts Logic."

Harcourt Brace and Company, Inc.: *A Passage to India,* by E. M. Forster, and *The Tyranny of Words,* by Stuart Chase.

Harvard University Press: *The Study of the History of Science,* by George Sarton.

Henry Holt and Company: *Liberal Education,* by Mark Van Doren.

Alfred A. Knopf, Inc.: *How New Will the Better World Be?* by Carl Becker.

The Macmillan Company: *The Case For Christianity,* by C. S. Lewis, *Science, Religion and the Future,* by C. E. Raven, and *Formal Logic,* by F. C. S. Schiller.

The New American Library: *Science and the Moral Life,* by Max Otto.

W. W. Norton and Company, Inc.: *The Scientific Outlook,* by Bertrand Russell.

Oxford University Press, Inc.: *The Essays of Montaigne,* translated by E. J. Trechmann.

Penguin Books, Ltd.: *Limitations of Science,* by J. W. N. Sullivan.

Random House, Inc.: *The Wisdom of Confucius,* ed. by Lin Yutang, and *The Male Animal,* by James Thurber and Elliott Nugent.

The editor of *Science:* Quotations from six articles.

The editor of *The Scientific Monthly:* quotations from two articles.

Sheed and Ward: a verse from *Sonnets and Verse,* by Hilaire Belloc.

Yale University Press: *The Folklore of Capitalism,* by Thurman Arnold.

Full references to the sources of the quotations will be found in the places of their occurrence in the text.

M. B.

CONTENTS

CONTENTS

PART THREE

Induction and Scientific Method

TO THE STUDENT

1. It is wise to get a general view of a chapter before studying details: read the summary at the end of each chapter *first*.

2. The "comprehension tests" at the end of each chapter can be of great help. Sometimes there is an important point of emphasis or interpretation involved which may have been missed on the first reading.

3. Many examples are discussed and analyzed in the text. To obtain full benefit, think about them and formulate your own conclusions before reading the printed comment.

4. The exercises are as important as the text. The group labeled "A" consist mainly of relatively straightforward application of method or doctrine. The remainder, headed "B," often raise critical questions about the doctrine of the chapters to which they are attached.

5. The use of words in precise senses is of the greatest importance in critical thinking: be sure you have mastered the technical terms. For your convenience, they are printed in boldface type on their first appearance, and definitions are assembled in the glossary.

6. The three parts of the book can be studied in relative independence of each other, but you are advised to read Part Three last.

CRITICAL THINKING

PART ONE

Deductive Logic

I

INTRODUCTION: THE AIMS OF LOGIC

It is foolish to study logic unless one is persuaded that one's own reasonings are more or less bad.
—C. S. Peirce.

LOGIC can be briefly defined as the study of reasoning. The study of any subject calls for thought, and every student is, or ought to be, a thinker; but he is not a student of logic unless he thinks about reasoning. Now reasoning is itself a special kind of thinking; hence the special kind of study known as logic is concerned with thinking about thinking.

These remarks will become more illuminating as we become clearer about the differences between reasoning and other types of thinking.

What is reasoning? A group of people waiting to be interviewed were once asked by a psychologist to answer the question, "What were you thinking about when the clock struck just now?" Among the answers received were these:

1. "I was wondering whether I would get the job."
2. "I was trying to remember what book I had to buy for the course."
3. "I was hesitating whether to wait any longer."
4. "I really can't say—I suppose I was just wool-gathering."
5. "My young brother asked me this morning how a heavy airplane could float in air—I was trying to figure out the answer."

All of these people were thinking, but only the last was engaged in reasoning. If he could have been made to think aloud, the following monologue might have been heard:

Nothing can float in a liquid or gas that is lighter than itself—that's certain. Yet an airplane *is* heavier than air—it's even *called* a "heavier-than-air machine" sometimes. (There's no problem with a balloon—it simply floats.) There must be some extra supporting force—an *upward* force. Where does it come from? Could it be the propeller? But doesn't it drive air *parallel* to the wings? Yes—that's it—the air current could still press *upward* on the plane.

The distinctive feature of this type of thinking is the use of *reasons:* Something known or believed to be true is repeatedly used in order to arrive at other supposed truths. The thinker knows (or believes) that airplanes are heavier than air, that a body cannot float in a gas lighter than itself, that the propellers drive a current of air past the wings of a plane, and so on. By using these items of information he is trying *to prove* that airplanes can stay aloft: he is engaged in a search for *evidence*. He is not, in this instance, much interested in the undoubted fact that airplanes do manage to fly, *considered as a fact in itself;* his puzzle is to square this known fact with other items of knowledge; he wants to find a set of facts from which it would *follow* that airplanes can fly.

The key words used in the last paragraph—'reasons,' 'to prove,' 'evidence,' 'follow'—all point to a certain kind of connection that sometimes holds between items of information. It sometimes happens that if the items of information A, B, and C are true, then another item of information, D, will also be true. We then say A, B, and C, are reasons for D; or D can be proved by means of A, B, and C; or they are evidence for D; or D follows from them. Whenever a man uses or searches for this type of relation between possible truths, he is said to be reasoning.

The answers to the psychologist's question, mentioned on the preceding page, illustrate the fact that not all thinking is reasoning in the sense explained. Among the mental activities referred to as "thinking" are guessing (answer 1), attempting to remember (answer 2), making up one's mind (answer 3), or daydreaming (answer 4). Nor does this exhaust the variety of activities properly called cases of thinking: a man listening to music is comparing and relating his experiences—is actively thinking. But none of these instances involve reasoning, since they do not involve *the use of supposed truths as evidence in support of other supposed truths.*

The importance of reasoning. In selecting reasoning for special study, the logician is not belittling the types of thinking he finds it convenient to neglect. His readiness to devote laborious hours to a study of reasoning does, however, imply a belief in the importance of the study. Should this belief be challenged, it would be sufficient to point to a number of familiar facts from everyday experience. It is a common and exasperating experience to be "in possession of the facts" without being able "to see what they mean": a doctor may observe a patient's symptoms without being able to diagnose the disease, a detective may have any number of clues and yet be helpless to appreciate their significance, a businessman may know he is losing money without being able to find a solution to his perplexities. One cure for such predicaments and the lesser problems encountered every day is reasoning. Indeed, we have only to consider the moronic behavior of a man unable "to put two and two together" in order to appreciate the importance of this activity. A man unable to reason would be restricted to the most superficial of external appearances; he would have no reason to believe that water was wet, or milk nourishing. Unable to learn from experience, he would be at the mercy of instinct and unreasoning habit. Capacity to reason is an essential ingredient in intelligence.

The tasks of logic. When the importance of reasoning is appreciated, it is natural to seek ways to improve the practice of reasoning. All men who are not imbeciles are able to reason with some degree of skill. Unless their reasoning prevented them from systematic belief in absurdities, they could hardly survive in a world not designed to provide an easy life for the stupid. But one may reason without being able to do so as well as could be desired. Reasoning is as natural and familiar a process as breathing, but it is also a skill in which indefinite improvement is possible for anybody who is not a genius. This book is not addressed to geniuses.

If logic is studied primarily as a means of improving skill in reasoning, it is natural to think of it as an *art,* like cooking, architecture, or swimming. From this standpoint, the interest in studying logic is the practical one of self-improvement: knowledge of logical principles and methods is sought not for its own sake so much as for its use in the betterment of reasoning. (The student may then think of himself as a kind of athlete, intent on improving his capacity to reason by the right kind of training and discipline). Logic may indeed be regarded as the *art* of proceeding correctly from truths to new truths.

But if logic is an art, it is also a *science.* Every art makes use of knowledge: the painter must know the properties of pigments and canvas, though such knowledge is not enough to make him a good painter; the reasoner must know what is *in fact* evidence, though such knowledge is insufficient to make him a skillful reasoner. Logic, therefore, may also be studied in as dispassionate a spirit as mathematics. The mathematician is wise to forget that he has a practical interest in using mathematics, for in this way he gets a firmer grasp of the objective relations between mathematical entities. The logician also often approaches his subject in the same spirit of detachment, anxious to understand first, so that his understanding may eventually enlighten and animate his practice.

A satisfactory approach to logic requires a proper balance between its practical and theoretical aspects. The student should regard himself as an artist, constantly developing his own power to reason. He should think of himself also as a scientist, seeking to uncover those truths of logic that are independent of his wishes and desires, and to which all his aspirations to be reasonable and intelligent must conform if they are to be fruitful.

Logic as criticism. The kind of thinking about thinking that it is the aim of logic to cultivate is a special kind—systematic, persistent, and, above all, *critical.* The word "critical" is often used to mean censure or faultfinding, as when a woman begs her husband to be less "critical" of her cooking. A film critic is not, however, expected to find fault with every film he sees, or held to be untrue to his profession when he breaks into applause.

Criticism, in this more generous sense, may result in praise or blame indifferently. And if we consider what is expected of the best kind of criticism—whether of cooking, films, or anything else—we see that judgment of praise or blame is but a small part of the business of a critic. A critic who practices his profession effectively is able to give reasons for his favorable or adverse judgments. Through wide knowledge of the subject under criticism, and long experience in comparing and relating examples of the art in question, he is able to see connections that are not obvious to inspection. A well-trained critic of music "understands what it is all about." He is in a position to appreciate what the performer was trying to achieve, how successful he was in overcoming the particular limitations and difficulties of the instrument, and so on. The critic's judgment of the value of a piece of music (or an omelet, or a piece of reasoning) is grounded in knowledge of principles and standards appropriate to the subject matter. And perhaps the greatest service that a critic can do those who wish to learn from criticism is to make explicit, if he can, the *reasons why* he approves or disapproves. Criticism, in this generous and educative sense, is the same as the *exhibition and defense of principles and standards.*

In the light of all this, our discussion of the aims of logic can be summarized by saying that *logic is the art and science of criticism of reasoning.*

The logician searches for *standards* of reasoning. To be in a position to improve reasoning means to be in a position to distinguish good reasoning from bad. A man who judges cattle has some specifications before him (often in a very precise form) of what constitutes a good specimen of the breed he is judging. A thinker who tries to improve his thinking must, likewise, have in mind some standard for discriminating good thinking from bad.

To express the matter in another way, the art of logic, like all arts, involves the use of *ideals*. It is possible, of course, to improve thinking without having any clear notions of what standards one is using, just as a reader may know what books he prefers without having any clear ideas of what tests he actually applies. But some standards must be involved if the discrimination of good from bad is not to be wholly capricious. Since logic involves the use of standards, it is sometimes called "normative," and the words "norm," "standard," and "ideal" have approximately the same meaning.

The logician searches for *principles* of reasoning. One of the ideals pursued by the logician is that of objectivity: he wants to certify chains of reasoning as "right" or "good" because they do in fact invariably yield truths and not falsehoods. He is therefore led to seek objective rules that determine when this condition is satisfied. To take the simplest illustration, he finds that a statement can be either true or false but not both: this is a (very simple) principle concerning truth, and it is an *objective* principle because its truth is independent of human desires or judgments. A statement *is* either true or false (but not both) whether we like it or not.

A logician's standards or ideals show how he means to exercise his freedom as a creative artist: truth, freedom from contradiction, clarity of discourse, are what he prizes, is free to pursue, and intends to achieve. A logician's principles show how his freedom to pursue his ideals is limited by the nature of things. Believing that consistency and the other logical ideals are desirable, he formulates the conditions that must be satisfied if the ideals are to be attained.

Standards are normative, principles factual; yet both alike are *general*. It is the essence of a standard that it should have *general application*. A judge of cattle who could determine the merits only of a bull belonging to his own herd would be of no help in a cattle show, and a logician who could decide whether Hitler's reasoning was good or bad without being able to apply the same standards to other cases would not have traveled far along the road to the critical understanding of right reasoning. The aim of logic is to discover standards that will apply to as many cases as possible.

In so doing, it is necessary to discover the general respects in which cases of good reasoning are alike, *i.e.*, the principles governing such cases. And it is obvious that such principles will be of interest and use in proportion to the generality of their scope. The logician is a connoisseur of generality, an admirer of the universal formula, an enemy of the exceptional case.

How far these handsome ambitions can be realized, only an examination of the fruits of logic will determine. But the patient inquirer need not be disappointed. Logic makes considerable demands upon its followers: it calls for close attention to detail and a capacity to enjoy strenuous mental activity. But logicians have not labored altogether in vain, and their achievements are not the least of man's mental conquests. To those who wish to think better, logic can be moderately useful; to those who know the pleasures of critical thought, it can provide a special enjoyment that is its own justification.

Summary

Logic is a study of reasoning. Reasoning is a special type of thinking, the latter term being commonly used to refer to almost any type of mental activity. Since all study requires thought, logic calls for thinking about thinking. Reasoning is an attempt to pass from certain items of information (or "supposed truths") to others for which they are *evidence*. Other terms used to refer to the connections between two such sets of items are "proof," "following," and "reason." The importance of reasoning arises from its use in "learning from experience" and other modes of intelligent behavior.

Logic may be thought of as the *art* of improving reasoning, and the *science* of the conditions to which this art must conform; it therefore serves the practical interest of self-betterment and the theoretical interest of understanding. Logic aims at the cultivation of the art and science of the *criticism* of reasoning. "Criticism" is intended to mean here the exhibition of *standards* and *principles.* The logician pursues certain ideals, and wishes to understand the objective conditions that have to be satisfied if those ideals are to be attained. The search for principles and standards of reasoning leads the logician to set a special value on *generality.*

Comprehension test

Note: This and the succeeding "comprehension tests" provided at the end of each chapter are intended to supply the reader with a check on his understanding of the text. Answers are provided in Appendix 6. Do not guess; items that cannot positively be identified as true or *partly* false should be omitted. Grade the performance by subtracting the number marked wrong from the number marked right. Thus if 7 were answered correctly, 2 incorrectly, and 1 omitted, the score would be 7 minus 2, or 5. The reader should aim at scoring at least 6 on each test.

1. Remembering is a special kind of thinking. (*true* *false*)
2. Nothing can be both praised and criticized at the same time. (*true* *false*)
3. Since logic is an art, the logician produces things of beauty. (*true* *false*)
4. Psychology is not a normative science. (*true* *false*)
5. Anybody who offers evidence for something is reasoning. (*true* *false*)
6. Since an ideal is something imaginary, it cannot influence behavior. (*true* *false*)
7. To discriminate good from bad is to use a standard. (*true* *false*)
8. Consistency is one of the ideals of logic. (*true* *false*)
9. Logic is an art, not a science. (*true* *false*)
10. The principles sought by logicians are such as are true for all thinkers. (*true* *false*)

Exercises in reasoning, 1st series

Note: The following puzzles and problems (mainly original) illustrate various aspects of the reasoning process. The methods used in their solution should be carefully noted in preparation for later work. Suggestions for solution will be found in Appendix 5 and a further series of such problems on page 156.

1. "The Fans have so primitive a language that they cannot converse unless they can make accompanying gestures. I have often heard them say 'We will go to the fire so we can see what they say' when any question had to be decided after dark." Is there any reason to doubt this account? (From Mary H. Kingsley, *Travels in West Africa* (1897), p. 504, adapted.)
2. "When a country has a 'favorable balance of trade' it is exporting more than it is importing, and therefore giving away the balance to its customers. Hence a nation ought to aim at getting an *unfavorable* balance of trade." Do you agree?
3. Assume (1) that there are at least 150 million living Americans, (2) that every human being has less than a million hairs on his head. Prove that at least 150 living Americans have exactly the same number of hairs on their heads.
4. An investigator interviewing a number of people for the Gallup Poll reported that he had spoken to 100 persons, of whom 70 were white, 10 were women and five were colored men. Why did he lose his job?
5. It is found that 99 per cent of people who smoke have bad teeth. Does this show that smoking is bad for the teeth?
6. Brave men tell only truths; cowards tell only lies. Three men meet on the street. The first speaks to the second, who turns to the third, saying, "He says he is a brave man. And he is." The third replies, "He is not a brave man. He is a coward." How many brave men and how many cowards are present?
7. There are three musicians: a violinist, a cellist, and a pianist. Each is the father of a grown son. The sons' names are Brown, Town, and Gown. The cellist and Town, Jr. are six feet tall. The pianist is five feet tall. Gown, Jr. is six inches shorter than Town, Jr. The violinist is five feet nine. The violinist has exactly one third as many phonograph records as that man (among the other five) who is nearest his own height. The pianist's son has 313 orchestral records and 409 vocal records. Brown, Jr.'s father has more false teeth than the cellist. What is the name of the violinist?
8. The game of Contact is played in the following manner: Both players have an inexhaustible supply of pennies. The first player places a penny on an empty table. The second player then places a penny without touching the penny already in position. The game then continues in the same fashion until one of the players is unable to deposit a coin without touching a coin already in position. Describe a method by which the first player can be certain to win.

9. A man, having mowed his lawn, has arranged the cut grass in four equal heaps along a north-south line down the middle of the lawn. He has a basket that will hold all the grass and is standing by the garbage can, immediately south of the heaps. Which method of collecting the grass will require the least expenditure of effort?
10. A certain bedroom has an electric light switch (A) by the door, and another (B) beside the bed. When the light is shining, it may be extinguished either at A or at B. But the light cannot be restored unless both A and B are in the "on" position. A man enters the room in complete darkness. Describe the most intelligent procedure for turning on the light.
11. A father wished to leave his fortune to the most intelligent of his three sons. He said to them: "I shall presently take each one of you away separately and paint either a white or a blue mark on each of your foreheads and none of you will have any chance to know the color of the mark on his own head. Then I shall bring you together again, and anybody who is able to see two blue marks on the heads of his companions is to laugh. The first of you to *deduce* his own color is to raise his hand, and on convincing me that his solution is correct, will become my heir." After all three had agreed to the conditions, the father took them apart and painted a *white* mark on each forehead. When they met again, there was silence for some time, at the end of which the youngest brother raised his hand, saying "I'm white." How was he able to deduce the color of the mark on his forehead?
12. Fair shares. When two children have to share a cake, they sometimes agree that one shall cut and the other choose the piece he prefers. State the assumptions underlying this procedure. How could the procedure be generalized for the case of three children? Or, more generally, for the case of n children?
13. Mr. Buick, Mr. Chrysler, and Mr. Ford owned a Buick, a Chrysler, and a Ford (not necessarily in that order). Buick often borrowed the Ford. The Chrysler's owner often beat Ford at cards. Ford was the brother-in-law of the Buick's owner. Chrysler had more children than the Chrysler's owner. *Who owned the Buick?*

2

DEDUCTION AND INFORMAL ARGUMENT

We know well that a fallacy that would be obvious to all in a three-line syllogism may deceive the elect in 400 pages of crowded fact and argument. . . . I think it is a useful exercise for any of us . . . to reduce any book of whose conclusions we are doubtful into a set of formal syllogisms and lay bare the bones of the argument.—Josiah Stamp.

1. How deduction is used in reasoning.

IN the first chapter it was explained that logic is confined to a study of the special kind of thinking known as reasoning. We said that reasoning was characterized by the search for evidence --that is to say, for items of information that can be made to yield new items of information.

We have now to recognize that what is commonly called reasoning is a complex affair. By examining an authentic example of reasoning we shall be able to isolate one aspect of it, known as *deduction*. Having done this, we shall be ready to get clearer ideas about what is involved in reasoning, and what principles are needed for its criticism.

An example of reasoning:

THE PROBLEM OF THE ALARM CLOCK

(The following account was supplied by a student in answer to a request for authentic experiences involving the use of reasoning.)

This semester it is necessary that I get up at 6:00 A.M. every morning. I was faced with the problem of how to waken at this time, at the beginning of the semester. Last semester my roommate called me every morning to get me up, but my roommate doesn't get up until 7:00. No one else in the house gets up at 6:00 regularly.

I borrowed an alarm clock from one of my friends, and thought my problem solved. However, I had a nightmare that night, and at about 3:00 I knocked the clock off of my bed accidentally. Of course, the clock could not stand much of this treatment, so the next night I put the alarm clock under my pillow. Even though I got some sleep in spite of the noise under my ear, the alarm did not go off at 6:00, for the little key on the reverse side that I wound the alarm with could not turn because it was pressed on the bed too hard under the weight of my head. I got up at 7:00.

The next day, I went to the dormitory and built a little shelf on the wall (which was in arm's reach from my bed), and that night I set my alarm clock on the shelf. The alarm went off at 6:00 and I got up on time.

The sequence of connected thoughts and actions here reported was certainly reasonable. And it would be commonly agreed that the person concerned was *reasoning* in the course of the events described. While the solution of the "Problem of the Alarm Clock" did not require an exceptional amount of intelligence and reasoning power, examination shows that the behavior reported involved considerable complexity and called for the use of several mental faculties in successful co-ordination.

Among other things, it was necessary to *make relevant observations* (*e.g.*, that the key on the alarm clock had failed to turn during the night), *to remember relevant experiences* (*e.g.*, that of having been told that "no one else in the house gets up at 6:00 regularly"), and to *test plausible solutions* (*e.g.*, that of putting the clock under the pillow). Inability to perform any of these processes adequately would have prevented the discovery of a solution. We shall be particularly concerned with another procedure not yet mentioned whose use was also essential to the solution.

When the girl in question *saw* that "the little key on the reverse side . . . could not turn" she knew that it "could not turn *because* it was pressed on the bed too hard under the weight of my head." How did she know this? She did not see, or remember, or find by trial, that the bed's pressure had prevented the key from turning. The obvious answer is, of course, that she "reasoned it out" or knew it *by means of an argument.* (The use of the word "because" sufficiently shows this.)

Let us try to make this particular fragment of reasoning plainer. If the girl had been asked, "*How* did you know that the bed's pressure prevented the key from turning?" she might well have replied, "Because I know that nothing else could have prevented it."

The argument would then run:

(A) Nothing but the bed's pressure prevented the key from turning (*reason*).

Therefore: The key was prevented from moving by the bed's pressure (*statement to be proved*).

We notice that here something believed to be true (the reason) is used as a way of arriving at some other supposed truth, *without independent investigation of the latter.* If the girl knew that "nothing but the bed's pressure prevented the key from turning," she did not need to *look* at the bed or the clock; *thinking alone* showed that it was reasonable for her to accept the statement to be proved, or as we shall now say, the **conclusion.** We shall call the process by which a supposed truth or truths (the reasons) are used to obtain another truth (the conclusion) by thinking alone, without independent investigation of the truth of the conclusion, an inference.

When we are justified in making an inference, there must be some relation between the reasons and the conclusion. In such cases we can truly say the conclusion **follows from** the reasons.

It is easily seen that a large number of inferences were made in the course of solving the Problem of the Alarm Clock. Here are a few of them (to which the reader should add any others he can discover):

(B) No one else in the house gets up regularly at 6:00.
Therefore: No one in the house will call me regularly at 6:00.

(C) I knocked the clock off my bed last night.
Therefore: I shall probably knock the clock off my bed on other nights.

(D) The clock went off at 6:00 when left on the shelf last night.
Therefore: It will go off regularly at 6:00 on other mornings.

These and other inferences that occurred by no means constituted the whole of the train of intelligent behavior reported, but they were a very important factor in its success. For they made it possible to use beliefs obtained by observation or memory in such a way as to produce justified *new* beliefs.

It is important to notice that in each of the inferences so far listed a *complete* justification of the conclusion would call for further reasons to be presented. Let us check this assertion against inference (A). We accept, for the sake of argument, the truth of the reason offered, viz.:

Nothing but the bed's pressure prevented the key from turning.

If *no more were known than this,* we should not even know that the key *was* prevented from turning; nor should we have been told that anything at all prevented the motion. If, however, we add two assumptions to the original reason, we get the following argument:

(AA) Nothing but the bed's pressure prevented the key from turning.
The key did not turn.
Something prevented the key from turning.
Therefore: The key was prevented from turning by the bed's pressure.

This inference, unlike the original, (A), is *conclusive.* For anybody who understands the words used can see *without appeal to any information except that given in the reasons* that the conclusion is justified. *If* the reasons were true, it would be *impossible* for the conclusion not to be true.

The reader should check that none of the inferences (B), (C), and (D) are conclusive; and should attempt to supply the additional assumptions that would make them so.

An inference that purports to be conclusive is said to be **deductive,** and such an inference is known as a **deduction.** (Notice, however, that in every day life the latter term may also be used to cover *any* kind of inference.) Deductive inferences need not arise in the course of solving some problem, as in the examples so far used. Whenever reasons are offered in conclusive justification of a statement, we have a case of deduction. This may happen when we are trying to change somebody's opinions, to test the soundness of our own convictions, and in many other connections.

Nothing so far said is intended to suggest that deduction is superior to other forms of inference. Indeed we shall see in the third part of this book that scientific method leans very heavily on *non*-deductive inferences.

2. *The elements of a deductive argument.*

Our first task is to discover the kind of things out of which a deductive argument is constructed. Let us consider a concrete example:

Whales are mammals. (1)
All mammals suckle their young. (2)
Therefore: Whales suckle their young. (3)

This very simple example illustrates certain important features common to all arguments. In the first place, the argument is a *complex* thing, having three parts in its make-up. Furthermore, we commonly distinguish these parts: we say that (1) and (2) taken together are *evidence for* (3), while we should not say that (3) is presented as evidence for (1) and (2). The parts of the argument are therefore *arranged* in a certain way, shown by the order in which the sentences are written, and by the use of the word "therefore." The argument:

Whales are mammals. (4)
Whales suckle their young. (5)
Therefore: All mammals suckle their young. (6)

is clearly a new one, even though it has exactly the same parts as the first example. (Thus the first argument would be recognized without hesitation to be "good" or "sound"; while the second can be seen just as readily to be "bad" or "unsound.")

But what, exactly, are these "parts" or elements out of which an argument is constructed? Let us say, for the time being, that they are *statements*.

Sentences and propositions. In examining specimens of argument hitherto, we have had on the paper before us certain *sentences,* and we might be tempted to suppose that the argument is composed of these sentences. But a little thought will show that this is wrong.

As logicians or critics of reasoning, we are interested in words or sentences in so far as they are used to express *thoughts* that might be true. Our interest is in right thinking and so in the best ways of arriving at truth; we leave concern with language for its own sake to the linguist or grammarian. We especially want to know, in such cases as those illustrated by our specimen arguments, whether anyone who believed (1) and (2) would be justified in believing (3); and, again, why anyone who believed (4) and (5) would not be justified, on that evidence alone, in believing (6).

Now the very same *thought* that is expressed by the sentence (1) could be just as well expressed by the sentence,

Everything that is a whale is a mammal. (1A)

but (1A) is certainly a different *sentence* from (1), though substitution of it for (1) in the first argument would clearly make no difference to the correctness of the process of thought. And again, the very same process of thought expressed by the sentences (1), (2), and (3), could be expressed by translating all three sentences into French or any other language. Since we are not interested in the particular words used, it would be better to say the elements of an argument are thoughts of a certain kind. But this is still vague. (For as we saw earlier, the word "thought" is ambiguous.)

Rather than speak of "thoughts of a certain kind," the logician prefers to use the technical term **proposition.** We shall not try to give an exact definition of this term; it will be sufficient for our purpose if we learn to use it correctly.

The following four points should be enough to make this possible:

1. Whenever we know, believe, doubt, or disbelieve something, whatever it is that we are knowing, believing, doubting, or disbelieving is a proposition. (Thus when I believe that pain is an evil, *what* I believe, *i.e., that pain is an evil,* is a proposition.)
2. If something *could* be either true or false, that thing is a proposition, and every proposition must be either true or false. (Thus if someone says, "That's a lie," I know that the person to whom he has objected must have asserted a proposition. For a question of *truth* has been raised.)
3. A proposition can be *expressed* in a sentence (and, as we have seen, the same proposition can be expressed by several sentences). Not every sentence, however, will serve as the expression of a proposition: "Shut the door," and "If only it were Monday" will not; nor will "Smith is at home" express a proposition unless we are told who Smith is. (If in doubt whether a sentence expresses a proposition or not, use the previous condition (2), *e.g.,* try asking whether "Shut the door" is *true.*) In general, sentences in the interrogative or the imperative (questions, commands or prayers) will not express propositions; nor will sentences that need to be supplemented in order to say something definitely true or false.
4. If John and Mary both believe that there will never be another world war, we may say that there are *two* thoughts occurring. John's thought is *his* thought, just as his toothache is *his* toothache, and Mary's thought is *her's.* John may have first believed on Monday that there will never be another world war. Mary may never have given the question any thought until John talked it over with her on the Tuesday. Nevertheless, no matter when or how often John and Mary were thinking or believing that there will never be another world war, there was always just *one* proposition before their minds.

In logic, we are not interested in the particular psychological facts as to which persons hold a certain belief, or when they hold the belief, or how strong the belief is. We pay attention rather to what a great many such beliefs have in common—*the* proposition with which they are all concerned. This notion of a single object being present to the minds of a number of persons engaged in discussing a question occurs also in everyday talk: we normally say that the parties to a debate are arguing about the *same* "proposition," even though each of the debaters has his own thoughts and degree of belief with regard to the proposition under debate.

3. The mutual relation of the elements of an argument.

We have seen that the elements out of which that complex object we call an argument is constructed are statements (or, more technically, *propositions*); and we have noticed that the propositions are arranged or *related* to one another in a certain way. We must now try to become somewhat clearer about the nature of the arrangement or relation that is involved.

It is obvious enough that some of the propositions that occur in an argument are *used,* in order to *obtain* another. Thus in the first argument taken as an example in the last section, propositions (1) and (2) were *used* in order to *get* (3). We are familiar with similar situations in other fields: We can use letters to construct a word; or flour, yeast, and water to make bread; or oxygen and hydrogen to produce water. In each case we have certain *materials* and a certain *product*. Similarly, in the case of our argument, we may look on the propositions (1) and (2) as the materials, and the proposition (3) as the product.

The technical terms used to mark this distinction between the materials and the product of an argument are **premise** and **conclusion.** Thus (1) and (2) are premises and (3) is the conclusion. The term *premise* is closely connected in meaning with the more familiar word *evidence:* the evidence for a proposition consists in the premises of an argument, of which the statement for which they are the evidence is the conclusion.

We have said that the conclusion is constructed out of, or is produced from, or is a product of, the premises. But what exactly is the method by which the premises are *used* in order to obtain the conclusion? We understand sufficiently clearly how a word is constructed out of letters, or a cake out of its ingredients; but it is absurd to suggest that the premises put side by side will themselves be a conclusion, or that we must physically or chemically mix up the premises to get the conclusion. What, then, *is* the relation of premises to conclusion?

Our first task is to be sure we can recognize the relation when we meet cases of it. (After this we can proceed to think about the nature of the relation involved.)

Let us then consider a few simple examples of groups of premises and their relations to alleged conclusions:

(a) Mercury is heavier than iron, and iron is heavier than water; therefore mercury is heavier than water.

(b) Some women are fond of children, and most mothers are fond of their children; therefore some women are mothers.

(c) Webster's dictionary says that a whale is a mammal, and I trust Webster's dictionary; therefore a whale is a mammal.

(d) Lincoln was assassinated, and he was a President of the United States; therefore at least one President of the United States has been assassinated.

(e) All men are either husbands or bachelors, and no bachelor is a husband; therefore no man is both a bachelor and a husband.

(f) Most languages are difficult to learn, and most languages are taught in some American universities; therefore some things that are difficult to learn are taught in some American universities.

If you will consider carefully the premises and their relation to the conclusion in each of the above six examples, you should be able to recognize that (a), (d), (e), and (f) differ from the remaining two in a very important respect. (But try to "see" this before reading any further.) In each of the four cases, we have, or ought to have, a feeling that the conclusion is *justified* by the premises. We also commonly use such expressions as "the conclusion *must* be true" or "the conclusion really does *follow* from the premises." Each of these expressions is a way of showing that we have recognized the relation in question. It is because this relation between the premises and the conclusion is not present in cases (b) and (c), that we are able to say that each of those arguments is "incorrect."

In such cases as (a), (d), (e), and (f), *where it is impossible for the premises to be true without the conclusion also being true,* we speak of a **valid** argument. For the time being, all we can do to become more expert in the recognition of validity is to practice with many examples, trying in each case to "see" whether it would be possible for the premises to be true without the conclusion being true.

4. Making arguments explicit.

We have seen that arguments are constructed out of propositions, and that while propositions can be expressed in sentences, they are not themselves sentences. If we are not to take too narrow a view of what reasonable thinking is like, we must recognize also that reasoning can be carried on without words, and that even when words are used, it is rare to have arguments expressed in full verbal detail.

Suppose that some evening a violent thunderstorm puts out the electricity in your house. You know that you have some candles in the kitchen closet, and grope your way to it in the dark. As you rummage around the shelves, your hand suddenly comes into contact with a cold, clammy, waxy-feeling object. At that instant you know you have found the candles you were looking for. Your knowledge *could be* expressed in some such words as "*There* are the candles." But it is quite unlikely that you will actually utter such a sentence, whether aloud or "to yourself." If you make any sound at all, it will more probably be some exclamation. But whether you grunt with satisfaction, or triumphantly say "Aha!" or *say nothing at all,* you are still aware at the moment of discovery that a certain proposition is true.

Or take another example. You are crossing a deserted road in an absent-minded way, when suddenly you hear a grinding of brakes and, looking up in alarm, notice that you are in immediate danger of being run down by an automobile. Only an imbecile would stay to formulate the situation in complete sentences. If you delayed long enough to say, "This car is moving at high speed and I am in its path. If I stay where I am, I shall be hit. When a car moving at high speed hits a stationary pedestrian he is often killed. *Therefore,* unless I get out of the way quickly I stand a good chance of getting killed." —the car would soon put an end to your argument and your life. Being a reasonable person, you jump out of the way "without stopping to think." Yet *something like* the thoughts suggested "pass through your mind in a flash," as we say. At the instant you become aware of your danger, you know that certain propositions are true, and correctly see the valid conclusions that result from them, even though these propositions are not fully expressed in words.

The examples we have used are not exceptional cases. On the contrary, practically all our reasoning (apart from occasions when we are formally arguing on paper or in public) takes this telescoped form. It may be that all thinking involves the use of symbols, but we express our thoughts by a private shorthand of gestures and unfinished words very different from the standardized forms prescribed for "correct" English.

And even when we are making a deliberate effort to express an argument in a formal way, with the premises and conclusion fully detailed in complete and unambiguous sentences, we are seldom wholly successful. It is tedious to have to write out reasons in full, and we normally take a great deal for granted in ordinary communication of ideas. Such talking or writing "between the lines" lends itself to abuse, especially when used as a device to conceal the weakness of an argument; but it would be foolish to try to persuade people to talk always in the style of a mathematical demonstration.

In the light of these facts, we can see that the examples of reasoning so far used (and the stock examples whose use is customary) can be very misleading to those unaware of their limitations. The examples of argument are made artificially tidy

—the premises neatly arranged above the conclusion and separated from it by a convenient "therefore," and all the propositions carefully expressed in plain and clear language. Now the samples of reasoning we meet with in ordinary life (even those written down in scholarly and well-argued books) are by no means so orderly and complete: the conclusion may come before the premises or even be omitted altogether, vital steps may be left for us to guess or understand, the language may be far from clear, and the use of rhetorical devices appealing to emotion and prejudice may add to the general disorder. While the consideration of simplified examples is essential to the progressive and orderly study of logic on which we have embarked, we shall do well to remind ourselves of the simplifications we find ourselves making, and it will be a good thing to test our principles and standards (as and when we discover them) on specimens taken from real life. (In the same way a medical student must learn by actual practice in the hospital what corrections are needed in the simplified anatomy and physiology that he has learned in the lecture room.)

5. *Analysis of specimens of extended argument.*

We shall here discuss two samples of actual argument, in order to illustrate the kind of problem that arises when we try to criticize the way people actually reason. The first is comparatively easy, the second relatively hard.

(A) Under normal conditions, air and other gases do not conduct electricity—otherwise power lines and electrical machines would not operate in the open as they do. (*Atomic Energy for Military Purposes,* Princeton University, 1945, p. 3.)

There is little trouble here in picking out the conclusion, as given by the first eleven words of the quotation, or in stating the reasons explicitly. We obtain the analysis:

Power lines and electrical machines operate in the open. (1)
Power lines and electrical machines would not operate in the open

unless air and other gases did not conduct electricity under normal conditions. (2)

Under normal conditions air and other gases do not conduct electricity. (3)

(Notice how verbose the extended argument becomes, even in this simple instance.)

It should be easy to see that the deduction in question is *sound, i.e.,* that *if* premises (1) and (2) are true, the conclusion (3) *must* be true. In this instance we have no choice but to accept (2) as true on the authority of the physicist who wrote the report.

Now for contrast we consider a more baffling argument:

(B) It looks in fact very much as if both parties to a quarrel had in mind some kind of Law or Rule of fair play or decent behavior or morality or whatever you like to call it, about which they really agreed. And they have. If they hadn't they might, of course, fight like animals but they couldn't quarrel in the human sense of the word. Quarreling means trying to show that the other man is in the wrong. And there'd be no sense in trying to do that unless you and he had some sort of agreement as what Right and Wrong are; just as there'd be no sense in saying that a footballer had committed a foul unless there was some agreement about the rules of football. (C. S. Lewis, *The Case for Christianity,* page 3. New York: The Macmillan Company, 1943.)

In criticizing this passage, we shall find it much harder to pick out the reasons offered, and those implicitly understood though not explicitly stated. We should begin by trying to understand *what it is the author is trying to prove.* This seems to be the proposition that men who quarrel are committed to accepting some rule of morality that they hold to be binding on both of them.

Next we look for the *main reasons* offered in support of the proposition. One such reason seems to be an alleged difference between *human* quarreling and mere *animal* fighting. And a second seems to be that quarreling is an attempt to show that the other man is *in the wrong.*

Having succeeded, to our own satisfaction, in identifying the main points of the argument, we now write it out formally, separating premises from conclusion. In so doing we try to *follow the author's language as closely as possible,* deviating only when we can offer good reasons for the change.

Finally we add any *assumptions required to complete the argument.*

Following this procedure, we find the argument in question can be broken up into two deductions, having identical conclusions:

If both parties to a quarrel had no sort of agreement as to what Right and Wrong are, they could not quarrel in the human sense of the word. (4)

[Parties to a quarrel can quarrel in the human sense of the word.] (5)

Both parties to a quarrel have some sort of agreement as to what Right and Wrong are. (6)

And again:—

Quarreling (in the human sense of the word) means trying to show that the other man is in the wrong. (7)

There would be no sense in trying to show that the other man is in the wrong unless both parties to the quarrel had some sort of agreement as to what Right and Wrong are. (8)

[There is some sense in trying to show that the other man is in the wrong.] (9)

Both parties to a quarrel have some sort of agreement as to what Right and Wrong are. (10)

Here sentences (5) and (9) express assumptions that are needed for the argument, though not actually stated in the original passage. *If* these assumptions were granted, the entire argumentation would be satisfactory. But it is very difficult to see how the author would establish these crucial assumptions (or some of the other premises) except by working in a circle.

The general pattern of argument here consists in *defining* "quarreling *in the human sense of the word*" in such a way that this kind of quarreling will have the characteristics required for the rest of the argument. But the language used is question-begging. No evidence has been produced to show that disputes between humans differ in any relevant respect from "fights" between "animals."

(To see what is essentially wrong with the argument, compare the following argument in which a similar mistake is committed: "Eating in the human sense of the word means choosing a diet in accordance with accepted principles of what is healthy and unhealthy. Therefore, human beings do actually choose their diet in accordance with accepted principles of what is healthy and unhealthy.")

The last example illustrates well the type of difficulty encountered in analyzing specimens of actual argumentation from newspapers, books, or the radio. Sometimes the type of argument is complex and correspondingly hard to judge correctly. More often the pattern of argument is relatively simple, but assumptions that play an essential part in the argument are withheld from the notice of a casual reader. Thus premises that conscious examination would show to have very little value tend to be accepted without question.

The most important practical rule to be followed in criticizing specimens of argumentation from real life is *make the assumptions explicit.*

Even at this early stage in our study, it is excellent practice to try analyzing passages of argumentative prose, with the special intention of bringing concealed assumptions to light. Further work of this type is illustrated on pages 66-73.

Summary

The term "reasoning" often refers to a complex pattern of thinking and acting. A typical example of reasoning was seen to involve observation, memory, and the testing of plausible solutions of a problem. Also involved was a process of *inference,* in which a supposed truth is reached by *argument.* In an argument, a supposed truth is derived from *reasons,* without independent appeal to observation or memory; a *conclusive* argument uses no information other than that contained in the reasons to which appeal is made. An argument or inference that purports to be conclusive is said to be a *deduction.* Not all arguments are deductive.

A deductive argument is composed of elements arranged in a certain fashion. The elements are *propositions.* Propositions are expressed by sentences, but a single proposition can be formulated by a number of different sentences. Propositions can be recognized by their capacity to be either true or false and to be doubted, believed or known. In a deduction, the propositions used as evidence or reasons are technically known as *premises;* the proposition derived from the premises by means of the argument is known as the *conclusion.* In a sound deduction, the conclusion is said to *follow* from the premises. When this is the case, it is impossible for the premises to be true without the conclusion also being true.

Not all reasoning is carried on in words, but the thoughts involved in reasoning *can be* rendered explicit in the form of propositions. The arguments encountered in conversation or writing usually take much for granted. Criticism of such arguments calls for making the unstated premises or *assumptions* explicit. The method to be employed in criticizing argumentative speaking or writing was illustrated by detailed examination of two specimens.

Comprehension test

(For instructions, see page 10.)

1. "Reasoning" sometimes refers to actions as well as thoughts. (*true* *false*)
2. Every sentence expresses a proposition, but several sentences may express the same proposition. (*true* *false*)
3. Two different arguments must be constructed out of different propositions. (*true* *false*)
4. The term "proposition" has been explained but not explicitly defined in this chapter. (*true* *false*)

5. If two persons are thinking two thoughts, they must be considering two propositions. (*true* *false*)
6. If a conclusion follows from premises, it is impossible that it should be false if those premises are true. (*true* *false*)
7. A good argument must be fully explicit. (*true* *false*)
8. An argument in which the same proposition is the conclusion and also one of the premises may be a good one. (*true* *false*)
9. In analyzing samples of argumentation, it is desirable to begin by establishing the writer's conclusions. (*true* *false*)
10. All reasoning is carried on in words. (*true* *false*)

Exercises

A

1. Formulate the conclusion, given premises, and unstated premises in each of the following arguments:
   a. He must be poor—look at his clothes.
   b. Since the snow has stopped falling, we can expect a rise in temperature.
   c. The defendant was absent from the scene of the crime. He is innocent.
   d. Sovereign States can be brought into a Federal Union. The experience of the United States proves it.
   e. Lincoln's career is a living demonstration that poverty is no obstacle to real talent.
   f. If the Republicans win the next election, I am a Chinaman.
   g. As all dogs are mammals and all mammals are vertebrates, Rover must be a vertebrate.
   h. A majority of the electorate prefer a lawyer for this office, and a majority prefer a man. Therefore a majority prefer a male lawyer.
   i. The easiest way to bring prosperity to this country would be to double all wages and incomes. For then everybody would be able to buy twice as many goods.
   j. "There is no point in my buying a war bond, for a hundred dollars will make practically no difference to the billions of dollars spent on the war."
   k. "If everyone thought as you do, nobody would buy any bonds."
   l. A college education is no use. College graduates earn very little more on the average than those who have not been to college.

2. Which of the preceding arguments do you regard as sound? Explain your reasons in detail.
3. The relation between conclusion and premises is sometimes shown by use of the words "since" or "because." Make as complete a list as you can of the other devices by which this relation is sometimes indicated.
4. Are you in favor of divorce by agreement between husband and wife? Write an informal defense of your position. Examine your statement carefully and determine which assumptions you have been using. Do any of them appear questionable on examination? Compose a reasoned defense of one of the most questionable of the assumptions.
5. Choose other controversial questions and follow the same procedure.
6. Explain the differences in meaning between "reason," "reasonable," "reasoning," "rational," and "rationalization."
7. Describe some experience of your own in which you used reasoning to solve a problem. (See "The Case of the Alarm Clock" on page 13.) Show in detail what arguments were used in the course of your efforts to find a solution.
8. A man is in the habit of reaching automatically for his keys when he approaches the front door of his house *after midnight*. Is he reasoning when he does this? Give a justification of his behavior in the form of an explicit argument that he might use if challenged to defend it. Suppose the front door sometimes happens to be unlocked after midnight: Does this make the habit unreasonable? Explain.
9. Criticize the following passages according to the methods explained in section 5 of the chapter:
   a. "Psychology and physiology show the mind to be nothing but the manifestation of the working of the brain, much as the moving picture on the screen is the manifestation of the working of the picture machine, and in no way independent of it, and they show too that the picture varies according to whether the machine has a high or low blood sugar, an excess of adrenal secretion, or a hyperactive thyroid. On top of all this, Freud, one of the truly great contributors of all time, showed that this mind can be shown by scientific observation not to be under the voluntary control of its possessor at all times; its thoughts can only be developed in those patterns determined for it by its hereditary capacity to think as developed and altered by past experience and present bodily well being. The synthesis of all of this is this: the human mind is not a reasoning mechanism at all, but the manifestation of a brain which is geared to produce THAT ANSWER WHICH IS MOST COMFORTABLE TO ITS OWNER, AND TO MAKE HIM BELIEVE THAT THIS ANSWER IS THE TRUTH. In the light of this

knowledge we can see how it is that men—even the most learned and wise—cling so dearly to so many versions of the truth, and mankind advances by slow fits and starts." (From a letter from a young naval officer to his father published in *Scientific Monthly,* July, 1945.)

b. The saying that a little knowledge is a dangerous thing is, to my mind, a very dangerous adage. If knowledge is real and genuine, I do not believe that it is other than a very valuable possession, however infinitesimal its quantity may be. Indeed, if a little knowledge is dangerous, where is the man who has so much as to be out of danger? (T. H. Huxley, *Science and Education,* p. 300. New York: D. Appleton & Co., 1895.)

c. The hunted fox suffers that death to which it seems that he was devoted by nature, without any added circumstances of torture, in which his death-struggle is not prolonged as is that of the mouse beneath the cat, in order that a large number of men may enjoy a sport which is by them thought to be salutary, noble, and beneficial. . . . The objection now urged is solely that of cruelty, and is so urged as to be intended to prevail even were the advantages of hunting confessedly very great. In answer to that objection, I plead that the end justifies the mean, that a minimum of suffering produces a maximum of recreation, and that the fox's life serves as good a purpose as that of any animal which falls that men may live. (Anthony Trollope in the *Fortnightly Review,* 1869.)

d. We often talk of the dead past. But we ought also to talk of the living past. What does that mean? It means that a set of ideas about the past—and especially the past of our own country—lives in our minds; colors our minds; moves our minds; and helps to determine the way in which we think and act on the current issues of the present. In that sense, and in the form of our set ideas about it, the past still lives, and not only lives but acts. It has hands and feet. It grasps us with its hands and hurries us along in the path of its feet.

If the past thus lives and if history is a part and parcel of our mind, we must all desire that this living past should be the real and actual past, and that the history of it should be a good and true history. We none of us want to live in a lie or even in a "legend" which is sometimes only a polite word for the same sort of thing. But the matter is not altogether simple. After all, the past of a particular country belongs in a peculiar way to that particular country: and it means something particular to that country.

George Washington and Abraham Lincoln mean something particular to the United States which they cannot mean—at any rate cannot mean so much—to any other country. That particular meaning is the real and actual past for Americans; and a good and true history must record that particular meaning. That is why there must always be a national history of each country. Each nation lives in its atmosphere; and its history must be part of its atmosphere. (From "The Historian, Too, Must Stand Trial," by Sir Ernest Barker, *New York Times Magazine,* December 9, 1945.)

e. The conception of pacifism is logical if I once admit a general equality amongst peoples and human beings. For in that case what sense is there in conflict? The conception of pacifism translated into practice and applied to all spheres must gradually lead to the destruction of the competitive instinct, to the destruction of the ambition for outstanding achievement. I cannot say, in politics we will be pacifists, we reject the idea of the necessity for life to safeguard itself through conflict, but in economics we want to remain keenly competitive. If I reject the idea of conflict as such, it is of no importance that for the time being that idea is still applied in some single spheres. In the last resort political decisions are decisive and determine achievement in the single sphere. For 50 years you can build up the best economic system on the basis of the principle of achievement, for 50 years you may amass wealth, and then, in three years of mistaken political decisions you can destroy all the results of these 50 years. (From one of Hitler's speeches, translated by N. H. Baynes.)

B

1. Make an outline for an essay to be entitled "Assumptions and How to Detect Them." Illustrate your main points by examples drawn from the field of politics.
2. "How do we know that there *are* any propositions? We can't see them, or touch them, or weigh them." What answer can be made to this objection?
3. Answer the following objections:
   a. "Men want their conclusions to agree with their *prejudices*. They'll tolerate any amount of inconsistency with their premises, no matter how much you criticize."
   b. "It takes so long to criticize any important argument that if everybody were a logician no serious thinking would ever get done."
   c. In criticizing an argument, the logician is *arguing*. Should not *his*

argument *also* require criticism? Where can the chain of criticism end?

4. Explain some of the respects in which logic differs from the *psychology* of reasoning.
5. Find two important propositions in the preceding chapter that are asserted without proof. Do you think they need proof?
6. Should it be an ideal of logic to demand proof of *every* proposition before it is accepted?

3

VALIDITY AND FORM

The distinction between sound and fallacious reasoning is another of those fundamental philosophical problems which admits of no solution in terms of any formula; it is finally a matter of critical judgment.—Frank H. Knight.

1. The distinction between deductive and other types of argument.

WE have seen that it is possible to have a certain relation between the propositions composing an argument, such that the premises could not be true unless the conclusion were also true. In such a case we say that the argument is **valid.** It is also convenient to be able to call the conclusion of such an argument a valid conclusion.

The relation between premises and conclusion that we recognize by using the word "valid" is of fundamental importance to right reasoning. And cases of the relation are constantly recognized in ordinary conversation and thought, even by people who are not students of logic. Here are some of the common phrases used to refer to the relation:

This statement *follows from* those.
If such and such is true, then so and so *must be* true.
These facts are *conclusive evidence* for what we are trying to prove.

Though the three phrases italicized are common ways of indicating the presence of the basic relation of validity, they are simply other ways of naming the same relation, and tell us nothing more about its nature. If we ask ourselves *why* a certain conclusion is valid, it will be futile to reply "because it follows from the premises"; for then we are simply saying, in slightly different words, "the conclusion is valid because it is valid."

What name we give to the relation is not very important (though it will help us think clearly if we agree to use the word "valid" in preference to the other names in common use): what we need to do is to be able to recognize its presence, so we may commit fewer mistakes in reasoning than we otherwise should. In order to improve in this respect, we shall now discuss the difference between valid arguments and other "good" types of argument.

"Don't go out: it's raining and you will be bound to get wet."

Here is a scrap of conversation the like of which might often be heard. Does it express an argument—is the speaker trying to *prove* anything? The words "you will be *bound to*" suggest that the speaker *is* passing from some proposition that he claims to be true (the premise "it is raining") to another proposition that he believes to be true (the conclusion). The conclusion seems to be "You will get wet *if you go out.*" (Notice the understood condition, printed in italics, that has been *supplied.*)

So far, then, our analysis suggests that the argument has this form:

It is raining now. (1)

Therefore: If you go out you will get wet. (2)

Let us call this argument *A*.

If you were to ask ordinary people whether *A* is a good argument you would probably get a unanimous vote in its favor (unless the fact that you asked the question at all aroused suspicion of there being some "catch" somewhere). And there is no reason why we should not share this opinion. (1) is a good reason for (2) to be true. If I am in a room from which I cannot observe the state of the weather and somebody coming in from the street says "You will get wet if you go out now, *because* it is raining," it would be quite reasonable for me to accept the conclusion without asking for more evidence.

It is important, however, for our purpose, to notice very carefully that *A* is *not* a valid argument. To begin with, the conclusion mentions *getting wet,* which is not referred to in the premise; we are not *told* the connection between rain and people getting wet. Now we *know,* of course, that rain *is* wet, but the argument, *A,* if explicit, is supposed to be complete; it is intended to contain *enough* reasons to justify the conclusion. (This is part of our notion of an explicit, as distinguished from a "telescoped" or fragmentary argument.) Ought we not then to add a further premise? If we do, we might get the expanded argument:

It is raining now. (3)
[Rain is wet.] (4)
Therefore: If you go out you will get wet. (5)

We may call this argument *B.* (Here, as always, brackets show premises that have been supplied.)

But even this is not valid yet. We decided, a little while ago, that another premise should be added to *A* in order to get some reference to *getting wet* into the premises. The same line of thought consistently pursued will now lead us to add still further premises. For the conclusion mentions a person ("you"), and there is no reference to any persons in the premises of *B.* Ducks "go out" in the rain without "getting wet"—the rain slides off their backs. Let us then try a further expansion:

It is raining now. (5)
[Rain is wet.] (6)
[Persons who go out when something wet is falling get wet.] (7)
Therefore: If you go out you will get wet. (8)

which we may call argument *C.*

Have we done enough—is this argument in which our original single premise has been supplemented by two more, now *valid? Not if we confine ourselves to the reasons given.* For nothing has been said to show whether "you" are a person. And if you regard this as too obvious to mention, you will hardly think the same of the assumption that it will *still* be raining when "you" go out. These considerations might lead us to add two further premises, and to write the argument:

It is raining now. (9)
[It will still be raining when you go out.] (10)
[Rain is wet.] (11)
[Persons who go out when something wet is falling get wet.] (12)
[You are a person.] (13)

Therefore: If you go out, you will get wet. (14)

If the words, "it is raining" mean the same as "rain is falling" (as they do), this argument, *D,* is valid—a judgment that may relieve us of the fear that the type of elaboration of a simple piece of reasoning here illustrated can continue indefinitely.

Now just because the word "valid" inevitably carries with it a suggestion of rightness or goodness, there is some tendency for the logician to say that arguments *A, B,* and *C,* are all *bad*—or at least, not as good as they ought to be. This is, however, unjustified. According to the standards of common sense, even *A,* with its single premise, is a very satisfactory argument. It states the one piece of new information that is not perfectly trivial and familiar to us, the one fact that will in practice rightly lead us to believe the conclusion.

We must not, however, make the mistake of supposing that since arguments *A, B,* and *C* are satisfactory and good for all ordinary purposes, they are therefore *valid.* The notion of validity is intended to be a narrower and more precise one than that of the "goodness" or "soundness" of an argument. We use the notion of validity when we want to determine whether *stated* premises *without appeal to further knowledge* are enough to determine the truth of the conclusion.

Even (5), (6), and (7), *by themselves,* are not enough to ensure the truth of (8). Something else, the proposition (10), must also be true, whether or not we find it necessary and convenient to mention that further proposition.

The question whether an argument is sufficiently well expressed for a practical purpose must therefore be carefully distinguished from the other question whether it is valid. The latter question refers to a certain relation between premises and conclusion (that holds when the truth of the premises assures the truth of the conclusion without reference to any further evidence), which is either present or not, quite independently of our convenience in thinking or talking.

If you are still unclear concerning the difference between cases *A, B, C,* and *D,* this final comment on the example may help. Anybody who objected to the argument *A,* or *B,* or *C,* *while admitting the premises to be true* (*i.e.,* anybody who objected to the *passage* from premises to conclusion) would presumably do so because he disagreed concerning a *question of fact.* He might, for example, believe that the rain was on the point of stopping. But anybody who objected to the *valid* argument *D,* while admitting the truth of the premises, must fail to understand fully the meaning of the words used. For anybody who clearly understood the meaning of the words used in the sentences (9), (10), (11), (12) and (13), should be able to see, *even if he did not know that the premises were true,* that the conclusion (13) would necessarily be true, *if* those premises were true. While you, the reader, are now pondering argument *D,* it is very likely not raining at all. Yet by this time you can no doubt see that argument *D* is valid, in spite of the fact that you do not know all the premises to be true. Such dependence of the validity of a deductive argument on the meaning of the words used, and its independence of the actual truth or falsity of the premises, is characteristic of *all* valid arguments.

We have seen that one argument at least can be "satisfactory" without being valid. We should mention here that a great many of the arguments we use in ordinary life are not, and do not try to be, valid. An old story tells of a student who used to toss a coin each evening to determine whether to study. If the coin came down heads, he went to the movies; if it came down tails, he listened to the radio; if it stood on edge, he studied. The point of this mildly amusing anecdote (if we may allow ourselves to spoil it by comment) is the belief that tossed coins do not land on their edges. If this belief were to be challenged, an excellent way to prove it to be true would be actually to toss a number of coins. Imagine that a thousand persons tossed a thousand different coins in a variety of different ways without causing a single one to rest on its edge. Then the argument would run:

In a million different tosses of a variety of coins, tossed in a variety of ways, not one of them landed on its edge.

Therefore: A tossed coin does not land on its edge.

This is not merely a good argument, but an excellent one. But it is, nevertheless, *not valid.* For there is no logical contradiction in supposing that the premise is true and the conclusion nevertheless false; appeal to the meaning of the premise will not guarantee the truth of the conclusion.

The kind of argument in which the truth of the premises guarantees (or is intended to guarantee) the truth of the conclusion without appeal to other reasons is commonly called *deductive.* Our discussion in this section can therefore be briefly summarized by saying that not all satisfactory, or "good," or "sound" arguments are valid. A sound and fully explicit deductive argument must, however, be valid; and the study of deductive argument, while it does not coincide with the study of all good argument, is nevertheless a very important part of that study.

2. *The relations between validity and truth.*

When we were pointing out that an argument consisted of elements (propositions) arranged in a certain way (Ch. 2), we used the analogy of a cake. The ingredients of a cake must be brought into relation with each other in a certain way (mixed and baked) before a cake results; and the premises of a deductive argument must be related in the way we refer to by the use of the word "valid" before a sound argument can result.

This analogy may help us to further discoveries about validity. There are two ways in which an unskillful cook can spoil a cake—either by using bad ingredients or by putting the ingredients together in the wrong way. Wrong cooking will ruin even the best of sugar and flour; on the other hand, a good cook may do the right thing even with inferior materials. In fact, the quality of the materials, and the soundness of the methods adopted to prepare them for eating, can to a considerable extent be considered and criticized separately.

Is there anything analogous to this in deductive argument? Here the "goodness" of the material will be the truth of the premises. The soundness of the means adopted to bake the logical cake will be the same as the validity of the alleged conclusion. Is it possible then to consider separately the truth of the premises and the validity of the conclusion?

The following arguments will lead us to the right answer:

(a) Cats are animals, and all animals need food; therefore cats need food.
(b) Dogs are reptiles, and reptiles are warm-blooded; therefore dogs are warm-blooded.
(c) Fish are vegetarians, and vegetarians eat nothing but bread; therefore fish eat nothing but bread.
(d) Birds build nests, and sparrows build nests; therefore sparrows are birds.
(e) Snakes are harmful, and snakes are popular; therefore harmful things are popular.
(f) Horses are becoming stronger, and anything that becomes stronger needs more to eat; therefore horses need more to eat.

(Before you go any further, decide carefully which of these six arguments are valid.) Let us note the truth and falsity of all the propositions that have been used in these arguments, and see how these are related to the validity of the conclusion in each case. The results of this examination are shown in the following table:

Argument	*First Premise*	*Second Premise*	*Conclusion*
(a)	true	true	valid & true
(b)	false	false	valid & true
(c)	false	false	valid & false
(d)	true	true	invalid & true
(e)	false (?)	false	invalid & false
(f)	?	?	valid & ?

A careful inspection of this table will teach some important lessons about validity and its relation to truth. In the first place, *there is no direct relation between the truth and the validity of a conclusion.* A conclusion can be valid and true (a,b), valid and false (c), invalid and true (d), or invalid and false (e). A particularly interesting case is the sixth, (f), where the conclusion can be seen to be valid *even though the truth of both the conclusion and the premises is unknown.* These examples show that knowledge of the validity or invalidity of a conclusion provides no definite knowledge concerning its truth or falsity.

There is nothing surprising in this in view of the fact, already mentioned many times, that "validity" refers to a certain *relation* between the premises and the conclusion. Consider a parallel case, where mention is made of a geographical rather than a logical relation. The fact that New York is north of Miami does not of itself determine the exact geographical location of New York—so far as this one fact goes, New York might be anywhere on the earth's surface (except at the South Pole!). What the geographical fact shows is that the location of New York *depends on* the location of Miami. When the exact position of Miami is known, knowledge of the geographical relation between the two cities will in some degree determine the position of New York. (Thus, if the latitude of Miami were known to be 24 degrees N., the latitude of New York would be known to be more than 24 degrees N.)

A similar situation arises whenever we have knowledge of any kind of relation between objects. If we are told that John is taller than Mary, we know as yet nothing definite concerning

John's height; but if we should find out in some other way what Mary's height actually is, we should be in a position to determine more exactly what John's height must be.

We may expect then that knowledge of the validity of an argument reveals how the truth or falsity of the conclusion is *connected* with the truth or falsity of the premises. What is the connection?

Suppose we are told that the conclusion is valid but we have no more information concerning the truth or falsity of the propositions composing the argument. The following three possibilities are consistent with our information:

The premises are all true and the conclusion is true. (Case (a) above)
Some or all of the premises are false and the conclusion is false (Case (c) above)
Some or all of the premises are false and the conclusion is true. (Case (b) above)

(The last of these is the most surprising to beginners in logic, and you should construct other examples to convince yourself that a statement that validly follows from premises, some of which are false, is not itself necessarily false, but may be true.)

The one possibility *excluded* by our supposition that the argument is valid is: All the premises are true and the conclusion is false. For it was part of our conception of the meaning of validity that the truth of the premises should guarantee the truth of the conclusion.

Here we have the answer to our question as to the relation between premises and conclusion that is referred to by the word "validity." *A valid conclusion cannot be false when the premises are true.* It is important to remember the exact meaning of this statement; it does not mean that when some or all of the premises are false, the conclusion has to be false. *When some or all of the premises are false, knowledge of the validity of the argument gives no information concerning the truth or falsity of the conclusion.*

If you have followed this discussion, you will be ready to see how the results obtained can be used in three different, and equally important, situations:

1. We may have reason to know that certain premises are all true, and may be able to discover that a certain argument is valid. Then our information justifies us in asserting that the conclusion is *true*.

2. We may know that a certain statement validly follows from certain premises and is itself false. Then we are justified in asserting that *at least one* of the premises is false.

3. We may know that all the premises are true and an offered conclusion is false. Then we are justified in asserting that the argument is *invalid.*

These situations are, respectively, those in which we try to get new information from truths in our possession, those in which we correct assumptions, and those in which we prove that a line of reasoning is incorrect.

So far we have no methods for establishing the validity of arguments, though we have just seen how an argument may sometimes be shown to be *in*valid. The discovery of positive ways of establishing validity must await the discussion of logical form in the next section.

3. *The use of logical analogies.*

At the famous mad tea-party in *Alice in Wonderland,* Alice, it will be remembered, made a logical blunder:

"Then you should say what you mean," the March Hare went on. "I do," Alice hastily replied; "at least—at least I mean what I say—*that's the same thing,* you know."

Immediately she gets hauled over the coals by her infuriatingly logical companions:

"Not the same thing a bit!" said the Hatter. "Why, you might just as well say that 'I see what I eat' is the same thing as 'I eat what I see'!" "You might just as well say," added the March Hare, "That 'I like what I get' is the same thing as 'I get what I like'!"

And even the Dormouse, who has been asleep throughout the party, cannot miss a wonderful chance like this:

"You might just as well say," added the Dormouse, who seemed to be talking in his sleep, "that 'I breathe when I sleep' is the same thing as "I sleep when I breathe'!" "It *is* the same thing with you," said the Hatter, and here the conversation dropped.

The method used by Alice's companions to convince her of a mistake in reasoning is very useful. The crucial words "you might just as well say" give a clue to what is involved: other *analogous* pairs of propositions are used to show that the step from

I say what I mean

to

I mean what I say

is not justified.

But what is it that makes the analogies used by Alice's companions *good* analogies? Suppose Alice were to reply to the Hatter's objections: "It isn't the same thing at all. *I* wasn't talking about eating and seeing, but about saying and meaning!" Probably the Hatter would think this a sign of stupidity, and he would be right. What is important in determining the correctness of Alice's reasoning is not the nature of the particular *subject-matter,* but as we say the "shape" or "pattern" of the argument. And the Hatter, the Hare, and the Dormouse were making this logical shape or pattern obvious by bringing forward other cases, having different subject-matter but the *same shape.*

This "you-might-just-as-well-say" technique is so important in the study of logic that we shall do well to consider another example. Here is an ancient text against prohibition:

> I hear many cry when deplorable excesses happen, "Would there were no wine!" Oh, folly! Oh, madness! It is the wine that causes this abuse? No . . . If you say "Would there were no wine," because of the drunkards, they you must say, going on by degrees, "Would there were no steel," because of the murderers, "Would there were no night," because of the thieves, "Would there were no light," because of the informers, and "Would there were no women," because of adultery. (From St. John Chrysostom.)

In this argument, also, a persuasive attempt is made to show t nature of a certain *relation* (between the existence of wine ar the occurrence of drunkenness) by the use of parallel cases ha ing the same logical "shape."

The word "shape" suggests primarily the notion of *physica* shape—the shape of a house, a tree, or a knife. The elements of an argument, however, are not physical things—it is absurd to ask for the length or weight of a proposition. What then can we mean when we talk of the *logical* "shape" of a *proposition?*

4. Analysis of the meaning of "shape" or form.

Anything which has physical shape also has a certain material or stuff out of which it is constructed. In order for a pencil to have a certain shape, there must be some stuff (wood and graphite) out of which the pencil is made. Let us agree to call the pencil a **structure.** Since the pencil is made of a certain stuff arranged to have a certain shape we may write an equation:

$$\text{structure} = \text{stuff} + \text{shape}$$

(But of course the shape is not literally *added* to the stuff.) We notice that exactly the same stuff or material could be arranged in many different shapes (*e.g.,* to produce short and stubby, or long and thin pencils); and that different materials (*e.g.,* mahogany and oak) could have exactly the same shape.

It is easy to find other examples of the structure-stuff-shape equation. Thus a sonata is not just a collection of musical tones, thrown together higgledy-piggledy; the various sounds used are *arranged* in a careful and deliberate order. Here the "structure" is the whole piece of music; the "stuff" is the set of tones and rhythms used; and the "shape" is the system of melodic and harmonic relations produced by sounding the tones in the right orders and at the right times. We notice that, as in the previous example, the materials can be preserved unchanged while the shape is altered—the very same notes could be regrouped to make other tunes. The materials can be altered while the shape remains unchanged—the whole piece could be "transposed" to a different key.

Literature provides many other examples of this combination of "stuff" and "shape." When a certain poem is called a "sonnet," reference is made to a certain arrangement of the component elements. Thus there must be fourteen lines, divided into two groups; in the first group the first, fourth, fifth and eighth—and the second, third, sixth, and seventh, lines must rhyme, and so on. The definition of a sonnet gives the specification of a certain literary form. Here the materials are the words, stresses, and possibly ideas and images used by the poet; as before, the matter and the form can vary independently of one another.

It would be easy to multiply examples; for practically every object that we could imagine would turn out to be a "structure," *i.e.,* some material in a certain arrangement or form. A book, a flower, a man's character, a battle, a baseball game, a thought, a nation, are all objects in which certain materials are shaped or formed.

Indeed a little thought will show that stuff and shape, or material and form, cannot be separated except in thought. Every stuff must have *some* shape, and every shape must be the shape of *something, i.e.,* of some material or kind of material. The pair of words "shape" and "stuff" resemble such pairs as "husband" and "wife" or "north" and "south." *Two* persons must be in a certain *relation* (that of marriage) before one can be described as a husband, and so whenever there is a husband there is bound to be a wife; two positions must be in a certain geographical relation in order for one to be north of the other, and so whenever there is a north there is bound to be a south; finally, two things must be present before one of them can be described as a shape or form, and so whenever there is a form there will be some material or stuff that has that form. Words used in pairs, in this way, will be called **polar words.** (We may remember that magnetic and geographical poles come in pairs.) It is characteristic of a pair of polar words that the meaning of one of the pair involves the meaning of its partner.

You will have noticed that in the course of this discussion, we have come gradually to talk of "material" and "form," rather than "stuff" and "shape." The reason is that the latter pair of words suggest too strongly the notion of *physical* shape and *physical* material. In thinking of the more general notion, we shall, from now onwards, prefer the word "form," and our basic equation will read:

$$\text{structure} = \text{material} + \text{form}$$

If we wish to indicate the special kind of material and form that is under discussion, we use an appropriate adjective—thus we may talk of *musical, mathematical, grammatical,* or *logical* form. What distinguishes logical form from, say, musical form is the nature of the materials concerned and the nature of the relations by which those materials are related. When the materials are tones and rhythms, standing in the kind of relations referred to by the use of such words as "harmony" and "melody," we have a case of musical form; when the materials are propositions or the elements out of which propositions are made, and the relations are those that determine conditional truth and falsity, we have a case of logical form.

The great importance of logical form in the criticism of reasoning is due to the fact, with which we shall become familiar, that *the validity of deductive reasoning depends only on the logical form of reasoning.* It will therefore be necessary for us to consider how logical form can be revealed and made prominent.

5. *Methods for showing logical form.*

The first way to demonstrate form, which we have already used, is to present a variety of things (structures) having different materials but the same form. Examination of a number of different sonnets will show the characteristic arrangement of rhymes that constitutes the sonnet-form; comparison of a number of sonatas will reveal the typical division of such music into "allegro," "scherzo," "minuet," and other movements. In logic, what we called the "you-might-as-well-say" technique (#3, above) makes use of this method. Thus, we can see a common logical form in these three arguments, though the subject matter (the premise and conclusion) is different in each case:

I mean what I say, therefore I say what I mean.
I see what I eat, therefore I eat what I see.
I breathe when I sleep, therefore I sleep when I breathe.

Since the second and third arguments are cases of true premises and false conclusion, we are able to see that this *form* of argument is invalid. (This is typical of the fashion in which examination of logical form can help in the detection of invalidity and validity.)

Instead of using *formal analogies* (other structures with the same form), we can make good use of special devices for drawing attention away from the material and toward the form. An income tax statement, for instance, shows the form of the declaration that the taxpayer is to make, by supplying *fragmentary statements* that he is expected to complete. In such an entry as:

My gross income for the year . . . was . . .

the two *gaps* or *blanks* (shown by the use of dots) indicate the *form* of the statement that is required. When an individual inserts a definite date and a sum of money in the spaces supplied, he produces a specific statement having the required form. The familiar use of the word "form" to refer to income-tax declarations, and other official documents, in which spaces are left to be filled by definite items of information, may serve as a reminder of this way of exhibiting form.

The use of blanks to exhibit *logical form* can be illustrated by an example—the form of the argument:

If Harry is in Washington, he cannot attend tomorrow's meeting.
He is in Washington.

Therefore: He cannot attend tomorrow's meeting.

can be shown as:

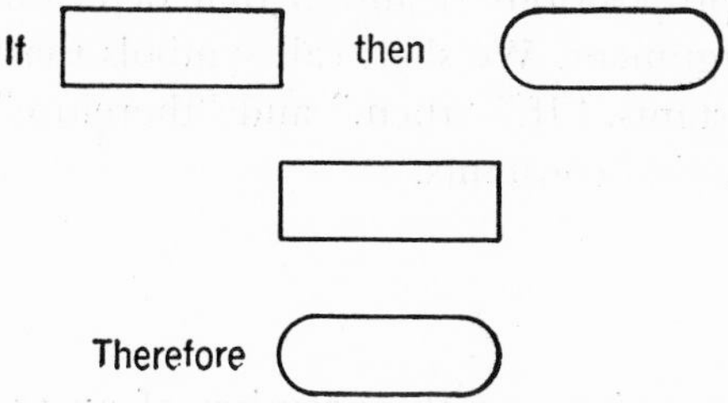

If [ ] then ( )

[ ]

Therefore ( )

Here the rectangular and oval spaces are understood to be reserved for sentences expressing *propositions.* By inserting in the spaces provided any sentences that express propositions, we can obtain any number of arguments having the same form. It should be easy to see that all these arguments are valid. (Notice carefully that the use of a rectangular blank in both the first and second lines of the argument is an indication that the same proposition is to be inserted in both places.)

Closely allied to the use of "blanks" is the use of *variables.* Instead of leaving a hole in a statement, we may agree to use special symbols which will leave those places *open* for subsequent insertion. Thus the income-tax entry might be presented as

My gross income for the year X was Y dollars.

And the argument about Harry's presence in Washington could be analyzed more concisely as:

If A then B
A
Therefore: B

It is important to notice that 'X' and 'Y', or 'A' and 'B', have no independent meaning that could be explicitly given. They are used, exactly as the "blanks" were, to show a certain form. We shall call such symbols **variables** or **place-holders.** (Other meanings of the term "variable" that are important in mathematics and the sciences will not concern us here.)

The symbols "if," "then," and "therefore" are not placeholders or variables: they indicate the *definite* logical relations between the propositions A and B that determine the logical form of the argument. We shall call symbols that have definite meanings **constants.** "If," "then," and "therefore" are our first examples of *logical* constants.

Summary

When it is impossible for the premises of an argument to be true unless the conclusion is also true, the argument is said to be *valid.* In such cases it is also convenient to say that the conclusion is valid. An argument need not be valid in order to be satisfactory for many purposes. Yet an argument that claims to offer *complete* justification of its conclusion is one that claims to be valid. Every fully explicit *deductive* argument must be valid in order to be acceptable.

There is no direct relation between the truth and the validity of a conclusion. A valid argument may have true premises and true conclusion; or false premises and false conclusion; or even false premises and true conclusion. A valid argument cannot, however, have all its premises true and its conclusion false. Three useful results follow: (1) If the premises of an argument are known to be true and the argument is known to be valid, the conclusion must be true (use of argument to obtain new information); (2) If the premises are known to be true and the conclusion known to be false, the argument must be invalid (disproof of a line of reasoning); (3) If the conclusion is known to be valid but false, at least one premise must be false (correction of unsound assumptions).

The use of logical *analogies* requires the presentation of arguments having the same *logical form.* Many objects can be regarded as composed of a *material* and a *form;* they may then be referred to as a *structure.* 'Material' and 'form' are *polar words.* If *A* and *B* are polar words, nothing can be an instance of *A* unless something else is also an instance of *B* (thus there cannot be a husband unless there is also a wife). Logical form is distinguished from musical, mathematical, or other form by the nature of logical *material*. Logical material consists of propositions (and elements of propositions); logical form consists of relations involving relative truth and falsity.

Logical form can be made prominent in three ways: (1) By presenting a variety of logical structures (arguments) having the same form in common; (2) by the use of *blanks* or gaps to produce fragmentary statements; (3) by inserting *variables* or "place-holders" into such gaps. A variable is a symbol having no meaning apart from its function of helping to indicate the form of a logical structure. Symbols having definite meanings (such as "if," "then," and "therefore") are known as *constants.*

Comprehension test

(For instructions, see page 10.)

1. Every good argument must be valid. (*true* *false*)
2. An argument having a false conclusion and true premises cannot be valid. (*true* *false*)
3. An argument may sometimes be known to be valid when the truth of its premises is not known. (*true* *false*)
4. A valid argument having false premises must have a false conclusion. (*true* *false*)
5. Validity has nothing to do with truth. (*true* *false*)
6. "Uncle" and "nephew" are polar words. (*true* *false*)
7. Appeal to logical analogies requires the use of different arguments having the same form. (*true* *false*)
8. Two arguments having identical form must be identical. (*true* *false*)
9. A variable is a place-holder. (*true* *false*)
10. A poem cannot have *logical* form. (*true* *false*)

Exercises

A

1. Which of the following arguments are valid *as presented?* (Explain what tests you are using.)

a. The sun has always risen in the past, so it will rise tomorrow.
b. Since John is a man, he must have a heart.
c. As Liberia is a republic, it must have a President.
d. All wise people are happy; therefore no unhappy people are wise.
e. Atomic bombs are so destructive that no nation can hope to fight a major war in the future without suffering severe damage.
f. Not all men reason well and not all men are educated; therefore some uneducated men do not reason well.
g. John is taller than Mary and Mary is taller than Jane. Hence John is taller than Jane.
h. Since there is no lightning without thunder, there can be no thunder without lightning.

2. Construct examples of arguments satisfying the following conditions:
a. True premises, true and valid conclusion.
b. True premises, false and invalid conclusion.
c. False premises, true and valid conclusion.

3. Criticize the following arguments by using the "you-might-as-well-say" method (page 48).
a. A man who eats meat is a murderer because he causes animals to be killed.
b. Most men drink whisky and most whisky drinkers pay taxes, so most men pay taxes.
c. There is no point in improving the condition of Negroes because they are not used to better conditions.
d. Eating oysters hasn't killed me yet. The doctor can say what he pleases!
e. We shall always have wars—human nature does not change.

4. Indicate the nature of the material and the form of the following structures:
A house; a pack of cards; a business letter; a film; a book; the 1947 Ford; the Constitution of the United States; a jury.

5. Use blanks and variables to show the logical form of arguments d, f, and g in question 1 above.

6. Which of the following symbols are variables? John Doe, Superman, the next man who telephones my home, he, somebody, X-rays, X (marking the spot where a crime was committed), X (in the formula $X = 100X cents).

7. Determine the pairs of polar words in the following list:
Parent, child; life, death; Monday, Tuesday; true, false; black, white; smoke, fire; debtor, creditor; poverty, wealth; argument, conclusion.

B

1. Criticize the following statements:
   a. "I might say (1) All physical laws are identities, (2) Maxwell's laws are physical laws, (3) therefore, Maxwell's laws are identities. The above argument is a deductive one provided (1) and (2) be stated as true." (B. Stevens, *Psychology of Physics,* Stechert, 1939, p. 48.)

   b. "The arguments by which conclusions are reached may be logically flawless. In that case, the conclusions will be what the logicians call 'hypothetically necessary.' That is to say that, granted the truth of the assumptions, the conclusions are necessarily true. If the assumptions are false the conclusions are necessarily false." (Aldous Huxley, *Proper Studies,* Doubleday, Doran, 1928, p. 23.)

2. "You admit that my premises are true and my conclusion true. Yet you object that my argument is *invalid.* Aren't you interested in getting at the truth about this matter? And haven't I succeeded in getting the truth?" Answer this argument.
3. Is it possible for a single object (structure) to have *more than one* form? Illustrate your answer by reference to examples of musical form.
4. It has been said that political rights and political duties are "polar notions." What does this mean? List some of the political rights of an American citizen; then list some of the duties automatically created by the existence of these rights.
5. a. Use a dictionary to find the etymology of the words "form," "material," and "structure."
   b. Investigate the common elements of meaning in the following italicized words or phrases:
   "he is playing *in good form*"; "*formal* dress"; "*information*"; "it is *bad form* to interrupt"; "*formula*"; "a printer's *form*"; "*form* fours."

4

CONDITIONAL ARGUMENT

I would have you realize very clearly that all discussion, all criticism, whether wise or unwise, is reasoning. The blunderers who warn you against reason are simply bad or temporarily confused reasoners. There is no getting away from reasoning, save by way of insanity, and insanity simulates the process of reasoning.—J. M. Robertson.

1. The importance of the if-then relation in reasoning.

A GOOD reasoner is a man who is able to judge correctly of the relations between *propositions.* The advice to "stick to the facts" is good so far as it goes. In order to arrive at sound conclusions that are both valid and true, it *is* necessary to use "facts" or true premises. But nobody who confined himself to drawing valid conclusions from premises that are facts would be a successful thinker.

In a situation in which we are trying to think reasonably about a practical problem, we usually have to choose between alternatives. To think reasonably about the problem means to explore in detail the *consequences* of each of these alternatives, and to choose between them in the light of these consequences. We may for instance be weighing the relative advantages of traveling to some place by train or by bus—our thinking will then be partly expressed in such propositions as "If I go by train, I will have to wait for two hours to make a connection" or "If I travel by bus, I shall find it difficult to write those letters that I want to send away."

If we were to "confine ourselves to the facts," we should be unable to formulate such statements of *connected possibilities,* for we do not *know* in advance that we shall travel by train—if it were a settled fact, it would be a waste of time to reason about it. We need, rather, to determine what *would* be the case *if* a certain possibility were realized. Our knowledge of such a connection is normally expressed by a compound proposition having the form

If A then B.

Since the truth of condition B is thereby presented as depending on the truth of condition A, we shall call propositions having the form *If A then B* **conditional** propositions. And arguments in which conditional propositions are used as premises will be called **conditional arguments.** (We shall also use "conditional argument" more loosely to refer to arguments containing premises that can be *transformed* into the "if-then" type.)

The importance of the use of conditional propositions in reasoning may be further illustrated by an interesting historical example. In the confusion of the first year of the Civil War, we find President Lincoln arguing the merits of a proposed plan of campaign in these terms:

Executive Mansion, Washington
February 3, 1862

Major-General McClellan:

My dear Sir:—

You and I have distinct and different plans for a movement of the Army of the Potomac—yours to be down the Chesapeake, up the Rappahanock to Urbana, and across land to the terminus of the railroad on the York River; mine to move directly to a point on the railroad southwest of Manassas.

If you will give me satisfactory answers to the following questions, I shall gladly yield my plans to yours.

First. Does not your plan involve a greatly larger expenditure of time and money than mine?

Second. Wherein is a victory more certain by your plan than mine?

Third. Wherein is a victory more valuable by your plan than mine?

Fourth. In fact, would it not be less valuable in this, that it would break no great line of the enemy's communications, while mine would?

Fifth. In case of disaster, would not a retreat be more difficult by your plan than mine?

Yours truly,
Abraham Lincoln

Here we have a vivid illustration of exploration of the consequences of possibilities that is characteristic of good reasoning. President Lincoln, by means of a series of five questions, invites McClellan to prove, if he can, a number of *conditional* propositions. The evidence required for a decision in favor of McClellan's plan will take the form of propositions such as "If the McClellan plan is adopted, there will be a smaller expenditure of time and money than is involved in the alternative plan," or "If the McClellan plan is adopted, victory will be more certain than if the other plan is adopted." Good reasoning in this fateful moment of American history depended partly on the ability to establish the truth of conditional propositions and perceive their connections with other propositions. Conditional propositions will be found equally important in all reasoning, whether in the most trivial decisions of everyday affairs or the most complex investigations of science and technology.

It is not the business of logic to prove the truth of specific conditional propositions about travel, the disposition of armies, or the nature of the physical world. The logician can, however, usefully concern himself with those properties of conditional arguments that are manifested in *all* subject-matters. Such a study will be concerned with the *formal* properties of conditional argument. We may hope in this way to get results applicable to all reasoning in which reference is made to conditions and consequences.

2. *Analysis of the if-then operation.*

If we are given two numbers, say 6 and 2, we can combine them in various ways to get other numbers. Thus we may get $6 + 2$, $6 - 2$, $2 \div 6$, 6×2, 2^6, 6^2, and so forth. When we study simple arithmetic, we need to refer to these different ways of combining numbers, and learn accordingly to speak of the **operations** of addition, subtraction, multiplication, and exponentiation.

If we are given two propositions rather than two numbers, we may proceed similarly to combine them in various ways to get other propositions. Thus if the propositions should be *Today is Monday* and *The weather is fine today* (which we will represent by 'M' and 'W' respectively) we can form the propositions:

If M then W
M and W
W if and only if M

and many more. In each of these, the elements are combined by a certain *logical operation,* which can be referred to by a convenient name. For the time being we are interested only in the operation indicated by the use of the words "if . . . then"; we shall refer to this operation as **implication.**

So far, we have given examples of operations on two things at a time: It is possible also to have operations that involve just one thing. Thus 5 is converted by the operation of *negation* into −5 (minus or negative five); and 8 is converted by the operation of *reciprocation* into 1/8. The most important logical operation involving a single proposition is that of **contradiction** (a kind of logical negation). The operation of contradiction converts M and W into *Today is not Monday* and *The weather is not fine today,* respectively. In general, if P is a proposition, the contradictory of P (*i.e.,* the result of applying the operation of contradiction to P) will be the proposition that is true when P is false and false when P is true.

Operations can be applied to the result of operations. Thus in arithmetic we may have $-(4 \div 3)$ or $7 \times (3 + 2)$. Let us follow the practice of arithmetic and use simple symbols for the logical operations we have named. Thus let "$A \supset B$" mean the same as "If A then B" and let "A'" mean the same as the contradictory of A (to be read aloud as "not-A"). With the help of these two simple symbols of the horseshoe and the prime we can proceed to construct all manner of complex propositions, such as $A' \supset B$, $(A' \supset B)'$, $(A \supset B)'$, $(B' \supset A)'$. (Note the use of parentheses to show the order in which the operations are performed.)

We have named the operation of implication and explained a convenient short-hand symbol by which it may be shown; we have now to learn something of its properties. A little thought will assure us that the truth or falsity of the compound proposition $S \supset H$ depends in some way upon the truth and falsity of the separate propositions, S, and H. (It is the connection between the truth and falsity of the three propositions that makes conditional propositions useful in reasoning.) But what exactly *is* the connection?

To make our ideas more definite, let us suppose that S is the proposition *The sun will shine today,* and H the proposition *I will be happy today;* and let us represent the conditional proposition, $S \supset H$, by using 'C'. Consider the answers to the following questions:

If C is true, must S necessarily be true?
If C is true, must S necessarily be false?
If C is true, must H necessarily be true?
If C is true, must H necessarily be false?

It is not hard to see that the answer to all four questions is "No!" (Thus, to take the third question, though it be true that *If the sun shines today, I will be happy,* it by no means follows that I *will* be happy today.)

Let us call S and H the **antecedent** and **consequent** respectively of the conditional proposition (from Latin words meaning that which goes before and that which follows). Then we have reached the interesting result that *Although the truth of a conditional proposition is connected with the truth and falsity of its components, the truth of the conditional proposition determines nothing with respect to the truth and falsity of the antecedent and consequent considered separately.*

The key to the understanding of this result lies in the word "separately." Let us now consider the possibilities of truth and falsity of S and H *together*. We shall have four *complex* cases: S-true-and-H-true, S-false-and-H-true, S-true-and-H-false, and S-false-and-H-false. We can show them pictorially in this way:

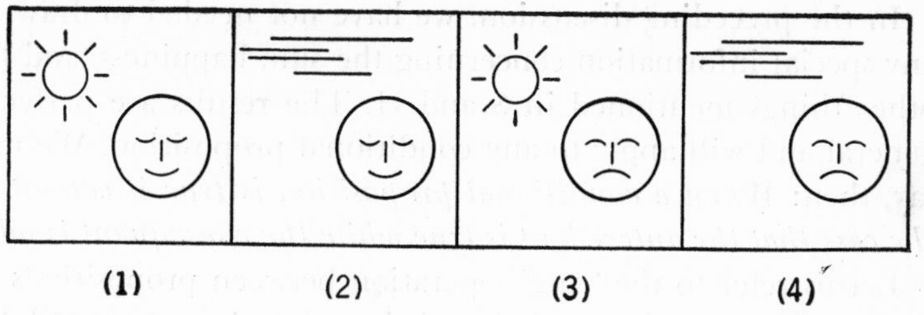

Now supposing C (or S ⊃ H) to be true: Is anything determined with respect to these four cases? First, the complex situation (1) might certainly occur; our supposition is quite consistent with the sun shining while I am happy. Next, it is equally obvious that the situation (4) might occur; the sun might not shine and I might then be unhappy. Situation (2) will require a little more thought. Supposing it to be true that if the sun shines I will be happy, could it happen that the sun should not shine and I should still be happy? The answer is, of course, "Yes." The conditional statement, C, tells what is to happen if the sun does shine—it says nothing concerning what is to happen if the sun does *not* shine: I might in that case have other reasons for being happy. Thus situation (2) also is not excluded by the truth of S ⊃ H. Finally, it is easy to see that the truth of S ⊃ H *does* rule out the occurrence of situation 3.

We have then at last arrived at an interpretation of the bearing of the truth of S ⊃ H on the truth and falsity of its components, S and H. The truth of S ⊃ H simply rules out the complex situation S-true-while-H false. This very important result can be shown pictorially thus:

When S ⊃ H is true:

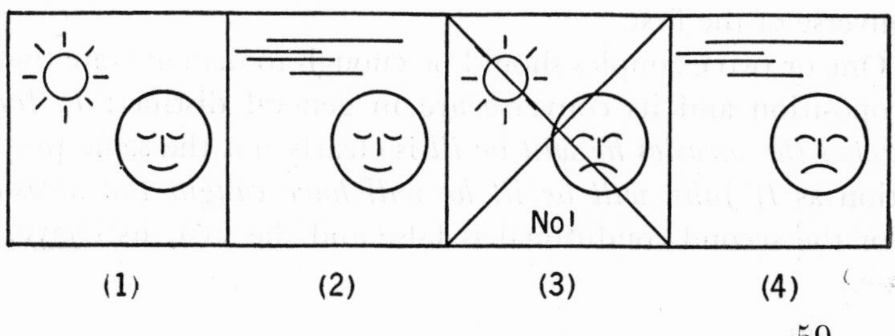

In the preceding discussion, we have not needed to draw on any special information concerning the sun, happiness, and the other things mentioned in S and H. The results are perfectly general and will apply to any conditional proposition. We may say, then: *When a conditional proposition is true it cannot be the case that the antecedent is true while the consequent is false.*

Let us refer to the "and" operation between propositions by the word **conjunction,** and show it by using the ampersand, '&'. Then the result just obtained can be concisely shown in the form:

$$\{\square \supset \bigcirc\} \supset \{\square \;\&\; \bigcirc'\}'$$

or, more concisely still, by the use of variables, as:

$$(X \supset Y) \supset (X \,\&\, Y')'$$

3. Some formal properties of implication.

The results just obtained will help us recognize certain important formal properties of implication, and thereby decide the validity of some simple conditional arguments.

In using *some* arithmetical operations, the order in which we take the numbers makes no difference to the final result: thus $2 + 6$ is the same as $6 + 2$. Other arithmetical operations yield different results according to the order in which the terms are operated on: thus $2 \div 6$ is not the same as $6 \div 2$. The logical operation of implication resembles arithmetical division in this respect: $P \supset Q$ will *not* in general be the same proposition as $Q \supset P$. We shall call the second conditional proposition the **converse** of the first.

One or two examples should be enough to demonstrate that a proposition and its converse are in general distinct: *If John catches the measles he will be ill* is clearly not the same proposition as *If John will be ill he will have caught the measles.* (For the second conditional is false and the first, its converse, true.)

Examination of the second figure shown on page 59 will confirm this result. We saw that the truth of $S \supset H$ excluded situation (3), that in which S-is-true-while-H-is-false. The arguments we used in showing this will obviously lead us to say that the truth of the converse, $H \supset S$ will require the exclusion of the situation H-is-true-while-S-is false, in other words case (2).

Confusion between a proposition and its converse is one of the commonest causes of mistakes in reasoning.

If we try to construct simple arguments in which the operation of contradiction does not occur, and implication occurs only once, we shall arrive at the following two forms:

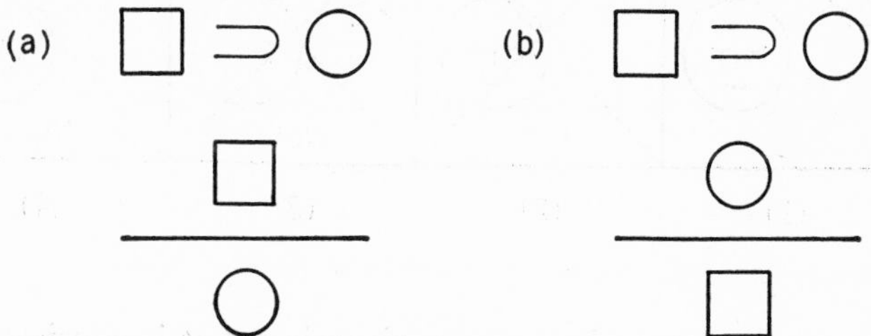

(Notice that we are now using a horizontal line, in place of the word "therefore," to separate premises from conclusion.)

Expressed with the help of variables, the two forms will be:

(a) $$\begin{array}{c} X \supset Y \\ X \\ \hline Y \end{array}$$

(b) $$\begin{array}{c} X \supset Y \\ Y \\ \hline X \end{array}$$

Suppose we insert names of the definite propositions, S (*The sun will shine today*) and H (*I will be happy today*) into these forms, so that we obtain the two *definite* arguments:

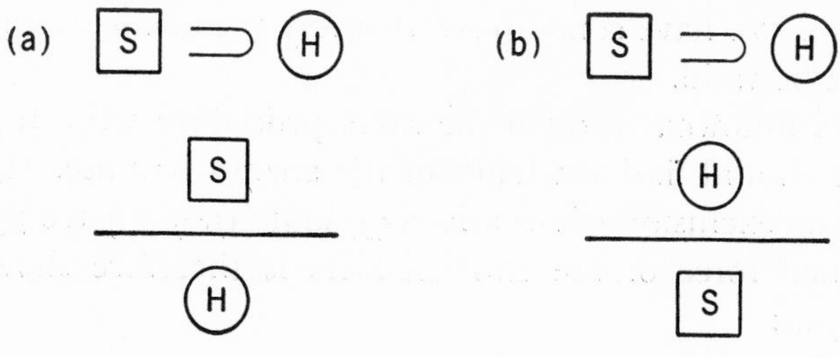

Let us represent argument (a) pictorially, again. If the first premise were true, situation (3) (see page 59) would be excluded as before. If in addition the second premise, S, were true, situations (2) and (4) would *also* be excluded; for both of these are cases in which the sun is *not* shining. Pictorially, these results are shown as follows:

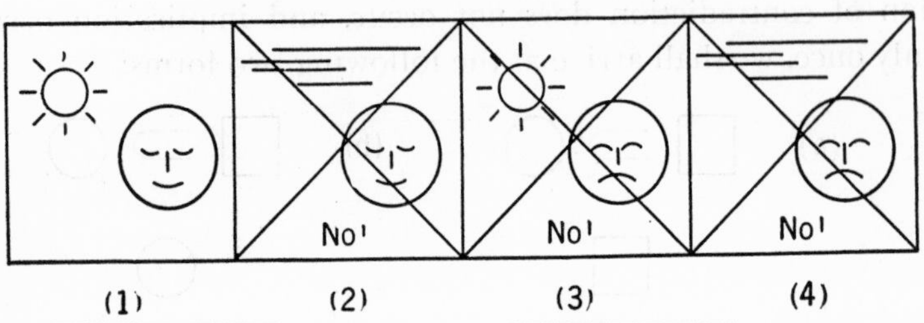

We see that there is only one situation that is consistent with the premises both being true, that in which S-is-true-and-H-is-true. But if this is the *only* situation, it is bound to occur: in other words, both S and H must be true. Half of this (S is true) we knew from our second premise; the rest, that H must be true, is new information.

This line of reasoning in no way depends on any knowledge we may have concerning sunshine, happiness, and people's reactions to them. We have used only the analysis of the notion of implication set out in the previous section, and the result would have been the same whatever propositions were inserted in the form (a). We have come to see that *any* argument having form (a) will be valid.

If we followed through the same procedure with argument (b), we should find the truth of the second premise, H, to require the exclusion of situations (3) and (4), (see page 59). The combined force of the two premises is therefore shown pictorially as:

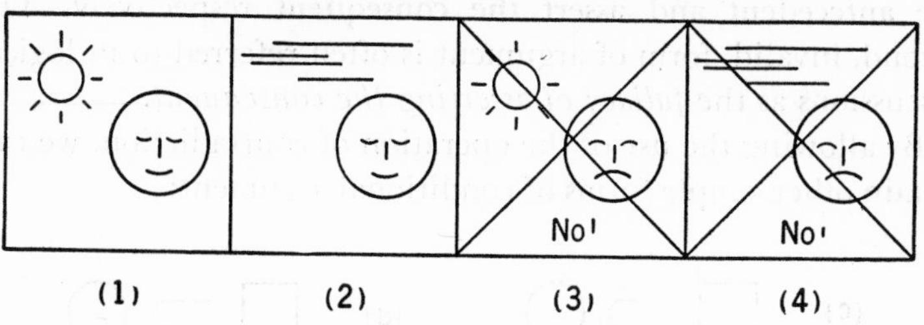

In this case we are left with the two situations, S-is-true-while-H-is-true (1), and S-is-false-while-H-is-true, (2). What information do we have, when both premises are true? First, that H is true (in both remaining situations); but this we knew already from the second premise; secondly, that S is either true or false. We are certainly *not* entitled to deduce from the premises that S is true—the argument is *invalid*. (It may be noticed that the conclusion *S is either true or false* would be not invalid but rather *logically obvious:* the meaning of the word 'proposition' already shows that every proposition must be either true or false. It would therefore be fatuous to use specific premises in order to establish this truth.)

The difference in the verdicts that we have made in the two cases confirms our previous judgment that a proposition is distinct from its converse. For the only difference between *form* (a) and *form* (b) is that in the latter the conditional premise has been replaced by its converse. (To check this, interchange circle and square in figure (a) of page 61.) We notice, again, the importance of distinguishing between a proposition and its converse, since their interchange is sufficient to turn a valid argument into an invalid one.

It is useful to have some terms by which we can refer to the forms (a) and (b) and distinguish them from one another. Both forms contain a single conditional premise; in the first, the antecedent of that conditional is asserted as a second premise, while in the second form it is the consequent that is detached for separate assertion. We may say, briefly, that the forms **assert the antecedent** and **assert the consequent** respectively. The second, invalid, form of argument is often referred to in logical discussions as the *fallacy of asserting the consequent.*

By allowing the use of the operation of contradiction, we can obtain other simple forms of conditional argument:

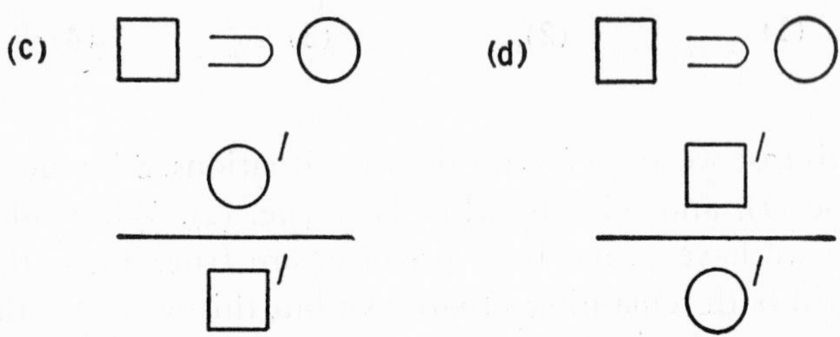

An analysis similar to that used on forms (a) and (b) will show that (c) is a valid and (d) an invalid form of argument. The latter is commonly known as the *fallacy of denying the antecedent.*

It is unwise to rely on memory to distinguish the valid forms, (a) and (c), from the invalid ones, (b) and (d). Appeal to examples illustrating the forms is a much more reliable procedure. Thus if you are in doubt concerning the validity of the argument in which the consequent is asserted, you may construct the example:

If I am Chinese I am human
I am human
____
I am Chinese

Here is a case in which both premises are true while the conclusion is false: the argument must be invalid. (We are here using the procedure for detection of invalidity previously explained on page 43.) More generally, it is easily seen that *many different antecedents are conditions for the same consequent:* so, to be given the conditional and the consequent is to be left in doubt concerning the antecedent.

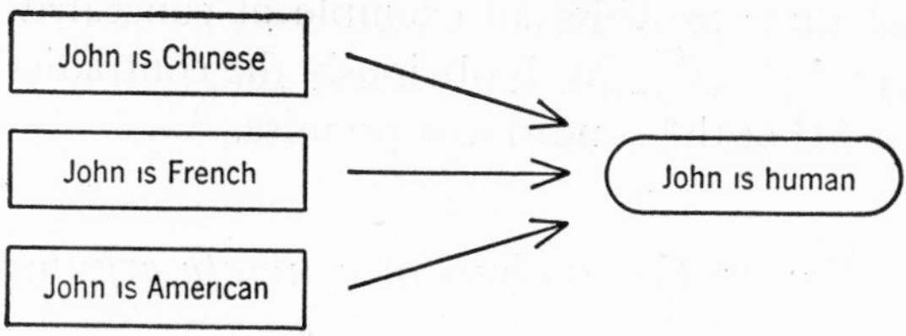

In the same way, doubt whether the argument involving the denial of the antecedent is valid can be resolved by the choice of a suitable example. The argument:

If my name is Archibald I am a male
My name is not Archibald

I am not a male

is clearly invalid for the same reason as before. (If the reader is a lady, she may be invited to make another, more convincing example!) In general, a conditional statement informs us of what will be true when the antecedent is *true,* and gives no information concerning the case in which the antecedent proves to be false. Thus, to be given a conditional and the denial of its antecedent is to be left in doubt concerning the truth of its consequent.

The reader would do well to practice inserting different kinds of propositions into the blank forms (a), (b), (c), and (d), in order to be able to recognize these forms in more complex surroundings. The following are a selection from the cases which can occur:

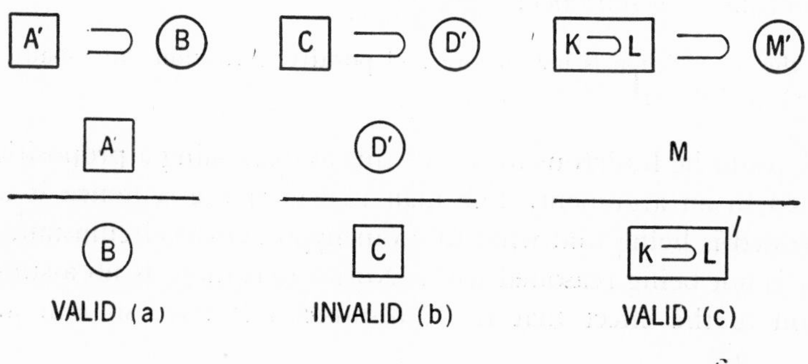

The last of these provides an example of concealed negation: for the second premise, M, is obviously the contradiction of the consequent M′ of the conditional premise.

4. Application to the analysis of concrete arguments.

The examples of conditional argument so far used in this chapter have been of an artificial character deliberately invented to illustrate the properties of implication. When we come to apply the results obtained to the analysis of concrete arguments, as they occur in writing or conversation, we normally meet with certain diffculties that must be recognized and overcome before the argument's form can be established and its validity determined. For arguments are often expressed in obscure or elliptical form with important premises left unstated. We shall illustrate the methods to be used in dealing with these difficulties of interpretation by formulating a set of suggestions for procedure, following each rule with comments and examples of its application.

1. Determine that the passage to be analyzed really expresses an argument and is not a mere set of assertions. There is a tendency for the beginner to suppose that the occurrence of an "if-then" sentence is an infallible sign of the presence of an argument. The "if-then" sentence may, however, be used simply to make a conditional *assertion,* without serving as the conclusion or a premise of an argument.

An "Owner's Manual" for a well-known automobile contains the following sentence:

> If the transmission is not smooth and positive, correction can usually be made as follows:

It would be ludicrous to regard this as expressing a proposition used in an argument. The man to whom the sentence is addressed is being told what to do in hypothetical circumstances; he is not being reasoned with. (Notice that there is no assumption to the effect that the transmission is *not* "smooth and positive.") The remark, known to be made by exasperated parents, "I'm not arguing—I'm telling you," shows an understanding of the same distinction between saying and reasoning.

A more serious instance occurs in the text of the United Nations Charter:

> The General Assembly may nevertheless permit such a member (in arrears in the payment of its financial contributions) to vote if it is satisfied that the failure to pay is due to conditions beyond the control of the member.
>
> (*Article 18*)

Here the context makes it clear that the intention is to lay down a general rule of procedure in the form of an *assertion*. The conditional proposition expressed in the quotation is not being put forward as resulting from accepted principles, nor is it being used to prove some other proposition.

Contrast with this example the passage:

> If there was anything against these men as individuals, if they were deemed to be guilty of criminal offenses, they should have been charged accordingly. But I understand that the action is not directed against these five elected members as individuals but that the proceeding is virtually an attempt to indict a political party and to deny it representation in the Legislature. This is not, in my judgment, American government... (C. E. Hughes, quoted in the *Bulletin of the American Association of University Professors,* Autumn 1949, pp. 410-411.)

In this instance the writer is not merely making a conditional assertion (expressed by his first sentence). His use of the word "But" shows that he does *not* believe that the men "were deemed to be guilty of criminal offenses" and there would be little point in his stating what would happen if something *were* the case which he knew *not* to be the case. By "reading between the lines" we see that he is trying to *disprove* the proposition *These men were deemed to be guilty of criminal offenses.* Let us represent this proposition by D; and let C stand for the proposition *These men were* (*later*) *charged accordingly* (*i.e., with having committed criminal offenses*).

Part of the argument can then be properly symbolized as:—

$$\frac{\begin{array}{c} D \supset C \\ [C'] \end{array}}{[D']}$$

The square brackets, as usual, show that propositions have been supplied. Clearly, the reasoning is valid. (We notice that the premise C′ is itself supported later in the passage quoted.)

2. *Be sure that the "if-then" sentences express conditional propositions.* Many a current advertisement uses an appeal of such a kind as this:

If you want to be strong (or beautiful or popular, etc.)
BUY KREEPIES

Here the second clause ("Buy Kreepies") gives advice and does not describe a situation; the whole sentence, therefore, is not one that expresses a conditional proposition—or, indeed, any proposition at all.

A sentence may, however, take an "if-then" form and express a proposition without that proposition's being of the form we have called conditional. The sentence:

If any adult citizen fails to observe the laws, he is liable to penalties

expresses a true proposition. We cannot, however, symbolize it in the form $A \supset B$. For "A" would have to be an abbreviation for *Any adult citizen fails to observe the laws,* which does not express a proposition, since the presence of the indefinite word "any" makes it impossible to raise a question of its truth or falsity. The occurrence of such "if-then" sentences does not render arguments automatically invalid, as the following example shows:

If any adult citizen fails to observe the laws, he is liable to penalties.
The President is an adult citizen.
―――――――――――――――――――――――――――――――――――
The President is liable to penalties if he fails to observe the laws.

(Valid)

But this argument is not an instance of any of the valid forms yet considered and must be carefully distinguished from them.

We must not make the mistake of supposing that conditional arguments are the only form of valid deductive argument.

3. *If necessary, rephrase sentences to convert them into the standard "if-then" form.* Sentences in which conditional propositions are expressed are not always conveniently offered in the form *If A then B:* the consequent may be stated before the antecedent ("I will accept your offer if you lower the price"); one or even both of the words "if" and "then" may be omitted ("You agree with him? He will agree with you"); or equivalent phrases such as "provided that," "only if," and "not . . . unless" may be used.

The reader will be able to check the correctness of the following translations:

A provided that B	means the same as	$B \supset A$
A only if B	means the same as	$A \supset B$
not A unless B	means the same as	$A \supset B$

The second of these deserves especial attention. Just as the word "if" when attached to a clause indicates that the clause expresses an *antecedent,* the words "only if" when attached to a clause usually indicate the occurrence of a *consequent.* Sometimes, however, "only if" is used loosely to mean "if and only if." In that case two conditionals will be required:

A if but only if B means the same as $(A \supset B) \& (B \supset A)$

For brevity, the double conditional may be shown with a sign of equivalence, thus: $A \equiv B$. (Read aloud as "A if and only if B.") There are corresponding variations in the meanings of "provided" and "unless."

4. *Make certain that all unexpressed premises have been included.* This is the hardest of the four rules to apply, yet it is in many ways the most important. For unless we are able to exhibit all the premises a thinker is using, we can have little hope of coming to a just verdict concerning the soundness of his reasoning. Let us illustrate by an example that is not too trivial:

What exactly is meant by saying that the white man must get out of the Far East? I suppose it does not mean that the Australians must get out of the Far East, although the Australians are white men and Australia is in the Far East. I take it to mean that the white man must abandon political and military control of those Far Eastern countries that are chiefly inhabited by other people. (C. L. Becker, *How New Will the Better World Be,* p. 98. New York: Alfred A. Knopf, Inc.)

The part of this argument that concerns us here may be set out as follows:

Those who say that the white man must get out of the Far East do not wish this to apply to Australians. (S)

What is intended is that the statement shall apply only to those Far Eastern countries that are chiefly inhabited by non-white peoples. (N)

There is clearly an unexpressed further premise needed to complete the argument. Let us put it in this way:

If S then N.

This proposition, needed to make the argument valid, is clearly a debatable assumption. It is not at all certain that those who would not wish Australians to be included among the white men "who ought to get out of the Far East" would make the exception *on the ground that the population of Australia is almost wholly white*. Becker may be, indeed probably is, right in assuming this. But he is, nevertheless, making an undefended assumption, and the deduction and evaluation of the assumption is essential to the criticism of his argument.

5. *Some model analyses of concrete conditional arguments.*

We will conclude this chapter by analyzing some further examples of argument, ranging from the trivial to the difficult:

1. "If the next president is a Republican, I will eat my hat."

Comment: This statement is not made merely for the sake of expressing an interesting connection between two unrealized situations; it is rather an effective, though indirect, way of asserting that the next president will not be a Republican. Let 'B' and 'E' stand for the propositions *The next president will be a Republican* and "I" (the speaker) *will eat my hat,* respectively. The analysis is:

$$\begin{array}{c} B \supset E \\ \underline{[E']} \\ [B'] \end{array}$$

The argument is *valid* (see form (c) on page 64). We could hardly consider this a *good* argument, however: We are given no reasons for believing the premises, and while we may accept the first on the basis of the speaker's veracity, the second is a mere prediction. (It is said that a radio commentator who once made a similar claim over the radio was compelled to eat his hat when the prediction was not upheld.*)

2. "Smith must be educated—he's a professor."

Comment: A case where the if-then connection is not explicitly shown. Using 'P' and "E' for *Smith is a professor* (note the change of wording) and *Smith is educated,* we get:

$$\begin{array}{c} P \\ \underline{[P \supset E]} \\ E \end{array}$$

The argument is *valid.* Whether we shall accept the conditional assumption will depend upon our interpretation of the ambiguous word "educated." If education means more than the possession of a Ph.D., some unkind critics would hold the assumption to be at best doubtful.

3. If Congress passes the bill, trade will improve, provided measures are taken to make the bill effective. The prospects are hopeful, therefore—trade *will* improve.

Comment: A more complex argument than any yet examined. We ignore the sentence "The prospects are hopeful" as being immaterial to the argument, and use 'C', 'T', and 'M', for the

* But he went to work wearing a cabbage on his head for the occasion.

three propositions that occur in the argument. The analysis is:

$$\frac{\begin{array}{c} M \supset (C \supset T) \\ [M] \\ [C] \end{array}}{T}$$

We can appeal twice to the valid form in which the antecedent is asserted, as shown in case (a) on page 61, to test the argument. First,

$$\frac{\begin{array}{c} M \supset (C \supset T) \\ M \end{array}}{C \supset T} \quad \text{(VALID)}$$

Next, using this *intermediate* conclusion as a premise, and also the premise hitherto unused, we have:

$$\frac{\begin{array}{c} C \supset T \\ C \end{array}}{T} \quad \text{(VALID)}$$

Thus the original argument was valid. (We have insufficient information concerning the circumstances to decide whether the premises are true.) This example illustrates well the possibility of successive application of our simple patterns of valid and invalid argument in the examination of arguments of more complex type.

4. If the long-range policy is to have any success at all it must depend upon help from inside Europe. That is the reason why American propaganda is seeking to calm the rising tide of rebellion in occupied countries. (*The New York Times,* June 13, 1943.)

Comment: An interesting example of a leap in argument. Let us use the following symbols:

S: The long-range policy of defeating the Nazis will have some success.

H: Help will be received from inside Europe by the Americans and their allies.

P: American propaganda seeks to calm the rising tide of rebellion in occupied countries.

If the propositions actually formulated in the extract be symbolized with the help of these symbols, we have:

$$\frac{\begin{array}{c} S \supset H \\ ? \end{array}}{P}$$

There is clearly an important premise missing. In order to make the argument valid, it would be sufficient to add the premise $(S \supset H) \supset P$. The argument seems, however, to suppose there is some connection between the receipt of help by the Allies and the subduing of rebellion in the occupied countries. We shall therefore use another symbol:

C: The rising tide of rebellion in the occupied countries will be calmed.

and shall symbolize the entire argument as:

$$\frac{\begin{array}{c} S \supset H \\ [H \supset C] \\ [(S \supset C) \supset P] \end{array}}{P}$$

It should not be hard to see that this argument is *valid.* We may regard the third premise (that if the calming of rebellion is a necessary condition for the success of long-term American policy, American propaganda will seek to calm rebellion) as very plausible on general grounds, and the newspaper may be taken as good authority for the truth of the first premise. The second premise was, however, a very dubious assumption at the time this argument was published. It is not at all obvious that more help will be given to an invader in an occupied country in which the "tides of rebellion" have been calmed, and British and American policy received a great deal of criticism at the time for making the assumption. The analysis of this argument illustrates well how an attempt to establish the validity of a piece of reasoning may help to expose unsound assumptions in the form of unstated premises.

Summary

Reasoning requires the consideration of the consequences of alternative possibilities. The consequence of a possibility is normally expressed in a complex proposition having the form *If A then B.* Such a proposition is technically known as a *conditional proposition;* arguments in which one or more conditional propositions occur as premises are known as *conditional arguments.*

When two propositions, A and B, are combined to produce the complex proposition *If A then B* (symbolized as '$A \supset B$'), they are said to have been subjected to the *operation of implication.* (Similarly, numbers may be combined by the arithmetical operations of addition, subtraction, etc.). Operations may be performed on *one* thing at a time. Thus the proposition P may be converted into its *contradictory* ('not-P', symbolized as 'P'') by the operation of *contradiction* or logical negation. Operations can be applied to the results of operations—in this way we get such complex propositions as $A' \supset B$ and $A \supset (B \supset A)'$. In $A \supset B$, A is known as the *antecedent* and B as the *consequent.*

The truth of a conditional proposition determines nothing with respect to the truth and falsity of the antecedent and consequent considered separately. Analysis shows, however, that the truth of *If A then B* precludes the occurrence of the complex situation *A-true-while-B-is-false.*

The proposition $B \supset A$ is said to be the *converse* of $A \supset B$. The truth of a proposition does not guarantee the truth of its converse.

The simplest types of conditional argument have the forms: (a) $X \supset Y$, also X; therefore Y: (b) $X \supset Y$, also Y; therefore X: (c) $X \supset Y$, also Y'; therefore X': (d) $X \supset Y$, also X'; therefore Y'. Of these (a) and (c) are valid, and (b) and (d) are invalid. Arguments having form (b) are said to commit the *fallacy of asserting the consequent;* arguments having form (d) commit the *fallacy of denying the antecedent.*

In analyzing the reasoning embodied in given passages, it is necessary to determine that the specimen contains arguments and is not a mere string of assertions. Since not all "if-then" propositions are compounded of two propositions, care must be taken to see that the use of the symbol 'A ⊃ B' is justified. It may be necessary to rephrase sentences to exhibit propositions in the conditional form. It is usually necessary also to formulate a number of unexpressed premises (assumptions). Each of these points has been illustrated by examples.

Comprehension test

(For instructions, see page 10.)

1. Many different antecedents can be conditions for the same consequent. *(true false)*
2. An implication is an unexpressed premise. *(true false)*
3. If a conditional proposition is true, it is impossible for its antecedent to be false while its consequent is true. *(true false)*
4. *Jones is a bachelor* is the contradictory of *Jones is married.* *(true false)*
5. An argument in which "the antecedent is asserted" is invalid. *(true false)*
6. If $C \supset D$ is true, C *only if* D is true. *(true false)*
7. A proposition expressed by a sentence in which the words "if-then" occur may not be a conditional proposition. *(true false)*
8. If a proposition is true, its converse is not true. *(true false)*
9. The converse of the converse of a proposition is the original proposition. *(true false)*
10. A conditional proposition can sometimes be known to be true when its antecedent and consequent are not known to be either true or false. *(true false)*

Exercises

A

1. Let B ⊃ F be the proposition *If the bough breaks the cradle will fall,* and suppose this proposition to be true. Illustrate what can be the case with regard to the truth and falsity of B and F by drawing pictures similar to those on page 59.

2. When $A \supset B'$ is true, which of the following propositions are true, which false, and which perhaps either true or false?
   a. A & B. b. A′ & B. c. $B' \supset A$. d. $A \supset B$. e. $B \supset A'$.
3. What are the contradictories of the following propositions?
   a. All dogs are mammals.
   b. The next conference will be held in Boston or Chicago.
   c. Some conditional arguments are invalid.
   d. Some of the people can be fooled all the time.
   e. Yesterday's temperature ranged between 50 and 70.
   f. "Lectures, like sermons, are usually unprofitable." (Santayana.)
4. Perform the following operations on each of the arguments stated below: (1) Indicate any propositions supplied by you but not explicitly included in the argument; (2) Use the symbols suggested to show the form of the argument. *Let the symbol stand for a positive proposition;* (3) Decide whether the argument is valid.
   a. If Jock is a terrier, so is Rover. But Jock is a terrier. Hence Rover is a terrier. (J,R)
   b. If you answered the telephone he heard you. Since he did not hear you, that proves you could not have answered the telephone. (A,H)
   c. If yesterday was Monday, today must be Tuesday. Yesterday was not Monday, thus today cannot be Tuesday (M,T)
   d. He acted very suspiciously, and surely if he were guilty he would have acted very suspiciously. He must be guilty. (S,G)
   e. You will not get an answer if you write. You will be miserable if you do not get an answer. It follows that if you write you will be miserable. (A,W,M)
   f. If the weather does not change, we shall have a picnic. The weather will not change. We *shall* have a picnic. (C,P)
   g. If the postman is not late, I shall not miss my class. The postman will be late. I am bound to miss my class. (P,C)
   h. He will certainly be inducted. For if he is not inducted, he cannot be physically fit. And he *is* physically fit. (I,F)
   i. If the *Daily Gossip* can be trusted, pigs can fly. And pigs cannot fly. . . . (T,P)
   j. All men are liars. Hence, some women must be gullible. (L,G)
   k. He is an Italian because he was born in Rome (I,R)
5. Express each of the following propositions in the "if-then" form:
   a. You cannot hope to be admitted unless you have a ticket.
   b. For another Ice Age to occur, a change in the sun's radiative power will be necessary.
   c. Japan will be helpless to wage war, provided her industries are not allowed to recover.

d. It is not possible for him to be in New York City without being in the State of New York.
e. A careful diet will be sufficient to restore this patient to health.
f. Either world trade will expand or another depression will hit this nation.

6. The following were among the answers supplied by students who were asked to identify the consequents of given statements. Explain what is wrong with each of these answers:
   a. "Use Lux."
   b. "Anybody would be pleased."
   c. "Then he would be happy."
   d. "Prosperity."
   e. "The next day must be Tuesday."
7. Symbolize each of the following arguments, showing unexpressed premises where necessary. Say whether the argument is valid or not, indicating the nature of the mistake committed where a mistake occurs.
   a. If the Federal government is to stay in business, it must continue to levy taxes; and if taxation is not to defeat its purpose, it must not be exorbitant.
   b. If woodpeckers fed on farmers' crops they would deserve to be exterminated. But if insects do the damage to the crops, as we know to be the case, it is they who ought to be exterminated. My views are well known—I believe that woodpeckers should not be slaughtered.
   c. It is quite wrong to say that mistakes were made at the Yalta conference, for it is plain that nothing could have saved us from the position we face today.
   d. We know that if the invalid had been in the hands of an expert doctor and believed implicitly in him, he would have had a good chance of recovery—provided that the tumor was not malignant. The patient had every confidence in the doctor, the tumor was not malignant, and yet the patient failed to recover. It must have been the doctor's fault.
   e. If the premises of an argument are true and the conclusion is valid, the conclusion must be true; and if the premises are false and the conclusion is valid, the conclusion must be false. Now a self-contradictory conclusion is both true and false; so if the argument is valid the premises must be both true and false, *i.e.*, self-contradictory.

B

1. The proposition *Today is Sunday* (S) is said to be a **contrary** of the proposition *Today is Monday* (M), because while S and M cannot both

be true it is possible for both to be false. Show that every proposition has several contraries. Explain carefully the difference between *contradictory* and *contrary*. Would the forms of argument (c) and (d) on page 64 be valid if a contrary of the consequent were substituted for the contradictory?

2. Is it possible to assert both $A \supset B$ and $A \supset B'$ without contradicting oneself? What would follow with respect to the truth of A?
3. Use the method of "logical analogy" (page 43) to prove that arguments in which the "antecedent is denied" or the "consequent is asserted" are invalid.
4. A student who was asked to solve the arithmetical equation $X + 4 = 7$ is said to have commented: "I can see how to solve this *if* $X + 4 = 7$. But what happens if $X + 4$ does *not* equal 7?" Clear up his confusion.
5. "The argument having premises A and B and conclusion C is valid." Assuming the truth of this statement, formulate a true conditional proposition containing A, B, and C.
6. Give a full analysis and criticism of the passage (by C. E. Hughes) quoted on page 67.

5

TRUTH-TABLES AND CHAIN-ARGUMENTS

Don't think in exclusive abstract, for then we fall in a set pattern of thought.
—From a student's essay.

1. *The construction of truth-tables.*

WHEN we were analyzing the meaning of implication, we used pictures to make vivid the various complex cases of truth and falsity of the antecedent and consequent (page 59). It would be impracticable to draw pictures to illustrate the various situations consistent with every given complex proposition: we look therefore for some other, more abstract, way of analyzing the meaning of such propositions.

Our previous analysis showed that when A $\supset$ B is true the one case excluded is that the antecedent should be true while the consequent is false. We can therefore show the various possibilities, in verbal form, in this way:

When A $\supset$ B is true: (1)

A-true-while-B-is-true	(no information)
A-false-while-B-is-true	(no information)
A-true-while-B-is-false	NO
A-false-while-B-is-false	(no information)

A still more condensed way of showing these results is:

When A $\supset$ B is true: (2)

(A)	(B)	
T	T	?
F	T	?
T	F	NO
F	F	?

A diagram such as (2) is known as a **truth-table** for A ⊃ B. We can make truth-tables for other forms of complex propositions, and they will be found to be a very useful device for the criticism of complex arguments.

You should notice the following points: The truth-table, (2), is intended to mean exactly the same as the expanded diagram, (1); it is advisable to practice writing diagram (2) in the fuller form (1). Exactly the same information supplied by (2) would be given if the four complex cases were arranged on the page in a different order; nevertheless, we shall make fewer mistakes by agreeing to list the cases always in the order shown. Indeed we shall try always to preserve intact this part of the truth-table:

(A)	(B)
T	T
F	T
T	F
F	F

Thus suppose we want to show the truth-table for A ⊃ B′. We might show one of the four situations as

A-true-while-B′-is-true;

we shall prefer to write this, however, as

A-true-while-B-is-false,

thereby using A and B (the simplest propositions), rather than A and B′, as our elements of description. The truth table will accordingly be:

When A ⊃ B′ is true: (3)

(A)	(B)	
T	T	NO
F	T	?
T	F	?
F	F	?

Comparison of diagrams (3) and (2) will at once confirm that A ⊃ B and A ⊃ B′ are different propositions. For while each excludes *one* complex case of truth and falsity of A and B, the cases excluded are not the same.

Let us use the truth-table technique to examine the meaning of $B' \supset A'$. The truth table resulting will be:

When $B' \supset A'$ is true: (4)

(A)	(B)	
T	T	?
F	T	?
T	F	NO
F	F	?

We can see this to be correct as follows: Our discussions have shown that a conditional proposition excludes a *single* complex situation. Now $B' \supset A'$ tells us that when B is false, A must be false, *i.e.* cannot be true. Hence the case excluded is B-false-while-A-is-true, which is shown in the *third* line of the truth-table.

Comparison of diagram (4) with diagram (2) will show that $A \supset B$ and $B' \supset A'$ *exclude* exactly the same cases and *permit* exactly the same cases. We can therefore say that they describe the same possible states of affairs. We shall call $B' \supset A'$ the **contrapositive** of $A \supset B$.

Since a contrapositive is obtained by interchanging and *negating* antecedent and consequent, we may show the result just obtained in this way:

$$\{\square \supset \bigcirc\} \equiv \{\bigcirc' \supset \square'\}$$

A contrapositive must be carefully distinguished from a converse. We have already seen that if $A \supset B$ is true, the same is not necessarily true of the converse $B \supset A$ (page 60). But the truth of $A \supset B$ does automatically guarantee the truth of the contrapositive $B' \supset A'$, and vice versa.

It is easy to see how truth-tables may be constructed for more complex statements such as $A' \supset (B \,\&\, C)$, in which three or more elements occur. We will show the truth-table for this proposition as an example.

When A′ ⊃ (B & C) is true:

(A)	(B)	(C)	
T	T	T	?
F	T	T	?
T	F	T	?
F	F	T	NO
T	T	F	?
F	T	F	NO
T	F	F	?
F	F	F	NO

It is seldom necessary to consider cases as complicated as this, however.

2. *Final analysis of the meaning of implication.*

In introducing the logical operation of implication, we used the analogy of such arithmetical operations as subtraction. There is an important difference, which will repay attention, between the mathematician's notion of subtraction and that of "common-sense." An ordinary person who has not studied algebra is inclined to say that a combination such as 5 − 9, in which a larger number is subtracted from a smaller number, "doesn't make sense." The unmathematical "ordinary person's" idea of subtraction is subject, therefore, to a restriction; when he uses the symbol X *minus* Y, we know that he is not merely referring to some number which, if added to Y, would give X but is, *in addition,* supposing that X is greater than Y. This restriction is, however, most inconvenient to a mathematician interested in developing a general theory of numbers; it would be awkward for him to be always stopping to determine whether X were greater than Y in order to be assured of the right to form the combination X − Y. He accordingly drops the restriction, and *gives a meaning* to the combination X − Y in *all* cases. (How this leads to the definition of so-called "negative numbers" does not concern us here.) By taking a *part* of the common-sense meaning of subtraction, the mathematician succeeds in giving the idea wider application. In cases where X *is* greater than Y the mathematician's notion will agree with that of the "ordinary person," but he will also be able to use it in other cases, *viz.*, those in which X is less than Y. Such modification of common notions in order to give them a wider field of application is very characteristic of mathematical method.

Let us now see whether there is anything analogous to all this in the common notion of "if-then." The many examples we have already considered show that *part* of the common meaning of *If A then B* is *It is not the case that A-is-true-while-B-is-false.* But this is not always the *whole* meaning. Take A to be *The earth is round,* and B to be *Water is wet.* In this instance it certainly is not the case that A-is-true-while-B-is-false—for the good and sufficient reason that here we know B is not false. (If we know, as we do, that water is wet, we also know that the situation *The-earth-is-round-and-at-the-same-time-water-is-not-wet* cannot be realized.) Yet we should feel reluctant to say that *therefore* the following proposition is true:

If the earth is round then water is wet.

We feel there should be some further connection between the antecedent and the consequent. But what is the nature of the connection between A and B in cases in which we should have no hesitation in asserting *If A then B?*

Consider the following examples of true conditional propositions:

(a) If John is a husband, then John is married.
(b) If the temperature of this water is more than 90 centigrade, it will scald your skin.
(c) If a lizard is a reptile and all reptiles are cold-blooded, then a lizard is cold-blooded.
(d) If the weather improves, I will go fishing.

The connection between antecedent and consequent can be seen to differ in each case. In (a) the consequent is connected with the antecedent in virtue of the *definition* of the words "husband" and "married"; in (b) the connection is based on sufficient *experience* of what has been found to happen when boiling water is allowed to touch the skin; the third example shows the relation that has elsewhere been referred to by the word "validity"; while in the last example the only connection between antecedent and consequent seems to be that of the speaker's *determination* to make the consequent true if the antecedent should prove to be true.

While *If A then B* commonly means something more than *It is not the case that A is true while B is false,* this additional meaning seems to vary widely according to circumstances. If the logician (who wants to develop *general* principles and standards of reasoning) were to try to take account of all these variations in meaning, his results would be hopelessly complicated.

We prefer, therefore, to take the common element of all these different meanings of "if-then" and *define* A ⊃ B to mean *nothing more than:*

It is not the case that A-and-also-not-B.

In so doing we shall extend but not *falsify* the common meanings of "if-then." For the "if-then" relation is usually employed in reasoning to make it possible to pass from true antecedent to true consequent, and this our definition will permit. We have preserved all the meaning of "if-then" that is needed for most forms of deductive reasoning. And if a case should arise in which we need to make explicit use of a particular kind of connection between antecedent and consequent (whether that connection is based on definition, experience, resolution, or some other thing), we can always add further premises, making the nature of the connection quite explicit.

Our definition of the meaning of the horseshoe symbol will require some modification in the typical form of a truth-table. Thus the truth-table for A ⊃ B will now appear as:

A ⊃ B means the same as: (5)

(A)	(B)	
T	T	true
F	T	true
T	F	false
F	F	true

This is to be read as: A ⊃ B is the case in situations 1 (A and B both true), 2 (A false, B true), and 4 (A and B both false); and is not the case only in situation 3 (A true, B false). Compare diagram (2) on page 59. The changes are necessitated by our recent decision to *define* the operation of implication by means of the truth-table. Corresponding changes will be made in all truth-tables used from this point onwards.

3. The "chain argument" or hypothetical syllogism.

The simple forms of deductive argument so far analyzed have all contained a *single* occurrence of the horseshoe symbol in the premises. A very common type of conditional argument has a form that differs from those already studied in having two instances of implication in the premises.

Thus, a student at college who is trying to decide which subject to choose for his major may argue in this way: "If I major in a science I shall need some calculus. If I need calculus I must take a class at eight o'clock in the morning. So if I major in a science I must take a class at eight o'clock in the morning." With an obvious choice of symbols, the argument will be displayed as:

S ⊃ C
C ⊃ E
―――――
S ⊃ E

This type of argument we shall call a **chain argument;** a more usual, though less vivid, name is **hypothetical syllogism.** It will be noticed that a chain-argument has as its two premises a pair of implications, such that *the same proposition occurs once as an antecedent and once as a consequent.*

Direct inspection suggests that a chain-argument is valid. We shall do well, however, to confirm this suggestion by explicit argument.

According to our definition of the horseshoe symbol, S ⊃ C means that the situation

S-but-not-C

is excluded. And C ⊃ E similarly means that the situation

C-but-not-E

is excluded.

In the light of these two exclusions, is it possible to have

S-but-not-E?

If this situation should occur, we must have either

S-while-not-E-*and-not-C*

or

S-while-*not-E-but-also-C*

But the first of these cases, as we have seen, is excluded by the first premise; and the second is excluded by the second premise. Hence the two premises together exclude

S-but-not-E

and the conclusion S ⊃ E is *valid.*

The chain-argument must be carefully distinguished from conditional arguments containing two conditional premises with the same proposition occurring in the *same* position in both. We can easily prove these other forms invalid by the method of formal analogy explained on page 48.

Here is an instance of the use of this method: The argument "If John is a Frenchman, he is human, and if he is a German, he is human; therefore if he is a Frenchman, he is a German" has two true premises and a false conclusion, and is therefore invalid. The following form is accordingly *invalid.*

$$\begin{array}{l} X \supset Y \\ Z \supset Y \\ \hline X \supset Z \quad \text{(INVALID)} \end{array}$$

Similarly we may use the argument "If Jane is a wife, she is a woman, and if she is a wife, she is married; therefore if Jane is a woman she is married" to prove the *invalidity* of the form:

$$\begin{array}{l} U \supset V \\ U \supset W \\ \hline V \supset W \quad \text{(INVALID)} \end{array}$$

By using our previous results concerning the contrapositive of a conditional proposition page 81), we can often transform other types of argument into one of the three forms just examined. Thus the argument "If the call came from Chicago, it was important; but if it was not about business, the call was unimportant; therefore if the call was about business, it must have come from Chicago," can be symbolized:

$$\begin{array}{l} C \supset I. \\ B' \supset I' \\ \hline B \supset C \end{array}$$

This is not yet a case of the chain-argument, but replacing the second premise by its contrapositive yields:

$$\begin{array}{l} C \supset I \\ I \supset B \\ \hline B \supset C \quad \text{(INVALID)} \end{array}$$

The argument is clearly *invalid,* though the converse conclusion, $C \supset B$, would have been valid. We may check this result by taking the contrapositive of the original first premise, obtaining:

$$\begin{array}{l} I' \supset C' \\ B' \supset I' \\ \hline B' \supset C' \quad \text{(VALID)} \end{array}$$

where the conclusion obtained is, of course, the contrapositive of $C \supset B$, rather than of the conclusion given in the original argument.

4. Indirect argument.

The time is 3 P.M., the place any office. Miss Smith, a stenographer, is trying to decide whether she can leave a little earlier than her usual time of 5 P.M. She reasons in the following way: "If I am to leave early, I must get all these letters typed first." But an inspection of the letters convinces her she has two hours' work ahead of her; she continues, sadly, "If I am to get these letters typed, I must work two hours more." A look at the clock convinces her that "If I am to work two hours more I cannot leave early." What conclusion follows from the three premises?

The argument is symbolized as:

$$\begin{array}{c} L \supset T \\ T \supset W \\ \underline{W \supset L'} \\ ? \end{array}$$

This is an obvious case of an extended chain-argument. The first two premises will give $L \supset W$, so this conclusion can be added to the remaining premise, yielding:

$$\begin{array}{c} L \supset W \\ \underline{W \supset L'} \\ ? \end{array}$$

which is another chain-argument, leading to the valid conclusion $L \supset L'$.

When beginners meet a proposition of this form for the first time, they are inclined to suppose it is self-contradictory, because they confuse it with the *different* proposition $L \mathbin{\&} L'$. But when we say that $A \supset B$ is true, we are not saying that A *is* true: and so in saying, with Miss Smith, that $L \supset L'$ is true, we are not saying that L is true. What then *is* the import of $L \supset L'$?

A little thought will show that Miss Smith has demonstrated to her own reluctant dissatisfaction that she cannot leave the office early, *i.e.,* that *L is false.* We can easily check this result in general. For

	$A \supset B$	means	A-true-while-B-false is excluded
Hence:			
	$L \supset L'$	means	L-true-while-L′-false is excluded
			i.e., L-true-and-L-true is excluded.

The proposition we are examining means, therefore, that it is not the case that L-is-true-and-L-is-true; *i.e.,* it means that *L is false.*

We have accordingly the following valid form of conditional argument:

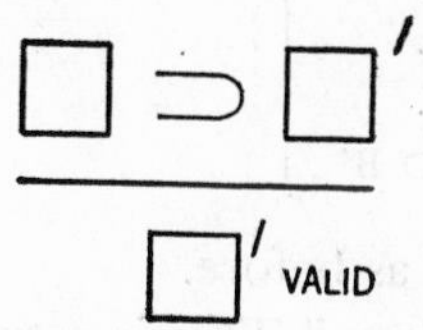

By inserting P′ into the blank supplied, we can see that a special case of this form is:

$$\frac{P' \supset P}{P} \qquad \text{(VALID)}$$

The rule, therefore, is: If a proposition is such that if true its contradictory is true, then its contradictory *is* true. We shall call an argument of this form **indirect.**

As an example, let us take 'R' to stand for the proposition *Every rule has an exception.* Now R is itself a rule; hence if every rule has an exception, R must have an exception. But if R has an exception, it is not true as it stands. Hence, if *every* rule has an exception, R is false, which can be symbolized as

$$R \supset R'.$$

Thus we can, by indirect argument, draw the valid conclusion, R′. We have therefore proved that R must be false. (The argument would not, however, apply to the proposition *Every rule except this one has an exception.*)

The method of indirect argument is a particularly powerful form of deductive argument. By taking, as its first antecedent, the contradictory of what is to be established, it provides a suggestive starting point for the discovery of useful premises. Thus, if Jones wants to prove that he is innocent of a suspected burglary, he might do worse than start thinking along the lines "If I were the burglar . . . (what?) . . . " With sufficient ingenuity he might be able to establish an argument of form

$$\left.\begin{array}{l} B \supset K \\ K \supset L \\ L \supset M \\ \quad\cdot \\ \quad\cdot \\ \quad\cdot \\ P \supset B' \end{array}\right\} \text{(extended chain)}$$

which would prove B′, as before.

"Reductio ad absurdum." This is a type of argument closely resembling indirect argument. It consists in showing that some proposition, A′, implies a *self-contradiction* (*i.e.*, yields as valid conclusions *both* B and B′). This being so, it follows that A′ cannot be true, and so, indirectly, that A is true. Arguments of this form are particularly useful in mathematics.

Here is a relatively simple example, being a proof by *reductio ad absurdum* of a proposition that has been of great importance in the history of thought. This example is worth following carefully, as an illustration of how comparatively simple trains of deductive argument can result in surprising and important results.*

We want to prove that *it is impossible to express the square root of* $2(\sqrt{2})$ *as an exact fraction* (proposition A). In other words, we want to show that there are no *whole* numbers, *k*, and *l*, for which the following equation is true.

$$\sqrt{2} = \frac{k}{l} \qquad (1)$$

* The rest of this section can be omitted by those allergic to even the simplest mathematics.

We assume that A is false, i.e., take A′ as a premise, the characteristic first step in an indirect argument. In that case, there *are* two numbers, k and l, for which the equation (1) holds. If k and l have any common factors, we can divide the top and bottom of the fraction k/l by such factors, until we get

$$\sqrt{2} = \frac{m}{n} \tag{2}$$

And now, on the basis of our previous assumptions, *m and n have no factors in common* (proposition B).

From equation (2), we get

$$2 = \frac{m^2}{n^2}$$

or

$$2.n^2 = m^2 \tag{3}$$

The left side of equation (3) is an even number; hence the right side must also be an even number. This is possible only if m is even, *i.e.*, if $m = 2.m_1$

So we have

$$2.n^2 = (2.m_1)^2$$

or

$$2.n^2 = 4.m_1{}^2$$

or

$$n^2 = 2.m_1{}^2 \tag{4}$$

Since the right side of (4) is even, we must conclude, as before, that n is an even number. Hence both m and n are even, and hence *they do have a factor in common, viz.,* 2. But this is proposition B′.

Thus we have proved that if A′ were true, *both* B and B′ would have to be true. Hence, A must be true.

Proofs by elimination. Sometimes we may know that of several alternatives *at least one must be true*. It is often convenient in such cases to take the alternatives in turn, disproving each of them until only one remains to be examined. If this can be done, the one alternative that has not been disproved must be true. Such proof by elimination can be regarded as a generalization of indirect argument (as described above) in which only *two* alternatives (A and A′) are considered.

Here is a simple illustration: A murder was committed in a locked office to which only four men and the victim had access on the day of the crime. Three of them are able to establish alibis for the time at which the murder is known to have occurred: the fourth suspect must therefore be guilty.

Summary

Truth-tables are diagrams for showing the compound cases of truth and falsity of components of complex propositions. If only two components, A and B, occur in the complex proposition, there will be *four* compound cases of truth and falsity of A and B, and the truth-table will have four lines. It is convenient to write the four complex cases always in the same order (*viz.,* A-true-and-B-true, A-false-and-B-true, A-true-and-B-false, A-false-and-B-false).

If the antecedent and the consequent of a conditional proposition are negated and interchanged, there results the *contrapositive* of the original proposition. Examination of truth-tables shows that a proposition and its contrapositive describe exactly the same state of affairs.

When we assert "If A then B" we usually mean something more than "It-is-not-the-case-that-A-while-not-B." This extra meaning however varies considerably. The logician therefore finds it convenient to *define* "$A \supset B$" as meaning *just* "It-is-not-the-case-that-A-while-not-B." Substitution of "$A \supset B$," so defined, for "If A then B," will do no harm to any given argument. As explained in the text, the adopted definition requires a slight modification of the standard form of a truth-table.

A *chain-argument* or "hypothetical syllogism" is an argument having premises of form $A \supset B$ and $B \supset C$ (*i.e.,* two occurrences of implication, and a proposition occurring once in the antecedent- and once in the consequent-position). It has the valid conclusion, $A \supset C$. The arguments having premises

$A \supset B$ and $C \supset B$ or $B \supset A$ and $B \supset C$ have no simple valid conclusion.

An *indirect argument* is one using a premise having the form $A \supset A'$ (*i.e.,* one whose consequent is the contradiction of its antecedent). From $A \supset A'$, one can validly deduce A'.

In *reductio ad absurdum* a premise of form $A \supset (B \,\&\, B')$ is proved (*i.e.,* it is shown that some proposition implies a self-contradiction). In such a case, A must be false.

In *proof by elimination* it is known that one of several alternatives must be true. Each of these possibilities is then disproved in turn, until only one remains, which must then be true.

Comprehension test

(For instructions, see page 10.)

1. The truth-tables of propositions having the same logical form look similar. (*true* *false*)
2. If a proposition is true its contrapositive is also true. (*true* *false*)
3. Every conditional proposition has a contrapositive. (*true* *false*)
4. In a chain-argument the antecedent is asserted. (*true* *false*)
5. "If A then B" usually means more than "$A \supset B$." (*true* *false*)
6. "$A \supset B$" is defined to mean it-is-not-the-case-that-A-while-not-B. (*true* *false*)
7. *If A is false, A is true* is a self-contradictory proposition. (*true* *false*)
8. In "reductio ad absurdum" a contradiction is deduced from the premises. (*true* *false*)
9. In using "proof by elimination," it is necessary to know that at least one of several given possibilities is true. (*true* *false*)
10. A chain-argument always involves at least three components (say A, B, C). (*true* *false*)

Exercises

A

1. Draw truth-tables for the propositions $A' \supset B$ and $A' \supset B'$ respectively.
2. Translate the whole of the truth-table for $A \supset B$ into words, using no symbols except "A" and "B".

3. Symbolize the following arguments, using the suggested symbols to stand for positive propositions. Supply appropriate assumptions, and decide which of the arguments are valid.
   a. "If polar air moves down from Canada, we shall have snow. Many traffic accidents can be expected this weekend." (P,S,T)
   b. "If I stay at home I shall listen to the radio, and if I listen to the radio I shall neglect my work. So I shall neglect my work if I listen to the radio." (H,R,N)
   c. "If he is not in Boston he is in Chicago. If he is not in Chicago he is in New Orleans. So if he is not in Boston he must be in New Orleans." (B,C,N)
   d. "If all people were clever, there would be no need for examinations." (C,E)
   e. "If Smith did not write the article, he did not accept the bribe and will not be imprisoned. If the prosecuting attorney's evidence is accepted he will be imprisoned. Smith did not write the article. Hence, the prosecuting attorney's evidence will not be accepted." (W,B,I,A)
   f. "If MacDonald was the murderer, he must have been in Los Angeles on December 12. In that case he was the man who bought the railroad ticket on December 11. But if he bought the railroad ticket on the 11th, he had no chance to buy the poison. MacDonald is innocent!" (M,L,R,P,I)
   g. "Jones says nobody should ever be trusted. If he is right we ought not trust his statement. If he is telling the truth he must be lying. He is not telling the truth." (T,S)
   h. "We shall have a holiday for New Year's Day or Easter. The New Year's holiday has been cancelled. We *shall* have an Easter holiday. (N,E,C)
   i. "If we have no peace-time conscription we shall have to fight a war eventually. If we have peace-time conscription we turn our young men into soldiers. The nation is bound to be militaristic." (C,F,S,M)
4. Determine which of the following forms of argument are valid:
   a. $A' \supset B$ *and* $B \supset C'$, *therefore* $C \supset A$.
   b. $K \supset L$ *and* $M \supset K$, *therefore* $M \supset L$.
   c. $P \supset Q$ *and* $P' \supset R'$, *therefore* $R \supset Q$.
   d. $U \supset V$ *and* $W' \supset U'$, *therefore* $V \supset W$.
   e. $(A \& B')'$ *and* $(B \& C')'$, *therefore* $A \supset C$.
   f. $A \supset (B \supset C)$ *and* $(B \supset C) \supset D$, *therefore* $A \supset D$.
   g. $F \supset G$ *and* $F \supset F'$, *therefore* F'.
   h. $(K \& L) \supset (K \& L)'$, *therefore* K'.
   i. $P \supset Q$ *and* R' *and* $Q \supset R$, *therefore* P'.
   j. $U \supset V$ *and* $U \supset V'$ *and* $W \supset U$, *therefore* W'.

k. $A \supset (B \& B')$, *therefore* A'.

l. $A \supset (B \& C)$ *and* $B \supset D$ *and* $C \supset D'$, *therefore* A'.

5. Invent ten more problems of about the same difficulty as those given in the last question and solve each of them.
6. Given only the following propositions, compose as many arguments as possible having the forms indicated below.
   $R \supset T'$, P, C, D, E, L', $B \& R$, $C \supset P'$, $Q \supset P$, $S \& T$, $P \supset Q'$, $L \supset L'$, P', $B' \supset S'$, $P \supset R$, $L \& S$, $R \supset Q$.
   a. Indirect argument.
   b. Reductio ad absurdum.
   c. Denying the consequent.
   d. Chain-argument.
7. Show the form of the following complex argument and determine its validity:
   "Thus absolute truth is indestructible. Being indestructible, it is eternal. Being eternal, it is self-existent. Being self-existent, it is infinite. Being infinite, it is vast and deep. Being vast and deep, it is transcendental and intelligent. It is because it is vast and deep that it contains all existence. It is because it is transcendental and intelligent that it embraces all existence. It is because it is infinite and eternal that it fulfils or perfects all existence." (*The Wisdom of Confucius,* ed. by Lin Yutang, p. 113. New York: Random House, Inc., 1943.)

B

1. Construct truth-tables for $(A \& B) \supset A$, $(A \& B) \supset C$, $(A \& C) \supset B$. Could all three propositions be simultaneously true? Simultaneously false?
2. What complex proposition having A and B as components has a truth-table whose last column reads "true; false; false; true"?
3. Use truth-tables to show that $A \supset (B \supset C)$ and $B \supset (A \supset C)$ describe exactly the same state of affairs.
4. Is it possible for a complex proposition having A and B as components to have a truth-table whose last column reads "true; true; true; true"? What is the significance of such a truth-table?
5. How many different truth-tables are there in which two components (A and B) are mentioned? How many involving three components? How many involving *n* components?
6. A man has assumed both A and A' to be true. He then argues as follows: $(A \& B) \supset A$. *But* A'. *Therefore* $(A \& B)'$. *Hence* $A \supset B'$. *But* A. *Therefore* B'. Is this argument valid? Take A to be *There will be another war* and B to be *Pigs cannot fly;* what does the argument show in this case? Explain how this result illustrates the importance of the logical ideal of consistency.

6

ARGUMENTS INVOLVING ALTERNATIVES

On the horns of a dilemma—Common saying.

1. The operation of alternation.

NOT all connections between propositions involve the "if-then" operation. It is, for instance, very common for reasoning to be concerned with plausible *alternatives,* expressed in a sentence using the words "either . . . or." Thus a boy, on the point of graduating from high school, may argue in the following manner: "Either I go to college or start working right away. But I don't want to start working right away if I can earn enough to work my way through college. And I *can* earn enough to work my way through college. I *will* go to college." In this particular argument every proposition except the first has a form of a kind already examined, but we need now to learn enough about propositions of type *Either A or B* to be able to say with confidence whether the arguments in which they occur are valid.

The "either-or" operation will be called **alternation.** We very soon notice that the words "either . . . or" are used in two ways in our language. The boy whom we imagined arguing about going to college was taking for granted that his choice lay *between* going to college and working right away, *i.e.,* that he would not be able to do both. In this case, then, *Either A or B* means the same as *A or B but not both.* But sometimes we use "or" in a different sense.

Here is a typical example. The philosopher, John Stuart

Mill, ends an eloquent defense of freedom of thought and discussion with these words:

> If there are any persons who contest a received opinion, or who will do so if law or opinion will let them, let us thank them for it, open our minds, and rejoice. . . . (*Essay on Liberty,* Everyman Edition, p. 105.)

Let us use 'P' for *There are some persons who contest a received opinion,* 'Q' for *There are some persons who will contest a received opinion if allowed,* and 'T' for *We should be thankful.* Then part of what Mill is saying is that

$$(P \text{ or } Q) \supset T$$

Does he mean that we should be thankful only if just *one* of P and Q is true? Clearly not. If some persons "contest a received opinion" *and also* "will do so if law or opinion will let them," there is still every reason, according to Mill, to be grateful. In this instance P *or* Q means the same as P *or* Q *or both.* Similarly we can see that the words "law or opinion" in the same quotation mean the same as "law or opinion *or both.*"

In ordinary conversation, we usually leave it to the context to determine which of the two senses of alternation is in question. In business correspondence, the symbol "and/or" is sometimes used when it is essential to state that "A or B *or both*" is intended. In criticizing arguments involving alternation, it will be necessary to distinguish between the two types, and to have convenient ways of referring to their different properties.

We shall refer to the operation occurring in the proposition *A or B but not both* as **exclusive alternation;** and the operation occurring in the proposition *A or B and perhaps both* as **inclusive alternation.** (The first proposition *excludes,* while the second *includes,* or allows, the situation in which both A and B are true.) We shall use, as symbols for the two types of alternation, '⩔' and '∨' respectively.

The difference between the two operations can be clearly shown by constructing truth-tables for each of them:

A ⩒ B means:

(A)	(B)	
T	T	false
F	T	true
T	F	true
F	F	false

A ∨ B means:

(A)	(B)	
T	T	true
F	T	true
T	F	true
F	F	false

Comparison of these tables will show that A ⩒ B *says more* than A ∨ B; for the second says that A-false-while-B-false cannot occur, and the first says, *in addition,* that A-true-while-B-true cannot occur. We may therefore also refer to exclusive alternation as *strong* alternation and to inclusive alternation as *weak* alternation. We notice that a strong alternation can be expressed by means of two weak alternations, for A ⩒ B means the same as

$$\{(A \vee B) \ \& \ (A' \vee B')\}$$

2. *Relations between alternation and implication.*

Having now defined two operations of alternation, we could proceed as we did in examining implication in the previous chapters, *i.e.,* we could gradually develop all the properties of the two types of alternation relevant to decisions of the validity of arguments in which they occur. We can save ourselves this trouble, however, by learning how to translate statements involving alternation into statements involving implication. For if we can change "either . . . or" statements into "if . . . then" statements, we shall not need to burden ourselves with further theory.

Let us then construct the truth-tables for A′ ≡ B and A′ ⊃ B respectively. (Here the three lines are used to show an "if-and-only-if" connection.)

A′ ≡ B means:

(A)	(B)	
T	T	false
F	T	true
T	F	true
F	F	false

A′ ⊃ B means:

(A)	(B)	
T	T	true
F	T	true
T	F	true
F	F	false

(For the first proposition says that when A is false B cannot be false, and when B is true A cannot be true, while the second says only that when A is false B cannot be false.)

Comparison of these truth-tables with those on the previous page will show that

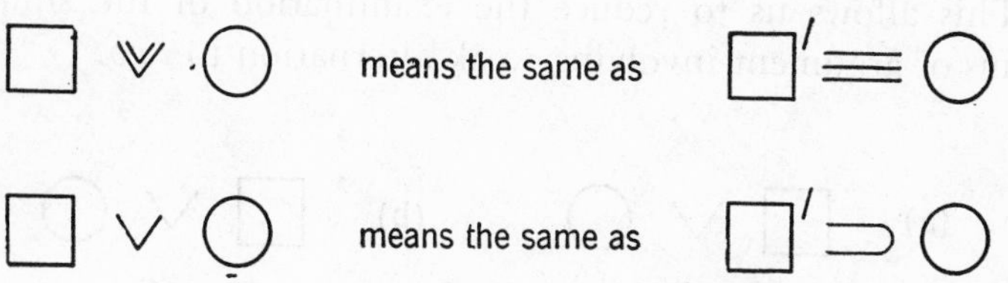

Since every strong or exclusive alternation can be expressed by means of two weak or inclusive alternations, as we have already seen, we shall chiefly use the second of these operations. We notice the rule of translation is: *To change a weak alternation into an implication, take the contradictory of one term as antecedent and the other, unchanged, as consequent.* (We shall see immediately why it does not matter which term we choose to negate.)

The relation just obtained can obviously also be looked at in reverse as a way of translating an "if-then" statement into an "either-or" one. Thus we must have:

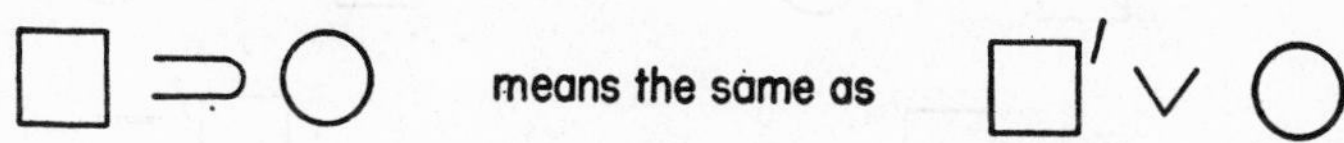

The method we have discovered of passing from (weak) alternation to implication allows us to get a number of useful results concerning alternation with very little trouble. As an example, we may try to compare the meanings of A ∨ B and B ∨ A. (Our discussion of the converse of a conditional statement on page 60 has warned us not to assume that the order of terms is indifferent in a logical operation.)

According to the results proved, A $\vee$ B means the same as A′ $\supset$ B, and B $\vee$ A means the same as B′ $\supset$ A. But A′ $\supset$ B and B′ $\supset$ A are contrapositives of one another, and therefore have the same meaning. We see therefore that A $\vee$ B *does* mean the same as B $\vee$ A, *i.e.*, that the order of the terms in alternation does not affect the meaning of the whole proposition.

This allows us to reduce the examination of the simplest forms of argument involving weak alternation to *two:*

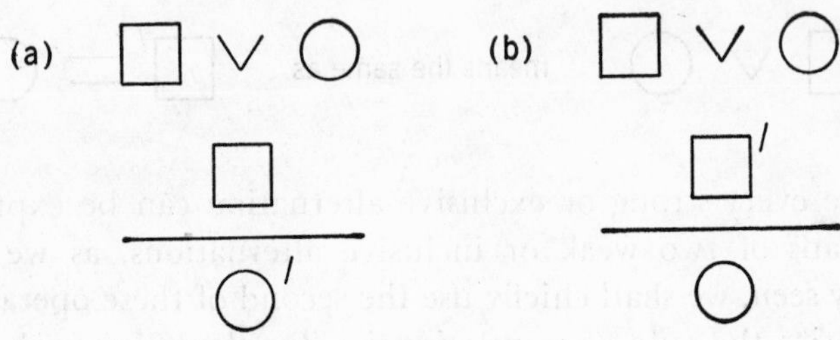

(This should be contrasted with the need for four cases in the discussion of implication—see pages 61, 64.)

On converting each of the alternative statements into the equivalent conditional, we have:

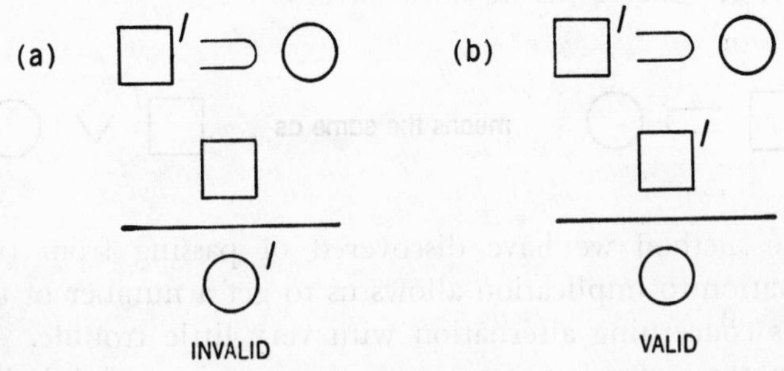

The corresponding results for strong or exclusive alternation, it is easy to verify, are:

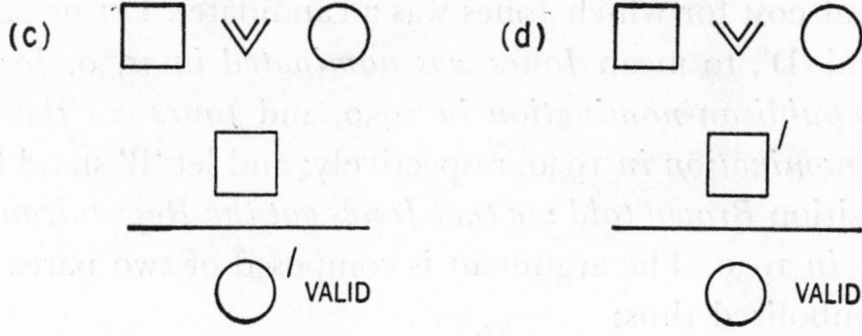

(It should be noticed by comparing (c) with (a), how the stronger premise, A $\veebar$ B, gives a valid conclusion, where the weaker premise, A $\vee$ B, fails to do so.)

The results with respect to the validity of simple arguments in which alternation occurs are, therefore, simpler than in the case of corresponding arguments containing implication. We need only to guard against supposing that the truth of one component in an either-or statement guarantees the falsity of the other. Whether it does or does not depends on the character of the alternation—whether exclusive or inclusive. Most mistakes of reasoning involving alternation arise from a failure to make clear the distinction between the weak and strong types.

3. *Specimens of analysis of concrete alternative arguments.*

Before this section is read, it would be useful to review the suggestions for the analysis of concrete arguments given above in Chapter 4 (pages 66-70). We shall give a selection of brief arguments, arranged in order of approximate difficulty, and followed in each instance by comment and analysis.

1. Jones was nominated for Senator in 1930, and so he got either the Republican nomination or the Democratic nomination in that year. But Brown has just told me that Jones got the Republican nomination in that year. Therefore, Jones could not have got the Democratic nomination.

Comment: The language is unusually explicit in this argument (though we are not told the full circumstances of the political post for which Jones was a candidate). Let us take 'N', 'R', and 'D', to mean *Jones was nominated in* 1930, *Jones got the Republican nomination in* 1930, and *Jones got the Democratic nomination in* 1930, respectively; and let 'B' stand for the proposition *Brown told me that Jones got the Republican nomination in* 1930. The argument is composed of two parts, which are symbolized thus:

$$
\begin{array}{ll}
(1) & N \\
(2) & [N \supset (R \vee D)] \\
\hline
(3) & R \vee D
\end{array}
\qquad\qquad
\begin{array}{ll}
(3) & R \vee D \\
(4) & B \\
(5) & [B \supset R] \\
\hline
(6) & D'
\end{array}
$$

We have chosen to show *inclusive* alternation involved in (2), in order to obtain a true assumption. (The same man has been known to get both the Republican and the Democratic nomination for a political office.) On this interpretation, (3) is a valid intermediate conclusion. On examining the remainder of the argument, we notice that (4) and the assumption (5) yield R, which, taken in conjunction with the remaining premise, (3), does *not* validly produce (6). Thus the argument is *invalid.*

We notice, however, that the validity of the argument could be saved, if we substituted for (2) the *false* assumption, $N \supset (R \veebar D)$. This sort of connection between the truth of the premises and the validity of a vague argument is typical; it is very often possible to render an argument valid by comparatively slight modification of the premises (*e.g.,* by replacing a proposition by its converse). But this will usually have the effect of introducing a false premise in place of a true one. Where the language or thought is not fully explicit, we often have a choice between deciding that the argument is unsound because the conclusion is invalid or because the conclusion, while valid, is deduced from false premises.

2. (I am hunting in a library catalogue for a book written by a man named DeWitt): The book will be indexed among the D's or the W's. It is not indexed under the D's. It must be indexed under the W's.

Comment: Let 'D' and 'W' stand for *The book is indexed among the D's* and *The book is indexed among the W's.* We might begin by symbolizing the argument as:

$$\frac{\begin{array}{c} D \vee W \\ D' \end{array}}{W}$$

In this case, the argument would be valid, whether inclusive or exclusive alternation were chosen (see forms [b] and [d] on pages 100, 101). By choosing the weaker interpretation, we allow the person arguing to have the better chance of asserting a *true* first premise.

This analysis could however be improved, for the truth of the first premise is conditional on the book being in the library in question. A better analysis would therefore be:

$$\frac{\begin{array}{c} [L] \supset (D \vee W) \\ D' \end{array}}{[L] \supset W} \qquad \text{(VALID)}$$

This form is more complex than any of which examples have been yet provided. It would be a good exercise in the understanding of the principles of this chapter to *prove* that the form is valid.

3. One ought never to complain about summer weather. If the sun shines, holiday-makers are happy; and if it rains, the farmers are happy.

Comment: Using the symbols 'O', 'S', 'H', 'R', and 'F', with meanings which will be obvious, we get:

(1)	$[S \veebar R]$	(4)	$H \vee F$
(2)	$S \supset H$	(5)	$[H \supset O]$
(3)	$R \supset F$	(6)	$[F \supset O]$
(4)	$[H \vee F]$		O

By converting premises (1) and (4) into the "if-then" form (as on page 100), the argument can be presented as a series of "chains" and can eventually be seen to be *valid*. (See also the next section of this chapter.) Assumption (1) is, however, false; and assumptions (5) and (6) are very doubtful.

4. *The dilemma.*

A man is arguing against some proposed Labor legislation: "If the Labor Unions have the confidence of the workers, they don't need any help from Congress; and if they have lost the confidence of the workers, they don't deserve such help." An argument of this form is called a **dilemma.**

Let 'H', 'L', 'N', 'D', mean *The Labor Unions have the confidence of the workers, The Labor Unions have lost the confidence of the workers, The Labor Unions need help from Congress,* and *The Labor Unions deserve help from Congress,* respectively. The form of the argument then appears as:

$$\begin{array}{c} [H \lor L] \\ H \supset N' \\ L \supset D' \\ \hline [N' \lor D'] \end{array} \quad \text{(VALID)}$$

An argument of this form has three premises, of which one is an alternative proposition. Each component of this premise also appears as an *antecedent* of a conditional proposition. The conclusion is an alternative proposition whose parts are consequents of the two conditional premises. Thus a dilemma may be looked on as an argument in which one alternative proposition (the first premise) is converted into another (the conclusion).

The simplest way of checking the validity of the dilemma is to convert the alternative propositions into conditionals in accordance with the formula previously obtained (page 99).

$$\text{(a)} \quad \begin{array}{c} X \lor Y \\ X \supset V \\ Y \supset W \\ \hline V \lor W \end{array} \qquad \text{(b)} \quad \begin{array}{c} X' \supset Y \\ X \supset V \\ Y \supset W \\ \hline V' \supset W \end{array}$$

The first and fourth propositions of (b) are equivalent to the first and fourth propositions of (a), according to the formula on page 99 above. Also (b) can be easily converted into a valid chain argument, for the first and third propositions yield $X' \supset W$, which may then be combined with $V' \supset X'$, the contrapositive of the remaining premise, to give the desired result.

In the general form of the dilemma, shown in (a), X, Y, V, and W may of course be any four propositions chosen at random. If Y is taken to be X′, the contradictory of X, only three propositions are involved in the argument's make-up; the same happens if V is taken to be identical with W. In this way we can obtain two *special cases* of dilemma, both of which are very common:

$$(a_1)\qquad \frac{\begin{array}{c} X \vee X' \\ X \supset V \\ X' \supset W \end{array}}{V \vee W} \qquad\qquad (a_2)\qquad \frac{\begin{array}{c} X \vee Y \\ X \supset V \\ Y \supset V \end{array}}{V \vee V} \quad (\textit{i.e. } V)$$

Since every proposition must be true or false, the first premise of (a_1) gives no information especially relevant to the conclusion to be established, and is therefore often omitted. By combining the procedures used to change (a) into (a_1) and (a_2), we get the still more specialized form of the dilemma:

$$(a_3)\qquad \frac{\begin{array}{c} X \supset V \\ X' \supset V \end{array}}{V}$$

(Here the first premise, X ∨ X′, has been omitted, as previously suggested.)

It should be noticed that the term *dilemma* refers in logic only to a certain *form* of argument. In ordinary life, the term is restricted to arguments whose conclusion is unpleasant in some way to the speaker (or to whomever the argument is addressed). A person who had the choice between staying at home and listening to the radio or going out to hear a concert would not commonly be said to be "faced with a dilemma"; the situation of such a person could, however, be expressed in the form of a *logical dilemma.*

Although the dilemma, whether in the general form (a) or the more special forms (a_1), (a_2), (a_3), is always valid, it has been regarded with much suspicion. For while *any* valid form of argument may be, and often is, used to support false conclusions, the dilemma is perhaps particularly liable to such abuse. We may therefore profitably spend a little time considering the three traditional methods that have been suggested for refuting unsound dilemmas (*i.e.*, those in which false premises occur). It should be emphasized at the outset that these are all methods for objecting to the *truth* of the conclusion. They are not to be thought of as objections to the *validity* of the dilemma.

"Slipping between the horns."

This picturesque description refers to a procedure that may be suspected to be more effective in logic than in bull-fighting. The "horns" are the two components of the alternative premise of the dilemma.

Quite often, the alternative premise of a dilemma is false because its parts express propositions that are contraries but not strict contradictories. Thus it might be argued: "John is either stupid or clever. If he is clever he doesn't need teachers, and if he is stupid he can't profit by them. Hence teachers will do John no good." Here we have two dilemmas, the conclusion of the first appearing as a premise of the second:

(1)	$S \vee C$	(4)	$N' \vee P'$
(2)	$C \supset N'$	(5)	$[N' \supset G]$
(3)	$S \supset P'$	(6)	$[P' \supset G]$
(4)	$[N' \vee P']$	(7)	G

If we want to show that this argument is a bad one, we may admit "for the sake of argument," that there is *some sense* of "clever" and a corresponding sense of "stupid," according to which premises (2) and (3) will be true. "John might be so clever that he wouldn't need teaching, or so stupid that he couldn't profit by it," we might say, "but these are not the only alternatives. John is much more likely to be of average intelligence, somewhere between genius and imbecility."

In this objection, we are proposing to replace the first premise by the *new* one, $(S \vee C) \vee A$. The valid conclusion is now $(N' \vee P') \vee A$, and the original argument collapses. In "slipping between the horns," then, the original alternative premise, rejected as false, is replaced by a new premise that takes account of an intermediate case.

"Taking the dilemma by the horns."

Sometimes it is difficult or impossible to challenge the alternative premise. "If I don't go to the dentist, my tooth will continue to ache; if I do go, I shall get hurt." Here there is no plausible middle way between going to the dentist and not going. The dilemma may, however, be challenged *by rejecting one of the conditional premises.* Thus I may recall previous experiences at the dentist, and decide that I shall not get hurt if I do go. The premise, $G \supset H$ is, therefore, rejected as false, and replaced by $(G \supset H)'$ or, perhaps, $G \supset H'$. In either case the original argument collapses.

"Rebutting a dilemma."

It is sometimes possible to challenge a dilemma effectively by presenting another dilemma, based on much the same grounds, but apparently leading to an opposed conclusion. Thus an opponent of an International Security Organization might argue: "If the nations remain at peace, the Organization will be superfluous, and if they don't it will be ineffective." To which one might reply "If the nations remain at peace the Organization will not be ineffective, and if they don't it will not be superfluous." The two dilemmas can be symbolized as:

(c)
$$\begin{array}{l} P \supset S \\ P' \supset I \\ \hline [S \vee I] \end{array}$$

(d)
$$\begin{array}{l} P \supset I' \\ P' \supset S' \\ \hline [I' \vee S'] \end{array}$$

As this example shows, the rebuttal of a dilemma is obtained by interchanging and *negating* the consequents of the conditional premises in the original dilemma. The term "rebuttal" is misleading, however, since the conclusion, $I' \vee S'$, does *not* contradict the original conclusion $S \vee I$.

This can be made clear by the following scrap of dialogue. Patient: "According to your diagnosis, Doctor, I have either measles or scarlet fever. What a cheerful prospect!" Doctor: "Come, look on the bright side. My diagnosis shows that either you have *no* scarlet fever or else *no* measles!" There is, plainly, very little comfort for the patient in such a "rebuttal." For the possibility remains that he will have measles or scarlet fever (though not both). It is easy to verify that $M \vee S$ and $S' \vee M'$, instead of contradicting each other, can be asserted simultaneously. Together, they are equivalent to $M \veebar S$.

While the rebuttal of a dilemma is effective in debate, or other situations in which there is little time or inclination for careful logical analysis, it is a fallacious method of disproving an argument.

Summary

Many arguments contain propositions of the form *Either A or B*. The either-or operation will be called *alternation*. In ordinary usage, "Either A or B" sometimes means "Either A or B *or both*" and at other times "Either A or *B but not both*"; in the first case we speak of *inclusive* alternation, in the second of *exclusive* alternation. These operations are symbolized by '$\vee$' and '$\veebar$', respectively. Since $A \veebar B$ asserts *more* than $A \vee B$ (namely that A and B cannot both be true), we may also speak of *strong* alternation (exclusive) and *weak* alternation.

Any alternative proposition can be converted into an equivalent conditional proposition. For $A \vee B$ means the same as $A' \supset B$, and $A \veebar B$ means the same as $A' \equiv B$. By means of these equivalences, questions concerning arguments containing alternative statements can be answered by using the theory of conditional argument developed in previous chapters.

It is found that $A \vee B$ means the same as $B \vee A$; hence there are only *two* types of argument containing a single weak alternation. The form $A \vee B$ *and* A *therefore* B' is invalid, while the form $A \vee B$ *and* A' *therefore* B is valid. The two corresponding forms having strong alternation in one premise are both valid. In analyzing concrete alternative arguments, it is necessary to take especial care to determine the type of alternation involved.

The dilemma is a form of argument containing an alternative and two conditional premises. Its most general form is $A \vee B$, $A \supset C$, $B \supset D$, *therefore* $C \vee D$. Special cases are $K \vee L$, $K \supset M$, $L \supset M$, *therefore* M; $P \supset Q$, $P' \supset R$, *therefore* $Q \vee R$; and $U \supset V$, $U' \supset V$, *therefore* V. All of them are valid.

Dilemmas are often used to render unsound reasoning plausible. Three methods are in common usage to expose the *falsity* of the premises used in such cases. In "slipping between the horns" the alternative premise is rejected ($A \vee B$ is replaced by $A \vee B \vee C$); in "taking the dilemma by the horns" one of the conditional premises is rejected. In "rebutting a dilemma" a counter-dilemma is proposed, having a form explained in the text. But this method is fallacious.

Comprehension test

(For instructions, see page 10.)

1. "Either A or B or both" means the same as "If A is true B is false." (*true* *false*)
2. "$C \supset D$" means the same as "$C \vee D'$." (*true* *false*)
3. Exclusive alternation is "weak" alternation. (*true* *false*)
4. If P-or-Q is true and P is false, Q must be true. (*true* *false*)
5. If $K \veebar L$ is true $K \vee L$ must be true. (*true* *false*)
6. The conclusion of a logical dilemma presents alternatives, all unpleasant or unacceptable. (*true* *false*)
7. An exclusive alternation can be expressed as two conditional premises. (*true* *false*)
8. The dilemma is an invalid form of argument. (*true* *false*)
9. It is always possible to "slip between the horns" of a dilemma. (*true* *false*)
10. A dilemma and its "rebuttal" may lead to conclusions that are consistent with each other. (*true* *false*)

Exercises

A

1. Find ten examples of "either-or" propositions from newspapers. Characterize each as a case of inclusive alternation, exclusive alternation, or "doubtful."
2. Prove the validity of the arguments involving exclusive alternation (c) and (d), on page 101. Explain in detail what principles you have used in your proof.
3. Convert each of the conditional propositions used in a "chain-argument" (page 85) into an alternation. Give an independent proof of the validity of the type of alternative argument thus obtained.
4. Perform the following operations on the arguments below: (1) Symbolize the propositions, using the symbols supplied to stand for *positive* propositions; (2) add any assumptions that may be appropriate; (3) decide whether the argument is valid.
   a. He said he would arrive on Monday or Tuesday. It is too late to expect him on Monday. He will arrive on Tuesday. (S,M,T,L)
   b. The unknown is a multiple of 2 or a multiple of 5. We have proved it is a multiple of 2. Therefore it is not a multiple of 5. (T,F,P)
   c. "The dessert is pie or cheese. You prefer pie? Very well. No cheese for this customer." (P,C)
   d. "You are suffering from influenza or pneumonia. In either case, you need rest." (I,P,R)
   e. "In order to be eligible for this job, Tom must be a high school or college graduate. I happen to know he graduated from college. He is eligible." (E,H,C,K)
   f. Either the President can execute his own policies or not. If he cannot execute his own policies, he is weak. If he can execute his own policies, he must either follow other people's advice or not. If he *must* follow other people's advice he is weak; if not he is an autocrat. Thus the President must be an autocrat if he is not to be weak. (E,F,A,W)
5. Give concrete illustrations of each of the following types of argument. Which of them are valid?
   a. $K \vee L'$, L, *therefore* K.
   b. $M' \vee N'$, M', *therefore* N.
   c. $A \mathbin{\underline{\vee}} B$, *therefore* $B \supset A'$.
   d. $X \vee Y$, $Z \supset X$, *therefore* $Z \vee Y$.
   e. $P \supset Q$, $R \supset Q'$, *therefore* $P' \vee R'$.
   f. $F' \vee G$, $G' \vee H$, *therefore* $F' \vee H$.

g. $U \supset W$, $V \supset W$, *therefore* $(U \vee V) \supset W$.
h. $J \vee K \vee L$, *therefore* $J \vee (K \,\&\, L)$.

6. Criticize the following dilemmas, using whatever method seems to you most appropriate. Explain your reasons for choosing the preferred method.
   a. "Enter at once for the competition. If you win you get a handsome prize. If you don't you have the fun of competing. Either way you can't lose."
   b. If wages are held at their present level, workers will have to accept lower incomes than they received during the war. Yet a rise in wages will produce increased prices and thus fail to produce any improvement in *real* wages.
   c. I must live in town or in the country. If I live in the country I shall be lonely, and if I live in a town I shall be uncomfortable.
   d. If you make your living honestly you must work hard, but if you decide to become a crook you will have to work still harder.
7. Discuss the following passages of argumentative writing:
   a. "Science cannot long remain free in a society of slaves. If technological science must continue to throw men out of work and there is no remedy, the day must come when science itself must go on relief. If the meaninglessness which theoretical science has read into the universe must, as science advances, be read into the human spirit in its entirety, the scientific spirit cannot survive.... We face a critical dilemma. One horn is the destruction of *man by science;* the other the destruction of *science by man;* and a third possibility, a path of escape between the horns, is untrammeled study of fact in union with the hunt for the most promising means of general happiness." (Max Otto. *Science and the Moral Life,* p. 109. New York: New American Library, 1949.)
   b. This nation must be prepared to follow one of two policies with respect to the atomic bomb. Either we decide to keep the secret or to share it with the rest of the world. The objection to the first policy is that there is really no secret to keep—all the major powers will solve the problem of producing atomic bombs in a few years' time. The second policy, the only one that remains, means giving up some part of our sovereignty.
   c. "There are two ways of looking at our duty in the matter of opinion —ways entirely different.... *We must know the truth;* and *we must avoid error*—these are our first and great commandments as would-be knowers; but they are not two ways of stating an identical commandment, they are separate laws. Although it may indeed happen that when we believe the truth *A,* we escape as an incidental

consequence from believing the falsehood *B,* it hardly ever happens that by merely disbelieving *B* we necessarily believe *A*. We may in escaping *B* fall into believing other falsehoods, *C* or *D,* just as bad as *B;* or we may escape *B* by not believing anything at all, not even *A*." (William James, "The Will to Believe," reprinted in *Selected Papers on Philosophy*. Everyman Library, p. 113. New York: E. P. Dutton & Co., Inc.)

d. "Either you are for Nationalism or for Internationalism. But if you love your country, you cannot hesitate for a moment. This argument is only a little sillier, because more shortly stated, than many an argument I have heard. We must ask 'What does it *mean* to be "for Nationalism"?' and 'What does it *mean* to be "for Internationalism"?' " (L. S. Stebbing, *Thinking to Some Purpose,* p. 141. England: Allen Lane [Pelican Books], 1939.)

e. "In defending my client against the charge of libel, I shall show that the article was not written by Jones. Or if it was, that the passages in question were not. Or if they were, that he did not mean them in the plaintiff's sense. Or if he did, the passages in question had substantial truth. Or if they had not, my client did not and could not at the time know them to be untrue. Or if he could and did, we could not then and cannot now know them to be untrue. Or if we can and could, and he could and did, and they had not, and he did, and they were, and it was, then my client is not Jones." (Based on an answer to a competition in *"The New Statesman and Nation,"* 12 March, 1949.)

f. "Some people, who maintain the existence of a creative omnipotent God, maintain also that the choice of the human will between motives has no cause, and, therefore, is not ultimately caused by the creator. They admit, however, that God could have dispensed with the freedom of the human will, if he had chosen to do so.

"We may therefore say that an omnipotent God could have prevented all the evil in the universe if he had willed to do so. It is impossible to deny this, if omnipotence is to have any meaning, for to deny it would be to assert that there was something that God could not do if he willed to do it." (J. McT. E. McTaggart, *Some Dogmas of Religion,* p. 210. London: Arnold and Co., 1930.)

8. Collect examples from advertisements or elsewhere of fallacies depending upon confusion between exclusive and inclusive alternation.

B

1. Prove that if one premise of a dilemma involves exclusive alternation (so that the premises are $A \veebar B$, $A \supset C$, $B \supset D$), the valid conclusion is still $C \vee D$, *not* $C \veebar D$.
2. "All over human life we find properties which show continuous variation . . . and find this property obscured by the use of words implying sharp distinctions. 'Sane' and 'insane'; 'good' and 'bad'; 'intelligent' and 'unintelligent'; 'proletarian' and 'capitalist', are pairs of opposites which show this property of continuous variation . . . Any argument, therefore, which begins in some such way as follows: 'A man must be either sane or insane, and an insane person is absolutely incapable of reasonable thought . . .' is a dangerous piece of crooked thinking, since it ignores this fact of continuity." (R. H. Thouless, *Straight and Crooked Thinking,* pp. 179-80. London: Hodder and Stoughton. 1930.) Discuss these remarks. Do you think it possible to make true alternative propositions involving such vague notions as "sanity," "goodness," and "intelligence"?

7

THE FINER STRUCTURE OF PROPOSITIONS

Logic, which is, as it were, the Grammar of reasoning . . . consequently serves the purpose (when we are employing Logic as an art) *of a test to try the validity of any argument; in the same manner as by chemical analysis we develop and submit to a strict examination the elements of which any compound body is composed, and are thus enabled to detect any latent sophistication or impurity.*

—Archbishop Whately.

1. The need for other types of analysis.

THE types of arguments studied in the last three chapters have always contained one or more compound propositions, such as $A \supset B$, $C \& D$, $E' \vee F$. If simple propositions (*i.e.,* those not themselves constructed out of other propositions) are looked on as a kind of logical atom, we may consider ourselves as having been engaged in analysis of logical *molecules.* This has resembled in some ways the analysis performed by chemists when they seek to establish the structure and physical properties of chemical compounds, without using any knowledge of the structure of the interior of the atom itself. The need for more precise understanding of the properties of matter leads chemists and physicists to investigate the internal structure of atoms. In logic also there soon arises a need for methods that will reveal how "simple" propositions are themselves constructed out of elements.

A trivial example will reveal the limitations of the methods so far studied. Suppose a man has written some letters that he decides to send by air-mail. He may reason, more or less explicitly, "Air-mail letters require a six-cent stamp; therefore each of these letters will need a six-cent stamp." This argument becomes, when set out in full:

(a) All air-mail letters require a six-cent stamp.
All the letters I have written are air-mail letters.
———————————————————
All the letters I have written require a six-cent stamp.

None of the three propositions involved are compound. Since they are not constructed out of other propositions, the methods so far used require them to be symbolized by simple symbols, such as 'S', 'A', and 'W'. The argument is accordingly analyzed as

(b)

$$\frac{\begin{array}{c}S\\A\end{array}}{W}$$

The form, as so far analyzed, is that of an *invalid* argument. For it shows a conclusion, W, quite unrelated to the premises, S and A. [If we need any confirmation, we can take S and A to be *any* two true propositions, say *September has 30 days,* and *Alexander was a general*—and W any false proposition, say *Whiskey is a kind of milk.* This instance of the form (b) has true premises and a false conclusion, hence the form is that of an invalid argument.]

Nevertheless, the original argument, (a), is *valid;* it is logically impossible that the premises should be true while the conclusion is false. If our analysis (b) fails to show this, the reason is that we have not yet succeeded in showing how the three propositions are related to one another. Repetition of such phrases as "six-cent stamp," "air-mail letter," etc., shows that the three propositions are not *any three* propositions selected at random, as form (b) misleadingly suggests; they are, instead, three propositions whose parts, or elements, are related to one another in a definite way. In order to criticize arguments similar to (a) we shall need a "finer" or sub-atomic analysis of propositions.

Argument (a), in fact, has a certain logical form, not yet revealed by our symbols, on which its validity depends. (It would be good to re-read at this point what was said about logical form in Chapter 3.) The argument (a) we have been using as illustration should be compared with the following two:

(c) All plants need sunlight.
All roses are plants.
―――――――――――――
All roses need sunlight.

(d) All air-mail letters require a six-cent stamp.
All the letters I have written require a six-cent stamp.
――――――――――――――――――――――――――
All the letters I have written are air-mail letters.

The first of these is constructed out of materials quite different from those occurring in (a); yet (a) and (c) have the same logical form, and are both valid. We might try to show the form crudely by writing:

(e) All *so-and-so* are *such-and-such*.
All *thus-and-thus* are *so-and-so*.
――――――――――――――――
All *thus-and-thus* are *such-and-such*.

(Notice carefully the point of using three *different* phrases in this analysis.) The fact that the *so-and-so's* were air-mail letters in the argument (a), and plants in the argument (c), obviously makes no difference to the validity of the arguments.

Turning now to argument (d), we find that it has the same *materials* as (a), arranged in a different form. With the crude devices used above, the form appears as:

(f) All *such-and-such* are *so and so*.
All *thus-and-thus* are *so-and-so*.
――――――――――――――――
All *thus-and-thus* are *such-and-such*.

[Be sure you see the difference between this and (e) above.] This form is that of an invalid argument.

We have now seen that propositions that are not constructed out of other propositions may nevertheless have a logical form that is relevant to the validity of certain types of arguments. Our immediate task is to become clearer about the elements and forms of "simple" propositions than we can be so long as we use the vague language of "so-and-so," "such-and-such," or "thus-and-thus"; and then to go on to determine the principles that govern the validity of arguments similar to those used as illustrations above.

2. *The subject-predicate analysis of propositions.*

What *kind* of object were we describing by the italicized phrases in "all *so-and-so* are *such-and-such*"? Consider the sentence "All Texans are Americans." Here the "so-and-so" are Texans, a certain *group* of men, all of whom are being thought about at one time; and the "such-and-such" are another *group* or *class* of men, united by the fact that they are all citizens of the United States. Instead of using words "group" or "class" to identify the subject-matter of the proposition, we might have used "set," or "collection," or one of the other words available in the English language for referring simultaneously to a number of individual persons or things. In logic, the term preferred is **class;** we say, therefore, that the subject-matter of the proposition in question consists of the *class of Texans* and the *class of Americans;* these two classes are also said to be the **terms** of the proposition. (Let us refer to them, for brevity, as *t* and *a,* using small italics to remove any risk of confusion with our previous use of capital letters to stand for *propositions.*)

The proposition *All Texans are Americans* makes an assertion about *t* and *a*—and not about these classes separately, but rather about their relation to one another. What is this relation? Obviously the proposition claims that *t* is *wholly within* or is *included in a.*

Other propositions may be easily analyzed as expressing a relation of *exclusion* between classes. Thus the proposition *No mules are intelligent* may be thought of as claiming that the *whole* of the class of mules is outside (or is excluded from) the class of things that are intelligent. Each of these two **types** of propositions, having the forms *all a's are b* and *no a's are b,* respectively, are called **universal** propositions.

Two interpretations of universal propositions.

At this point we encounter a troublesome ambiguity. When a man says, "All Texans are Americans," both he and his hearer know that *some Texans exist.* The statement does not refer *only* to the Texans who already exist, however. It implies that *any* Texan (whether now alive or not) *would be* an American. We can therefore break up the original statement into two parts:

There are some Texans *and* if anything is a Texan, that thing is an American. (1)

Now for contrast consider the true statement, "All giants are tall." This time it may be supposed that neither the speaker nor the hearer claims that *some giants exist.* Since they believe the statement nevertheless to be true, it must be interpreted as

If anything is a giant, that thing is tall. (2)

On comparing (1) and (2), it is seen that the words "all A are B" can mean in some contexts:

There are some *a's and* if anything is an *a,* it is also a *b.* (3)

and, in other contexts, only:

If anything is an *a,* it is also a *b.* (4)

Of these two forms, (4) is the weaker. Since we want a *definite* meaning of "all" for our discussion, we shall choose the weaker form as standard.

So, when we say, "All *a* are *b*" we shall mean, in the future, "Any *a would be* a *b,*" or, in other words, "*If* anything is an *a* it is also a *b.*" We shall not be asserting that there *are* any *a*'s, or that any *a*'s exist. (Consequently we shall likewise not be assuming that any *b*'s exist.) If, however, we want to claim (as we sometimes may) not merely that the class of *a*'s is included in the *b*'s but also that there *are* some *a*'s, we shall be able to do so by making the *two* assertions: "All *a*'s are *b*'s" *and* "There are some *a*'s."

When the sentence "All *a*'s are *b*" is used by a person to imply the existence of some *a*'s, we shall say an **existential universal** statement is made; when "All *a*'s are *b*" is used without any implication that some *a*'s exist, we shall say a **hypothetical universal** statement is made.

According to the convention we have adopted, whenever *we* use the words "all *a* are *b*" we are to be understood as wishing to assert a hypothetical universal statement. If we are interpreting the use of these words by a speaker who has not adopted our convention, we shall have to decide, in each case, whether he is committed to the weak hypothetical or the strong existential form of the universal statement.

Corresponding remarks apply to the negative universal propositions of form *No a's are b.*

The interpretation of particular propositions.

The two propositions: *Some Europeans are Frenchmen* and *Some vegetables are not fit to eat* are clearly not universal propositions. But they resemble the universal propositions previously discussed in expressing relations of inclusion and exclusion between *classes.* The first proposition does not claim that the *whole* of the class of Europeans is included in the class of Frenchmen (as would be required to make it a universal statement). It says, instead, that *part* of the first class is included in the second. Similarly, the second proposition says that *part* of the class of vegetables is excluded from the class of edible things.

Propositions of form "some *a* are *b*" or "some *a* are not *b*" are called **particular.**

Once again we have to decide whether to adopt an existential or hypothetical interpretation of our use of the words "some *a* are *b*." Normally this phrase is used so as to imply that some *a*'s exist, and we shall follow this usage. When we use the words "some *a*'s are *b*" we shall imply that some *a*'s exist. Consequently, we must also be implying that some *b*'s exist.

Corresponding remarks apply to our interpretation of the negative particular proposition of form *Some a are not b.*

Some technical terms.

We have seen that four kinds of propositions involve a relation of inclusion or exclusion between classes. We shall say a proposition is expressed in **subject-predicate form** when the following conditions are satisfied:

The proposition is expressed by a sentence that begins with "some" or "all" (the **quantifier**), is followed in turn by the name of one class (the **subject**), the name of the relation of inclusion or exclusion (the so-called **copula**), and finally the name of the second class (the **predicate**). We shall show the occurrence of inclusion or exclusion by using the symbols '$<$' and '$\nless$', respectively. (These should be read as "is included in" and "is excluded from," respectively.)

These definitions are summarized in the following diagram:

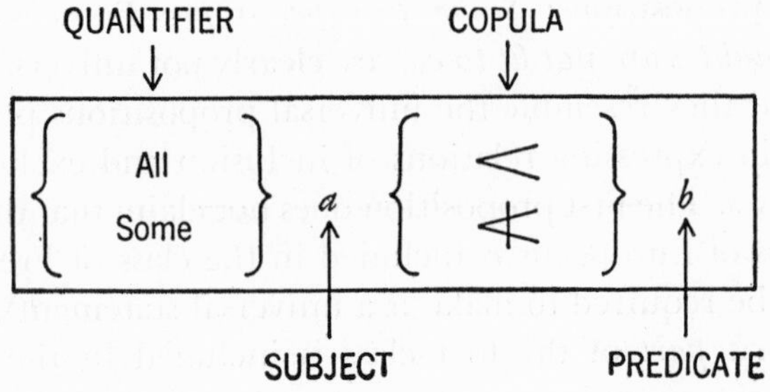

Each of the four standard forms has a distinctive label, as shown in the following diagram:

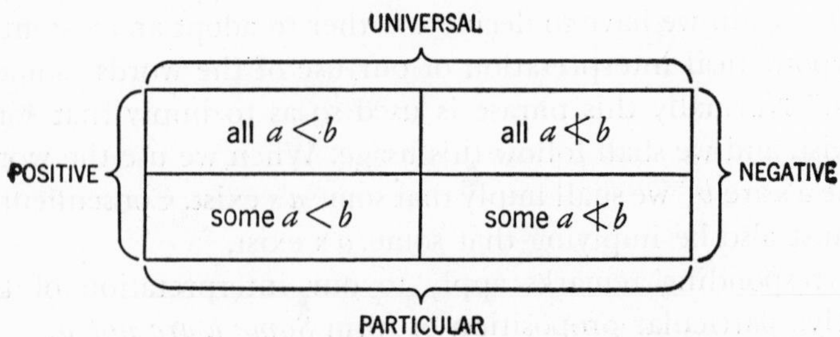

The meanings of the standard quantifiers.

Many other words besides "some" and "all" are in common use to indicate how much of a class is referred to in a proposition. "Most," "a few," "half," "a majority," "three," and all adjectives of number, are examples. We are neglecting all of these in our analysis—thus any argument that depends on the difference in meaning between any of these and "some" or "all" will have to be left uncriticized at this stage. The valid argument:

(a)

Most dogs like meat.
Most dogs are tame animals.
――――――――――――
Some tame animals like meat.

could at this stage be symbolized only as:

(b)

Some $d < l$.
Some $d < t$.
――――――
Some $t < l$.

which is an invalid form. In this example the fact that "most" means more than "some" is essential to the validity of (a); in other cases "most" can be replaced by "some" without harm to the argument.

The words "some" and "all," which we are to use as our only quantifiers, are themselves used ambiguously in ordinary situations. We shall take them to mean *at least one and possibly more* (*even all*) and *each and every one,* respectively. When we say "Some people are bad-tempered" we shall, therefore, mean that at least one person, unspecified, is bad-tempered, and shall be making no assertion concerning the other men; one or more, even all, of them might be bad-tempered or otherwise.

It is especially important to notice that the quantifier "all" indicates, in conjunction with the rest of the sentence in which it occurs, something that is true of each *individual* of the subject-class. The argument "Americans are numerous, therefore the President is numerous" is unsound because the premise asserts something that is true of the class of Americans *con-*

sidered as a unit. The class is a numerous or large class. Since we cannot say "each and every American is numerous" we have accordingly no right to represent the premise in the form *All* $a < n$.

Before proceeding further it would be good to work some (*i.e.,* at least one!) of the exercises on the analysis of propositions into standard subject-predicate form supplied at the end of this chapter.

3. *The Venn diagrams.*

In this section and in the next chapter we shall explain some pictorial devices for displaying the logical properties of propositions having subject-predicate form. We shall eventually find them a useful aid to the criticism of arguments whose validity depends upon the "fine structure" of propositions.

The English logician Venn invented the following way of representing relations of exclusion or inclusion between classes by means of simple geometrical diagrams.

Suppose a man has just arrived in a new house and his books are piled in confusion on the floor. In order to get some preliminary order, he draws two chalk circles on the floor, in this way:

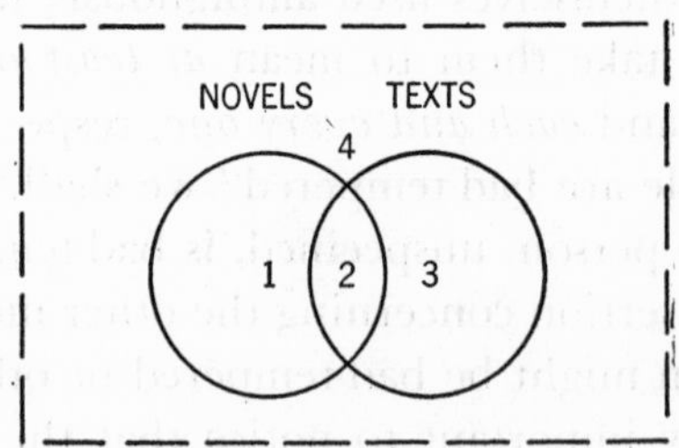

This gives him four compartments, as indicated by the numbers we have inserted. In compartment 1, he will place *things that are novels but not texts;* in compartment 2, *things that are both novels and texts;* in 3, *things that are texts but not*

novels; and in 4 (the space outside both circles), *things that are neither novels nor texts.*

Now we know that *No novels are texts, i.e.,* that compartment 2 must be empty. This can be shown by shading the corresponding space in the diagram, thus:

Any universal negative proposition can, of course, be represented in this way, by placing appropriate labels on the two circles. Notice carefully that according to our *hypothetical* interpretation of universal propositions (page 119) the Venn diagram does *not* say that compartments 1, 3, or 4 are occupied.

The corresponding representation of *positive* universal propositions is easy. Thus, the proposition *All cattle are animals* would be shown as:

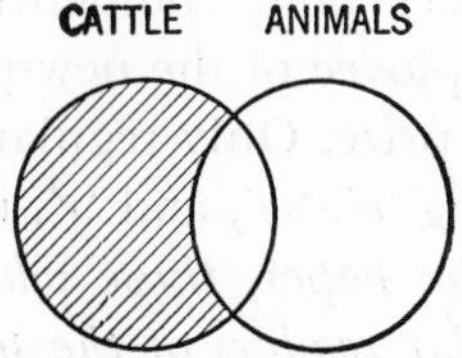

Notice again that this diagram does *not* claim that compartment 2 (reserved for things that are both cattle and animals) *is* occupied.

In order to show the particular proposition *Some birds swim* in a Venn diagram, we need some way of indicating that compartment 2, which is reserved for things that are birds and can swim, *has at least one occupant.* This is done in the following way:

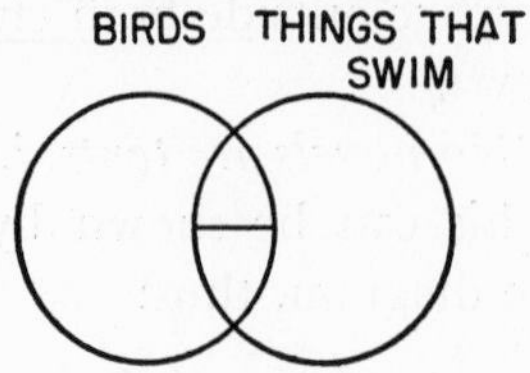

(Some writers prefer to place a cross or an asterisk in the compartment that is known to have at least one occupant.)

The only type of standard subject-predicate proposition not yet discussed, the *negative particular,* gives us no difficulty. Thus, the proposition *Some men are not married* will be shown as:

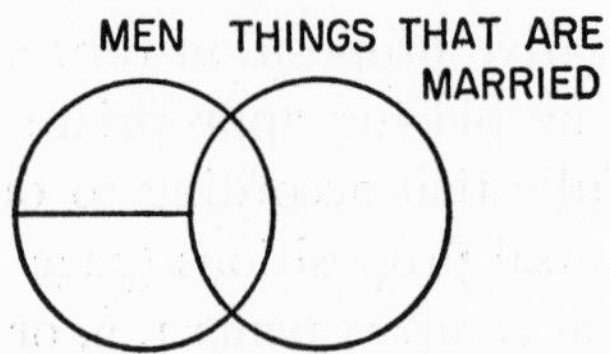

Extension of the diagrams to cases where more than two classes are concerned.

Newspapers sometimes hold competitions with some such rules as these: "No employee of the newspaper can win a prize. Somebody must win a prize. Only regular readers of the newspaper can win." Taking *'e'*, *'w'*, and *'r'*, to stand for the three classes *employees of the paper, those who win a prize in the competition,* and *regular readers of the paper,* respectively, we have the diagram:

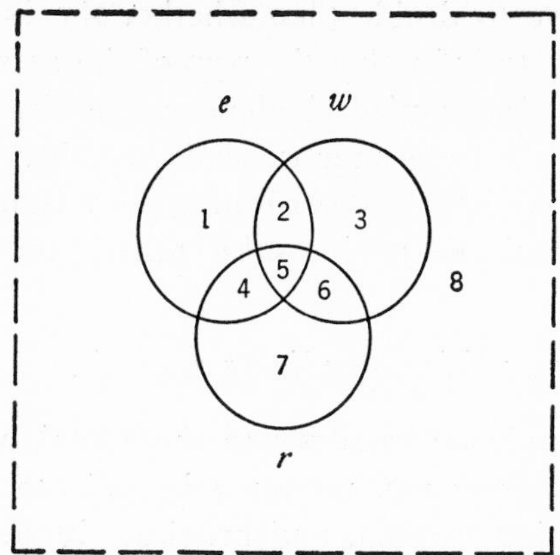

We have to show that compartment (2 + 5) is empty, compartment (2 + 3 + 5 + 6) has an occupant, and compartment (2 + 3) is empty. *It is wise to insert data concerning empty compartments before inserting data concerning occupied compartments.* Following this hint, we might get:

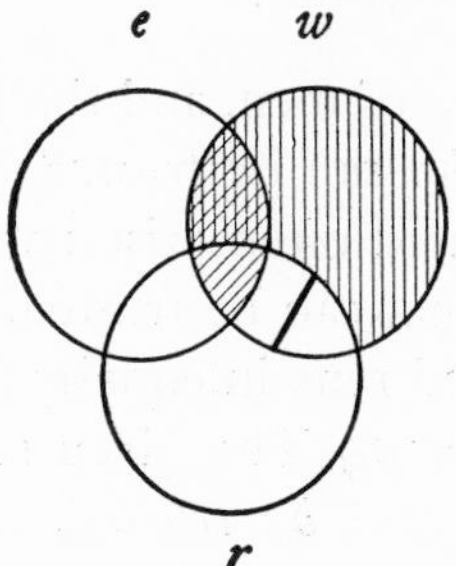

It should be carefully noted how the elimination of compartments (2 + 5) and (2 + 3), as shown by the shading, makes it sufficient to apply the "bar" *only* to compartment 6.

The chief use of this Venn diagram, as of the others we have illustrated, is to make it easy to answer questions concerning validity. Thus, we might be interested in knowing whether the information given permits as a valid deduction the conclusion *Some regular reader of the newspaper is not an employee of the paper*. We have to decide then whether the information provided allows us to infer that the part of the *r*-circle outside the *e*-circle ($6 + 7$) is occupied. A glance at he diagram shows that this is the case. A little later we shall be using Venn diagrams systematically as a help in determining the validity of arguments involving propositions having subject-predicate form.

4. *Exercises on subject-predicate analysis.*

In order to apply our analysis to the actual propositions we encounter in arguments, we must be able to determine the quantifier, subject, copula, and predicate in such cases. In so doing we should bear in mind (a) that many propositions not expressed in standard subject-predicate form can nevertheless be so expressed without harm to their content, (b) that nevertheless many propositions cannot conveniently be expressed in subject-predicate form at all. The examples that follow will illustrate these opposing maxims.

(1) "Not all men can be trusted."

The subject is the class of men, and the predicate is the class of *things* (or persons) *who can be trusted.* (The ambiguity of the predicate here illustrated often arises: we can say the predicate is the class of *things* that can be trusted, or the class of *persons* that can be trusted, and remain equally faithful to the meaning of the original statement.) The given sentence clearly implies *At least one man cannot be trusted,* which we symbolize as "*Some* $m \nless c$." Does it also imply the further statement *some* men *can be trusted* (*some* $m < c$)? We are unable to say, without further knowledge of the context. *Not all a are b* sometimes means *Some* $a \nless b$ and sometimes *Some* $a \nless b$ *and some* $a < b$.

(2) "Only high school graduates will be admitted to the college."

The two classes involved are *high school graduates* (*g*) and *those persons who will be admitted to the college* (*pa*). According to the sentence supplied, it is clearly intended that every *pa* will be a *g*, for which the correct symbols are "All $pa < g$" (note the reversal of the order of the symbols as compared with the original sentence). Is it also intended that every *g* is a *pa*? In this case, surely not. On the other hand, the sentence "Only regular customers will receive a discount" should be symbolized as "All *rc* are *dr and* all *dr* are *rc*." *Only a are b* sometimes means *all* $b < a$ and sometimes *all* $b < a$ *and all* $a < b$.

(3) "Tom is married."

There is reference here to the class of *married persons*. But Tom is not a class—it is absurd to ask whether something or other "is *a* Tom" (unless we are punning!). Tom is a member of the class of married persons, but is not *included* in that class in the way one class can be included in another. The subject-predicate analysis does not apply. We can, however, sometimes replace (3) by the proposition *All members of the class containing Tom and nobody else are married.*

(4) "The cause of our present distress is war."

We may try taking *the causes of our present distress (c)* and *wars (w)* as the two classes concerned, obtaining *all* $w < c$. But this is clearly wrong, since it means that *every* war is a cause of our distress. Since reference is made to the class of wars *as a whole,* the sentence resists our analysis [But see (3) above].

(5) "To have a hobby is to be happy."

This can be re-worded, "Those who have a hobby are happy persons," and can accordingly be represented as *all* $hh < hp$. The reader should be prepared to make such translations as this, when necessary.

Summary

Propositions not constructed out of other propositions may be called *simple* (as opposed to *compound*) propositions. Simple propositions have elements out of which they are constructed, these elements being arranged in a logical form. The validity of many arguments depends on the logical form of simple propositions.

Many propositions have the so-called *subject-predicate form.* When this is so, the proposition can be expressed by a sentence consisting of four parts: the *quantifier,* name of the *subject, copula,* and name of the *predicate.* The subject and predicate are two *classes* of objects; the quantifier is the word "all" or "some"; the copula is the name of the relation of inclusion or exclusion. The copula may be replaced by '$<$' or '$\nless$', and classes are symbolized by lower-case italic letters. The four types of subject-predicate proposition described are accordingly symbolized as "(some, all) a ($<$, $\nless$) b." If *all* of the subject is involved, the proposition is called *universal,* otherwise *particular.* If the relation connecting subject and predicate is that of inclusion, the proposition is called *positive,* otherwise *negative.* It follows that each of the four standard types of subject-predicate proposition has a distinctive technical label.

For the purpose of the theory of the syllogism (developed in the next chapter) special attention must be given to the following points in the interpretation of the four standard forms: (1) The sentence "All a are b," as ordinarily used, sometimes does and sometimes does not imply that some a's exist. In the first case it is said to express an *existential universal,* in the second a *hypothetical universal* proposition. We shall always take the *symbols* "all $a < b$" and "all $a \nless b$" to express *hypothetical* universal propositions. (2) A corresponding ambiguity arises in connection with the meaning of "some." We shall always take the symbols "some $a < b$" and "some $a \nless b$" in the *existential* sense. (3) The quantifier "all" is to be interpreted as meaning "each and every one." Sentences such as "Americans are respected" (in which reference is made to a property of the class of Americans considered *as a whole*) will not be taken to express propositions of standard subject-predicate form. (4) We decide that the quantifier "some," *as we use it,* shall mean "at least one, possibly more, even all." Thus *some* $a < b$ is compatible with *exactly one a is b, some but not all a are b,* and *all a are b.*

Venn diagrams are geometrical devices for showing relations between classes in a vivid fashion. Their use is explained in the text.

Comprehension test

(For instructions, see page 10.)

1. All propositions have logical form. (*true* *false*)
2. Some propositions may be considered to have two different logical subjects. (*true* *false*)
3. *All* $a < b$ is a particular positive proposition. (*true* *false*)
4. *Any a is b* means the same as *If there are any a's they are all b's.* (*true* *false*)
5. The word "some" always refers to at least two objects. (*true* *false*)
6. The sentence "Tom is happy" can be replaced by an equivalent sentence that is in the standard subject-predicate form. (*true* *false*)
7. A "particular" proposition is always to be interpreted in the "existential" sense. (*true* *false*)
8. "All $a < b$" is compatible with "Some $a < b$." (*true* *false*)
9. A Venn diagram for two classes consists of three compartments. (*true* *false*)
10. A Venn diagram has to be constructed out of circles. (*true* *false*)

Exercises

A

1. Which of the following sentences express subject-predicate propositions? (Give reasons.)
   a. Blessed are the merciful.
   b. Not all drugs are reliable.
   c. If there is no answer, he is not at home.
   d. All men over the age of twenty-one can vote.
   e. Nothing is impossible for the courageous.
   f. Einstein is an American.
   g. Half the population are undernourished.
   h. It takes all sorts to make a world.

   j. Stop that!
   k. Only club members admitted.
   l. A man may be old without being wise.
   m. There are more Americans than Frenchmen.

2. Pick out the quantifier, subject, copula, and predicate of each of the following propositions:
   a. All geese are fat.
   b. No men are women.
   c. At least one person has been here before me.
   d. Somebody is not telling the truth.
   e. Art is a luxury.
   f. Medicine is no cure for lack of exercise.
   g. Nobody has ever seen a ghost.
   h. Not every valid argument can be analyzed by the methods hitherto explained.

3. Give the correct technical name for each of the subject-predicate propositions in the preceding question.

4. Draw Venn diagrams for each of the following:
   a. No sailors are farmers.
   b. Some fishermen are wealthy.
   c. All fish are organisms and some organisms are mammals.
   d. No animals laugh, and all who laugh are happy.
   e. Some heavy stones are valuable; some heavy pearls are not valuable.
   f. Students will take one, but not more than one of the following subjects—French, German, Spanish.

5. Let *'A'*, *'E'*, *'I'*, *'O'* stand for "all $a < b$," "all $a \nless b$," "some $a < b$," and "some $a \nless b$," respectively.
   a. What are the contradictories of A and E?
   b. If A is true, which of the three others *must* be true? Which *must* be false?
   c. Repeat b substituting E, I, O, in turn, for A.
   d. Which of the four propositions remain true (or false, as the case may be) if subject and predicate *'a'* and *'b'* are interchanged?

B

1. Find examples to illustrate each of the following true statements:
   a. A valid argument can consist of simple propositions, none of which are of standard subject-predicate form.
   b. The word "few" may sometimes be replaced by "some" ("at least one") without detriment to the argument in whose expression it occurs.

c. A given proposition may sometimes be analyzed into the four elements of subject-predicate form in more than one way.
d. The word "is" does not always mean "is included in."
e. A class may contain only a single number.
f. Some statements express relations of inclusion and exclusion between *three* classes.

2. On being asked to identify the classes mentioned in given statements, a student supplied the following answers. Which of them are obviously wrong?
   a. "Everything that exists"
   b. "Animals"
   c. "Happy"
   d. "No dogs"
   e. "The class of awe-inspiring ghosts"
   f. "Can succeed"
   g. "Several people"
3. Explain carefully the difference between a *grammatical* subject and a *logical* subject.
4. What kind of a Venn diagram would be needed to show the relations between *four* classes? Use such a diagram (or any other method) to solve the following problems:
   a. Simplify the following regulations: "Every student who takes chemistry but no physics must take botany. No student may take more than one of these three courses."
   b. In a certain library there are no new foreign publications, none of the magazines are bound, and all the foreign magazines are new. What information do we have about the magazines in the library?

8

THE SYLLOGISM

The rationalization of knowledge is its reference to principles sufficiently secure from criticism; and it is the Syllogism which helps us to force these principles into explicitness in any given case, and so enables us to inquire into the foundation on which the thesis rests.—Alfred Sidgwick.

1. Definition of a syllogism and related notions.

"FROGS can't be mammals—they're cold-blooded." This scrap of conversation illustrates one of the most common of all types of argument. On supplying the implicit assumption, we get:

[all cold-blooded animals $\nless$ mammals]
all frogs $<$ cold-blooded animals

(all) frogs $\nless$ mammals

This is a special kind of **syllogism** (sometimes also called "*categorical* syllogism"). We notice that it contains *two* premises, that all three propositions have subject-predicate form, and that three classes in all are involved.

Sometimes an argument seems to be of this form, but actually refers to *more* than three classes, as in the following (invalid) argument: "Husbands are men. It takes plenty of courage to be a man. Therefore husbands have plenty of courage." (In this instance there is a subtle shift in the meaning of "man," as may be seen by considering the difference between saying "X is of the masculine sex" and "X is *manly*.")

In order to include such (invalid) cases, we define a syllogism as: *An argument composed of two premises and a conclusion, each capable of presentation in standard subject-predicate form, and purporting to contain three classes in all.*

The number and arrangement of the terms of a valid syllogism. Examination of a number of instances of syllogisms will soon make evident the truth of the following assertion: In a *valid* syllogism, exactly three classes (the **terms**) must be involved, and of these one must occur in both premises, and each of the others must occur once in a premise and once in the conclusion.

It is customary to call the class that occurs in both premises the **middle term;** the predicate of the conclusion is the **major term,** and the subject the **minor term.** The premise in which the major term occurs is the **major premise,** and that in which the minor term occurs is the **minor premise.** The use of these few technical labels makes it easier to compare syllogisms with one another and to determine the rules of validity that govern them.

A single illustration may show sufficiently how the major, minor, and middle terms are determined in a concrete case. Let the argument be: "Sailors are unsatisfactory parents—they spend so much time away from home." We see that the first sentence expresses the conclusion. The minor term is accordingly the subject of that proposition, *i.e.,* the class of sailors, and the major term the predicate, *i.e.,* the class of those who are unsatisfactory parents. The remaining class mentioned in the argument, *i.e,* that of those who spend much time away from home, must therefore be the middle term. If we represent these three classes by '*s*', '*u*', and '*a*', respectively, and add the unstated premise, *All who spend much time away from home are unsatisfactory parents,* we get:

$$\begin{array}{l} [\text{All } a < u] \\ \text{All } s < a \\ \hline \text{All } s < u \end{array} \qquad \text{(VALID)}$$

It will be noticed that the major premise has been written *first;* it is convenient to do this regularly when analyzing syllogisms. In the future, therefore, the first line of the *analysis* of a syllogism will be understood as intended to express the major premise.

2. *Determining the validity of syllogisms by Venn diagrams.*

In order to determine whether a given syllogism is valid, we represent the data contained in the premises by means of three Venn circles. Inspection of the diagram will then usually show at a glance whether the alleged conclusion is justified. *It is advisable to insert the data supplied by any universal premises first,* for otherwise it may prove difficult to insert unambiguously the "bars" indicating the occupancy of regions.

The following examples will illustrate some of the variety of cases that arise in practice. We use symbols at present ('s', 'p', and 'm', standing for the minor, major, and middle terms respectively), leaving difficulties that arise in the interpretation of arguments expressed in ordinary language for later consideration (sections 5 and 6 of this chapter).

First we insert a diagram to make it easier to discuss the cases considered:

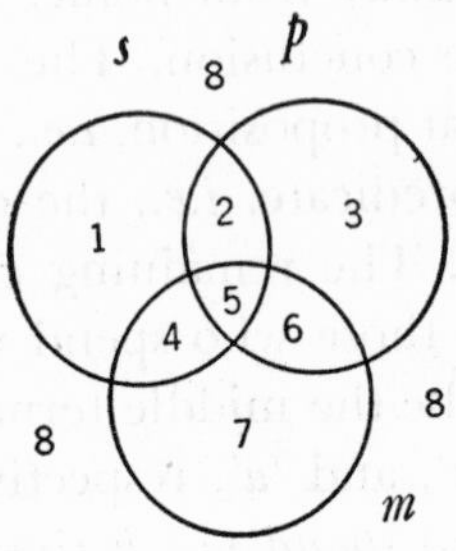

Case 1

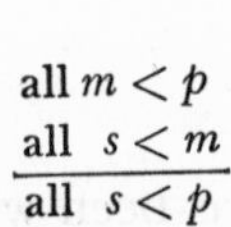

$$\begin{array}{l} \text{all } m < p \\ \text{all } s < m \\ \hline \text{all } s < p \end{array}$$

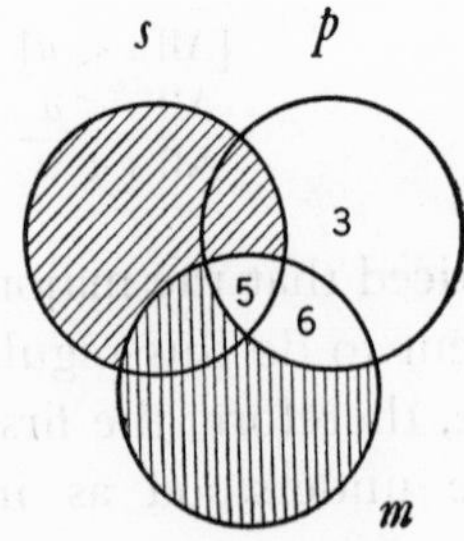

Comment: The conclusion requires all s to be contained in the p-class. The Venn diagram shows the surviving s to be contained in compartment 5, and the surviving p in compartment $(3 + 5 + 6)$. The argument is *valid.*

Case 2

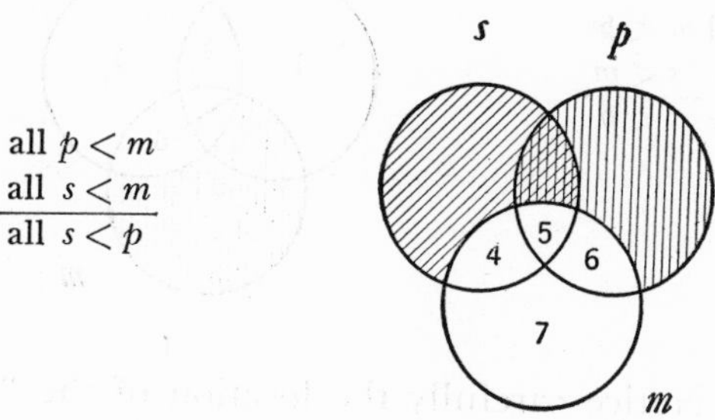

Comment: We are asked to conclude that the s [compartment $(4 + 5)$] are included in the p [compartment $(5 + 6)$]. The diagram shows that this conclusion is unjustified. An *invalid* argument. We can easily see that no valid connection between s and p can be deduced from the data supplied.

Case 3

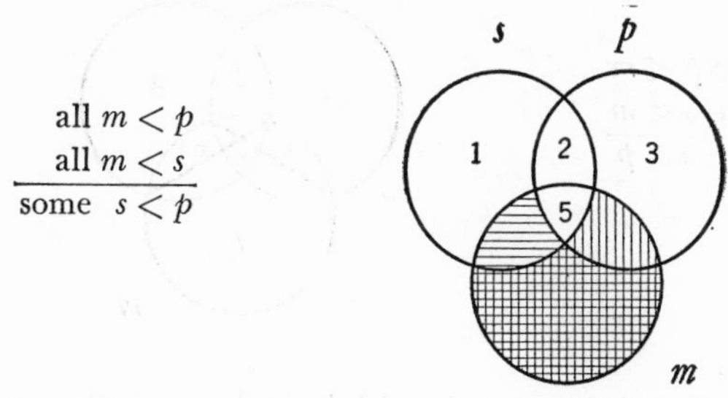

Comment: The conclusion asserts that something exists that is both s and p, *i.e.*, that the space $(2 + 5)$ is occupied. *Invalid.* This result is to be expected since both premises are hypothetical, and therefore make no reference to the existence of anything. Since the surviving m are in space 5, we notice that the addition of a premise to the effect that *some m's exist* would provide a valid conclusion.

Case 4

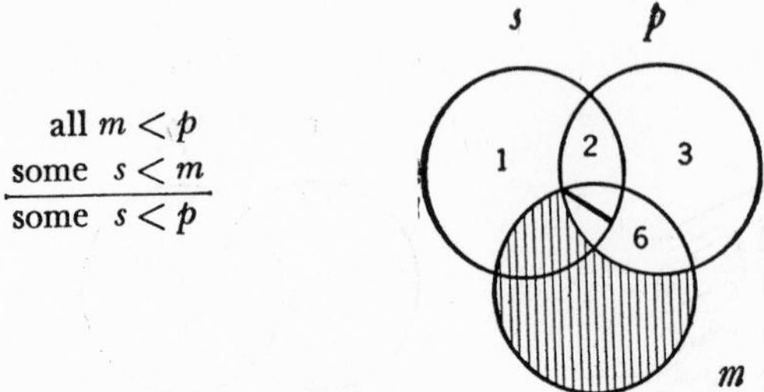

Comment: Notice carefully the location of the "bar." Symbolizing the universal (major) premise first permits the bar to be located in compartment 5 instead of compartment (4 + 5). (Why?) The conclusion, viz., that there is at least one occupant of compartment (2 + 5) is clearly justified. The argument is *valid.*

Case 5

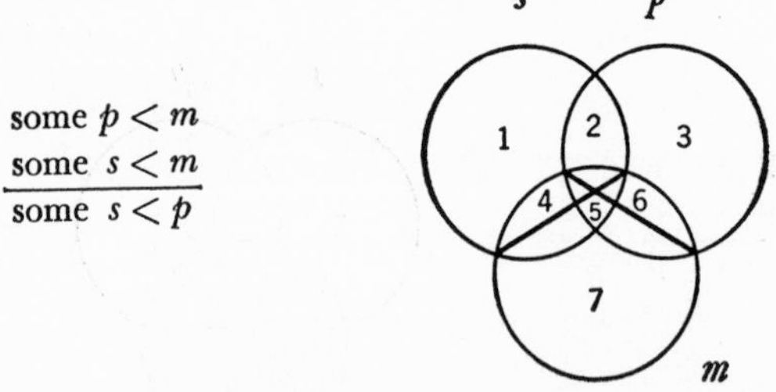

Comment: Careful note should be taken of the manner of insertion of the two "bars." We have to show compartment (5 + 6) as occupied and also compartment (4 + 5) as occupied. Does it follow that compartment 5 is occupied? Clearly not. Hence we do not know that compartment (2 + 5) is occupied and the argument is *invalid.*

Case 6

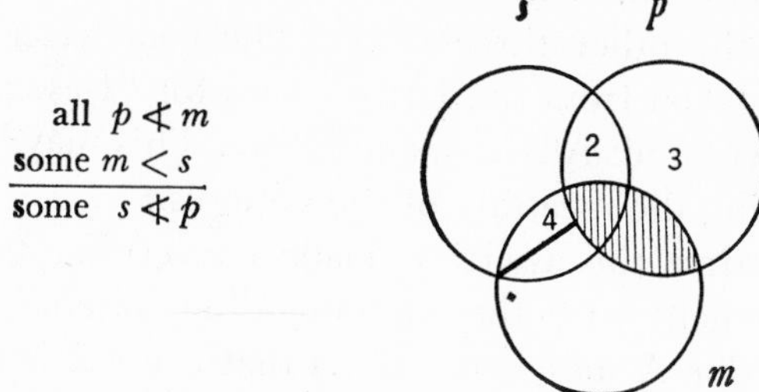

Comment: By first inserting the data supplied by the universal premise, we are able to show that space 4 is occupied. Since the surviving p are in (2 + 3), we are justified in asserting that some s (viz., that or those located in space 4) is excluded from p. The argument is *valid.*

3. *Distribution of terms.*

The examples discussed in the last section illustrate the point that the Venn diagrams, while useful, are not foolproof. For this reason, and because it is somewhat tedious and inconvenient to be always drawing sets of overlapping circles, it is advisable to have available some general principles of validity of the syllogism. In this section we prepare the ground for the formulation of such principles.

From now on it will be time-saving to be able to refer to the four standard types of subject-predicate propositions by using the **code-letters** 'A', 'E', 'I', 'O' according to this scheme:

A:	all $k < l$	(universal positive)
E:	all $k \nless l$	(universal negative)
I:	some $k < l$	(particular positive)
O:	some $k \nless l$	(particular negative)

Thus, an A proposition will be understood to be a universal positive proposition, *i.e.*, one having the form *all* $k < l$, and similarly for the other three cases. (The code-letters are said to have been taken from the Latin words for "I assert" and "I deny" as shown here: AffIrmo, and nEgO. This may be of help in remembering the meaning of the symbols.)

Let us contrast the assertion made concerning the subject in an A statement with the corresponding statement in an I proposition. The A statement asserts that every *k* is a member of *l*, *i.e.*, makes an assertion about the *whole* of the subject. Following the traditional terminology, we shall say the subject of an A proposition is **distributed.** In an I statement we are told only that *at least one k* is *l*. All of *k* might in fact be included in *l*, but we are not told that it is. We shall say that the subject of an I proposition is **undistributed.** (Notice carefully that to say a term is undistributed means only that the proposition in which it occurs does not *claim* that the whole class is involved.) The use of the quantifiers "all" and "some," respectively, shows that *the subject is distributed in universal propositions, undistributed in particular propositions.*

In which types of propositions is the *predicate* distributed? The E and the O propositions assert that all or some of *k* are excluded from the *whole* of *l*. (If you are doubtful about this, consider that for a man to be excluded from the United States it is necessary to keep him out of *every* state of the Union.) Finally, the remaining forms, A and I, give information only about *some* members of the predicate, *l*; for the A proposition claims, at best, that *some l* are *k*, and the I proposition that *at least one l is k*. The predicate in these cases is undistributed. *The predicate is distributed in negative propositions, undistributed in positive propositions.*

We shall show these results by using the two letters "D" (distributed) and "U" (undistributed). The four standard types of propositions accordingly have **distribution-patterns** shown below:

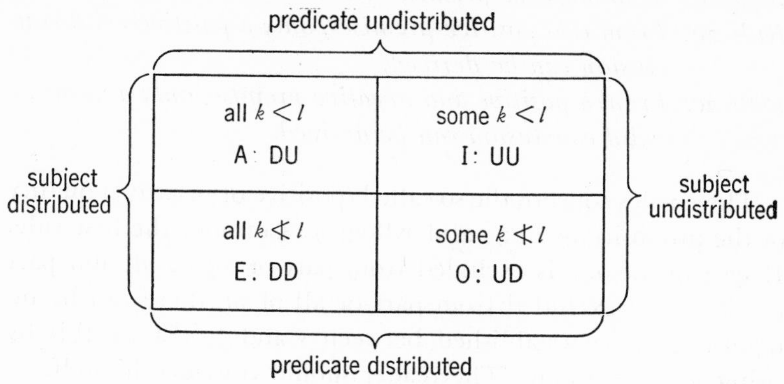

The reader should study this diagram (and work appropriate exercises from those provided at the end of the chapter) until able to supply the characteristic distribution pattern of each standard form unhesitatingly.

4. Principles of the valid syllogism.

In this section we shall introduce a set of eight rules, to which any syllogism must conform if it is to be valid. After each rule we add explanatory comment and justification.

Rule 1: In a valid syllogism there must be three terms.

(This rule should be compared with the definition of a syllogism, given on p. 132.) Suppose there are four classes mentioned in the syllogism, and let them be *s*, *p* (subject and predicate of the conclusion), *k*, and *l*. If both *k* and *l* occur in the same premise, that premise is clearly irrelevant. If, however, *k* occurs in one premise and *l* in another, *s* and *p* are related (by inclusion or exclusion) to two different classes, and there is no link between them for which a valid conclusion may be obtained. This rule is often broken by the occurrence of four terms. When this happens the **fallacy of four terms** is said to have been committed.

Rule 2a: Two negative premises yield no valid conclusion.

Rule 2b: From two positive premises, only a positive valid conclusion can be derived.

Rule 2c: From a positive and negative premise, only a negative valid conclusion can be derived.

These rules concern the so-called (positive or negative) **quality** of the propositions in a valid syllogism. Consider the first rule. If part or all of *s* is excluded from part or all of *m*, and part or all of *p* is excluded from part or all of *m*, there can be no definite relation established between *s* and *p*. (Check this by using Venn diagrams. The reader should convince himself, by testing assorted samples with the aid of Venn diagrams, that the other two rules are also needed.

Rule 3a: In a valid syllogism, the middle term must be distributed at least once.

Rule 3b: In a valid syllogism, the minor term canot be distributed in the conclusion unless it is distributed in the minor premise.

Rule 3c: In a valid syllogism, the major term cannot be distributed in the conclusion unless it is distributed in the major premise.

These rules, relating to the distribution of terms, are the so-called rules of **quantity.** Suppose the first rule broken, *i.e.*, that the middle term is *un*distributed in each occurrence. Then we are told that (part or all of) *p* and *s* are related (by inclusion or exclusion) to *some m*, but we have no assurance that the *same* members of *m* are involved each time. Such a syllogism is invalid (as should be confirmed by using Venn diagrams.) A breach of the second rule could occur only if *s* were U in the minor premise and D in the conclusion. In such a case we should proceed from data concerning *some s* to a conclusion concerning *all s:* The syllogism would be invalid (as is easily confirmed by use of Venn diagrams.) Similar argument applies to the last rule.

Notice that rules 3b and 3c do not prohibit passage from D in the premise to U in the conclusion (passage from "all" to "some"). (But see exercise 3 on page 156.)

Breach of these rules is very common. The corresponding mistakes in argument are entitled **fallacy of undistributed middle** and **fallacy of illicit process** (of the minor or major, respectively).

Rule 4: In a valid syllogism, the conclusion cannot be particular unless one premise is particular.

To see that this rule is necessary, consider the following type of syllogism:

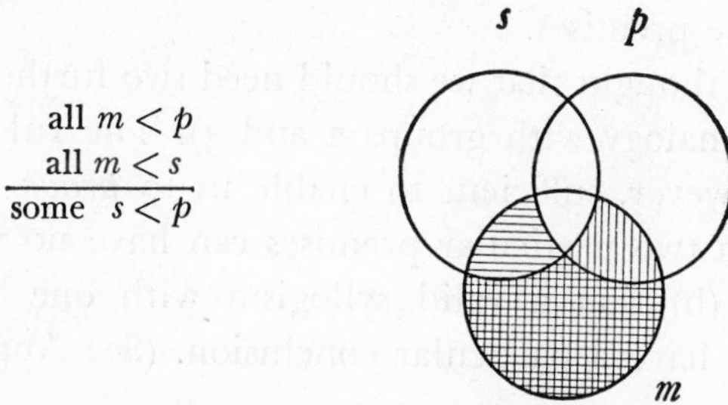

The distribution patterns for the three propositions are DU, DU, and UU respectively. Let us use a circle, square, and flattened M to show the location of the minor, major, and middle term respectively. The syllogism can then be analyzed as follows:

A	+	D (M)	U (square)
A	+	D (M)	U (circle)
I	+	U (circle)	U (square)

This diagram shows at a glance that the seven rules of the valid syllogism previously explained are all satisfied. (We have two positive premises and a positive conclusion, satisfying the rules of quality; the middle term *is* distributed "at least once" and neither the minor nor the major terms proceed from U to D as forbidden by the rules of quantity.)

Yet the syllogism is *invalid*. This is confirmed by the Venn diagram; it is also easily seen by considering that the premises are *hypothetical* (and accordingly do not assert that any *s*, *m*, or *p* exist), while the conclusion is existential.

We shall call this rule the **existential rule** of the valid syllogism, in order to emphasize its function of ensuring that the conclusion makes no assertions about existence that are not justified by the premises.

It might be thought that we should need two further rules in group 4 (by analogy with groups 2 and 3). The rules already given are, however, sufficient to enable us to *prove* (a) that a syllogism with two particular premises can have no valid conclusion, and (b) that a valid syllogism with one particular premise must have a particular conclusion. (See Appendix 1.)

5. *The criticism of concrete syllogistic arguments.*

In the examination of arguments suspected to be syllogistic in form, the difficulties are partly linguistic and partly formal. The *formal* difficulties are those that arise in determining whether a syllogism is valid *after the original argument has been adequately symbolized.* We now have powerful tools (the Venn diagrams and the rules of the valid syllogism) for overcoming *this* type of difficulty. The most troublesome aspect of arguments actually encountered in the course of reading or conversation will therefore be connected with the elliptical character of the language normally used. Special attention should therefore be given to the methods illustrated in this section for the removal of ambiguity and the detection of unstated premises.

This would be an excellent time to review the suggestions previously made in connection with the analysis of concrete conditional arguments (pages 66-70) that apply with little modification to the analysis of syllogisms. As in the analysis of conditional argument, it will be wise to begin by making certain that the statements examined are intended as an argument, rather than as a set of unsupported assertions. The exhibition of unstated premises will again be an important part of the work to be done.

In dealing with conditional arguments, it was suggested that special care be taken to verify that the premises can be expressed in the "if-then" form, and it was seen to be often necessary to rephrase a given sentence in order to exhibit it in this form (page 69).

In the analysis of syllogisms, the corresponding suggestions will be:

(a) *Be sure that the argument depends only on relations of inclusion or exclusion between classes.*

(b) *If necessary, rephrase sentences to convert them into the standard subject-predicate form.*

(a) You should guard against the false assumption that every valid argument consisting entirely of *categorical* (*i.e.*, unconditional) premises must be a syllogism. The argument, "John is taller than Mary, and Mary is taller than Jane; therefore John is taller than Jane," is clearly valid, but its validity depends on certain properties of the relation of relative height. To try to exhibit *this* argument as a syllogism or a chain of syllogisms would be to fail to see its relevant logical form.

(b) It is rare for a premise of a syllogism to be fully expressed in the standard form *All* (*or some*) *a is included in* (*or excluded from*) *b*. The quantifier is often left out altogether and must be supplied (as in "Cats are friendly animals"); it may be necessary to change such a quantifier as "most" or "few" into "some," in order to make our analysis applicable; and the copula is often unsymbolized (as in "Dogs love meat"), or expressed with the help of such words as "only" and "none but."

6. *Model analyses of concrete syllogistic arguments.*

The general procedure adopted in analyzing the following examples is this:

A. The argument is identified as a syllogism.
B. The terms involved in the premises are picked out and represented by appropriate symbols.
C. The premises and conclusion are exhibited with the help of the symbols.
D. Any unstated premises needed in the argument are stated explicitly.
E. The Venn diagrams and the "distribution-analysis" are constructed.
F. The validity of the argument is determined by inspection of the Venn diagram, and by verifying in the distribution-analysis that all the rules of the valid syllogism are satisfied.
G. Where appropriate, comments are made concerning the truth of the premises.

1. "*Some* turtles certainly cannot be regarded as fish, for no fish live on land, and some turtles do."

Comment: We take the first sentence to be an emphatic way of putting forward the conclusion *Some turtles are not fish.* The terms occurring in the argument are the class of turtles, the class of fish, and the class of things living on land, which we represent by '*t*', '*f*', and '*l*', respectively. The analysis is:

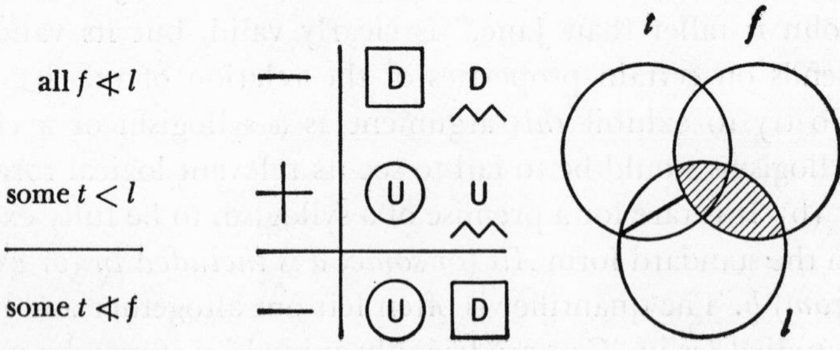

It will be noticed that the major premise has been written first, and the cirle, square, and flattened M show the location of the minor, major, and middle terms respectively. The distribution-analysis on the right shows at a glance that all the rules of the valid syllogism have been satisfied, and the Venn diagram confirms the judgment that the argument is *valid.*

2. "These books must be valuable—they were printed in 1660."

Comment: A typical case of a "telescoped" argument. The speaker must be assuming that all books printed in 1660 are valuable. The three classes involved are: that consisting of "these books," that consisting of valuable books (or, if we prefer, valuable things in general), and that consisting of books printed in 1660. Using 't', 'v', 'p' for these, we get:

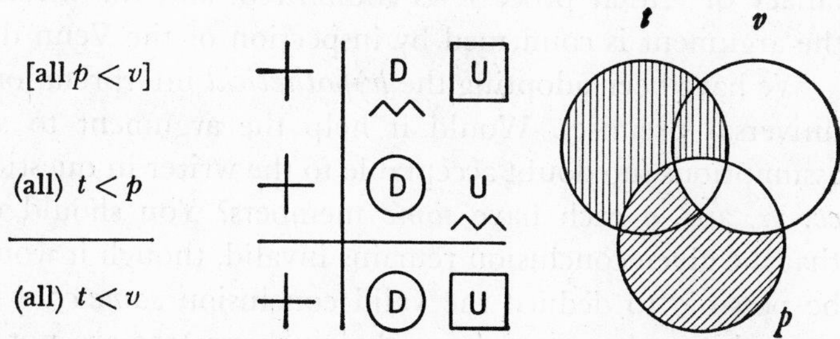

It is easily seen that the argument is *valid.* (The major premise is, however, false.)

3. "Quinine comes from the cinchona tree, but no rubber trees yield quinine. We must not expect any product of the cinchona from rubber trees."

Comment: It is not certain that the writer is putting forward the last sentence as expressing a valid deductive conclusion from his premises. Let us suppose for the moment that he *is* doing this. Examination of the first two sentences shows that the class of things that are quinine must be the middle term. The remaining terms must accordingly be the class of things that "come" from the cinchona tree, and the class of things yielded by rubber trees. We may interpret the last sentence as expressing the proposition *No things that come from cinchona trees are yielded by rubber trees.* The analysis is:

all q ≮ yr
(all) q < cc
all cc ≮ yr
D
D
D
U
D
D
cc
yr
q

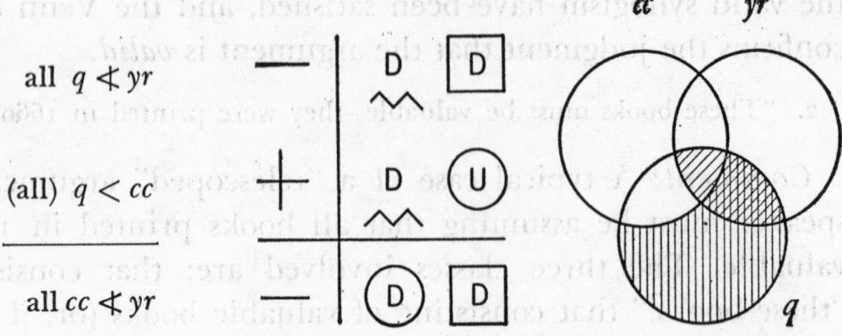

We see at once from the distribution-analysis that the minor term is U in its premise and D in the conclusion, whereby the fallacy of "illicit process" is committed, and the *invalidity* of the argument is confirmed by inspection of the Venn diagram.

We have been adopting the *hypothetical* interpretation of the universal premises. Would it help the argument to add the assumptions (no doubt acceptable to the writer in question) that *cc, yr,* and *q* each have *some* members? You should confirm that the given conclusion remains invalid, though it would then be possible to deduce the valid conclusion *some cc* $\nless$ *yr* (*i.e.,* some things that come from the cinchona tree are not yielded by rubber trees). But this is still very far from constituting a proof that cinchona and rubber trees have *no* products in common.

4. "All college students are high school graduates. All high school graduates have studied arithmetic. Hence some who have studied arithmetic are college students."

Comment: On the hypothetical (non-existential) interpretation of the premises, the analysis is:

all cs < hg
all hg < sa
some sa < cs
D
U
D
U
U
U
sa
cs
hg

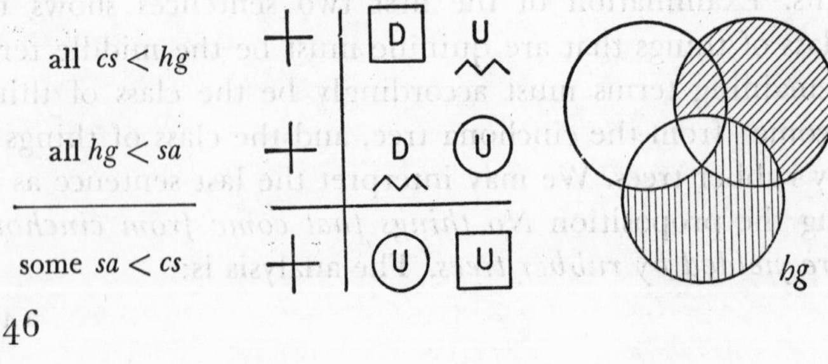

So far the argument breaks the existential rule of the valid syllogism (p. 142), but we are no doubt expected to assume that *some* college students exist. This gives us the following Venn diagram:

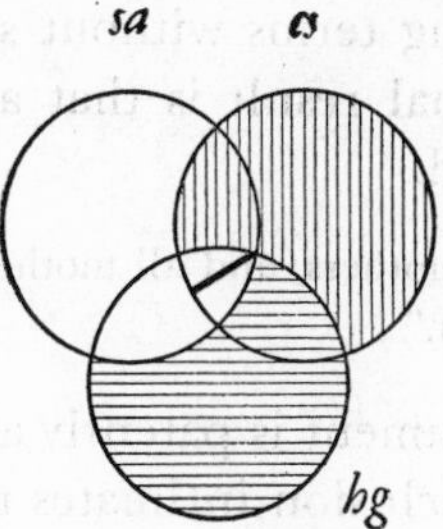

and allows us to certify the argument as *valid, provided the assumption is admitted.*

5. "All zebras wear stripes, and all prisoners wear stripes; therefore some zebras are prisoners."

Comment: There are here *four* classes involved, including the class of those who have striped *skins,* and the class of those who have striped *clothes. Invalid:* An instance of the "fallacy of four terms" (page 139).

One way of modifying the argument deserves attention. Suppose the speaker says, "Very well: Since you object to the ambiguity of my words, I propose to mean by 'wearing stripes' the same as either having a striped skin *or* having striped clothes." The effect of this is to coalesce the two classes, *ss* and *sc,* into a single combined class, *s.* The argument then no longer commits the fallacy of four terms and is analyzed as:

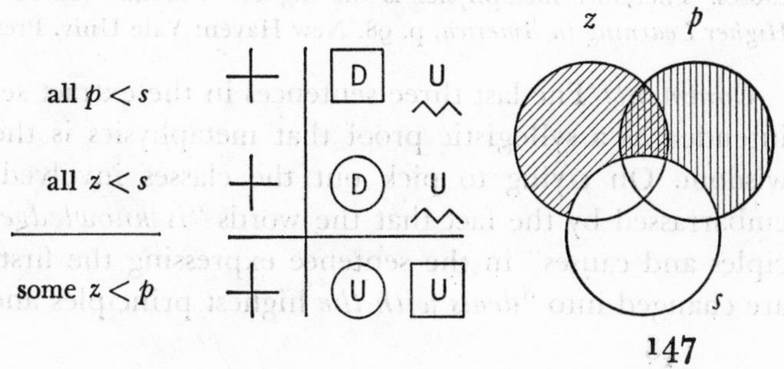

It is easy to see that the amended argument now breaks the rule for the distribution of the middle term (rule 3a, p. 140). This is typical of what occurs when a thinker tries to save an unsound argument by redefining terms without substantially improving his premises. The usual result is that a different type of mistake is then committed.

6. "All children have mothers, and all mothers have children; therefore all children have children."

Comment: The argument is patently absurd, for the premises are true while the conclusion intimates that everybody must be not merely a parent, but actually a grandparent! We might be inclined to say the mistake is due to the presence of four terms, but this would be over-hasty. For the class of those who have mothers is also the class of children. If we notice also that the class of those who have children is the class of parents, we get as our analysis:

$$\begin{array}{l} \text{all } c < c \\ \text{all } m < p \\ \hline \text{all } c < p \end{array}$$

(where 'c', 'm', and 'p' stand for the class of children, the class of mothers, and the class of parents, respectively). The mistake arose from confusing the class of those who *have* mothers (c) with the class of those who *are* mothers (m).

7. "The aim of higher education is wisdom. Wisdom is knowledge of principles and causes. Metaphysics deals with the highest principles and causes. Therefore metaphysics is the highest wisdom." (R. M. Hutchins, *Higher Learning in America*, p. 98. New Haven: Yale Univ. Press, 1936.)

Comment: The last three sentences in the extract seem to be intended as a syllogistic proof that metaphysics is the highest wisdom. On trying to pick out the classes involved, we are embarrassed by the fact that the words "*is knowledge of* principles and causes" in the sentence expressing the first premise are changed into "*deals with the* highest principles and causes" in the next sentence. Let us give the author the benefit of the doubt, and suppose that the second premise could be expressed by the sentence:

Metaphysics is knowledge of highest principles and causes.

We now have the following classes involved in the argument:

wisdom (*w*)	knowledge of principles and causes (*k*)
metaphysics (*m*)	
highest wisdom (*hw*)	knowledge of highest principles and causes (*kh*)

These classes are clearly all different; our best hope of saving the argument is that there may be unstated premises that will provide some connections between the classes. The argument as stated is:

$$\begin{array}{l} \text{(all) } w < k \\ \text{(all) } m < kh \\ \hline \text{(all) } m < hw \end{array}$$

We need connections between *k* and *kh* and between *w* and *hw;* the only plausible ones are *all kh is k* (all knowledge of highest principles and causes is knowledge of principles and causes) and *all hw is w* (all highest wisdom is wisdom). The argument then becomes:

$$\begin{array}{l} \text{all } w < k \\ [\text{all } kh < k] \\ \text{all } m < kh \\ [\text{all } hw < w] \\ \hline \text{all } m < hw \end{array}$$

By combining the first and fourth premises, and the second and third, we get:

$$\begin{array}{l} \text{all } hw < k \\ \text{all } m < k \\ \hline \text{all } m < hw \end{array}$$

With all this assistance, the argument is still guilty of the fallacy of undistributed middle (since *k* is undistributed in each occurrence) and is therefore *invalid.*

We ought to note finally the play on two meanings of "highest," which gives the argument such plausibility as it has. The "highest" principles of which knowledge is sought in metaphysics are the most *general* principles—those that come earliest or "highest" in the logical order of deduction; but "highest" wisdom is, of course, most *valuable,* most precious wisdom. We notice also the suggestion (for it is no more than that) that "higher" education should deal with the "highest" wisdom, and so are presented with still a third sense of "height." For "higher" education means education at a more difficult or more complex level. The argument is, therefore, permeated with ambiguities.

Lest we have done violence to the argument by squeezing it into the syllogistic form, we end our examination by constructing a formal analogy (see page 48). "Engineering is knowledge of the properties of material bodies. Aeronautics deals with the highest material bodies. Therefore aeronautics is the highest engineering." This transparently unsound argument sufficiently confirms our adverse judgment of the original.

Summary

One of the most common forms of argument is the *syllogism.* A syllogism is defined as an argument composed of two premises and a conclusion, each capable of presentation in subject-predicate form, purporting to contain three classes in all.

A valid syllogism must involve exactly three classes. The subject of the conclusion (or *minor term*) and predicate of the conclusion (or *major term*) must each occur once in a premise; the remaining class (the *middle term*) must occur in both premises.

The validity of syllogisms can be conveniently determined by drawing Venn diagrams. In so doing we symbolize *only the premises,* inserting data for universal propositions before data for particular propositions. The types of cases arising were illustrated in detail.

Every subject-predicate proposition may be assigned one of the four *code-letters,* A, E, I, O. The first two of these refer to *universal* propositions, the first and third to *positive* propositions. When a subject-predicate proposition makes a statement about every member of a class, that class is said to be *distributed* in that proposition. Examination shows that *universal propositions have distributed subjects* and *negative propositions have distributed predicates.* It follows that the four standard types of propositions have the following distribution-patterns: (A), DU; (E), DD; (I). UU; (O), UD.

A valid syllogism must conform to the following eight rules: (1) it must have three terms; (2a) it cannot have both premises negative; (2b) if both premises are positive, the conclusion must be positive; (2c) if one premise is negative, the conclusion must be negative; (3a) the middle term must be distributed at least once; (3b,c) the major (minor) term cannot be distributed in the conclusion unless it is distributed in the premises in which it occurs; (4) the conclusion cannot be particular unless one premise is particular.

2a, b, c are often called rules of *quality* and 3a, b, c rules of *quantity*. We call 4 the *existential rule* of the valid syllogism.

In applying these principles to the criticism of concrete syllogistic arguments, it is necessary to pay special attention to the expression of propositions in standard subject-predicate form and to the explicit formulation of assumptions. The procedure to be adopted and the type of problem arising were illustrated in the text.

Comprehension test

(For instructions, see page 10.)

1. No syllogism has four terms. (*true* *false*)
2. The major term of a syllogism must be the predicate of the major premise. (*true* *false*)

3. Every proposition has a major term. *(true false)*
4. A negative subject-predicate proposition has an undistributed predicate. *(true false)*
5. A negative universal proposition has the distribution pattern UD. *(true false)*
6. In a valid syllogism, the major term cannot be distributed in the conclusion if it is undistributed in the major premise. *(true false)*
7. A valid syllogism may have its middle term distributed twice. *(true false)*
8. One rule of the valid syllogism forbids the conclusion to be universal unless at least one premise is universal. *(true false)*
9. In using Venn diagrams to analyze syllogisms, the information given in the conclusion should be entered in the diagram. *(true false)*
10. No syllogism having an "undistributed middle" is valid. *(true false)*

Exercises

A

1. What are the minor, major, and middle terms of the following syllogisms?
   a. Some fallacious arguments are syllogisms; no syllogisms are dilemmas; therefore some dilemmas are not fallacious.
   b. No man in continual fear is free; every miser is in continual fear; therefore no miser is happy.
   c. "What is related in the Talmud is unworthy of credit; miraculous stories are related in the Talmud; therefore miraculous stories are unworthy of credit."
   (Whately.)
   d. Some fools speak the truth; whoever speaks the truth deserves to be imitated; therefore there are some who deserve to be imitated who are nevertheless fools.
   (Port Royal Logic.)
   e. Your sisters are terribly old-fashioned. They don't smoke.
   f. Vitamins are good for you. And VITAVIM is full of vitamins.
   g. Anybody who trusts communists is a fool. But the officials of our State Department are not fools.

h. Not all unnatural things are bad. For it is not natural to take medicine.

i. Some servants need not be spoken to politely. For horses are servants.

j. Penicillin is very useful. But it is hard to produce, and all things that are hard to produce are expensive.

k. Some of the things alleged by spiritualists are incredible, because they contradict the laws of nature.

l. Only sensitive people resent criticism, and, since only sensitive people are musical, it follows that all musical people resent criticism.

m. Agreeable companions do not ask questions or make criticisms. Hence animals are agreeable companions, for they do neither.

n. The existence of sensations consists in being perceived; material objects are not sensations, therefore their existence does not consist in being perceived.

2. Determine which of the preceding arguments are valid.
3. Make a list of all the universal propositions occurring in the arguments of Question 1 and determine whether they should be interpreted existentially or hypothetically.
4. What rules are broken by syllogisms composed of the following types of proposition (the first in each case being the major premise and the last the conclusion)?
   a. EOA.
   b. EAO.
   c. OEE.
   d. III.
   e. IEO.
   f. AIA.
5. Determine what type of valid conclusion can result from the following types of premises (the first being the major premise in each case).
   a. AI.
   b. EI.
   c. AA.
   d. EA.
   e. AO.
   f. IO.
6. Draw Venn diagrams to illustrate the following sets of premises:
   a. all $a < b$, no $b < c$.
   b. all $c < d$, all $c < e$.
   c. all $f < g$, all $f < h$, some f exist.
   d. all $h \not< k$, some $k < l$.

e. all $m < n$, all $p < n$.

f. all $q < r$, all $s < r$. some things are not r.

g. all $v < u$, everything which is both u and v is w, nothing is both w and u.

7. What valid conclusions can be obtained from the premises supplied in Question 6?

8. Construct valid syllogisms having the following propositions as conclusions:

   a. Some winter days are sunny.
   b. Arsenic is poison.
   c. Only price control can prevent inflation.
   d. Not all education is enjoyable.
   e. Conscientious men (and there are some) examine both sides of a question.
   f. There is no disputing about tastes.

9. Examine the following arguments. Consider both the validity of the argument and its soundness as a whole.

   a. In matters that really interest him, man cannot support the suspense of judgment which science so often has to enjoin. He is too anxious to feel certain to have time to know. We had better therefore reconcile ourselves to the fact that education must consist largely in the inculcation of the right dogmas. To treat a fundamentally irrational creature such as man as if he were reasonable is itself a symptom of irrationality.

   b. *Idea of Keeping Hirohito on Throne Affronts Logic*
   The proposal that we should promise to keep Hirohito on the throne of Japan, to shorten the war, and to help keep order afterward, is certainly an unlovely one. There is nothing taking, or fetching, about the idea; it seems like the typical heavy thought of a light intellect, gadgety, and smeared all over with a kind of lowgrade cunning. It is, perhaps, bush-league Machiavelli. If nothing else were wrong with it, the idea (as has been pointed out) rests on a logical fallacy; we excuse Hirohito for working with the Japanese militarists on the ground that he has no real power and can't help himself; then we demand that he be retained, so that he can use his power, which he doesn't have, on our behalf. (Samuel Grafton in *The New York Post,* July 10, 1945.)

   c. Opponents of 'pacifism' make much of the well-known argument about the criminal attack upon your sister. Would you fight to protect her virtue? If so, you are no pacifist and not really opposed to war. Our old friend logic:

Major premise: War involves violence.
Minor premise: Those who defend their sisters use violence.
Therefore: They are warriors.

Though the context of a criminal attack is entirely different from that of organized, deliberate warfare, both are cheerfully lumped together. (Stuart Chase, *Tyranny of Words,* page 341. New York: Harcourt, Brace & Co., Inc., 1938.)

d. *Definition.* Science is systematized positive knowledge or what has been taken as such at different ages and in different places.

Theorem. The acquisition and systematization of positive knowledge are the only human activities that are truly cumulative and progressive.

Corollary. The history of science is the only history that can illustrate the progress of mankind. In fact, progress has no definite and unquestionable meaning in other fields than the field of science. (George Sarton, *The Study of the History of Science,* page 5. Cambridge, Mass.: Harvard University Press, 1936.)

e. *Murray Bill Offers Jobs and Freedom*

We have begun to witness some fascinating crawfishing on the full-employment issue. Some of the gentlemen over on the right are not nearly so certain as they were a year ago that full employment after the war would be a good thing.

A nearby contemporary, for example, has concluded that one is "dishonest" when he cites the $200 billion annual production in wartime as evidence that our national economy can provide full employment if it is managed right. That level of output, we are told, may be sufficient to provide jobs for all who want them, but it was only achieved at the cost of "regimenting the entire nation," controlling raw materials, wages, hours, prices, and so on. The by-products are distasteful, and therefore we ought to quit aspiring to a capacity operation in peace-time.

They used to teach us in logic class that this was the fallacy of the undistributed middle. Regimentation is a bad thing; full employment at present involves regimentation; therefore full employment is a bad thing. (Robert Lasch in *The Chicago Sun,* June 11, 1945.)

B

1. Prove that a term *a* can be undistributed in a valid syllogism, even though no *a*'s exist.
2. Prove the following consequences of the rules of the valid syllogism:

a. The conclusion of a valid syllogism cannot be universal unless both premises are universal.
b. A valid conclusion cannot result from two particular premises.
c. No valid conclusion can result if the major premise is I and the minor premise E.

3. Show that in fact no syllogism is valid in which a term is D in a premise but U in the conclusion.
4. Have we shown that any syllogism conforming to the eight rules given in the text must necessarily be valid? Does this throw any doubt on the correctness of our procedure?
5. Does appeal to a Venn diagram constitute a *proof* of validity or invalidity? (Before answering, consider what you mean by "proof.")
6. What is an "axiom"? (Consult a good dictionary.) Would it be correct to describe (a) the rules of the valid syllogism, (b) the "Ten Commandments," as axioms? Compare and contrast the rules of the valid syllogism with rules of morality.
7. Show that if universal propositions are interpreted *existentially,* Rule 4 (page 141) of the valid syllogism becomes incorrect.

Exercises in reasoning, 2nd series

(*Note:* This is a second series of puzzles and problems illustrating various aspects of the process of reasoning. The first series appeared on page 10.

1. The surprise quiz. An instructor who meets his class six days a week announces one Saturday that a "Surprise Quiz" will be given in the course of the following week. (A Surprise Quiz is defined as one whose date canot be known ahead of time.) Is the instructor guilty of self-contradiction?
2. Find the digits represented by letters in the following division sum:

```
ab)cdeeb(bfb
   ceb
   ---
    gge
    gch
    ---
     ceb
     ceb
     ---
```

3. "Let us suppose that I am looking at a star, Sirius, say, on a dark night. If physics is to be believed, light-waves that started to travel from Sirius many years ago reach (after a specified time which astronomers calculate) the earth, impinge upon my retinas and cause me to say I am seeing Sirius. Now the Sirius about which they convey information is the Sirius that existed at the time they started. This Sirius,

may, however, no longer exist; it may have disappeared in the interval. To say that one can see what no longer exists is absurd. It follows that, whatever it is that I am seeing, it is not Sirius." Is the argument sound?

4. "Any object begins to fall as soon as its support is removed. Hence a stone begins to fall as soon as it leaves the hand of the man who throws it. Therefore no stone can be thrown upward." Criticize this argument.
5. An ordinary chessboard has had two squares—one at each end of a diagonal—removed. There is on hand a supply of 31 dominoes, each of which is large enough to cover exactly two adjacent squares of the board. Is it possible to lay the dominoes on the mutilated chessboard in such a manner as to cover it completely?
6. The logician's will: "I leave $1,000 to be divided among my four daughters. Some of the money is to go to Annabel or Beatrice. I know that Beatrice and Clarissa are under Deirdre's thumb, so if any of the money goes to either of them, she is to have none. I want Beatrice and Clarissa treated alike—in fact all four, or as many as possible, are to receive equal treatment." Who was the logician's favorite daughter, and what was the size of her legacy?
7. A ship of the Blue Star Line sails each noon from New York to Liverpool, and another sails at the same hour each day from Liverpool to New York. Each ship takes exactly a week to make the crossing. If an officer of the line takes passage on one of these boats, how many ships belonging to his line will he meet during passage?
8. Amy, Beryl, Cecily, and Dorothy are married to Arthur, Basil, Cyril, and David (not necessarily in that order) and each of the four husbands is brother to one of the ladies. Dorothy has no brothers. Amy's brother-in-law is married to Cecily. Beryl is married to Basil. Cecily's husband was at school with Arthur and David. Which of the ladies is Cyril's sister?
9. A certain suburban railroad line to Chicago operates under the following conditions: (1) There is exactly one train per day to take passengers from any given suburban station to any other given suburban station. (2) No two trains in the same direction have more than one stop in common. (3) Each train stops at exactly three suburban stations. (4) More than one train per day in each direction stops at each suburban station. How many trains per day are there in each direction and how many stations are there on the line?
10. Nine men—Brown, White, Adams, Miller, Green, Hunter, Knight, Jones, and Smith—play the several positions on a baseball team. Determine from the following data the position played by each: (1)

Smith and Brown each won $10 playing poker with the pitcher; (2) Hunter was taller than Knight and shorter than White but each of these weighed more than the first baseman; (3) The third baseman lived across the corridor from Jones in the same apartment house; (4) Miller and the outfielders play bridge in their spare time; (5) White, Miller, Brown, the right fielder and the center fielder were bachelors, and the rest were married; (6) Of Adams and Knight, one played an outfielder position; (7) The right fielder was shorter than the center fielder; (8) The third baseman was brother to the pitcher's wife; (9) Green was taller than the infielders and the battery, except for Jones, Smith, and Adams; (10) The second baseman beat Jones, Brown, Hunter and the catcher at cards; (11) The third baseman, the shortstop, and Hunter made $150 each speculating in U.S. Steel; (12) The second baseman was engaged to Miller's sister; (13) Adams lives in the same house as his own sister but dislikes the catcher; (14) Adams, Brown and the shortstop lost $200 each speculating in copper; (15) The catcher had three daughters, the third baseman had two sons, but Green was being sued for divorce. (A. A. Bennett and C. A. Baylis, *Formal Logic*. New York: Prentice-Hall, Inc., 1939.)

11. In a certain village it was decided that the barber should shave all those and only those who did not shave themselves. Did the barber shave himself?
12. The maze. Show that by proceeding so as always to "keep to the right" (*e.g.*, by always touching a wall with one's right hand) one is bound to emerge eventually from any maze, no matter how complicated.
13. Matching pennies. A and B play the following game. Each places a penny on the table without showing it to his opponent. The pennies are compared. If the upper faces are unlike (one head, one tail) B pays A two pennies; if two heads are shown, A pays B three pennies; if two tails are shown, A pays B one penny. Is this a fair game? What is A's best strategy?
14. Consider any two-handed game of skill in which the rules provide that each game must be won by one of the two players (*e.g.*, chess or checkers played with the understanding that a "draw" counts as a loss for the player having first move). Prove that such a game is "unfair," *i.e.*, that there must be a procedure by which either the player moving first or his opponent can *force* a win.

PART TWO

Language

9

THE USES OF LANGUAGE

In every tongue the speaker labours under great inconveniences, especially on abstract questions, both from the paucity, obscurity, and ambiguity of the words, on the one hand, and from his own misapprehensions, and imperfect acquaintance with them, on the other.—George Campbell, 1776.

1. Introduction.

EVER since men began to reflect critically upon their own thinking, the wisest of them have been acutely aware of the imperfections of the language in which their thought must be expressed. The greatest of the Greek philosophers often returned to this theme, and centuries later we find Francis Bacon echoing the ancient complaint and listing "false notions" generated by the "common tongue" as one of the main hindrances to the advancement of knowledge. Every important advance in science and scholarship has required a reform in terminology. Thinkers, as ingenious as they were public-spirited, have labored to invent artificial languages, systems of notations, and a bewildering tangle of other symbolic aids to accurate thinking. Yet after thousands of years of criticism and improvement, the chorus of complaint continues, and experts insist today, more emphatically than ever, on the importance of critical study of language and its relation to thought. The brave new science of "semantics," though still in swaddling clothes, already has many interesting results to its credit, and its many enthusiastic followers are actively exploring its implications for logic, aesthetics, education, psychiatry, and other subjects.

Philosophy of language, for all its importance, is too intricate a subject to be fully discussed in an elementary introduction to "critical thinking." We shall therefore not attempt a sys tematic account of the nature of language and its relation to the objects of thought. Nevertheless, our dealings with specimens of actual reasoning have shown us the importance of attention to the language in which ideas are expressed; since ideas are communicated in language, criticism of thought must also be criticism of its vehicle. We shall undertake the relatively modest task of developing just so much theory of language (or "semantics") as will be useful in criticizing the types of reasoning we are most likely to encounter.

This part of the book may therefore be regarded as a practical guide to *the linguistic problems that arise in the criticism of reasoning.*

2. *The complexity of language.*

When we read a sentence, or understand conversation, we are responding to **signs.** It is characteristic of a sign that a person who understands it is led to attend to *something other than the sign itself;* the headline "HURRICANE DUE TOMORROW," considered as an object in its own right, is a mere string of ink blotches; it is a sign for the reader because it leads him to think of things quite other than printer's ink—the approaching storm, the precautions that need to be taken, and so forth.

Signs need not be *linguistic.* A herd of animals taking flight on hearing a warning cry from a sentinel, a man entering a dining room at the sound of a gong, a doctor diagnosing the visible symptoms of a disease, a spider set in motion by a twitch of its web, are all interpreting signs. These examples also illustrate the point that quite primitive organisms can interpret non-linguistic signs.

If such instances of elementary sign-interpretation are contrasted with the processes of reading a book, hearing a speech, or otherwise responding to complex uses of language, a number of important points of difference may be noticed.

1. *Linguistic signs are artificial, while the simplest kinds of non-linguistic signs are natural.*

If a flash of lightning causes me to expect a clap of thunder, it is because the two kinds of event normally occur together; but the presence of pepper in a can would not result in the appearance of the word "pepper" on the can *but for human intervention.* Men have to agree that certain noises and marks shall cause interpreters to attend to certain other objects (their "meanings") before there can be *language.* We notice, however, that some non-linguistic signals (such as the cones hoisted to warn of the approach of a storm) can also be artificial.

Let us agree to use the word **signal** as an abbreviation for the phrase "the simplest kind of sign." (This agrees fairly well with the customary meaning of the word "signal.")

2. *Response to signals is stereotyped and undifferentiated, while response to linguistic signs is variable and complex.*

The presence of a dog will cause a cat to bristle with anticipatory fear, but a man's response to the remark "a lion has escaped from the circus" will vary with circumstances. The spoken sentence is constructed out of *component signs* (the words) arranged in a conventional *order,* and the man responds to the components and to their arrangement as well as to the sentence as a whole. He is able to understand an isolated word (such as the word "lion" appearing alone on a sheet of paper); and he can interpret a sentence *he has never seen before,* if it is composed of known words in a known arrangement. The natural signals to which animals respond always occur in association with the things to which they refer. But the users of a *language* have learned to deploy and re-deploy linguistic signs in an endless variety of sign situations; they can therefore anticipate novelty and respond to situations of radically new types.

3. *Signals normally serve a single purpose, while linguistic signs tend to serve a number of different purposes simultaneously.*

The spoor of a wild animal may tell the skilful hunter a great deal about the beast that made it, yet consider how much more is conveyed to the sensitive listener by even the most trivial remark. If we hear a stranger say "I've missed that train again!" we may learn something about a train, but we may sometimes learn even more about the speaker—that she is annoyed, is not disposed to be friendly, is in a hurry to go somewhere, and was educated in the Middle West! Nor is this an exceptional case. Because men and women express their feelings and attitudes as well as their beliefs by means of language, all talk conveys information about much more than its ostensible subject. And because language is a social product, the result of interaction between persons sharing common purposes, any individual utterance also conveys information about the *community of language users* to which the speaker belongs.

These three differences between fully developed language and the simplest kinds of non-linguistic signs give us but a glimpse of the full complexity of language. No doubt they are differences of degree, and "The metaphysician," as Anatole France said, "has only the perfected cry of monkeys and dogs with which to construct the system of the World." Yet the differences are important: we shall find that failure to be aware of them, and to appreciate some of their consequences is responsible for much fallacious reasoning.

3. The many purposes served by language.

Any spoken utterance will usually express feelings, attitudes, desires, and beliefs, and will convey information (either true or false) about the speaker and other objects. But there is such a tremendous variety of human transactions in which language is used, that the appropriate response to a particular utterance may vary widely according to the circumstances of its use. Everybody understands that the spoken words "Pass down the bus, please" are primarily intended to cause the passengers to move and are not said for the purpose of giving information about the conductor; and it is equally obvious that the remark "This bus is over-loaded" is an *assertion,* not a request or command, even though it, too, causes the passengers to move. When we contrast "assertions" with "questions," "requests," "commands," "exclamations," or "prayers," we are recognizing *different ways in which language can be used.* Such crude distinctions, however, hardly begin to do justice to the variety of different uses of language.

In order to see how variable the correct response to language may be, let us examine the following two utterances, *both of which are "statements":*

(1) "A body immersed in a fluid is acted upon by an upward force equal in magnitude to the weight of the fluid displaced." (From a text.)

(2) "The apples were falling like great drops of dew to bruise themselves an exit from themselves." (D. H. Lawrence.)

The first statement makes a certain *claim* concerning the behavior of solid bodies and fluids: it is intended to produce in us (the readers) a definite belief that can be tested and confirmed by actual observation of the weight of bodies immersed in a fluid. If observation proved that the belief does not accord with the facts, we should be justified in calling the writer a liar. In formulating a supposition to be tested against experience in this way, we are behaving in the way intended by the scientist who made the statement. Since the statement (1) was used in order to produce such beliefs and testing procedures, our interpretation was *appropriate.*

It would, of course, be absurdly inappropriate to interpret the second statement in similar fashion. Only a very stupid reader would ask "What apples is he talking about? How big are the drops of dew? How can an apple *make an exit from itself?*" Such questions are stupid because the poet has no intention of producing beliefs that could be tested in a manner appropriate to a scientific statement. And to call him a "liar" because his statement could not be confirmed in the laboratory would serve only to reveal our own misunderstanding of what poetry "is all about." For the poet's intention, here as elsewhere, is to embody and communicate an aesthetic experience in words that will give pleasure as well as insight.

And there are many other ways in which language can be used.

Consider, for instance, these words, which might be spoken by any departing guest to his hostess:

(3) "Thank you for a nice party—we've had a wonderful time."

Sometimes the guest has had anything but a pleasant time,* but he is not on that account to be regarded as dishonest. To insist that "a really truthful person" would, if necessary, say "Good-bye, I've had a very dull and uncomfortable time," would be to repeat the mistake that occurs when poetry is treated as if it were science. A formula of polite thanks is not intended, or understood, as a factual claim (nor as a snatch of poetry). Questions of truth and falsity are no more applicable to such *ceremonial* uses of language than they are to a handshake.

The moral of such examples is that *all intelligent criticism of any instance of language in use must begin with understanding of the motives and purposes of the speaker in that situation.* Unfortunately, the type of case that causes trouble in practice is that in which the kind of use made of language is not as transparently clear as in our examples. Language is often used to *conceal* motives and purposes, and human motives and purposes are notoriously mixed. One and the same utterance may convey factual information (true or false), embody aesthetic insight, express social conformity, or do a number of other things *all at the same time.* For this reason, any attempt to isolate "pure" types of language uses (such as "scientific," "poetic," "ceremonial," and so on) would be of little help to us. In the next two sections we formulate distinctions applying, in varying degree, to *all* uses of language.

4. Some working distinctions.

Personal and impersonal aspects of utterance. We have already said that any utterance normally gives some information about the speaker himself, as well as other matters. Let us, therefore,

* The actress, Beatrice Lillie, is reported to have made the parting remark: "Don't think I haven't had a wonderful time—because I haven't!"

refer to the **personal** and **impersonal aspects** of an utterance. By the first term we shall mean the information given about the speaker, and more especially about the attitudes, feelings, and wishes that caused him to make the utterance; by the second, whatever other information may be conveyed by the utterance. The personal aspects may be further divided into **expressive** and **dynamic** aspects. The utterance is expressive insofar as it is caused by the speaker's feelings or attitudes, *without any desired effect on a hearer*. An involuntary cry of pain or joy is markedly expressive in this sense. The utterance is dynamic insofar as it is caused by the speaker's desire to produce actions or other effects in a hearer; a command or a question is markedly dynamic in this sense. Actual utterances vary widely in the relative importance of their expressive, dynamic, and impersonal aspects.

Statement and suggestion. No human speaker explicitly symbolizes all that he conveys to the hearer; we must constantly "read between the lines." One important consequence of this has already been mentioned. A speaker very rarely says: "I want you to feel that I am a thoroughly likable person of the sort you can trust; I am not much interested in tariffs (or whatever it may be) except insofar as some knowledge of this subject is necessary to persuade you to trust me." Such devastating frankness would be self-defeating, but many a speaker talks in such a way as to convey the same impression. Intelligent understanding of the utterance requires an awareness of much more than is "said in so many words." The *general setting* of the utterance (whether it is predominantly "scientific" or "poetic," intended to produce approval, result in actions, and so on) is not usually symbolized explicitly.

Let us examine a striking instance of "reading between the lines." In answering a letter not long ago, a certain Senator began his reply with the words "My dear Wop"—an action that led to considerable indignation on the part of his correspondent and many of the lady's sympathizers. Furious letters were written to Congress and the newspapers, and the Senator's action was denounced at meetings of protest as "undemocratic" and "un-American."

Why all this fuss about three words? A foreigner, not thoroughly familiar with the subtleties of the American language, would find on enquiry, that "Wop" means about the same as "Italian" or "person of Italian origin." "Well, well," he might wonder, in his naive way, "is it so insulting to an American to be accused of having Italian ancestors?" The answer, of course, is that "Wop" is a term of powerful *abuse,* conventionally used as a way of expressing a high degree of contempt for the person addressed. The three words might be expanded in some such way as this: "Madam, the usual rules of politeness require me to use the words 'My dear so-and-so.' I show my contempt for you and your opinions by refusing even to call you by your name. I am pretty sure that you can't be an American; I suspect that you are of Italian origin; and I regard Italians in general as inferior and degenerate."

Yet the abusive Senator did not *say* all this "in so many words"—even though much of it is quite clearly understood by his readers. Offense is properly taken at the insulting suggestions of the utterance, rather than at its explicitly formulated content.

The unformulated implications and suggestions of an utterance are not always abusive. Often we convey feelings of approval, enjoyment, or appreciation by gesture, tone of voice, and choice of words. The means employed are so flexible and variable that usually we are hardly aware of them, even while constantly responding to their influence. A large part of the information conveyed by utterance is *suggested, not stated.*

When a purported fact, a wish, a judgment of value, and so forth, are conveyed by means of a symbol conventionally used for that purpose we shall say the fact, wish, and so on, has been **stated;** when information is conveyed by means not conventionally reserved for that purpose we shall say that that information has been **suggested.** Thus, a **statement** is an explicitly formulated assertion, command, desire, judgment, and so forth, while a **suggestion** is conveyed, though not explicitly formulated. (It is, however, hard to draw a sharp line between suggestion and statement, as here defined. Sometimes, of course, there can be no doubt at all that an important part of a given utterance has been suggested, though not explicitly symbolized. The man who asks "When did you start smoking so heavily?" has not *actually* said "You are smoking heavily.")

All human languages rely, to an astonishing degree, on what is understood, though not said "in so many words." It has been reported of the Eskimoes that "Their phrases are as sober as their faces. A gleam in an Eskimo's eye tells you more than half a dozen of our sentences concerning desire, repugnance, or another emotion. Each Eskimo's word is like that gleam: it suggests at once what has happened and what is to come. . . ." (Gontran de Poncins, *Kabloona,* page 247.) The more articulate languages of Western civilization, though not as suggestive as those of the Eskimo, still retain enormous suggestive power.

Emotive and neutral language. Among the most effective suggestions conveyed in human utterance are those expressive of the speaker's *feelings* (and especially feelings of approval or disapproval). Not only *feelings* are conveyed by suggestion: Any statement about "impersonal" matters of fact makes use of tacit assumptions, which are suggested, not stated. Nevertheless, the uses of suggestion to communicate the nature of a speaker's feelings are particularly important, for the following reasons:

1. Suggested feelings concerning a person or object can powerfully influence people's opinions. To call a man a "Red" is already to turn an audience against him; to call him a "dirty Red," in certain contexts, is practically to condemn him outright. Such "name calling" is usually more successful than explicit statement or reasoned argument.

2. Feelings, especially strong feelings, concerning a person or object spontaneously find expression in the use of "satisfying" symbols. (All praise and abuse tends to become poetic.) An angry man tends to *show* his anger rather than talk *about* it: thus the means by which he expresses his feelings will be a

suggestion, not a statement. In general, suggestion is a very "natural" way of conveying a feeling.

Much attention has accordingly been given, in recent times, to the use of those signs that particularly lend themselves to the expression and communication of feelings. Such symbols are termed **emotive**, and are contrasted with **neutral** symbols. An emotive word, then, is one expressive of strong feelings (especially of approval or disapproval) on the part of the speaker. The use of emotive words has a tendency to produce similar feelings in the hearer.

The English language has a few words reserved for the expression of feeling and used for no other purpose—exclamations like "Shame!" "Hurrah!" "Encore!" While these words are highly emotive according to our definition, they express very generalized feelings. For this reason (and because they are so seldom used in discourse) they have negligible influence in determining people's views concerning *specific* topics.

If an advertiser wants to predispose the man in the street in favor of his product, he will probably adopt more subtle means to recommend it. Suppose he is selling a dentifrice consisting of powdered beef bone (an actual case): the slogan "Hurrah for powdered beef bone!" is unlikely to enlist many customers for the new product, even though repeated thousands of times in newspaper advertisements and on the radio. For the words "powdered beef bone" have suggestions that are unfavorable to the advertiser's purpose: we have all seen raw bones, and we are led to think of an unappetizing mess of blood-stained splinters, not at all the sort of stuff we would choose for cleaning the teeth. How much better then from the advertiser's standpoint to label the product "Numin" (the name actually chosen). Instead of the *negative* emotive force of "powdered beef bone," we have a *positive* emotive appeal of the substitute term, "Numin." For the latter has a scientific flavor, as of some new vitamin, and can therefore be relied upon to attract the man in the street.

The device used in this instance to stimulate a favorable

reaction to a certain object (the dentifrice) consists in *the choice of a name having agreeable associations.* The English language is very rich in words approximately equivalent in *explicit* meaning, while markedly divergent in their emotive associations and suggestions.

The terms "government official," "bureaucrat," and "public servant" have much the same explicit meaning, yet the first is neutral, the second abusive, and the last honorific. "Liquidation of the opposition" sounds a great deal more agreeable than "torture and murder of the minority." A man may "talk eloquently" or "jabber"; a statesman may "have the gift of compromise" or be a "slippery trimmer"; a friend is "understandably confused," an enemy "has gone a bit off his noodle"; all these examples were in a single newspaper editorial.

The list of examples could be indefinitely extended, for nearly all the words we use are colored with some shade of respect or contempt, and every notion can be so worded as to make its subject seem either admirable or ridiculous.

The expression and influence of attitudes by means of such highly emotive words as those we have cited should be too obvious to escape notice. *But these cases are not exceptional.* The view that only in "propaganda" and abuse is language used emotively is none the less profoundly mistaken for being widely held. We must insist, to the contrary, that language is *normally* used to express attitudes and exert influence as well as to convey explicit statement; it is as much of an exception for language to be "uncolored" or neutral as for matter to be without odor.

Since the emotive and suggestive influence of language is so strong, we must take account of it in our general program of establishing principles and standards of right thinking. (If, on the other hand, we were to neglect these aspects of language, and pay attention only to what is explicitly stated in neutral terms, we should be behaving like a pilot who refused to take account of any part of an iceberg that was not visible above the water.) By discussing a concrete example in detail, we shall now illustrate the types of critical procedure that are appropriate.

5. *Analysis of a specimen of highly emotive writing.*

A recent newspaper editorial opened with this sentence:

(A) "A fabulously rich playboy, who got tired of his ponies, got the idea that he would like to repudiate the free enterprise that privileged his grandfather to endow him with so many million dollars he could never hope to count them."

This passage tells us a good deal more about the editorial writer (or his employer) than about the millionaire who is the target of his abuse. Yet the passage does contain a little *impersonal* information (true or false), and the first step in analysis is to make this context explicit. An experienced journalist who happened to read (A) would immediately "discount" much of what was said. What this probably means, he might comment, is:

(B) "The rich man in question is supporting federal control of industry."

After the invective of (A), this partial translation appears insipid. Clearly the writer had little interest in conveying the information expressed by (B).

We proceed, therefore, to identify the *emotive suggestions* of the original passage. A convenient way of doing this is to begin by picking out (say by underlining) all the words and phrases that make a notable contribution to the total impression intended. After this has been done, we try to state explicitly the nature of the suggestion conveyed in each case. Proceeding in this fashion, we get the following analysis:

Language used	*Suggestion conveyed*
"playboy," "ponies"	X (the man in question) is an idler and gambler
"fabulously rich" *"so many million dollars he could never hope to count them"*	X is excessively wealthy
"got tired of" *"got the idea"* *"would like to repudiate"*	X is irresponsible—makes decisions for no good reason
"privileged" *"endow"*	X has received special and unearned favors

It will be seen that these suggestions reinforce each other in painting the picture of a most unattractive character. The malice of the writer's intention is obvious when the various suggestions are combined in a single explicit statement, in some such fashion as this:

(C) The man in question is an idle gambler, who has far more money than he deserves, and is now irresponsibly using the vast financial power that he did nothing to earn.

This last statement, if made explicitly, might well be libellous and expose its author to a legal suit for damages. Yet even so it would probably be less effective than the hints and innuendoes of the original passage (A). In all such cases the rule holds that the outspoken accusation is less dangerous than the whispered calumny.

A good way of neutralizing the suggestive power of the original passage is to replace the crucial emotive terms and phrases by others having *opposite emotive tendency* (but approximately the same explicit content). In this way we get the following substitute for (A):

(D) A very wealthy American sportsman has decided to oppose the system of unregulated commercial trading that enabled his grandfather to leave him his large fortune.

(You would do well to compare versions A and D very carefully, in order to decide for yourself whether the latter can be regarded as a "fair translation" of the former.)

It still remains for us to determine whether the suggestions contained in the original passage (and explicitly formulated in C) are to be regarded as justified. *We must guard carefully against assuming that the implicit suggestions of an utterance can be automatically rejected without further examination, just because they are suggested and not explictily stated.* Such an assumption would be grossly mistaken, for there are many occasions on which the expression of our feelings is perfectly justified.

We take as a second instance of highly emotive language a passage from one of Garrison's addresses to the public:

> I am aware that many object to the severity of my language; but is there not cause for severity? I will be as harsh as truth, and as uncompromising as justice. On this subject, I do not wish to think, or speak, or write, with moderation; No! no! Tell a man whose house is on fire to give a moderate alarm; tell him to moderately rescue his wife from the hands of the ravisher; tell the mother to gradually extricate her babe from the fire into which it has fallen; But urge me not to use moderation in a cause like the present. I am in earnest—I will not equivocate—I will not retreat a single inch,—AND I WILL BE HEARD.

This is the language of a man laboring under strong emotions, conveyed in words well fitted to communicate indignation. Shall we say he is wrong to have the feelings or to attempt to communicate them? Or that he ought to resort to the pallid and ineffective use of "neutral" language? Surely not. But to grant the right of Garrison or anybody else to express feelings and attitudes towards a subject by the most effective means he can find at hand is a very different thing from admitting without further examination that the specific emotion or attitude is justified. The suggestions of eloquence, rhetoric or poetry, insofar as they consist of claims that might be true or false, must submit to enquiries into their evidence, general credibility, consistency; if their moving appeals to our feelings are justified, they should survive such examination without detriment or loss of eloquence.

Returning to our original example, then, we must ask *what evidence* is provided for the claim formulated in (C). In this particular instance, the answer is quickly given: for *no reasons at all* are brought forward in support of the scurrilous accusation. Even while we admit the editorial writer's general privilege of accusing his subject of idleness, irresponsibility, and so forth, in the manner he has chosen, we must object strenuously that in the case at issue his accusation is presented as a bare assertion, destitute of any supporting evidence in its favor. Our summing up of the value of passage (A) might take some such form as this: "The passage is intended to arouse prejudice against its subject, by representing him as idle, irresponsible, and undeservedly wealthy. It appeals successfully to the reader's presumed dislike of these qualities. But it offers no particle of evidence in support of its hostile contention."

6. *Suggested rules of procedure for the criticism of emotively toned utterance.*

The painstaking analysis illustrated in the last section will be too elaborate for everyday use—life is too short for us to be always ferreting out the full emotive implications of what we read and hear. It is nevertheless of much value as a training in critical awareness of the suggestive overtones of human utterance to perform a few such exercises in great detail. When this is done, the following suggestions for procedure may be helpful:

1. *Begin by reading the passage slowly, carefully, and calmly several times, noting any points in the utterance that seem to deserve further examination.* (The reader will pardon this insistence on so elementary and obvious a point. Experience shows that once the excitement of the chase has been aroused, there is a tendency to "discover" sinister or profound implications in a passage, *before even reading it with any degree of attention!*)

2. *State the general intention and context of the utterance.* [*E.g.*, "This is a report of a new scientific discovery made to an audience thoroughly familiar with the general background, and made by a man who is trying to suppress all that is personal in the circumstances he is describing." Or "This is an advertisement whose main object is to arouse curiosity concerning a mysteriously labelled new product; it is designed to appeal especially to women to make them more receptive to later 'follow-ups.'" It is useful also to try to determine *the evidence used in arriving at this verdict concerning the general nature of the symbolic situation.*]

3. *Extract the words and phrases in the passage that are particularly effective in conveying the desired suggestion.* [Crude instances of this, such as those discussed in the last section, are easily detected. More subtle suggestion, *e.g.,* those due to the general style of a passage, may easily escape notice. It is an excellent practice here, as throughout this training, to compare one's results with those of others working independently on the same

passage. Hunting down the reasons for disagreement will often bring to light unsuspected resources of the language used.]

4. *Make the suggestions of each word explicit, and combine the partial suggestions in a single statement.* [This has been illustrated by the analysis preceding version (C) above. You will soon find, on trial, that the suggestions of a word or phrase can be made explicit only in a rough and approximate way. Paraphrasing the implicit content largely neutralizes its emotive influence. Instead of extracting the implicit content in this way, a useful variation is to rewrite the original passage *reversing the emotive effect of the critical terms,* as illustrated in statement (D) above.]

5. *Formulate, in neutral language, the impersonal content of the original passage.* [The products of steps 4 and 5 should together approximate in informative content to the original passage.]

6. *Determine the evidence in favor of the original passage, as now elaborated.* [But beware of assuming that the speaker *is* arguing, and not "just telling." Compare what was said on this point on p. 66. At this stage anything said in part 1 concerning the criticism of thought may be relevant. But what are we to say about the criticism of *feeling?* When is a man justified in expressing hate, indignation, approval, etc.? These questions, important as they are, take us out of the subject matter of this book into the fields of ethics and aesthetics. They illustrate the limitations of logic.]

Summary

Adequate criticism of thinking requires special attention to the influence of language on thought. This has been a favorite theme of scholars throughout the ages, and is today a major preoccupation of the new discipline of "semantics." We discuss only such aspects of language as are most immediately useful in the criticism of reasoning.

The understanding of spoken or written language is a special case of the *interpretation of signs.* But signs need not be linguistic, and the simplest signs (here called *signals* for convenience) can be interpreted by insects and other "lower" animals. A sign is characterized by the fact that its presentation leads its interpreter to attend to *something other than the sign itself.*

The most complex of *linguistic* signs are different from *signals* in three important respects: (1) They are artificial; (2) They evoke a variable and complex response to the nature and order of the sign components as well as to the total sign; (3) They tend to serve a variety of purposes simultaneously.

Some of the different specialized forms taken by human utterances are marked by the familiar distinctions between "assertions," "questions," "commands," etc. More subtle differences were revealed by contrasting the appropriate interpretation of a scientific with a poetic assertion—and each of these with the *ceremonial* utterances required by the conventions of politeness. Intelligent criticism of any utterance should begin with understanding of the motives and purposes of the speaker.

Any given utterance may be interpreted as giving some information about the feelings, attitudes, intentions, and so forth of *the speaker himself* (the *personal aspects* of the utterance). The personal aspects may be further divided into *expressive* and *dynamic* aspects: An utterance is expressive insofar as it is caused by the speaker's feelings or attitudes, without any desired effect upon a hearer; it is dynamic in the degree to which it is caused by the speaker's desire to produce a certain reaction in a hearer.

We are constantly required to "read between the lines" of human speech. Whatever is conveyed by symbols conventionall allocated for that purpose may be said to be *stated;* whatever else can be understood in the utterance is *suggested.*

Among the most potent of suggestions are those of feelings of approval or disapproval. Signs that particularly lend themselves to the expression and evocation of feelings are termed *emotive;* the remaining signs are *neutral.*

Detailed hints were given for the analysis of highly emotive writing. The suggestions of a passage (emotive or otherwise) may be justified or unjustified; they are not to be *automatically* rejected, but must be submitted to tests of credibility, consistency, and the like, insofar as they make truth-claims. The evaluation of *feelings,* however, takes us outside the province of logic.

Comprehension test

(For instruction, see page 10.)

1. "Signal" means the same as "non-linguistic sign." *(true false)*
2. Animals are unable to interpret signs. *(true false)*
3. "Statement" is used in the text in such a way that a command can be expressed in a statement. *(true false)*
4. A speaker who makes a "ceremonial" statement without believing it may properly be called dishonest. *(true false)*
5. It is wrong to make suggestions unbacked by evidence. *(true false)*
6. The same form of words can have different suggestions when used by different speakers. *(true false)*
7. Every utterance has "personal" aspects. *(true false)*
8. The personal aspects of an utterance are always "suggested," not "stated." *(true false)*
9. The emotive effects of an utterance do not usually depend on the speaker's intention or the context of utterance. *(true false)*
10. A word can be both "emotive" and "neutral." *(true false)*

Exercises

A

1. Describe instances from your own experience in which intelligent reasoning about some problem involved the interpretation of *non-linguistic signs.*
2. In the text, reference was made to three types of discourse: "scientific," "poetic," and "ceremonial." Add to this list by describing other types of discourse, giving examples, and explaining your reasons for making the new distinctions.
3. "The mathematician Babbage once wrote to Tennyson (after the publication of the latter's poem *The Vision of Sin*) in this way:

 'Every moment dies a man.
 Every moment one is born.

 It must be manifest that were this true, the population of the world would be at a standstill. In truth the rate of birth is slightly in excess of that of death. I would suggest that in the next edition of your poem, you have it read:

 Every moment dies a man.
 Every moment $1\frac{1}{16}$ is born.

Strictly speaking, this is not correct. The actual figure is a decimal so long that I cannot get it in the line, but I believe $1\frac{1}{16}$ will be sufficiently accurate for poetry. I am, ...' " (H. Hankin, *Common Sense and its Cultivation,* page 6. New York: E. P. Dutton & Co., Inc., 1926.)

Compose a reply to this letter.

4. "The remark that did him most harm at the club was a silly aside to the effect that the so-called white races are really pinko-grey. He only said this to be cheery, he did not realize that 'white' has no more to do with a colour than 'God save the King' with a god, and that it is the height of impropriety to consider what it does connote. The pinko-grey male whom he addressed was subtly scandalized; his sense of security was awoken, and he communicated it to the rest of the herd." (E. M. Forster, *A Passage to India,* p. 62. New York: Harcourt, Brace & Co., Inc. (Modern Library Ed.), 1940.)

   Make a list of other words to which taboos are at present attached. Explain why the literal interpretation of such words might "scandalize" the hearer.

5. Many dentists avoid using the word "pain," preferring such remarks as "A little *sensitive?*" Leprosy is often referred to as *Hansen's disease* (after the Norwegian who isolated the bacillus). Find other instances of *euphemism.* Explain the point of using euphemistic synonyms.

6. According to Blake Clark, the Federal Trade Commission complained against the use of the word "toasted" in certain advertising matter. "[The tobacco] is not browned, made crisp, or made to touch flame, as the term 'toasted' suggests. The FTC says that use of the term misleads the public into thinking that Luckies are the only cigarettes heat-treated or that they are treated to a degree that makes a notable difference." (Blake Clark, *The Advertising Smoke Screen,* p. 26. New York: Harper & Bros., 1943.)

   Analyze other advertisements in such a fashion as to make their suggestions fully explicit.

7. "O'Donnell always uses the words *world-saver, do-gooder, internationalist, global-thinker, post-war planner* contemptuously, usually accompanied by the adjectives *dreamy, starry-eyed, breast-beating, sweaty* or *slobbering,* and alongside the phrase *pay roll patriot. Dumbarton Hoax, San Fiasco,* and the *crime conference* on the Crimea are O'Donnellisms." (*PM,* Sept. 23, 1943.)

   Make a study of the emotive terms used by some other newspaper columnist.

8. Use the methods of analysis explained in the last two sections of the chapter on the following passages:

a. "The South has lived too much in the past. It's time she rejoined the Union. She is entitled to be back in the house of her fathers. For her political and economic reverie the South has been paying a huge price. We have been content to blame many of our woes on the rest of the country, particularly the North, the damyankee. Gentle warnings, subdued alarms, polite suggestions have failed to awaken the rest of the nation to the fact that here is a great economic frontier, crying for development. Growing pains have not yet awakened all our own populace here in the South to our great potentials. It's time to make a rude noise.

"The narcotic that has been keeping the South in her twilight sleep is poverty. Her evasion of reality, her self-pity, her inertia have given her bad government, filled many of her important political offices with demagogues and incompetents. Here and there thieves who went into office penniless emerged millionaires—even went to prison for their racketeering....

"Since the War Between the States (the Civil War to the cold bread country), the South has at times given the rest of the country reason to think of some of her governors as clowns and of some of her legislatures as dominated by charlatans and scalawags. The South has sometimes elected to office noisy quacks and fantastic scatterbrains. Able men have had difficulty in being heard or seen in the burlesque played by some of our leaders." (*Collier's Magazine,* July 28, 1945.)

b. "The chief characteristic of the intellectual world during the last fifty years is its gradual loss of the old simplicity and integrity which went so deep, went right down to the roots of life with men like Milton and Wordsworth in literature, or Abraham Lincoln in statesmanship. This deep integrity of spirit has been replaced everywhere by a shallow cynicism, a spirit of mockery, sometimes a clever mockery, but none the less a surface with nothing behind it. It is no exaggeration to say that Matthew Arnold's vague stream of tendency flowing through literature and making for righteousness has been replaced by a stream of tendency which everywhere and on all sides in art and in literature is making for what again old-fashioned people used to call wickedness. Despite the occasional good work, and the gleams of beauty that occur here and there, as a kind of afterglow from the sunset of the great tradition, it is precisely true to say that in the literature of the pseudo-intellectuals we have developed a new and more horrible form of hypocrisy than history has every known; a hypocrisy which no longer says "Thank God, I am not as that Publican," but "Thank God, I am not as that

Pharisee." (Alfred Noyes, "The Edge of the Abyss," *Fortune Magazine,* October, 1942. Reprinted by special permission of the Editors.)

c. "We are apparently incorrigible victims of *hokum,* a term of our own used to designate the fraud that is common, intimate, and honored. An impartial observer can hardly fail to recognize that this hokum is the daily bread of the masses, and that at present they would refuse any other food. . . . From patent medicine 'ads' to class talk for *mademoiselle* the hokum is universal." (H. R. Huse, *The Illiteracy of the Literate,* p. 73. New York: Appleton-Century Inc., 1923.)

B

1. "I think that if we stripped all magical speech of its essentials, we would find simply this fact: a man believed to have mystical powers faces a clear blue sky and repeats: 'It rains: dark clouds foregather; torrents burst forth and drench the parched soil.' Or else he would be facing a black sky and repeat: 'The sun breaks through the clouds; the sun shines.' Or in illness he repeats, like Monsieur Coué: 'Every day and in every way it is getting better and better.' The essence of verbal magic, then, consists in a statement which is untrue, which stands in direct opposition to the context of reality. But the belief in magic inspires man with the conviction that his untrue statement must become true. . . . I have defined magic as the institutionalised expression of human optimism, of constructive hopes overcoming doubt and pessimism." (B. Malinowski, *Coral Gardens and Their Magic,* vol. 2, p. 239. London: Allen and Unwin Ltd., 1935.)
   Find illustrations from current advertising of the extent to which "verbal magic," as Malinowski defines it, is used in modern life.
2. Consult a good dictionary to determine the various senses in which the term *symbol* is used. How are these senses related to the meaning of *sign,* as used in this chapter?
3. Explain carefully the respects in which the "neutral" report of a scientist's investigations can be "dynamic."
4. Does "emotive" language necessarily generate emotions? Discuss.
5. Is "emotive" an emotive word? Discuss.
6. Words in common use can be roughly placed upon a "scale of heat" ranging from "high positive," through "neutral," to "high negative." Assign positions on such a scale to some of the emotively toned words in a piece of highly emotive writing.
7. How would you set about resolving *disagreements* concerning the alleged emotive tone of certain words? Illustrate your discussion by reference to specific instances.

8. "Phatic communion—a type of speech in which ties of union are created by a mere exchange of words." (Malinowski.) Write an outline for an essay entitled "The value of phatic communion."
9. Discover the sense in which "suggestion" is used as a technical term in psychology. Is there any relation to the meaning of "suggestion" in this chapter?

10

AMBIGUITY

A word is not a crystal, transparent and unchanged; it is the skin of a living thought and may vary greatly in color and content according to the circumstances and the time in which it is used.
—Justice O. W. Holmes.

1. *The versatility of words.*

IN the last chapter, we emphasized the multiple purposes served by language. Much of the meaning conveyed by speakers to their hearers, we saw, is not explicitly "stated" by formal linguistic devices, but is left to be "suggested" by intonation, emphasis, choice of words, and other such subtle means. The learner of a foreign language begins by assimilating a stock of words (a vocabulary) and a set of conventional rules for their arrangement (a grammar), for these are easily recognized and manipulated. Further experience soon teaches him, however, the inadequacy of this conventionally simplified vocabulary and grammar. Only by repeated conversation with natives, and by prolonged reading of books in the foreign tongue, does he gradually come to learn the finer shades of meaning that cannot be reduced to mechanical rule. *The distinguishable noises that we call separate words have a simpler structure than the meanings conveyed by their use.* That is to say, every word has to play many parts (like an overworked artist in a small repertory company); *every* word has a variety of meanings "according to the circumstances and the time in which it is used."

This is obvious enough when there is a large shift of meaning from one use to another—as when "school" sometimes means a place of education and at other times a company of fish. But more subtle shifts of meaning easily escape notice. In the following settings, for instance,

he is only sixteen—not yet a *man,*
man is a vertebrate,
no *man* is allowed to take courses in cooking in this college,
get that *man!*
man the lifeboats!
what a piece of work is *man*—how infinite in capacity. . . . ,
the son of *Man*

careful analysis is needed to bring the shifts of meaning to full awareness.

The versatility of such a word as "man" is far from being a *defect.* In the case of many instruments it is true that specialization of function is a condition of efficiency. An efficient knife is good for nothing but cutting, and a pen that could also be used as a flashlamp would be a poor writing implement. But language is so nearly indispensable for *all* purposes requiring co-operation between the members of a social group, that it needs to be flexible in its resources in proportion to the variety of human needs and purposes. Thus, a relatively small stock of words has to serve for conveying information, arousing feelings, inciting to action, creating bonds of union—and much else. And since many of these activities are interdependent, the inconveniences resulting from the creation of a number of special "languages" for special purposes would in the long run outweigh the advantages of increased precision or definiteness. In cases where bodies of men come together for *specialized* purposes, however, the flexibility of ordinary language is a hindrance, and so we get the technical "languages" or notations of mathematics, music, aeronautics.

2. *The meaning of "ambiguity."*

Normally we are skillful in adjusting our responses to the shifting meanings of the words we use. But sometimes we find ourselves unable to determine which of a number of alternative and equally plausible meanings to adopt; the process of communication has then broken down and the offending words are *ambiguous.* We shall say that a word (or other sign) is **ambiguous in a certain usage** when in that occurrence the interpreter (or hearer) is unable to choose between alternative meanings of the word, any of which would seem to fit the context. Ambiguity, as here defined, is therefore relative to context and interpreter; a word may be ambiguous in one usage and unambiguous in another; a remark may be ambiguous for one hearer and unambiguous for another.

Ambiguity can occur whenever signs function defectively and there are as many kinds of ambiguity as there are kinds of ways in which signs are used. There are cases of ambiguity when an interpreter is unable to locate the object intended to be named by a sign, when he is puzzled about the motives of a speaker, when he is unable to decide between an "emotive" and a "neutral" interpretation, and so on through a great variety of types of situations.

Ambiguity distinguished from some related notions. When we say "Several classes in Speech are offered in this College," we are using the **vague** word "Speech." This can be shown by considering such questions as "May a class in *Speech* include work in writing—or in argumentation?" and *"How much* use of spoken language is needed to ensure that the class is one in *Speech* rather than some other subject?" These questions are unanswerable *in principle.* They are like the questions, "Where does the light from an electric lamp *end?"* or "How many hairs must a man lose in order to become bald?"

The word "Speech," like the word "bald," is vague, *i.e.,* borderline situations can arise in which it is impossible to say whether the word should or should not be used. But the word "Speech" is *not ambiguous* (for a normal interpreter) in the context quoted. For the speaker is not trying to refer to the exact nature of the work done, and the interpreter, understanding this, is not puzzled by trying to make a choice between equally plausible alternative meanings. For contrast, consider the remark "Senator Filibuster is famous for his speech," which may cause the hearer to doubt whether the Senator's diction or some special oratorical performance was intended.

When we say "*Somebody* has left the light burning" we are making an **indefinite** statement. By leaving out mention of the particular person who was responsible, we are giving less information about the situation than might be supplied. Yet here again the word "Somebody" is *not ambiguous* as used. The speaker is not trying to give more definite information, nor is his hearer hesitating between alternative meanings. The word "some," in "some cases of influenza can be cured by penicillin," may, however, be ambiguous (as we previously saw on page 121); for here we may not know whether "some and perhaps all" or "some but not all" is intended.

Vagueness and indefiniteness characterize most of the words we use, and in general are not to be regarded as defects. The reverse is true of ambiguity, subject to the exceptions noted immediately below.

The uses of ambiguity. Ambiguity is not always a hindrance to human purposes. The famous Delphic oracle of the Greeks was able to maintain a reputation for infallibility by the judicious use of ambiguity. Thus, after encouraging Croesus in his disastrous war against the Persians by the prophesy that "he would destroy a mighty empire," its spokesmen were able to point out after the event that the words referred to the empire of Croesus rather than to that of his enemy! This is a device that latterday politicians and soothsayers also use to good effect.

In the more literary uses of language, deliberate ambiguity is an effective means for evoking complex response. When Hilaire Belloc says:

> When I am dead, I hope it may be said:
> "His sins were scarlet, but his books were read." *

he is deliberately playing on two senses of a word.

Full appreciation of the literary, diplomatic, and humorous uses of ambiguity implies some skill in its detection. And for

* Hilaire Belloc, *Sonnets and Verse,* p. 147. New York: Sheed and Ward.

the sober purposes of "critical thinking," detection must be a prelude to removal.

The detection and removal of ambiguity. As already said, the detection of crass ambiguity gives little trouble. When a student writes "Philosophy takes nothing for granite" or "A proposition is expressed innocence" (actual instances from the writer's experience), the offending words are easily noticed and corrected.

In the more troublesome cases, there is usually some dimly perceived *analogy* between the competing meanings of the dangerously ambiguous word. Thus some writers have argued that the existence of "Laws of Nature" implies the existence of a "Law-giver" and so of a divine Judge of the Universe. The plausibility of the argument rests on similarity between a "Law of Nature" and the kind of "Law" created by a legislature. Effective correction of the argument requires the dissimilarity of the two meanings to be made explicit. (Thus, we might point out that man-made laws are *commands,* enforced by penalties, while natural laws are regular ways in which things actually happen.) In other words, we make *explicit distinctions.* In so doing we begin to *explain the meanings of words* or give *definitions,* a process studied in detail in the next chapter.

It is a great help in the detection and correction of ambiguity to be familiar with some of the most common shifts of meaning that words suffer. The next section explains some of the most important of these.

3. *Types of shifts of meaning. Procedure followed.*

Each of the general types of meaning shift to be discussed will be introduced by means of an argument, the unsoundness of which hinges on ambiguity of some central word or phrase. Explanation of the specific mistake committed precedes a more extended discussion of the type of meaning shift involved. (The discussions will be more useful to the reader if he will try to criticize each unsound argument for himself before reading further. The questions to be answered in each case are *What is the precise mistake committed?* and *What light does the mistake throw on a general mode of shift in the meaning of the key words in the argument?*)

Sign: referent.

"Mary is a girl. Girl ends with an L. Therefore Mary ends with an L." The absurdity of the conclusion in this simple example makes the deliberate ambiguity (or **equivocation**) starkly obvious. In the first sentence, the word "girl" refers to something non-verbal, while in the second sentence the same word refers *to itself*. Only a *word* can end with an L; only Mary or some other member of the female sex can *be* a girl. A useful way of crystallizing the difference in usage here revealed is to say that in the first sentence the word "girl" is *used,* while in the second the same word is *mentioned.*

The difference between a word and what it mentions might be supposed to be too obvious to mislead anybody. Certainly nobody is likely to confuse the *cat* Hodge (that has fur, meows, likes milk, and so on) and the *word* "Hodge" (that begins with a capital H, has five letters, is sometimes used ambiguously). Yet many writers are in agreement that confusion between a sign and the *thing-mentioned* by a sign is responsible for a great deal of muddled thinking. Perhaps no distinction presented in this chapter is more important than the one here emphasized.

It has become customary to use the term **referent** to stand for whatever is mentioned or referred to by a sign. Thus, the referent of the word "Hodge" is the *cat* Hodge; the referent of the word "red" is a certain *color;* the referent of the phrase "the Capitol" is a certain Washington *building*. Unambiguous signs have a single referent; cases of ambiguity arise when the interpreter is unable to identify a unique referent.

One reason for confusion between sign and referent is failure to be sufficiently aware of the fact that words are *artificial* signs —the relation between word and thing-mentioned having been established indirectly by convention. Since the connection between symbol and thing-mentioned is thought to be natural, in this primitive way of thinking, it is consistent to regard properties of the sign as indicating properties of the thing-mentioned. That we are by no means free from such "word-magic" is illustrated by such proverbs as "Speak of the Devil and he will appear" or the superstitions clustering around the word "Friday" and the number "13." A charming historical example is that of the riots set off by the so-called Gregorian reform of the calendar in 1582. (After it had been agreed to initiate the new calendar by calling October 5 [Old style] October 15 [New style] furious mobs paraded the streets shouting "Give us back our ten days!")

We should not fall into the trap of supposing that we ourselves are quite free from such confusions between sign and referent. Gibbon's remarks, in the following quotation, apply to us no less than to the ancient Romans:

> Augustus was sensible that mankind is governed by names; nor was he deceived in his expectation, that the senate and people would submit to slavery, provided they were respectfully assured that they still enjoyed their ancient freedom. (*The Decline and Fall of the Roman Empire,* ch. 3.)

Too often we are still "governed by names," and suppose that by changing the word we have changed the thing to which it refers. We *can,* of course, produce a change in the associated attitudes of those who use the word (compare the remarks about emotive symbols on page 173). And all whose livelihoods depend on successful persuasion (whether businessmen, lawyers, educators, or politicians) know how important it is to choose the "right names."

A sophisticated reason for confusion between sign and referent is the difficulty many thinkers have found in supposing that general or abstract words name any real aspect of the world. Some thinkers have thought that the "world outside us" consists only of things "real enough to be kicked,"and have consequently been led to say that "Liberty" or any other general term must be "only" a word. Where this leads is well shown in Stuart Chase's remarks about fascism:

> But should one not be afraid of fascism and fight against it? The student of semantics is not afraid of evil spirits and takes no steps to fight against them . . . he refuses to shiver and shake at a word, and at dire warnings of what the word can do to him at some unnamed future time. (Stuart Chase, *The Tyranny of Words,* page 193. New York: Harcourt, Brace and Co., 1938.)

We have here as clear a case as could be wished for of confusion between sign and referent. What farsighted people might reasonably have feared in 1938 was not the *word* "fascism" but the complex events and tendencies *mentioned* by using that word.

A clear distinction between the use and mention of a word (or between a sign and its referent) can be easily shown by use of quotation marks. Where any risk of confusion may arise we should write " 'Bird' has four letters" rather than "Bird has four letters."

Dictionary meaning: contextual meaning.

" 'And now abideth faith, hope, charity, these three; but the greatest of these *is* charity.' According to the New Testament, therefore, it is more important to give alms to the poor than to have faith in God."

Comment: The giving of alms to the poor is a well-established standard meaning of "charity"; but in the context of the Bible, the same word is used with the older meaning of the Christian love of fellow men. The argument equivocates upon these two senses of "charity."

Our example illustrates a constantly recurring difficulty. In interpreting a given specimen of writing or speech, we are bound to rely in the first instance on the *general* or *standardized* meanings of the words used. Naturally, we want to use these generally accepted senses as clues to the particular meanings of the words in the passage before us, for it is with the meaning of that particular passage that we are concerned. The standardized meaning of a word or phrase is, however, very flexible, as we have seen. There is, therefore, a tendency to confuse **dictionary meaning** with **contextual meaning**—the meaning that a word *normally has* with the meaning it *does* have in a particular use.

By the **context** of a sign we understand the signs by which it is accompanied and the other circumstances attending its use in a particular case. The *contextual meaning* of a sign is its meaning in a given context; its *dictionary* (or *standard*) meaning is the meaning it has according to the conventions of the language in which it occurs. (Contextual meaning is usually, though not always, more definite than dictionary meaning.)

The utility of words depends on their having both dictionary and contextual meaning; the word needs to be easily recognizable by any suitably trained person, but each speaker must be free to express the particular shade of meaning fitting the context in which he is using the word.

If there were complete uniformity of sign-using behavior, the difficulty of distinguishing dictionary from contextual meaning would not arise, and every speaker could be depended on to be using words in exactly the same sense. In actual practice, however, most words take on an individual coloration from the differences in experiences, purposes, intentions and ideals of their different users. "Liberal" means one thing for a man who is thoroughly familiar with the history of the past two centuries; it means something else when used as a vague synonym for "radical" or "red." In an argument between two people about "liberals" it may therefore be necessary to begin by discovering how each disputant is himself meaning "liberal" *in that context.* Appeal to the dictionary may help to provide agreement concerning meaning, if both parties to the dispute can agree to use the crucial term in the dictionary sense. But quite often the core of the dispute arises from an *unnoticed* shift of meaning away from a standardized meaning, and in such cases appeal to the dictionary is useful mainly as a way of showing the *difference* between the dictionary and the contextual meaning.

An example of serious equivocation arising from failure to observe the dictionary-context distinction is provided by Aldous Huxley's criticisms of the ideal of equality. Huxley begins an essay on "The idea of equality" with the statement, "That all men are equal is a proposition to which, at ordinary times, no sane human being has ever given his assent." (Aldous Huxley, *Proper Studies,* page 1. London: Chatto and Windus, 1929.) He then argues that the equality of man is disproved by the known facts of physical and mental inequality. Men are not equal in their abilities to lift weights, or to reason; therefore they are obviously unequal; therefore the "equality of man" was a "prejudice" or "metaphysical dogma," "elaborated, after the fact, to justify the interests and desires of certain individuals, classes or nations." It seems never to have occurred to Huxley to consider the possibility that the Founding Fathers were neither stupid nor dishonest, and that he might possibly have misinterpreted what "equality" meant *in the context* of the Declaration of Independence. If we interpret "equality" to mean in part the equality of *rights* (and more especially the rights of life, liberty and the pursuit of happiness) we shall find a very good sense of the "equality of man"—worthy of the allegiance even of sane human beings.

Connotation: denotation.

"The word 'God' has meaning. Therefore it refers to something. But the word, as we are using it, refers to nothing else but a supernatural being. Therefore, that supernatural being, God, exists." A sufficient criticism might consist in pointing out that an argument of the same form could be used to prove that giants exist. For the word "giant" undoubtedly has meaning, and refers to "nothing else but" men of extraordinary height.

The crucial ambiguity, on which the argument's plausibility depends, is in the words "meaning" and "refer." A simple example will convince us that we can use words to "refer" (or "have meaning") in two ways that deserve to be distinguished.

(a) "That chimpanzee looks unhealthy." Here the word "chimpanzee" is being used primarily as a way of *identifying* the animal in question. If somebody replies "But he isn't a chimpanzee," we might retort "Very well—that monkey, that animal. He still looks unhealthy. You know what I mean!" In such contexts, we are not concerned with the *general characteristics* of chimpanzees except as they help us to draw the hearer's attention to the object we wish to mention.

(b) Contrast this use of "chimpanzee" with that occurring in "That monkey is not a chimpanzee." This time we *cannot* replace "chimpanzee" by "monkey" or "animal" without quite changing the meaning of our utterance. The word "chimpanzee" is, in this context, used primarily as a way of referring to properties that all chimpanzees (and nothing else) have in common.

We shall say the word "chimpanzee" has **connotation** and **denotation.** The word **denotes** all the individual chimpanzees that exist, or have existed, or will exist, *i.e.,* all those animals that are correctly called "chimpanzees." And it **connotes** the properties (being an African Ape resembling man) that an individual must possess in order to be a chimpanzee. When it is necessary to refer to the class of all the things denoted by a word, it is usual to speak of the *denotation* of the word in question. Thus, the denotation of "King of England" consists of John, George I, Richard I, and so on.

Possibly the most important point to notice in connection with the distinction here under discussion is that *a word (or phrase) can have connotation without denotation.* Thus the phrase, "man with green skin and two heads" has connotation: we know how a thing would need to look in order to be a man with green skin and two heads, *i.e.,* we know the properties connoted by the expression. Nevertheless, the phrase in question has no denotation: There is no green-skinned two-headed man anywhere in the universe.

We are now ready to understand more clearly the nature of the mistake committed in our introductory example. When we say, as we should, that the word "God" has meaning, we are holding that the word "God" has *connotation.* But this alone will not prove that God exists, *i.e.,* that the word "God" has denotation. For we have just seen that a symbol may connote without denoting.

At this point it is natural to ask the converse question—whether a symbol can ever denote without connoting. A symbol having no connotation would have to draw our attention to something without saying anything about that thing. A name such as "Mary" approximately satisfies this condition, since to be told that something is Mary is to be told almost nothing about it—not even that Mary is a person, since cats and ships are also given that name. Nevertheless, a good case could be made for saying that "Mary" does connote a property, viz., the property *of being referred to by the sound* 'Mary' (*i.e.,* having the name 'Mary'). Perhaps the word "it," or "that," when used to point out something, comes nearer than a personal name to providing an example of a word that denotes without connoting any property whatsoever.

Process: product.

"Science includes nothing but truth. Hence Newton's work in Physics was not scientific. For his theory of gravitation has been overthrown by Einstein's theory."

Comment: We might be inclined to retort that the "rejection" of Newton's theory does not show his work to have been wholly untrue, and that his results are still useful as an approximation. This reply would not be very adequate, however. For other examples could be given of early scientists, still highly regarded, of whose work very little has survived the criticism of later generations. Such pioneers are honored because they sought the truth *according to the scientific method,* formulating theories that were good in the light of the knowledge and experimental techniques available at the time they lived. Science, in short, is a process, as well as a product (as we shall learn in more detail in the third part of this book). The weakness of the argument consists in its neglect of that sense of "science" and "scientific" in which the nature of the *activity* (rather than its immediate fruits) is stressed.

A great many words exhibit a similar fluctuation between emphasis on a **process** (a doing something) and an associated **product** (the result of an activity). When Pope wrote:

> 'Tis education forms the common mind
> Just as the twig is bent the tree's inclined,

he was emphasizing a conception of "education" as activity. But when we say of somebody that he "received his education" at some university or other, the language we use, with its suggestion of some*thing,* acquired in a certain place and at a certain time, tends to stress the notion of "education" as a finished product. (A similar usage was, doubtless, uppermost in the mind of the student who, on receiving a diploma at commencement, exclaimed with relief, "Gosh, I'm educated!")

Shift of meaning of the **process: product** type is especially characteristic of words ending in "-tion." (Thus "destruction" may refer to what is done while something is being destroyed or to the results of such activity; "selection" may mean choosing or what is chosen; and so on.) But any word referring to an activity is subject to this kind of shift and may generate a corresponding type of ambiguity.

4. Metaphor.

The types of meaning shifts so far considered can be described by a single formula. In each case there was some word or phrase, W, having sometimes one referent, A, and, at other times, some other referent, B. It was characteristic of each case that A and B were *not unrelated;* on the contrary, the alternative referents were always connected in some fashion. In "sign: referent" shifts, A was a word (or other sign) and B *its* meaning; in "connotation: denotation" shifts, A was a property and B the class of objects having *that* property; in "process: product" shifts, A was a certain activity and B the result of *that* activity.

The foregoing illustrates a general principle of the *spread of meaning of linguistic signs;* whenever two things are related to each other in some fashion, there is a tendency in a living language for any word referring to the one to be applied also to the other—*things related tend to acquire identical names.* (The history of the English language is rich in instances where such spread of meaning eventually leads to permanent change in the dictionary meaning of the original sign. Thus "board" shifts from "table used for meals" to "food served at table"; "bead" originally meant "prayer" before it was transferred to the balls of the rosary, and so on.)

Of the many ways in which the alternative referents, A and B, can be related, one of the most common is that in which they are *perceived as similar* in some respects. "Blade" is applied to a leaf of grass and to a sword (similarity of shape); a "cardinal" is a high officer of the Catholic Church and a scarlet bird (similarity of color); a man may be a "servant of a corporation" or a "servant of the truth" (similarity of function).

Among the most striking of meaning shifts based on such implicit comparisons are **metaphors.** A word is said to **occur metaphorically in a certain context** if it is there used to indicate a referent similar to but different from that to which it normally refers. Common language abounds in metaphors: "the *birth* of a nation," "a *glaring* light," "a *foxy* negotiator," "a *monumental* folly," "a *moving* speech"—to mention only those that come first to mind.

Sometimes the original meaning vanishes, resulting in so-called "dead" metaphors. Few will think of horses when reading of *"unbridled* fury," of a carpenter's square in connection with *"normal"* or a pair of scales when *"balancing* accounts." But much thinking is naturally expressed with the help of living metaphors (as many sentences in this section of the chapter themselves illustrate).

Metaphors deserve special attention in the criticism of thought, for the following reasons:

(1) The shock of surprise caused by an unhackneyed metaphor, due to the presence of a familiar word in strange company, focusses attention on the characteristics that underlie the implicit comparison. A metaphor is a particularly effective way of securing a desired emphasis: "A man of courage" would be a very flat substitute for "a *lion* of a man."

(2) The customary emotive and other associations of a word tend to remain attached to it when it is used metaphorically. When Churchill, in a famous speech, referred to Mussolini as "that *utensil*," he was conveying much more to his audience than he would have done by saying "that passive agent."

(3) The spread of meaning that makes metaphor possible has some tendency to extend (often indefensibly) to *all* aspects of the two referents compared. Because the same word is applied to both objects, there is some temptation to suppose them more similar than they in fact are. A speaker who refers to the the Americas as "a *family* of nations" inevitably conveys an impression of brotherly harmony that may be far from the truth. We should be on the lookout for illegitimate extension of metaphor. (See also the discussion of the dangers of analogy on pages 319-323 below.)

(4) Because the basis of comparison of a metaphor is not explicit, this rhetorical device is easily abused by muddled though fervent thinkers. While it is usually impossible to give a "literal" translation of a metaphor without destroying its force (compare the difficulty of "explaining" a joke), a metaphor, however legitimate, is no substitute for clear ideas. The nature of the relation of similarity involved in any given metaphor can be explicitly described (by the methods for the expansion of suggestion illustrated in the last chapter), and the ideas underlying the metaphor, when so revealed for inspection, must submit to the usual tests of clarity, coherence, and adequacy.

What was previously said in connection with the use of emotively toned language is also relevant here: While avoiding the folly of condemning all use of metaphor (as if dullness and poverty of content were virtues in thinking) we should examine each metaphor on its own merits before accepting its embodied suggestions.

Summary

Because so many purposes are served by a relatively small stock of words, words play many parts according to the circumstances in which they are used. The capacity of words to shift in meaning is a merit, not a defect. When an interpreter is unable to choose between alternative (and equally plausible) meanings of a word, we have a case of *ambiguity* (in that usage). Ambiguity is relative to context and interpreter.

Most words are *vague; i.e.,* they do not determine an exact boundary between cases where they are and cases where they are not applicable; and they are *indefinite*—fail to give as much information as could be supplied by other words. Vagueness and indefiniteness are not the same as ambiguity, nor are they defects in language (as is normally the case with ambiguity). Ambiguity may occasionally be useful, however, for literary, humorous, or other purposes.

The detection and removal of ambiguity is most difficult when there is some relation of analogy between the competing meanings. Ambiguity may be removed in such cases by making explicit distinctions, that is to say by *defining* the related senses of the offending word.

Four general types of meaning shifts were considered.

(1) *"Sign: referent."* The term *referent* is used for whatever is mentioned or referred to by a sign. It is customary to allow the same word to refer either to its referent or, on occasion, to *itself*. The type of ambiguity resulting can be removed by using quotation marks. Confusion between a sign and its referent encourages *word-magic,* of which some examples were cited. (2) *"Dictionary meaning: Contextual meaning."* By the "dictionary meaning" is meant the general or standardized meaning a word has in the language to which it belongs; by "contextual meaning," the individual meaning it has in a particular occasion of its use. (The *context* of a sign is the whole set of circumstances attending its occurrence.) Contextual meanings seldom coincide completely with dictionary meanings. (3) *"Connotation: Denotation."* The connotation of a term is the property (or properties) a thing must have in order that the term shall apply to it; the denotation is the class of objects having that property. Words may have connotation without denotation. (4) *"Process: Product."* This is the shift

from meaning an activity to meaning the result of that activity. Particularly characteristic of words ending in *"-tion,"* it is also shown by many other words.

All four types exhibit a common pattern. Each time a word, W, shifts from indicating one referent, A, to another, B, *that is related to it in some fashion.* This illustrates the *principle of spread of meaning,* that whenever two things are related, there is a tendency (in any living language) for the name of one to be applied also to the other. (Sometimes the original meaning comes to be displaced by the new meaning.) The most common relation between A and B is that of *perceived similarity* in some respect. This is the basis of the kind of implicit comparison known as *metaphor.* Metaphors may be "dead" or "living." Metaphors are emphatic ways of presenting the characteristics underlying the implicit comparison. The metaphorical term tends to transfer its original suggestions and to cause the hearer to extend the basic comparison illegitimately. Though subject to abuse, metaphors are not to be condemned without examination.

Comprehension test

(For instructions, see page 10.)

1. A vague word is necessarily indefinite. (*true* *false*)
2. Ambiguity, like vagueness, is a defect of language. (*true* *false*)
3. To judge whether a word is ambiguous we need to know its context. (*true* *false*)
4. Ambiguity is least dangerous when there is a wide difference between the competing meanings. (*true* *false*)
5. The contextual meaning of a word may be the same as its dictionary meaning. (*true* *false*)
6. In " 'Tom' has three letters," the word 'Tom' is *used,* not *mentioned.* (*true* *false*)
7. A word can have meaning without having denotation. (*true* *false*)
8. Every word has both a "process-" and a "product-" sense. (*true* *false*)
9. To speak of "dead metaphor" is to use a metaphor. (*true* *false*)
10. The emotive associations of a word tend to accompany its metaphorical uses. (*true* *false*)

Exercises

A

1. The following passages illustrate different uses of the word "free." Do the following things: (a) in each case find a word having a meaning *opposite* to the particular meaning of "free" (it may sometimes be necessary to rewrite the whole sentence); (b) make a list of the various meanings of "free" that are illustrated; (c) determine in which of the given contexts "free" is ambiguous.
   This performance is *free;* the bicycle has a *free* wheel; we favor *free* trade; he made a *free* gift of the money; the poem is in *free* verse; no man is *free* to sell himself into slavery; the convict is *free* again; none of my income is *free* from taxes; an airplane is *free* to fall; they are *free* from anxiety.
2. Make a list of contexts illustrating some of the different meanings of "common," and do the things suggested in the previous question.
3. Which of the following words are subject to "process: product" shifts of meaning: *photograph, law, thought, resolution, peace, journey, emotion, information, government?* Explain carefully the difference between the product- and process-senses (in cases where the two senses exist).
4. Discover the etymologies of the following words: *implicit, member, idiot, spirit, premises* (when used of a house), *hypocrite, person.* Which of these words have a metaphorical origin?
5. Pick out all the words used metaphorically (other than those used as illustrations) in the last section of this chapter.
6. Expand the following metaphors, *i.e.,* state the respects in which the things compared are similar: *flaring* anger, a soldier's *foxhole,* a *villainous* cold, the *core* of the problem, the *horns* of a dilemma, a *persuasive* argument, a *dead* metaphor, *scum* of the earth (title of a book about concentration camps), *polar* words, a *steering* committee, a film *star,* a *clutch.*
7. What mistakes are made in these arguments:
   a. Since the body is a *host* to its parasites it must clearly welcome them. Hence the body invites parasitic organisms.
   b. The fact that men are all called men proves that they have a common nature.
   c. Prohibitionists object to drinking. But we know we should die of thirst if we stopped drinking.
   d. Giants are men who are exceptionally tall. Therefore some men are very much taller than others.

e. Ambiguity is a defect. All words are ambiguous. Hence all words are defective.
f. The Bible is the Word of God and is written in English. Therefore God must speak English.
g. "An astonishing number of women in Shakespeare's plays are openly called 'mistress.' There must have been a great deal of unashamed immorality in his time."
h. "How clever of the astronomers to be able to discover the *names* of those distant stars."
i. "I mean to buy a lot of three-cent stamps before the rate of mailing is raised to four cents per letter."
j. True freedom is freedom to do what is right. A convict has no right to leave prison. Therefore he is truly free in spite of imprisonment.

8. Judges are often required to make decisions about the meanings of crucial terms. Thus it has been held that the term "newspaper" applies to "comic supplements" (*New York Times,* June 14, 1947: "Comics Win Case in Federal Court") and that a new baby is not an extra tenant within the meaning of the law (*New York Herald-Tribune,* March 25, 1948: "Birth of Baby Ruled No Basis For Rent Boost"). Find two other instances, from newspaper reports, of legal rulings involving decisions about meaning. Analyze in each case the considerations that prompted the ruling.
9. "Every word carries with it, in each speaker's mind in which it lives, certain associations other than its main association to what it indicates, associations to other things or associated emotions and attitudes. No dictionary can record these associations when they are peculiar to one or a few persons, or needs to." (R. Robinson, *Definition,* Oxford: The Clarendon Press, 1950, p. 57.)

   Choose five common words that have peculiar associations in your mind and describe these associations. Describe situations in which the existence of these special associations might give rise to ambiguity.

B

1. Explain the differences between *metaphor, simile,* and *analogy,* and give examples of each. How far are the remarks made in the text about the first also applicable to the second?
2. Which of the technical terms introduced into this chapter are *polar* words?
3. Apply the process: product distinction to the terms *connotation* and *denotation.*

4. Define "word magic." Is this term used metaphorically in the text?
5. Expand and illustrate the following points concerning connotation and denotation:
   a. In order for a word X to have connotation or denotation, it must be possible to say "some X," "this X," "the only X," or "no X."
   b. A word may denote without having denotation.
   c. The connotation of a word consists only of those properties associated with it *by definition.*
   d. As a word shifts in meaning, its connotation also shifts.
   e. It is possible to understand a word without being able to give its connotation.
6. A man accused of burglary objects that "burglary is *only an abstraction*" and that we ought to refuse to be "afraid of *mere words.*" Imagine yourself to be the prosecuting attorney, and compose a reply suitable for delivery in court.

11

DEFINITION

> *The light of human minds is perspicuous words, but by exact definitions first* snuffed *and* purged *from ambiguity.*—Hobbes.

1. The occasions of definition.

LANGUAGE is a complex social instrument. We learn to use it, in childhood and throughout adult life, by imitation, practice, and deliberate instruction.

For many purposes, imitation and practice are good enough; we learn to make ourselves understood by watching others and trying to do likewise. And this normally requires little conscious thought. A variety of situations arise, however, in which a deliberate and conscious attempt to explain the meanings of words must be made. The examples that follow illustrate some of the purposes thereby served.

Introduction of new terms. A flight instructor must be able to refer to the various parts of an airplane. If he left his students to discover the meaning of "aileron," and the other technical terms, by trial and error, their studies would end in crashes. It is easier and safer to *state explicitly* that an aileron is a "lateral-control flap at the rear of the airplane's wingtips." An intelligent hearer, to whom the words used in the explanation are familiar, will *immediately* know how to identify an aileron. Most technical terms, words introduced to serve a special purpose, need to be accompanied by deliberate instruction in their use.

Removal of ambiguity. Two men are talking about "socialism." The first claims that "socialism is here already," since the Federal Government controls prices, wages, and production of goods. The other retorts that socialism is a "logical absurdity":

"Imagine anybody sharing a toothbrush with millions of fellow Americans."

Disputes of this kind, in which the contenders are talking about *different matters symbolized by the same word,* are all too common. It is noteworthy that *no disagreement concerning matters of fact may be involved;* for both men may agree about the extent of the control exercised by the Federal Government, and also about the impossibility of sharing all personal belongings. If the dispute nevertheless continues with unabated fury, it may be because the disputants insist on using the crucial term "socialism" in different senses. By "socialism" one man understands federal control of economic activity; the other, the common use of personal property.

When people talk "at cross purposes" in this way, the normal assumption (that others use words as we do) breaks down, and no "meeting of minds" is possible. The cure for such failure in communication is *definition* of the key terms in the argument. (This topic is further discussed in the next chapter under the heading of "Verbal issue"—see page 234.)

Extension of meaning. When Marshal Pétain was on trial for treason, an important duty of the French court was to determine what meaning "treason" was to have *in that context.* Treason is generally understood to be breach of allegiance to the sovereign power of a state, but the lawmakers had not considered a case in which the head of a state himself gave aid and comfort to the enemy invader. The unusual circumstances made it necessary to give explicit definition of the crucial term. (For this reason, some of the chief witnesses were asked to explain their own conception of "treason.")

Similar situations constantly arise, and not only in legal practice. For our ideas must be applied in a constantly changing environment; a conscientious thinker must be prepared to stretch the meanings of the central terms of his thinking.

In the ancient cities of Greece, "democracy" meant a form of government in which a privileged minority (the "citizens") participated as a body in the conduct of civic affairs. As this type of democracy is unfeasible in a nation like our own with millions of citizens, we require some extension of meaning. Anybody who wants to preserve the values of ancient democracy will be led to ask such questions as: Is democracy compatible with minority rule? With *representative* institutions? Should it apply to economic as well as political matters? The answers adopted will provide the material for a *definition* of "democracy" in the contemporary context.

2. *The meaning of "definition."*

In the variety of situations illustrated above, we have seen that it is desirable to give explicit instruction in the use of words. We shall say that an explanation of the use of a word (or other sign) is a **definition.**

"Definition" is to be understood as having "process-product" variation in meaning according to circumstances (see page 194). It may mean either the activity of explaining how a word is to be used or the outcome of that activity—usually a certain *statement.* (We are, of course, explaining how *we* shall use the term "definition," and thereby establishing an "individual" or "contextual" meaning of the term. But in so doing we are remaining close to some important "dictionary" meanings of the term.)

Definition of WORDS, not things. A dictionary has the entry, "*fox:* Red-furred sharp-snouted bushy-tailed quadruped." This may be contrasted with "Foxes are swift runners." The first statement (A), unlike the second (B), is not intended to make an assertion *only about foxes.*

In order to see this we need only to consider how the two assertions could be tested. To establish the truth of B, we must observe *foxes,* or use the testimony of others who are in a position to do this; moreover, this is *all* we need to do. One way of establishing the truth of A would be to wait for opportunities of hearing people say "That's a fox!" checking in each such case whether the speaker did indicate a quadruped that was bushy-tailed, and so on. If this procedure were followed, we should, as in the first case, observe foxes; but we should also observe people using *the word* "fox"; and A could not be tested *without* direct or indirect reference to such linguistic behavior. To look at foxes alone in order to test the definition would be as futile as looking at the planet Mars through a powerful telescope to see if the word "Mars" were inscribed on it. The reason we must pay attention to linguistic behavior in testing A is that the connection between *being a "fox"* and *having red fur* (or the other characteristics mentioned in the definition) is artificial or man-made. For this reason, also, the definition, A, unlike the second statement, can also be established without attention to foxes at all—as by asking sufficiently competent speakers of English what *they mean* when using the word.

In short, a definition (in our sense) is always an assertion about a word, though it may also be an assertion about non-verbal things. It is to be carefully contrasted with statements in which *no* reference is made to words.

Standard forms for definition. As a reminder of the important point that definitions mention words, the definition examined might be written in the form:

The *word* 'fox' means a red-furred sharp-snouted bushy-tailed quadruped.

It is useful to have technical terms for referring to the different parts of such a definition. The word 'fox' is called the **definiendum** (from the Latin, meaning: "that which is to be defined"), and the phrase "a red-furred sharp-snouted bushy-tailed quadruped" is called the **definiens** (Latin: "that which does the defining").

Thus a standard form of definition will be

"X" MEANS Y

where appropriate words are to be inserted at the places held open by the letters 'X' and 'Y'.

In a useful variation, the definiendum is presented as equivalent to another set of words that can be substituted for it. Thus "pleonasm" may be defined as follows:

"Pleonasm" *means the same as* "redundancy of expression."

The general form for this type of definition will be:

"X" MEANS THE SAME AS "Y"

3. *The relativity of definition.*

Definition is a process in which the use of a word (or other sign) is explained *by somebody* and *for somebody*. As it "takes two to make a quarrel," so it takes *at least three* to make a genuine definition (the explanation and those who give and receive it). Definition, therefore, is more like a hand-shake than a sneeze: It is a social transaction.

The social transaction we call "definition" has as its purpose that the person to whom the definition is addressed shall be able to use the definiendum in the manner intended by the person supplying the definition. In order to be "good," a definition must achieve its purpose by causing the person to whom it is addressed to learn to use the definiendum in the way intended. A "good" definition is one that is good for the receiver of the definition. For the same reason, "good" medical treatment must cure the patient who receives it. The test of the medicine is its capacity to heal; the test of a definition is its capacity to enlighten *the person addressed*. A "good" definition that is not good *for somebody* is as much of an absurdity as a "comfortable" chair that makes nobody comfortable.

Important consequences follow from these simple considerations. First, it is plain that *different persons may need different definitions* (just as different patients may need different medical treatment even for the same disease).

A definition, as we have seen, uses words to explain the definiendum. In order to be adequate for the particular person addressed, the words used must be intelligible to him. And any definition that is understood is so far "good." A child has been heard to define "pepper" as "that sneezy stuff Mummy puts on my potatoes when she forgets." That might be good enough for a child, but it would not satisfy an analytical chemist. Yet a definition of "salt" as "sodium chloride with an admixture of impurities in amount not greater than one per cent of the total mass," while satisfactory for the purposes of the chemist, would be quite useless to the child.

By the **relativity of definition** we shall understand the principle that a definition ought to be formulated in a manner intelligible and useful to the particular hearer addressed. A "good" definition will be one that is both intelligible and *effective* in teaching its recipient the particular use intended.

Relativity of definition does not eliminate all uniformity of definition. Though men are diverse, and accordingly need diverse definitions, they are also similar and can often profit from the same definitions. This accounts for the usefulness of dictionaries, which are compilations of definitions *roughly* adequate for all who speak a certain language.

The truth of definitions. Consider, first, a case where a speaker invents a *new term* for his own use. His definition then has the form:

By 'S' *I* shall mean (such and such)

or alternatively:

By 'S' *let us* mean (such and such).

In this case, the definition clearly expresses a resolution (first form) or a proposal (second form). *A definition of this kind can be neither true nor false.* We can *accept* or *reject* it (on the grounds of its fitness for the purpose in hand), but to call it false would be as absurd as to call "Let us go for a walk" a lie. We shall call this kind a **stipulated** definition.

In sharp contrast is the case in which a speaker intends to give a definition conforming to some customary or contextual usage. The definition then takes the form:

Such and such speakers when using 'S' *customarily mean* (such-and-such)

or else:

When 'S' occurred *in this particular context* it meant (such-and-such).

This time the definition purports to be *true,* for it is not a proposal or resolution, but a report *about* the usage of the definiendum.

We shall call the latter types of definition **reported** definitions, of which "customary" or "dictionary" definitions will be a special case. All reported definitions are either true or false. (Thus the definition "In the English language, 'cow' means an inefficient admiral" is *false.*) Dictionaries are collections of reported definitions.

When occasion arises to give definitions of words *already in use,* there is seldom a clear-cut choice between adopting a stipulated or a reported definition. On the one hand it is important that we shall, so far as possible, choose *our* meanings of the words we use. But when handling words already used in relatively stable ways, to ignore the pre-existing meanings is to promote ambiguity and confusion. (It would be unwise to stipulate that "cow" should mean an inefficient admiral, so long as the same word continued to be used in the more familiar meaning.)

Freedom to assign meanings by means of a stipulated definition is therefore restricted by the definiteness of previous usage of the definiendum. When a word has relatively definite and precise customary uses (as in the case of "camera," say) there is almost no freedom to stipulate. When a word is used loosely (as in the case of "education"), freedom to stipulate is correspondingly greater. The art of definition consists in part in striking the right balance between the need to *make* our own signs (by assigning meaning to them) and the obligation to respect the meanings of signs already in use.

4. Rules of definition.

Most writers on logic follow an ancient tradition in providing a list of rules for good definitions. No doubt such rules are of use, or they would not continue to be given. Yet in view of what has already been said concerning the variety of purposes served by definition, and the need for adapting definitions to the background and needs of the hearer, infallible *recipes* for definition are not to be expected. Making a definition is like baking a cake; the artist's skill (whether he is a lexicographer or a cook) consists of making the best use of the materials available, and no one can learn how to do this by merely reading about the skills required. Nevertheless, there are some general maxims, which even the most skillful cooks do well to remember, and there are general hints on procedure in framing definitions that can help to forestall some common blunders.

1. *The definition should be adequate for the purpose it is to serve.*

This first rule is intended to help the reader clarify his purposes before attempting his own definitions or criticizing those of others. It is useful to ask such questions as "Am I trying to indicate the connotation of this word (or merely describing a part of its denotation)?" "Am I examining a stipulated or a reported definition?" and so on.

2. *The definition should be intelligible to the person addressed.*

The reasons for this rule have already been discussed under the heading of "relativity of definition." Among the most important implications are the following two:

2a: *The definiens should not contain any words that are as unintelligible (to the reader) as the definiendum.*

Since the definiens is intended to explain the use or meaning of the definiendum, it will not achieve its end unless composed of words that he understands relatively well. (Thus the definition " 'Dracocephalum' means the Dragonhead flower" will work only for a person who already knows how to recognize a Dragonhead.) Successful application of this rule requires accurate knowledge of the background of the person addressed. In situations where such knowledge is unobtainable (as when a writer addresses an unseen audience), it is necessary to rely on somewhat vague notions of the relative simplicity and familiarity of language. Nobody would regard the following as a satisfactory definition:

> "Net: a reticulated texture with small interstices."

For it is impossible to imagine somebody familiar with the meaning of the pretentious definiens who would not know already how to use the word "net." (Dr. Johnson, who included this definition in his famous dictionary, was of course perpetrating a mild joke upon his readers.)

2b: *The definiens should not contain any part of the definiendum.*

To define a demon as one having demoniacal powers will not help the person addressed. For "demoniacal" means the same as "demon-like," and a person in doubt about the meaning of "demon" will certainly be equally in the dark as to the meaning of the words offered as substitutes. Such definitions are commonly called **circular.**

Circularity of definition is not always as obvious as in the illustration used. Consider, for instance, the facetious definition of a lady as "a woman in whose presence every man behaves like a gentleman." If this were intended as a serious clarification, it might be objected that the notion of a "gentleman" is as obscure as that of a "lady." (We might say that a lady is nothing but a "female gentleman.") The definition is guilty of circularity, even though the word "lady" does not occur *explicitly* in the definiens.

Hidden circularity, of this more subtle kind, is common in prolonged argument, in which chains of definitions occur. Thus, a writer may define peace as "the absence of war." This should put us on our guard immediately, since "peace" and "war" are correlative or polar words. If the writer elsewhere defines "war" without using the term "peace," his definition will survive our criticism. It may be found, however, that he defines war, in effect, as "a breach of a state of peace." Inserting this in the definiens of the original definition, we obtain " 'peace' means the absence of a breach of a state of peace"—which is clearly circular.

3. *The definiens and definiendum should be equivalent, i.e., should be substitutes for each other in every context.*

This rule is usually separated into two parts:

3a: *The definiendum should not be wider than the definiens.*

3b: *The definiendum should not be narrower than the definiens.*

The second of these rules is broken by the definition of a house as "a structure consisting of walls and a roof, used for human shelter"—for the definiens applies to theaters and cinemas as well as to houses. The first is broken by the definition of a house as "a brick structure used by humans as a permanent living place"—since houses may also be constructed of wood or other materials.

Gross breaches of these rules can usually be detected quite easily. But the rules establish a standard of perfection that is rarely achieved, except in the artificially constructed technical languages of the sciences. Consider the definition of "parapet" as "low wall at edge of balcony, roof, etc., or along sides of bridge, etc." (Quoted from a dictionary.) This is about as good a definition for most purposes as we can expect to find. Let us next examine whether definiens and definiendum are here equivalent. A story might contain the sentence "the steeplejack climbed on the parapet of the tower." Insertion of the definiens in place of the definiendum gives us the sentence "The steeplejack climbed on to the low wall at the edge of a balcony, roof, etc., or along the sides of a bridge, etc.,—of the tower." This is, of course, nonsense. The point is that even the satisfactory dictionary definition of "parapet" describes the different kinds of substitution to be made for the definiendum in various contexts, and does *not* provide a single phrase that can always be substituted for it. This is the best to be expected in most cases. (The attempt to substitute definiens for definiendum is usually illuminating, however, and often reveals unsuspected inadequacies in the definition.)

As a special case of the rule of equivalence of definiens and definiendum, we have the rule:

3c: *The definiens should not be expressed in metaphorical or figurative language.*

In a newspaper competition for a definition of "Loyalty," a prizewinning entry ran: "Loyalty is the flame of the lamp of friendship." Such a "definition" (if it deserves the name) can make no pretense at providing a definiens equivalent to the definiendum. The chief objection to this specimen is that the metaphorical expression ("flame of the lamp of friendship") fails to explain the use of the definiendum. (Imagine yourself trying to teach a foreigner the meaning of the word "Loyalty" by using *this* definiens.) And this weakness is characteristic of the use of metaphors or other "figures of speech." (Very likely, however, the competition was not searching for definitions in our sense of the term.)

4. *The definition should be an explanation of the meaning of the definiendum, not a statement only about the things mentioned by the definiendum.*

This follows at once from our conception of definition as explanation of the meaning of words (or other signs). (See the discussion on page 205.)

It is not always easy to see clearly the difference between a statement about the *sign* S and a statement about the things referred to or *mentioned by* S. Consider, for instance, one dictionary's definition of "steel" as "kinds of malleable alloy of iron and carbon *largely used as material for tools and weapons.*" The first part satisfies the demands of the rule, for it is true that nothing would be *called* "steel" (according to the customary convention) unless it were a kind of malleable alloy of iron and carbon. But the same is not true of the rest of the definition. Steel *is* largely used as material for tools and weapons, but it would still be *called* "steel" even if it were not. Suppose aluminum and plastics were eventually to displace steel as a constructional materials; we should then no doubt say "steel is no longer used as a material for tools and weapons," and this would be an intelligible and self-consistent assertion. But if "steel" *meant* "material used for tools and weapons," the statement in question would be a *self-contradiction.* (Similarly, "This is a camera, but not designed for photography" is a self-contradiction, because "camera" *means* "apparatus for photography.")

Our discussion leads to the following test for determining whether the rule is obeyed. Suppose the definition to be inspected has the form "S is P." We examine whether "something is S but *not* P" is a self-contradiction. If it is, the rule has been observed. But if the statement is false without being self-contradictory, the rule has been broken. In the latter case, the original statement "S is P" expressed a *fact* about the referent of "S," not an explanation of the meaning of "S."

5. *Division and classification.*

Definitions conforming to our general specifications may take many forms. Among the most commonly useful are those in which the definiens determines the *connotation* of the definiendum. (All our examples have been of this kind, and some writers on logic refuse to apply the term "definition" to any other type of explanation of meaning.)

When giving a "connotative" definition (as we might call it), it is often convenient to follow a procedure known as **division.** This may be illustrated by a well-known indoor game, in which one player has to determine an object chosen by his friends during his absence from the room. The rules are that the single player may ask any questions, with the understanding that the only answers permissible are "Yes," "No," or, in cases where either reply would mislead, "Can't answer." (The player may not make more than two guesses at the solution.)

Here is a typical dialogue, as it might ensue under the direction of a skilful player: "Is it alive? *No.* Is it manufactured? *Yes.* Can it move around? *Yes.* Under its own power? *No.* Does it move above ground? *Yes.* In the air? *No.* On the ground? *Yes.* Does it sometimes contain people? *Yes.* Does it usually contain furniture? *Yes.* Is it a trailer? *Yes.* Any special trailer? *No.*" At this point the single player announces the correct answer as "a trailer." (The problem was an easy one: Good players are able to locate notions as elaborate as *the thoughts that Nero had while Rome was burning.*)

The speed and directness with which the correct answer ("a trailer") was reached was the result of following a systematic procedure. The first question used a *division* of all possible objects into the two classes of living and non-living things. The hidden object having been located in the class of non-living things, a further question located it among the *manufactured* things (in that class). The first two steps can therefore be shown in a diagram in this way:

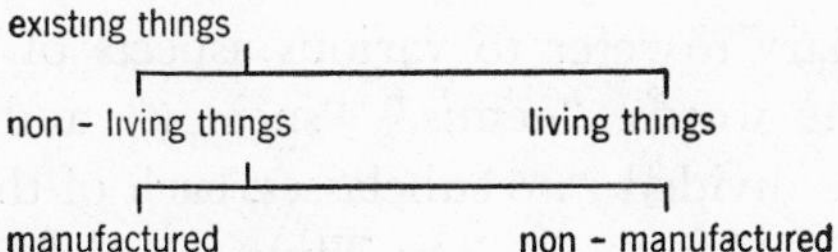

The remaining steps clearly follow the same pattern. In short, the expert player "narrows" down his search by successive division and subdivision of classes. (A poor player, however, asks questions at random, or fails to choose questions whose answers will appreciably reduce the field of search.)

The remaining steps will appear, diagrammatically, as:

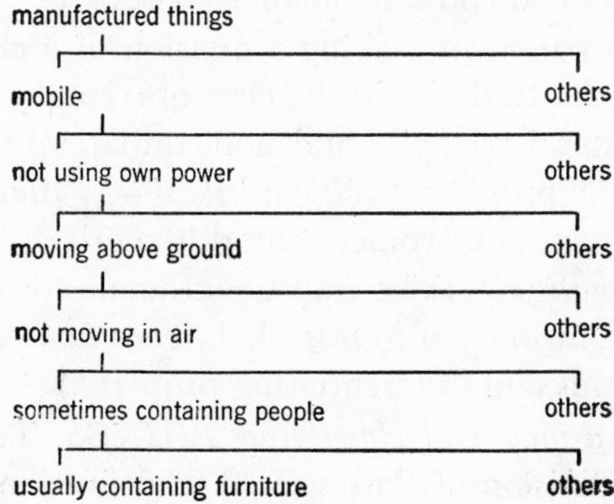

From this diagram we are now able to obtain a *definition* of "trailer," as "something inanimate, manufactured, mobile, not using its own power, on the ground, sometimes containing people, and usually containing furniture." This type of definition, in which the connotation of a term is given by progressive subdivision of a class, is known as **definition by division.**

For practical purposes, a definition of this type will usually contain fewer steps of division, and will begin with some class less inclusive than that of "all possible things." Thus, if one had occasion to explain to an English visitor the meaning of the word "trailer," one might telescope several steps by using the word "vehicle" and, taking a somewhat different route of definition, arrive at "a vehicle, drawn behind an automobile, and used as a place in which to live."

It is customary to refer to various aspects of the process of division by the words, "genus," "species," and "differentia." When a class is divided into subclasses, each of the latter is said to be a **species** of the larger class: Thus, white men are a species of men. Whenever A is a species of B, we say B is a **genus** of A: Thus, men are a genus of white men. It will be noticed that each class used in a process of definition by division (except the first and last) is both a genus *and* a species. Thus, in the example used, the class of manufactured non-living things is a genus of the class of mobile manufactured non-living things and a species of the class of non-living things. (Each class is included in larger classes and contains smaller classes.)

The property used in making a division of a class is known as the **differentia.** In dividing the class of triangles into the two species, equilateral triangles and non-equilateral triangles, the differentia is the property *having all its sides equal;* in dividing humans into men and women, the differentia is the property *being of the male sex*. (The traditional name for definition by division is definition *per genus et differentiam*—definition by means of a genus and differentiating property.)

Division as a means of classifying THINGS. The process of successive subdivision of classes, used in definition by division, is also widely useful as a means of organizing collections of *things*.

In this country, for instance, the F.B.I. organizes its collection of fingerprints according to the following system:

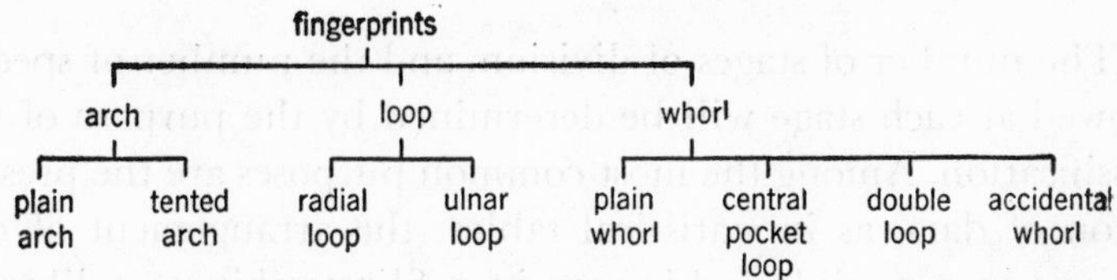

The terms used refer to certain distinguishable patterns in the prints: Thus in the "arch" pattern the lines run straight across the print; in the "loop" pattern they turn around and change their direction; in the "whorl" pattern, some of the lines make a complete circuit (the *full* directions are very complicated, however). It will be noticed that in this instance the first genus (the class of fingerprints) is divided into *more than two* species; it is usually convenient to allow this variation of our original pattern at any stage of the division.

Once the differentiae of the system of divisions are clearly understood, the division can be used in two ways. From it could be derived (stipulated) *definitions* of "plain arch," "tented arch," and the other terms used. But the same scheme can also be used as a way of sorting the fingerprints themselves into separate classes. When we are mainly concerned with sorting a given group of things into classes, we refer to the process of sorting as **classification.** But division and classification result in essentially the same end-product, a system of names for an orderly arrangement of classes and sub-classes.

Characteristics of satisfactory classification. It is sometimes recommended that a classification have the following features:

a. The basis of the classification will be made clear at each stage (*i.e.,* the differentiae used will be clearly described).
b. The division will be exhaustive at each stage (*i.e.,* all the members of the class being divided will occur in some one of the sub-classes). This is often achieved by having an Etcetera class, an "Omnium Gathe-

rum," into which are dumped the objects that fit into no other category.

c. A class will always be divided into non-overlapping sub-classes. (This is to ensure that each object to which the classification applies will go into a unique compartment.)

(The number of stages of division, and the number of species allowed at each stage will be determined by the purpose of the classification. Among the most common purposes are the presentation of data, as in statistical tables; the arrangement of collections in accessible fashion, as in a filing cabinet or library; the grouping of objects into classes that show regular properties, as in scientific classification.)

These are, however, counsels of perfection. In practice, it is usually impossible to make the basis of classification fully explicit, and the principles on which a classification is based gradually change in the course of time.

In chemistry, for instance, a major classification of substances is into the two classes of "inorganic" and "organic." As the names suggest, the differentia originally used in making this division was the place or origin of the substance. For it was then believed that certain complex substances were produced *only* by living organisms. With the discovery that urea and other "organic" substances could be synthesized in the laboratory, the original basis of classification no longer seemed important. Nowadays, a chemist would probably say that the distinction between organic and inorganic substances depended on the fact that the former are complex compounds of carbon. But since certain compounds of carbon are still called "inorganic" the basis of the distinction is not clear, *even though the distinction still has importance*. The two classes of "organic" and "inorganic" substances shade into one another instead of being divided by a clear-cut boundary.

The difficulties of classification are well illustrated by the procedures used for classifying fingerprints, to which reference has already been made. The problem of classification is here much simpler than that encountered in the sciences. The F.B.I.

is not trying to discover scientific laws *about* fingerprints; it is content to have some system by means of which any given fingerprint can be allocated to an appropriate category without excessive labor. But the great variability of fingerprint designs makes the division between these three main classes (and the smaller classes into which they are divided) one of degree rather than kind. It becomes necessary to give very precise and detailed instructions for locating a print in the right class. And even so, it is necessary to provide one class (that of "accidental whorls") in which are placed "those exceedingly unusual patterns that may not be placed by definition into any other classes." Those using the classification are also recommended to place very doubtful patterns in two categories *(e.g.,* to treat a pattern both as a loop and a tented arch.)*

The difficulties of classification illustrated in the analysis of fingerprints are a sufficient explanation of the extreme care given in all the advanced sciences to questions of classification and naming. And they illustrate once again the great importance that the right choice of names can have in assisting effective thinking.

6. *Criticism of specimen definitions.*

We shall end this chapter with some brief comments on a representative selection of the types of definition often met in practice. (As usual, the reader is advised to do his own criticizing before reading the discussion provided.)

a. *Gilbertian: Of the humorously topsy-turvy kind characteristic of Gilbert and Sullivan opera* (*a G. situation*).

This dictionary entry is circular in appearance only. For a person might well be familiar with the name "Gilbert and Sullivan," without knowing the meaning of "Gilbertian." The defin-

* Those interested can find more details in the pamphlet entitled "Classification of fingerprints," issued by the F.B.I.

iens offered combines a statement of the connotation ("of the humorously topsy-turvy kind") with a description of specimens. The definiens is vague, but so is the definiendum. A satisfactory definition.

b. A writer classifies education as "Specialized education; education for culture; and *charismatic education*" and goes on to explain the latter in a footnote as follows: "We must keep the unfamiliar term, as no other word quite so clearly conveys the idea. 'Conversional' is too clumsy, and 'inspirational' has been spoilt for any precise use. 'Education by infusion of grace' perhaps best conveys the idea to those reared in a Christian tradition." (F. Clarke, *Education and Social Change,* page 12. London: Sheldon Press, 1940.)

Here we have a technical term introduced that is not contained in standard English dictionaries and is not common in discussions of education. We might have supposed, then, that the writer would make a special attempt to tell us how he was using the term (which plays a very important part in his later argument). But it is not enough to be told that it is roughly equivalent to "conversional," and we are left guessing about several important details of the connotation. It would be especially important to know whether "charismatic" education is identical with what is commonly called "religious" education. The use of the phrase "education by infusion of grace" *suggests* a religious connotation, but does not explicitly identify "charismatic" and "religious." The definition is ambiguous and must be judged unsatisfactory.

c. *"A politician is a man who sits on the fence with his ear to the ground."* (Popular saying.)

This "definition" is of course a quip or an epigram rather than a sober attempt to explain the meaning of the word "politician." The humor of the remark depends on the malicious suggestion that indecision and lack of initiative are *defining* characteristics of a politician. It may be compared with "An expert is an ordinary man a long way from home" or similar remarks in which a terse comment is presented in the disguise of a definition.

d. "War is *by definition* nothing more than wholesale and organized murder."

The writer has obligingly told us that he is presenting a definition (or part of a definition). If he had left out the words "by definition," it would have been difficult to know whether he was offering a definition of "war" or a statement *about war*. We are clearly being offered a *customary* definition of "war." If the writer were to say "I propose to mean by 'war'. . ." his remarks would have little interest unless he went on to show that his stipulated definition agreed with customary usage. The short way with this definition would be to apply the test of equivalence (rule 3 on page 212), and to argue that the ordinary person would *not* understand by "Germany went into wholesale and organized murder" the same as he would by "Germany went to war." But this type of criticism would overlook the writer's object. He is probably quite aware of the fact that "war" does not *literally mean* "wholesale and organized murder." But war does *resemble* murder on the grand scale. And what he is saying is "*This* aspect of war is the important one—all the rest, the uniforms and the conventions of warfare—are so many unimportant incidentals." And by using the highly emotive word "murder" he is conveying his own abhorrence of war, and influencing us to have similar attitudes. This important example, therefore, illustrates a type of definition in which a part of the connotation of the word (or what is alleged to be part of the connotation) is selected as being especially important, in an attempt to influence the attitudes of the hearer.

e. "Prejudice is a biased attitude of mind."

This definition was given by a student who was asked to give a brief definition of "prejudice," and is quoted in G. C. Field's *Prejudice and Impartiality*.* As Professor Field points

* London: Methuen & Co., 1932. Page 3.

out, the idea of prejudice is "familiar and frequently used by us all." The definition must therefore be regarded as an attempt to clarify the meaning of a term already in use. Now "bias" means almost exactly the same as "prejudice"; so, if we want to *analyze* the meaning of "prejudice," it will hardly help us to be told that it involves bias. The definition must be rejected as circular.

f. "Prejudice is the influence on our thinking of any feeling, impulse, or motive which is not relevant to the immediate purpose of this thinking."

This is Professor Field's own definition of "prejudice," (page 9 in the same book) reached at the end of a detailed and careful discussion. As it stands, the definition is open to the objection of obscurity, since it contains the phrase "relevant to the immediate purpose" (of thinking). But the author has previously explained that "the immediate purpose" of thinking is "to arrive at a true conclusion, to find out something, to attain some piece of knowledge." According to him, any "feeling, impulse, or motive" is not "relevant" to this immediate purpose of thinking if it directs us away from it. The first objection is, therefore, removed.

A second objection might be that the definiens is too wide. If I am suffering from intense toothache, my feelings may make me so impatient of argument as to lead me to make a snap judgment about a question I am forced to consider. My feeling of toothache is then "irrelevant" to the "immediate purpose of thinking." But it would seem rather odd to say that the toothache *prejudices* me. The fact is that Professor Field has somewhat extended the common use of "prejudice" (which is more commonly used to mean approximately the same as "the holding of an opinion concerning a question not determined by the evidence"). But he does this for the purpose of emphasizing the importance of the notion of *relevance to the purpose of thinking* (as he explains in the course of his discussion). This may be regarded as a legitimate procedure.

Summary

When it is necessary to introduce new terms, remove an ambiguity, or extend the meaning of some word (or other sign), deliberate instruction in the use of signs is required. An explanation of the meaning of a sign is called a *definition.* (The word may be used in both "product-" and "process-" senses.) Any statement that is a definition, as here understood, *mentions* the word defined; it is to be contrasted with statements in which the word is used, but not mentioned. The standard forms adopted for definitions are *"X" means Y* and *"X" means the same as "Y."* The word (or other sign defined) is called the *definiendum,* the phrase by which its meaning is located the *definiens.*

Definition is a social transaction involving at least three factors—the explanation, and the persons by whom it is given and received. Satisfactory definitions must be adapted to the needs of the particular person addressed (the principle of *relativity of definition*).

A definition may take the form of a resolution or proposal that a word shall have a certain meaning (*stipulated* definition); or may record the way in which a word is already used in a language or some special context (*reported* definition). A stipulated definition will be neither true nor false; a reported definition must be one or the other. Freedom to stipulate meanings varies with the definiteness of the definiendum's previous usage: The more stable the pre-existing meaning of the sign, the less freedom to stipulate.

The rules of good definition specify that the definition shall be adequate for the purposes intended; shall be intelligible to the person addressed; shall not be circular; shall have a definiens neither wider nor narrower than the definiendum; shall not use metaphorical or figurative language; and shall mention, not use, the definiendum.

One of the most common types of definition is that in which the definiendum's connotation is located by successive division and sub-division of some initial class (*definition by division*). The sub-classes into which a given class is divided are known as its *species,* and it is known as their *genus.* The property that determines the division of the genus is known as the *differentia.*

A similar procedure may be used to sort *things* into a number of distinct classes and is then known as *classification.* In classification, the aim is to have non-overlapping species that together exhaust their genus, and are determined by precise and definite differentiae. But in practice this ideal can seldom be attained.

Comprehension test

(For instructions, see page 10.)

1. "Definition" was given a stipulated definition in this chapter. (*true false*)
2. Classification is a process of definition. (*true false*)
3. A definition of "man" uses rather than mentions the word "man." (*true false*)
4. The word to be defined is called the definiens. (*true false*)
5. *"X" means "Y"* is one of the standard forms of definition. (*true false*)
6. Cats are a genus of animals. (*true false*)
7. Good definitions may use figurative expressions. (*true false*)
8. Freedom to stipulate definitions is least in the case of words with well-established and definite customary meanings. (*true false*)
9. A definition may be false. (*true false*)
10. According to the principle of "relativity of meaning" there is no such thing as a correct definition. (*true false*)

Exercises

A

1. Each of the following accounts describes some occasion in which definition would be useful. Identify in each case the words to be defined; give definitions that you would regard as appropriate; state what type of definition you are using.
   a. On being asked to *prove* that "the sun will rise tomorrow," a student answered "The sun *will* rise tomorrow, because it is *already*

'tomorrow' at some places on the Earth. And at these places the sun has *already* risen."

b. Keller: "Americanism is what we want taught here."
Joe: "Americanism is a fine thing."
Tommy: "Fine! But how would you define Americanism?"
Keller: "Why-er-everybody knows what Americanism is!" (From *The Male Animal,* by James Thurber and Elliott Nugent. Random House, 1940.)

c. The owner of a tavern was appealing against the withdrawal of his license: "Revocation was on the ground that the tavern was closer than 100 feet to the Highwood Methodist Church—a distance which must be maintained under state law."
"Leo Bartolini, attorney for Snavely, cited legal precedent to show that courts have held that a church is the congregation and the room in which it meets to worship, but does not include church buildings, hallways and anterooms.
"If you measure from the One Hundred Club bar to the Methodist Church hymn-books, he argued, the distance is greater than 100 feet and therefore within the law.
"Bernard Juron, city attorney of Highwood, scoffed at this argument, and said he objected to having a church which had been at that location for 40 years 'split into infinitesimal hairs.' " (*The Chicago Sun,* Dec. 15, 1944.)

d. After an air-raid, the British announced that bombs had been dropped at random. German newspapers later carried the story that the British town of Random had been completely destroyed.

e. "One reason for the inability [of the Great Powers] to get together is their failure to reach a common definition of democracy. Without that, both sides argue completely beside the point on such issues as the Balkans, and nothing will ever bring them together so long as they continue arguing from entirely different premises. That is one of the great lessons of this conference. . . . The Russians claim that Bulgaria and Rumania have democratic governments that should be recognized, that have reformed and are now worthy to be treated as full allies and hence to arm as they please.
"The British, Americans, and French say these countries are not democracies, never were allies and are traditionally turbulent, and for safety's sake their armament should be restricted under the present circumstances. (*The New York Times,* Sept. 25, 1945.)

2. What points made in the chapter are illustrated by the examples used in the last question?
3. Which of the following are definitions, in our sense?

a. "Education is the process of driving a set of prejudices down your throat."
b. "When all the cows in a field are sitting down, the one standing up is an Irish bull."
c. "El-Be-Oral: Mouth wash which contained guaiacol, anise oil, alcohol, and water." (*Journal of the American Dental Association.*)
d. An alien is a foreigner.
e. Brevity is the soul of wit.
f. A man is his own best friend.
g. Logic is the Baedeker of reasoning.
h. A crab is a kind of ten-footed crustacean found near most sea-coasts.
i. Research is the process of finding out what we're going to do after we can't keep on doing what we're doing now. (C. F. Kettering.)
j. Poverty is absence of wealth.
k. "A *mistake* is something wrong. Tom said two and two make five. Tom made a *mistake.*" (From a children's dictionary.)
l. "I would define propaganda as the dissemination of interested information and opinion." (J. R. G. Wreford.)
m. Kleptomaniac. A rich thief. (Ambrose Bierce.)
n. Noise. A stench in the ear. (Bierce.)

4. Criticize the definitions used in the last question.
5. Construct your own definitions of *pencil, house, city, nation, society.*
6. Criticize a selection of the definitions contained in the glossary at the end of this book.
7. Display the classification of types of definition used in this chapter in the form of a table similar to that occurring on page 217. State the differentiae used in this classification.
8. Discover the main classifications used (a) in botany, (b) in the study of mental disease, (c) in determining the various kinds of mail. How far are the "principles of good classification" discussed in the chapter followed in these cases?
9. Give "definitions by division," where possible, of *automobile, coat, small business, bureaucrat, above, stipulated definition, syllogism.*
10. "It was Boehm who divided curare into three groups according to the container used by the natives—tube curare in bamboo tubes, calabash curare in gourds, and pot curare in earthenware pots. Today these distinctions are no longer reliable and most of the large amount of crude curare that has arrived in my laboratory has come in old tins, sometimes with widely known trademarks still visible upon them." (A. R. McIntyre in *Endeavour*, Vol. 8, p. 35, 1949.)

Find other examples of classifications that have ceased to be reliable and discuss the reasons for the changes.

B

1. Criticize and correct the following definitions supplied by students:
   a. "The referent, in logic, is the object referred to by a word."
   b. "The connotation of a word is concerned with the qualities of the referent, *e.g.*, a cow is a four-legged mammal that moos."
   c. "Denotation is when things are pointed out."
   d. "The suggestive aspect of language merely suggests one's opinion. In some cases it can arouse emotion, but this is not its main purpose. The suggestive aspect is used politely and often isn't true."
   e. "President: Washington, Roosevelt, and so on."
   f. "Democracy: Government of the people, by the people, and for the people."
2. Explain your reasons for agreeing or disagreeing with the following arguments.
   a. "You say a good definition must be intelligible to its receiver? In that case the definitions used in higher algebra are terrible—because *I* can't understand them."
   b. "No words can be defined without the use of other words. Hence either all definitions are ultimately circular or some words *cannot* be defined. Hence some words must be understood without being defined."
   c. "In accusing the Nazis of a crime against *international law,* we were stretching the meaning of those two words. For waging aggressive war was not a crime at the time the war broke out. It is unjust to twist language to our own purposes."
   d. "Definition is ordinarily supposed to produce clarity in thinking. It is not generally recognized that the more we define our terms the less descriptive they become and the more difficulty we have in using them. The reason for this paradox is that we never attempt to define words which obtain a proper emotional response from our listeners. Logical definition enters when we are using words which we are sure 'ought' to mean something, but none of us can put our fingers on just what that meaning is." (Thurman W. Arnold, *The Folklore of Capitalism,* p. 180. New Haven: Yale University Press, 1937.)
3. Discuss, with illustrations, some of the problems that arise in explaining (a) the emotive, (b) the metaphorical use of words.
4. It is sometimes difficult to define a word (or other sign) except as part

of a *larger* phrase. Thus, in order to define *minus* we say " 'A minus B' means the number that when added to B yields A." Here the word "minus" is defined in the *context,* "A minus B." Such definitions are sometimes called **definitions in use.** Find examples of "definitions in use" from the glossary at the end of this book. What kinds of words seem to need such definitions? Name some advantages and disadvantages of this type of definition.

5. What connection is there between the meanings of 'genus,' 'species,' and 'differentia,' and those of 'general,' 'special,' and 'differentiated'?
6. Locate *all* the mistakes committed in the following (an actual instance):

   The question: "Criticize the definition, 'Fox hunting is the pursuit of the uneatable by the unspeakable.' "

   The answer: "This definition is not good because it is false. The cannabals (*sic*) of African tribes eat men so men cannot be classified as uneatable. Also, words are symbols and maybe the barking of the fox are symbols, so could be classified as words. Therefore, the fox speaks, so cannot be classified as unspeakable."

12

ASSORTED FALLACIES

It would be a very good thing if every trick could receive some short and obviously appropriate name, so that when a man used this or that particular trick, he could at once be reproved for it.
—Schopenhauer.

1. The nature of fallacies.

THE use of studying fallacies. Since logic is the study of right reasoning, *mistaken* arguments might be expected to concern a student of the subject only as shocking examples of what to avoid. In fact, however, it proves difficult for even the ablest and best-intentioned thinkers to conform to the standards of right reasoning, and not all men have good intentions. The arguments of the market place or the classroom are more often than not unsound, and correct reasoning is as rare as perfect health. A lively awareness of the most common types of mistakes in reasoning and the means by which they may be remedied is, accordingly, useful both for self-correction and defense against the sophistries of others. In this chapter we follow the practice of logicians, from Aristotle onward, of identifying and classifying the main types of logical errors by which people are in practice misled.

The definition of a fallacy. The term "fallacy" is often used to refer to *any* kind of mistaken belief, however arrived at. In this sense it may be said, for instance, that the belief that women are illogical is a "fallacy." For our present purpose, this sense is too wide, and we shall consider only errors in *reasoning*. We need not spend time on *obvious* errors which, being easily detected, give little trouble. The kind of error in reasoning that deserves our closest attention is that which is *persuasive* to the speaker or hearer in spite of its unsoundness. We therefore adopt the following definition: A *fallacy* is an argument that *seems* to be sound without being so in fact. An argument is "sound" for the purpose of this definition if the conclusion is reached by a reliable method and the premises are known to be true. This definition agrees well with *one* common meaning of "fallacy."

Our definition admits an argument as a fallacy only if the conclusion is unsound yet *appears* sound. The reference to the impression that the unsound argument makes on the persons to whom it is addressed takes us out of the field of logic proper into that of the *psychology* of reasoning (*i.e.,* a study of how people actually behave). A good grasp of fallacies must be based, accordingly, on an understanding of the rules to which sound arguments conform, and factual information concerning the ways in which people react to the breach of these rules. Since people differ widely in their logical training and powers of criticism, the fallacies that flourish in a community will vary as much as the local speech or customs. It would be wise to supplement the simplified account of this chapter by personal observations on the fallacies particularly characteristic of the groups with which the reader is familiar.

Finally, "truth is one, but errors are many" (as we may be sure some sage has long ago remarked): There are infinitely many ways of deviating from the sound and justified conclusions of any given argument. The few types of fallacy we select for further inspection are a trifling sample from the great catalog of human error.

The classification of fallacies. A fallacy is an unsound but *persuasive* argument. It is disturbing but true that *the respect in which an argument is unsound may be the very feature commending it to the hearer.* Consider the unsound argument: "A mathematician is a man. Therefore a good mathematician is a good man." (The reader might pause here to decide *why* the conclusion is invalid.) The argument has a certain plausibility, or attraction, because it apes a *valid* argument; thus the unsound *form* of the argument is the source of its persuasive power.

We can roughly divide fallacies into two groups:

A: Those whose persuasiveness is connected with some intrinsic defect of the argument (**general fallacies**).

B: Those whose appeal arises from some features of the context in which the argument is used (**fallacies of circumstance**).

In the first group we place fallacies depending for their effect on lack of sufficient attention to the form of the argument, the falsity of unstated premises, and so on. Such fallacies are likely to mislead those to whom they are addressed, no matter by whom or in what circumstances presented. In the second group we place the fallacies that appeal especially to the prejudices and other vulnerable characteristics of the hearer, or make some special use of the situation in which they are uttered. (Thus a speaker may say to a group of strikers "The fact that you men are on strike proves that this strike is justified." It proves, of course, nothing of the sort. If the argument is highly persuasive nevertheless, the reason is that it appeals to the convictions of the particular group addressed.)

Both kinds of fallacies, according to our definition, consist of *unsound* arguments: Choice of the group to which a particular fallacy shall be assigned will, therefore, depend on our judgment as to the feature that makes the fallacy dangerous. If the circumstances of utterance seem relatively more important than the breach of the principles of right reasoning committed, we label it a "fallacy of circumstance"; if inattention to form or truth such as anybody might be subject to at any time is, in our judgment, the malignant symptom, we label it a "general fallacy."

We now further subdivide *general* fallacies into:

1. Those arising from mistakes about logical form.
2. Those due to ambiguity or other features of the language used.
3. Those dependent on mistakes concerning the truth of the premises or the possibility of knowing such truth.

These three types of **formal, linguistic,** and **material** fallacies are discussed separately in the next three sections. Afterwards we examine fallacies of circumstance (section 5).

2. *Formal fallacies.*

According to our discussion in the last section, a **formal** fallacy will be an unsound argument whose form nevertheless *seems* correct (to those, at any rate, who have not studied sufficient logic to know better). Four common examples of such fallacies, those "denying the antecedent," "asserting the consequent," "undistributed middle," and "illicit process" have been described in previous chapters.

Composition. This is the fallacy in which what is true of a part is therefore asserted to be true of the whole. Thus a speaker who argues "Everybody in this city pays his debts. Therefore you can be sure the city will pay its debts" commits this fallacy. For though it might be true that every citizen paid his personal debts, it would by no means be certain that the city *as a whole* would pay its debts. In order to see that the argument is invalid, it is sufficient to inspect the following argument having a similar form: "Every side of a square is a straight line. Therefore a square is a straight line."

The reverse fallacy, in which what is true of a whole is asserted, on that ground above, to be true of a part, is known as the **fallacy of division.** As an instance we offer: "America is powerful; hence Henry Ford, who is an American, must be powerful." Other examples should be constructed. (In constructing fallacies it will be noticed that arguments with true premises and a true conclusion have relatively more persuasive effect. For people are seldom hoodwinked by fallacies whose conclusions are conspicuously false.)

Accident. "Alcohol causes drunkenness. Therefore if you drink this bottle of whiskey, you will be drunk." The premises of this argument are true and the conclusion may be so if the bottle is sufficiently large and the resistance of the drinker sufficiently low. Yet the argument is *unsound,* for the assertion "Alcohol causes drunkenness," like most generalizations, is true only *if certain unstated conditions are fulfilled.* Not *any* dose of alcohol will cause *any* person to get drunk; the generalization is true only for a certain (specifiable) amount of alcohol (varying from person to person). The fallacy of accident is committed *whenever a general rule is applied to a special case to which the rule is not intended to apply.*

This fallacy should be carefully distinguished from that of "division" discussed above. Consider this instance: "Encyclopedias are heavy. Therefore this new encyclopedia will be heavy." The "new encyclopedia" is not a part of "encyclopedias" but is rather a *case* of *an* encyclopedia (it is a *member* of the *class* of encyclopedias). The fallacy here committed is that *of accident.*

Irrelevant conclusion. This phrase (or its Latin equivalent, "ignoratio elenchi") is the name commonly given to the fallacy in which the speaker establishes some other proposition than the one he claims to be proving. Thus, a man may set out to prove that the invention of the atomic bomb was on the whole a good thing and end by proving (at least to his own satisfaction) that it was inevitable for the bomb to have been invented. Yet a thing can be inevitable without being good. He has established neither the conclusion nor a proposition from which the conclusion follows. This type of fallacy depends on mistaken identity; some irrelevant conclusion is substituted and mistaken for the proposition debated.

This fallacy depends for its success on failure to notice the substitution of the irrelevant conclusion. In the course of extended argument concerning complex issues, such substitutions often happen.

Argumentative leap (more commonly known as *non sequitur,* literally "it does not follow"). This fallacy occurs whenever a reasoner leaps from premises to a consistent conclusion which, however, does not follow from them. An enthusiastic public speaker announces "The country is tired of the present administration—we shall have a change after the next election." The correct retort is "Non sequitur—it doesn't follow" (the alleged weariness of the public is not of *itself* sufficient to guarantee a change of administration at the elections).

An argumentative leap can be corrected by adding further premises to those in the original argument. Where the fallacy is most effective and dangerous, the required premises are untrue and can be seen to be untrue after being explicitly formulated. The fallacy depends for its plausibility on failure to be aware of the leap committed—jumping without looking, as it were.

3. *Linguistic fallacies.*

The three preceding chapters have provided many illustrations of fallacious arguments turning on misuse or misunderstanding of language. (Chapter 10 contained detailed criticism of a variety of such fallacies.)

Many linguistic fallacies, as we have seen, arise from the *deliberate* use of a word or phrase in more than one sense in the same argument. When this occurs a *fallacy of equivocation* is said to have been committed. If the shift of meaning is unintentional, we may say a *fallacy of ambiguity* occurs. The "fallacy of four terms" (discussed in connection with the theory of the syllogism, on page 139) is an instance of the fallacy of equivocation or the fallacy of ambiguity, according to the intent of the reasoner.

Closely related to these fallacies is the type of dispute known as **verbal issue,** in which two men unwittingly use the same word in different senses. (An example of verbal issue was discussed on page 204.) The occurrence of verbal issues calls for the provision of individual or contextual definitions, as previously explained. Thus, it is futile to argue about "God" unless we have reasonable assurance that our fellow-arguer attaches the same meaning to the term "God." Otherwise, we may end in the position of the theological student who burst out with the words "Now I see! Your God is my devil, and my devil your God!"

This brief reminder of the confusions resulting from insufficient attention to the influence of language on thought should include some reference to the use of "colored" or "emotive" language (see pages 169 and 175). Many fallacious arguments, as we have seen, depend for their effect on the illegitimate use of emotive terms.

4. Material fallacies.

According to our understanding, a fallacy is here called *material* when it depends for its appeal on a mistake concerning the truth of the premises or the possibility of such truth being known.

Tabloid formulas. The truth about any matter of importance is seldom simple. Yet most people would *like* the truth to be simple and will readily accept any short formula that seems to express the truth. The result is that much thinking is controlled by slogans or catchwords, accepted without examination. Sometimes, as in the case of certain epigrams and proverbs, the formula combines brevity with wit and truth. Too often, however, the "tabloid formula" slips as easily into the mind as the latest quack medicine down the gullet—and produces as little benefit.

A writer on the use of public speaking as propaganda significantly recommends that "A good slogan, besides being short and stylistically impressive, must seem so true, so apt, so absolutely unanswerable that *it discourages thought and argument.*" (Harold P. Graves.)

From among the many tabloid formulas popular today, we select two habitual offenders. We hear all too often that "the exception proves the rule." Probably not one person in a thousand who dishes up this ancient morsel of wisdom realizes that "prove" is here used in its older sense of "probe" or "test." What was originally intended was that the exception *tests* the rule—shows whether the rule is correct or not. The contemporary interpretation, that a rule is confirmed by having an exception, is absurd. This tabloid formula has the advantage of allowing a person to glory in the fact that his general principle does *not* square with the facts.

"It's all right in theory, but it won't do in practice," is another popular way of revelling in logical absurdity. The philosopher Schopenhauer said all we need to know about this sophism: "The assertion is based upon an impossibility: what is right in theory *must* work in practice; and if it does not, there is a mistake in the theory; something has been overlooked and not allowed for; and consequently, what is wrong in practice is wrong in theory too." (*The Art of Controversy*, #33.)

Begging the question. (Also known as "arguing in a circle.") This fallacy occurs when either the same proposition is used both as premise and conclusion or when one of the premises could not be known to be true unless the conclusion were first known to be true. In either case, the fallacious argument assumes as true what it needs to prove.

Suppose a man has to establish his credit at a bank, and the following dialogue ensues: "My friend Jones will vouch for me." "How do we know *he* can be trusted?" "Oh, I assure you he can."

This argument might be analyzed as follows: We have to establish X (*the speaker*) *can be trusted* (A). The evidence offered is *Jones will guarantee that* X *can be trusted* (B). But the only evidence for B is that X says B is true. Hence to establish B we must assume that X can be trusted, *i.e.*, that A is true. Thus, to prove that A is true, we are required to *assume* A is true.

This fallacy is often rendered plausible by more or less subtle changes in the language used—as when it is argued that "opium produces sleep because it is a narcotic" or that "new explosives should be controlled by the Army because the questions raised by their discovery are purely military ones."

Argument "in a circle" is likely to be most effective when many steps are involved. As one logician has said "the *narrower* the circle, the less likely it is to escape the detection, either of the reasoner himself (for men often deceive *themselves* in this way) or of his hearers. When there is a long circuit of many intervening propositions before you come back to the original conclusion, it will often not be perceived that the arguments really do proceed in a 'circle'; just as when any one is advancing in a *straight line* (as we are accustomed to call it) along a plain on the earth's surface. . . ." (R. Whately, *Logic,* 8th ed., p. 201.)

It should be noticed that circular arguments are not necessarily invalid; the ground for condemning such arguments is their *fruitlessness* as proofs.

Argument ad hominem. (Literally, "argument directed toward the man.") When arguing with an opponent, we may direct our energy toward establishing independently our view of the matter under discussion, or we may try to use the propositions already accepted by our adversary as a way of disproving his position. In the latter case, we are said to be arguing "ad hominem."

Thus, A may be arguing that the taking of life is evil, to which B replies "But you don't object to killing animals for food." On making B's argument more explicit, we find he is saying "You don't object to killing animals for food. Therefore you can't hold that the taking of life is never justified. Therefore you ought not to argue that the taking of life is evil." This is a typical argument *ad hominem;* supposing B's argument to be sound, he has shown only that his opponent's position is *inconsistent* with that opponent's premises. Yet this is formally irrelevant to the question whether the conclusion is *actually* true. (A might very well be wrong in not objecting to killing animals for food.)

Nevertheless, argument *ad hominem* may be justifiably used, provided its limitations are recognized. When the homo in question is oneself, it is a valuable device for revealing confusion of thought; when used against another it may properly serve to "shift the burden of proof," as we say.

5. Fallacies of circumstance.

These are the fallacies whose powers of deception arise from the special circumstances in which they are uttered or the special vulnerability of the persons to whom they are addressed. Among such fallacies must be counted appeals to pity, prejudice, vanity, ridicule, force—indeed to whatever can sway the judgment of an audience independently of its relevance to the matter in hand. There is little that can be usefully said about such modes of reasoning except to deplore them. There seems no point in giving them special names, as former logicians did when they spoke of arguments *ad misericordiam, ad ignorantiam, ad baculum,* and so on indefinitely. It is usually easy to detect such fallacious appeals to the irrelevant, and to understand the nature of the diversion involved. It is another matter, however, to be able to resist such appeals, or to have the logical conscience to refrain from imposing them upon others.

Considered as arguments, independently of the circumstances that lend them a specious appearance of correctness, the fallacies here discussed are all cases of *irrelevant conclusion* (or *irrelevant evidence*). A good antidote is any counter-argument that shows the irrelevance of the original argument and identifies the nature of the appeal made. Thus, in discussing the question whether colored workers should be entitled to receive the same pay as white workers *for equal performance,* public speakers have been known to dwell on the alleged lack of thriftiness of Negroes. A man who wished to expose the fallacy committed might insist that the question whether Negroes are thriftless, or have any other vices or virtues, *has nothing to do with the case,* since the question under discussion is whether they should receive equal pay for *equal* work. He might be tempted to add that such appeals to *prejudice* against a minority group "ought to be deplored by all right-thinking people." (Is our hypothetical speaker himself then guilty of irrelevance or appeal to prejudice? Is his attempt to enlist the support of the audience to be deplored? Is it ever justifiable to attack one dishonest argument by another?)

6. *An illustrative dialogue.*

We conclude this chapter with some light relief in the form of an imaginary dialogue illustrating various fallacies. It is to be hoped that discussion of important questions never sinks to the depths here displayed. The reader is invited to compare the dialogue with specimens of actual debate or the discussions of his friends.

The numbers sprinkled in the text refer to play-by-play comments on the course taken by the argument (they are assembled on page 240). It would be a good exercise to make one's own detailed analysis of the discussion before consulting the annotations.

Vegetarianism, or How Not to Argue

Scene: A restaurant. Two friends, Tom and Harry, are revealed eating. Tom is attacking an oversized porterhouse steak; Harry is toying with an even larger salad.

Harry: "How can you eat that revolting [1] food, Tom?"

Tom: "Revolting? This wonderful piece of juicy steak?" [2]

Harry: "I call it a piece of the scorched backside of a cow's carcase." [3]

Tom: "Now you're being disgusting! Whatever *you* call it, it's still the best steak I've tasted in a long while." [4]

Harry: "You're just a necrophagist.[5] In any really civilized country [6] you'd be locked up for murder."

Tom: "Necrophagist! I don't believe there's any such word.[7] What does it mean?"

Harry: "Eater of corpses."

Tom: "Now look, Harry, that's going too far. I know you're a fanatical vegetarian,[8] but that's no reason for abusing those who disagree with you. What the heck do you mean by calling me a murderer?"

Harry: "Isn't a man who causes a murder to be committed a murderer?" [9]

Tom: "I suppose so."

Harry: "Would manufacturers produce goods unless they were sure of customers?"

Tom: "No." [10]

Harry: "Aren't you a consumer of corpses—sorry, *steaks.*"

Tom: "You can see I am. Come on—get to the point."

Harry: "Animals wouldn't be killed unless people ate them. Therefore, you cause animals to be murdered. Therefore, you're a murderer." [11]

Tom: "Animals would have to be killed even if they weren't eaten. Otherwise there just wouldn't be any room for people to live." [12]

Harry: "Oh, yes, there would! Animals in a state of nature keep their numbers down. Darwin proved that!" [13]

Tom: "Well, if I'm a murderer, so are you! [14] What do you suppose your shoes are made of?"

Harry: "I wouldn't wear them if I could get equally warm shoes that weren't made of leather."

Tom: "You object to the taking of all life, don't you?" [15]

Harry: "Yes."

Tom: "Well, how do you justify eating vegetables. They're alive, aren't they? You disgusting vegetablophagist!" [16]

Harry: "You can't say 'vegetablophagist'—that's mixing Latin and Greek." [17]

Tom: "Of course I can say it—vegetablophagist.[18] Get back to the point—get back to the point." [19]

Harry: "Well, I suppose vegetables *are* alive. But you've got to admit that they're a low form of life." [20]

Tom: "I admit nothing of the sort. Julian Huxley says [21] that 'life is one and indivisible.' How can you draw a line between lower and higher forms of life?" [22]

Harry: "In that case you ought to approve of eating human beings." [23]

Tom: "Now you're being fantastic. When you start accusing me of cannibalism, I *know* you've lost the argument. Anyway, my steak's growing cold." [24]

(A silence falls,[25] broken only by the sounds incidental to the munching of meat and the crunching of lettuce.)

Notes

1. The argument begins, as so many do, by "name calling."
2. Tom prefers his own emotive language.
3. And Harry has his own way of reiterating real or pretended disgust. Such verbal fencing could continue indefinitely.
4. Diverting the talk to another issue.
5. (Harry refuses the bait.) This sounds very sinister.

6. A hidden assumption here.

7. Introduces another diversion.

8. More name calling.

9. Here Harry adopts the effective technique of drawing admissions by skillfully worded questions. ("If you want to draw a conclusion, you must not let it be foreseen, but you must get the premises admitted one by one, unobserved, mingling them here and there in your talk." Schopenhauer, *Art of Controversy*.)

10. An unnecessary admission.

11. A shift from "killing" to "murder" occurs in this argument.

12. Notice the assumptions here. (Compare Dr. Johnson's retort to one who said "A man must live"—"Sir, I don't see the necessity.") Tom is arguing that unavoidable killing is not murder.

13. Appeal to authority to prove the obvious. (Darwin proved nothing of the sort—the speaker must be thinking vaguely of the "struggle for existence.")

14. Argument *ad hominem* (in the special form sometimes known as the *tu quoque,* literally "you too").

15. Instead of meeting Harry's argument, Tom begins a counterattack. Notice how Tom *extends* the position that Harry has to defend (Harry did not need to maintain that *all* life was sacred).

16. Using Harry's name calling technique against himself.

17. Irrelevant diversion.

18. Equivocation.

19. Rejecting the opponent's attempt at diversion.

20. Tries to escape the force of the attack by making a distinction.

21. False appeal to authority (Huxley did not make the statement attributed to him).

22. Appealing to the popular "tabloid" notion that things that are continuous (between which "a line can't be drawn") must be identical.

23. *Ad hominem.*

24. Breaks off the argument in a final explosion of irrelevance.

25. None too soon.

Summary

The term fallacy is here restricted to mean a defective argument that *seems* to have true premises and a sound conclusion. The degree of plausibility of unsound arguments varies with the intelligence and logical training of the receiver; criticism of fallacies therefore requires understanding of human behavior as well as a grasp of logical principles. Fallacies are here divided into those whose appeal derives from some internal defect of the argument (*general fallacies*) and those directed to some special feature of the context in which they are uttered (*fallacies of circumstance*). General fallacies are subdivided into *formal, linguistic,* and *material* fallacies. Formal fallacies have a form that fails to guarantee the soundness of the conclusion; linguistic fallacies use ambiguity or the rhetorical resources of language; material fallacies depend on mistakes about the truth of explicit or implicit premises. The following fallacies received more detailed treatment: *composition* and *division* (ascribing properties of the part to the whole and vice versa), *accident* (application of a general rule to cases outside its scope), *irrelevant conclusion* (substitution of a proposition other than that to be proved), *argumentative leap* (omission of needed connections between premises and conclusion), *equivocation* (deliberate ambiguity of critical words), *tabloid formula* (use of slogans or other concisely expressed errors), *begging the question* (assuming what is to be proved), *argument ad hominem* (directing the argument against the opponent's admissions). The various fallacies that slide away from the question discussed by appeals to prejudice, prestige, authority, etc. are all formally guilty of irrelevance.

Comprehension test

(For instructions, see page 10.)

1. An error in reasoning is necessarily a fallacy. (*true* *false*)
2. An argument can be both a formal and a material fallacy simultaneously. (*true* *false*)
3. No argument whose conclusion is valid can be a case of fallacious appeal to prejudice. (*true* *false*)
4. *Ignoratio elenchi* is another name for the fallacy of irrelevant conclusion. (*true* *false*)
5. "My body is warm, therefore my hand is warm" is a case of the fallacy of accident. (*true* *false*)
6. No fallacy can have a valid conclusion. (*true* *false*)

7. A material fallacy is a special kind of fallacy of circumstance (*true* *false*)
8. Fallacies of circumstance are linked to some feature of the context in which they occur. (*true* *false*)
9. An argument *ad hominem* may be directed by a thinker against himself. (*true* *false*)
10. Verbal issue is a case of argument in a circle. (*true* *false*)

Exercises

A

1. Find out the meaning of the following words and phrases: paradox, quibble, sophist, playing upon words, special pleading, glittering generality, platitude, paralogism, logomachy, casuistry, amphiboly, burden of proof, cliché.
2. Make a collection of widely current fallacious beliefs about political or economic affairs.
3. Write a dialogue illustrating various types of fallacy.
4. Among the effective slogans used in recent political campaigns were the following: "Back to normalcy," "*the forgotten man* at the bottom of the economic pyramid," "*a new deal* for the American people." How far are these successful in "discouraging thought and argument"? Analyze the means employed to this end. Subject other examples of political slogans to similar scrutiny.
5. George Eliot referred to platitudes as "those undeniable general propositions which are usually intended to convey a particular meaning very far from undeniable." Illustrate the truth of this remark by analyzing some platitudes having a wide circulation.
6. Criticize the following arguments. If a fallacy is committed, explain the nature of the mistake committed:
   a. I never read the "latest" novels: They will all seem old-fashioned in a few years' time.
   b. A pacifist ought to disapprove of policemen. For policemen use force, and even kill if necessary.
   c. The defendant is accused of falsifying his income tax return. But is it worth making so much fuss about a few dollars?
   d. Miracles are so unlikely to happen that the chances are that a man who says he has witnessed a miracle is a liar.
   e. Miracles happen every day: A man on the tenth floor of a building is suspended in mid-air. There is no reason therefore to question the biblical stories of miracles.

f. Tigers are dangerous because they are inherently liable to attack other creatures.

g. Each cell of a man's body is renewed within ten years. Hence, no man is the same after ten years. No man should be held responsible for acts committed more than a decade ago.

h. A believer in the future life can never be disappointed, for if his belief is wrong, he will never live to find out his mistake. It is better to believe in immortality than to be sceptical.

i. It is not surprising that I was dealt a set of 13 spades last night. For every distribution of the cards was equally likely—why not this particular one?

j. Nothing is colder to the touch than ice. Nothing is up my sleeve. Therefore what is up my sleeve is colder to the touch than ice.

k. A man who has no choice but to perform a certain action cannot be held responsible for it. A perfectly good man cannot help but behave well. Therefore a perfectly good man cannot be responsible for his actions.

l. Unlikely things happen every day. What happens every day is certain to happen. What is certain to happen is not unlikely. Therefore unlikely things are not unlikely.

m. A hungry man eats the most. A man who has nothing to eat is hungry. Therefore, a man who has nothing to eat eats the most.

n. Professor Blank was born in China and has taught in a Chinese university. I am sure we shall find his views on the history of that country most interesting.

o. This country has many friends. For if you suppose that each inhabitant has only a single friend you still get a total of over a hundred million.

p. I need no evidence to convince me that your dog has been annoying my cat. For it is well known that dogs worry cats.

q. She's beautiful! She's engaged! She uses X powder!

r. A million people can't all be wrong—this book has had a million readers.

s. There's no sense in blaming me for getting the lowest mark in the examination—somebody *had* to get the lowest mark.

t. To call you an animal is to speak truth; to call you an ass is to call you an animal; therefore to call you an ass is to speak truth.

u. "You can't do what I am doing [said the speaker while touching his own head]. For if you imitate me, you are touching *your* head, not mine; and if you touch my head you are touching another person's head—not your own."

7. Annotate the following extract from the *Congressional Record* to reveal the fallacies involved.

The Bat's Eye Episode

(Members of the Senate were discussing an item of $13,000,000,000 appropriated for the War Department and returned unused.)

"Mr. BARKLEY. It is always impossible to sit down at a table and calculate to the fineness of a bat's eye just how much is going to be needed everywhere....

Mr. WHEELER. Mr. President, I do not wish to be understood as criticizing the War Department for turning back the money; but when the Senator talks about $13,000,000,000 being what can be put into a bat's eye....

Mr. BARKLEY. The Senator knows that I was not talking about putting $13,000,000,000 in a bat's eye. I was talking about Army officers sitting down at a table and working out to the fineness of a bat's eye everything they needed in the way of supplies and equipment.

Mr. WHEELER. The Senator was talking about a bat's eye, and I say he was talking about putting $13,000,000,000 in a bat's eye.

Mr. BARKLEY. I think the Senator is playing on words.

Mr. WHEELER. The Senator from Kentucky was playing on words.

Mr. BARKLEY. I do not understand that even the Senator from Montana thinks that $13,000,000,000 can be put into a bat's eye.

Mr. WHEELER. The Senator was playing on words when he was talking about the $13,000,000,000 which I mentioned. He said that Army officers could not sit down and work it out to the fineness of a bat's eye. I said that $13,000,000,000 could not be put in a bat's eye.

Mr. BARKLEY. Mr. President, for once the Senator and I agree. Thirteen billion dollars cannot be put in a bat's eye. That is settled. (Laughter.)

Mr. WHEELER. I am glad to have the Senator agree with me once in a while." (*Congressional Record,* Vol. 89, p. 9919, Nov. 22, 1943.)

B

1. Invent some other way of classifying fallacies, and contrast its merits with those of the scheme adopted in the text.
2. Show that the words "part" and "whole" are ambiguous by explaining some of the different senses in which they are used. What is the bearing of your result on the discussion of the fallacy of composition (p. 232)?
3. Signatures on wills or other important documents require witnesses.

Should not those signatures themselves be witnessed? Explain the theory underlying this legal requirement.

4. "Nothing has been accomplished in the world without interest, and, if interest be called passion, we may affirm that nothing has been brought about in the world without passion on the part of the actors." (Hegel.) Assuming this to be true, how far can appeals to passion be justified?
5. "Should an international security council have the power to compel America to go to war? It all depends on what you mean by 'international,' 'security,' 'power,' and 'war.' Since each of these words has at least two different meanings, there are at least sixteen questions raised. But anyhow it's a verbal issue." (From a student's answer to an examination question.) Point out some mistakes in this argument. How would *you* answer the question?
6. Show that an argument about words is not necessarily a verbal issue.

PART THREE

Induction and Scientific Method

13

THE GROUNDS OF BELIEF

It is open to any lunatic to know by intuition that he is the Angel Gabriel, just as it was formerly open to common sense to know that the Sun went round the earth or to feel that the Antipodes were a plain absurdity.—Alfred Sidgwick.

1. Need for the investigation.

THE theory of deductive argument which was studied in the first part of this book is concerned with the validity of conclusions and so with the *relative* truth of propositions. To know that some proposition is valid is to know that it must be true *if* the premises are true; a valid conclusion, as we have often emphasized, may well be *false.*

If we were to confine ourselves to the study of validity, we should be shirking the task of the "criticism of thought." For in real life we want our conclusions to be true as well as valid—irreproachable reasoning can be no substitute for well-grounded premises. We are led, therefore, to consider the ways in which the *truth* (as distinct from the validity) of conclusions may be established.

When a proposition is true, our belief in it is justified, provided we have arrived at that belief by a reliable method; but we may sometimes be justified in believing a proposition that may eventually prove to be false. We are justified in believing the historical data in an encyclopedia article. But even the best encyclopedias are *sometimes* mistaken, and some of our *justified* beliefs may therefore prove to be wrong. The relation between justified belief and truth is not simple, and needs analysis.

We shall formulate the central problem of this chapter as *When are our beliefs justified?* This shift from the determination of the truth of propositions to the justification of *beliefs* will help to bring our discussions down to earth, for the "truth" of which we have to take account in practice is usually that which is *believed to be true.*

What is a belief? We shall do well, at the outset, to agree, if possible, on how to use the term "belief." Like other familiar and important terms, "belief" is often used loosely. We say "I believe it is going to rain" when we would hardly be prepared to bet a nickel on the truth of the prophecy. In the same spirit of laxity, men of the most lukewarm convictions are said to be "believers" in some religious faith. It must be recognized, then, that *there are degrees of belief,* ranging from indifference to unshakable conviction.

A man's beliefs about a given topic may often be discovered by his affirmations. But in order to determine whether a man has a particular belief, it is unwise to rely solely on his own statements. He may try to conceal his opinions, and a man speaking in good faith may easily be mistaken about the beliefs he holds or the degree of conviction with which they are held.

The most reliable test is that of *conduct:* Faith is revealed by works. A man who takes an umbrella and a raincoat when going out for a walk may be presumed to *believe* that it will rain; conversely, we may question the genuineness of the charitable "beliefs" of a man who never spends a dollar to relieve the poor. The practical problems that sometimes arise in the determination of a person's beliefs will not concern us at present.

Reasons and causes of beliefs. Some beliefs undoubtedly have *reasons,* and all beliefs almost certainly have *causes.* Yet a reason for a belief is not the same as a cause of that belief. When a person is anxiously awaiting the arrival of a letter (or the occurrence of some other event), it is not uncommon for a strong conviction to arise that the hoped-for event will occur on a particular day. (The reader may be familiar with similar situations from his own experience.) If one asks of a person who has a "hunch" of this kind "How do you *know* the letter will come today—what reason do you have for expecting it?" the answer may well be "I can't tell you, I have no reasons, I am just positive that I shall not be disappointed today." Such a belief, though *unreasoned,* is the product of causes. Everybody knows that extreme anxiety for some event to happen tends to produce belief that the event *will* happen. The anxiety is a cause, but not a reason. We say that it is not a reason because anxiety for some outcome is unfortunately no reliable index of satisfaction.

The imagined instance of unreasoned belief in the arrival of a letter may be contrasted with the case in which somebody argues "There should be a letter today because Tom said he would write on Saturday and letters never take more than two days to get here from Chicago." This time the belief in the letter's arrival is based on two *reasons,* viz., the belief that Tom said he would write on Saturday and the belief that letters never take more than two days to arrive.

By a person's reasons for a particular belief we shall mean those propositions that he would honestly be able to offer in defense of that belief. Suppose the belief in question to be expressed in a proposition, P. Then anybody having reasons for the assertion of P believes that some other propositions, Q and R, are true and also believes that the truth of Q and R guarantees (or partly guarantees) the truth of P. To have reasons for a belief is to have what one imagines to be a sound argument in support of that belief.

We shall use the term **derived belief** to refer to beliefs having reasons, and **basic belief** to refer to those having no reasons. It should be noticed that in ordinary usage a man is sometime said to have a reason or a good reason for an assertion when th belief expressed is *not* derived from other beliefs. Suppose a man says "I have an awful pain in my tooth." If we believe him, we might say "I can see he has *good reason* to say that." In such a case we do not mean that he arrived at his assertion by argument; we mean, rather, that he *does* have an awful pain in his tooth. The statement that a man has a reason or a good reason for asserting a proposition P means, sometimes, merely that P is true. We shall, however, restrict the term "reason" to apply only to cases in which the belief in question is derived from other beliefs by inference. Only derived beliefs can have reasons, and basic beliefs will have no reasons. (Basic beliefs are sometimes called *direct* beliefs.)

Plan of the chapter. Whether a man has a certain belief is a question of *fact* about that man. Whether a man has any reasons for his belief is a further question of fact about him. Neither of these questions is the same as the question whether that man is *justified* in holding that belief. A man may honestly believe that the world will come to an end this year, on the ground that he believes this catastrophe to be foretold in the Bible. To criticize his belief adversely, by claiming that he *ought not* to believe what he does, is not to question the psychological facts *about* his belief; it is rather to challenge the belief by appeal to *standards of the justification of belief.*

Our task is now to survey the various procedures that have been used as approved ways of justifying belief, and to understand their respective advantages and limitations.

2. *The limitations of deduction.*

Whenever one is justified in having a derived or reasoned belief, it will always be appropriate to consider whether the proposition expressing the belief is a valid conclusion from the reasons. If the reasons are claimed to be *deductively sound* (*i.e.,* sufficient to prove the belief by a valid deductive argument), we may be able to challenge the belief by showing the argument to be *invalid.* The numerous examples studied in the first part of the book have illustrated the power of deductive logic in disciplining arguments that *claim to be valid.*

A great many of our beliefs are derived beliefs based on deductive argument. Yet it is easily seen that deduction alone cannot be expected to do more than provide *relative* or conditional justification of beliefs. Deduction can, at best, show that *some* beliefs are justified if *other* beliefs are admitted to be justified.

The difficulties that arise from exclusive reliance on deductive logic as a way of justifying beliefs is illustrated by an ancient explanation of the earth's position in space. The earth, said the sages, according to some accounts, is supported by an enormous elephant, whose feet rest on a tortoise swimming in a golden bowl. The golden bowl, in turn, is supported by a giant, and so on. But it is clear that it is just as hard to explain how a giant can be supported in mid-air as to explain how the earth can be so supported. The suggested "explanation" simply shifts the difficulty to a different point in space.

There is some analogy to this in the attempts to justify beliefs by appeals to deductive argument *alone*. A valid deductive argument assures us that the conclusion is supported by other premises, which may, by a fresh argument, themselves be supported by other propositions. If we insist on demanding reasons for the premises introduced, one of three things must happen: (1) Sooner or later we use the original conclusion as a premise, and in this case we are arguing in a circle or "begging the question" (see p. 236); *or* (2) the process of producing fresh reasons *never* comes to an end, and in this case nothing is proved except the dependence of the conclusion on a string of other propositions; *or* (3) we must be content at some stage with premises that need no justification by argument—or perhaps no justification at all. (The second case, in which a conclusion is made to depend on an unending series of conditions, is known as an **infinite regress.**)

Deduction, therefore, though a valuable aid, *cannot be relied on exclusively* for the establishing of beliefs. If it is to be of any use in establishing beliefs, deduction needs to be assisted by other procedures.

Another way of stating this conclusion is: In order to be in a position to justify *derived* beliefs, we must have some reliable ways of arriving at *basic* beliefs. Our discussion now turns, therefore, to the considerations that ought to guide us in formulating *basic* beliefs.

It might seem at first that no defense or criticism of *basic* belief would be possible. A man's basic beliefs are, according to our definition, those that he has not deduced from other reasons. Since he has no premises for the basic beliefs, it might seem impossible to criticize them. If they turn out to be true, they are justified; and they are unjustified when and only when they prove to be false. A little thought will show this to be a hasty verdict. Suppose a man to awake from a dream with the words on his lips: "General Electric shares will rise." If he were sufficiently credulous, he might believe the prophecy and proceed to buy General Electric shares; given the usual uncertainty of stock markets, he might even make a profit. Yet we should not say he was justified in his (basic) belief about the shares, *even though the belief turned out to be true.* For we should be inclined to say that dreams are an unreliable clue to the truth. (If the man's dreams about the stock market consistently came true, the case would of course be altered.) The basic belief is thereby criticized in the light of a general standard of reliability or credibility. The truth of a single belief is not enough to justify it: We require further that it shall be of a kind that *generally* proves to be true. This test of *general* reliability will be used in our examination of the different origins of basic beliefs.

3. Supporting basic beliefs.

The appeal to testimony. We shall use "testimony" in a very wide sense to refer to *any* assertion that another person makes concerning a topic. Thus, testimony includes tables of statistics, railroad time tables, the written statements contained in encyclopedias, and other works of reference, as well as spoken answers to requests for information. The testimony need not relate to matters concerning which the speaker or writer has personal knowledge: Thus, the person giving testimony need not be a witness to any event that he claims to describe.

A great many of our beliefs are determined by testimony, in this wide sense of the term. Much of what we learn as children comes to us because somebody "says so"; and, in adult life, our reliance on testimony grows with our increasing need for information of the most varied kinds. A man who tried to depend wholly on information obtained directly by himself would have a life that was, in the famous phrase, "nasty, brutish, and short." The records of history, the recipes of our various technologies, the accumulated ethical insights of our forefathers, must be *communicated* if society is to survive. We must, on the whole, be able to trust those who give the testimony on which our culture is founded. The insistence of most ethical codes on the duty of truth-telling is closely related to this fact. Willingness to appeal to testimony, and general reliability of the testimony to which appeal is made, are necessary conditions for the survival of any effective human society.

We may therefore take the following to be facts: (a) that a great many of any person's basic beliefs take the form of belief in testimony; (b) that without widespread readiness to develop basic belief in testimony, society could hardly survive.

Yet this does not mean that *all* testimony is to be trusted indiscriminately merely because testimony is indispensable to the acquisition of comprehensive knowledge; a man must eat to live, but he need not eat everything that comes his way. It is notorious that some men are incorrigible liars, that others have an interest in concealing the truth, and still more, with the best intentions, are in no position to give trustworthy testimony. It becomes, therefore, a matter of great practical import to set up ways of discriminating between reliable and unreliable testimony.

When a person is alleged to be qualified to speak on a certain topic, he is commonly called an **authority** on that topic. To be "qualified" to give testimony in a certain field is to have qualities that *generally* ensure the truth of the statements made. Testimony by an authority consists of statements made by a person whom there are general reasons to trust. (Notice, however, that belief in the testimony of a man who is an authority in this sense may still be *basic:* We may have general reasons for trusting him, yet our belief in any particular statement of his may arise in us directly and without argument.)

Among the most useful tests of qualification applied to alleged authorities are *recognition by other authorities* (especially as evidenced by such official signs of respectability as titles, diplomas, and degrees), *agreement with other authorities,* and *special competence* ("being in a position to know").

When deciding whether to have an inflamed appendix removed, we rightly pay more attention to the advice of a licensed doctor of medicine than to that of Aunt Jane. For the possession of a legal right to practice medicine is some assurance that the doctor's skill and knowledge have been scrutinized by other competent doctors (*i.e.,* by other authorities). And our confidence in the doctor's recommendation for an appendectomy is materially strengthened if we find that two or three other doctors independently arrive at the same judgment. Here we are applying the test of agreement of authorities.

If we want to know what it feels like to be in battle, we are rightly inclined to pay more attention to the report of a soldier who has been in the front lines than to the account of a man, however imaginative, who has never been exposed to the shooting. For, in such a case, we feel that the personal experience of the person giving testimony is essential to the reliability of his account. If we are wise, we do not pay much attention to the advice of a pianist, however celebrated, on matters of economics, for we have a stubborn notion that experience on the grand piano produces no important insight into questions of prices and wages. In these instances we are applying the test of presumed competence—in a wide sense of the term "competence," covering experience as well as training.

Still more important than these tests of authority is the *established credibility* of the testifier. A man may be in excellent standing among other authorities, and presumably in a position to know the truth, but if his judgments prove to be false more often than not, we should be gullible indeed to trust his testimony. History swarms with instances of absurd notions, promulgated by recognized authorities of the highest competence. And even in science, where distrust of authority has become a cardinal principle of method, every great innovator has had to fight against the inertia and hostility of false doctrine universally accepted on the basis of authority. By the "established credibility" of an authority, we mean simply *his demonstrated success in making true statements.*

To call an authority *good* is to say that he satisfies the tests outlined in the preceding paragraphs. When a person regularly submits the authority on which he relies to the tests described, the appeal to authority may be said to be critical or undogmatic. When the authority is held to have the last, unchallengeable, word on a subject, we have **dogmatic** appeal to authority.

Anybody who uses the Bible as an authority on the history of the early Israelites, but is willing to defend the general credibility of the text by reference to the work of archeologists, historians, and geographers, is appealing undogmatically to authority. If he can in this way make out a good case for the general credibility of the Bible on the subject of early Hebraic history, he will have established a valuable additional source of further knowledge concerning that subject. Whether he is right or wrong in his special contention, he will be making a use of authority that is unavoidable in all branches of science and scholarship. Should he, however, insist on grounding his beliefs on the Bible, for no better reason than his belief that the Bible cannot be wrong, he will be using his authority dogmatically. And even if he should sometimes arrive at true beliefs by such a method, his procedure would still be indefensible.

When the procedure involved in the dogmatic use of authority is set out baldly, it seems incredible that people should have trusted it. "I believe X because A says that X is true, and I believe in A because I believe that A ought to be believed"—this mode of reasoning seems quite uninviting to anybody who has the slightest feeling for evidence.

But appeal to dogmatic authority is seldom so starkly presented. However dogmatic the appeal to authority may in fact be, some pretense of undogmatic procedure is customary. Here, as elsewhere, vice pays to virtue the tribute of hypocrisy. It is common to find some reference, however perfunctory, to the alleged *credibility* of the dogmatic authority; even the most authoritarian of dictators claims that his predictions can be *trusted.*

Of still greater practical import is the fact that the actual *prestige* of a dogmatic authority is reinforced by factors that have nothing to do with his intrinsic credibility. If the practice of advertisers is any criterion, men have a tendency to act on any recommendation of a cigarette made by a pin-up girl. The assertions of somebody we admire, respect, or fear, come to us charged with an initial plausibility. And in general, the prestige of a source of testimony tends to spread to *all* statements of the person having that prestige. None of this is a reason for condoning the uncritical and dogmatic use of authority, but it may help to remind us of certain notorious facts of life and put us more on our guard against the abuse of the appeal to authority.

Our discussion has suggested that appeal to testimony and authority are useful and defensible ways of establishing basic beliefs. But the need to discriminate dogmatic from undogmatic appeals to authority calls for constant vigilance. A determination to exclude appeal to authority would impoverish our intellectual life intolerably. Yet uncritical use of authority can easily lead us into the most deplorable parroting of other people's errors.

The appeal to experience. By this title we mean first to refer to two kinds of ways in which we are sometimes led to certain beliefs. We may see, hear, smell, and feel something, and again, we may *remember* experiences of this sort. We are not yet considering the more complex methods by which we arrive at *general* truths "through experience." When we say that somebody has learned *by* experience, we imply that a great deal more has happened than simple sensation or memory. The type of man who has "seen everything and learned nothing" is unhappily all too familiar. *Learning* by experience requires an active sorting, comparison, and analysis of experience and memories; we reserve this process for later and more detailed examination.

So long as we confine ourselves to what we "actually see," "actually hear," or "actually remember," we seem to be using a method that comes close to being infallible. The dentist might inform us, with all the authority that comes from the recognition of his colleagues, his professional expertness, and his general reliability, that our tooth does not hurt; but none of this avails against our actual experience that the tooth hurts agonizingly. The politician's assurance that there are "enough jobs for everybody," echoed by every economist, governmental bureau and newspaper in the land, is cold comfort for the man who knows, *by actual experience,* that no work is to be found. A thousand proverbs in all languages testify to the common understanding of this somewhat cynical truth: Only the man who wears the shoe knows where the pinch comes, the proof of the pudding is in the eating—and so on indefinitely.

Yet, if we examine more carefully the limitations of this method, we shall see that the appeal to experience, while it is of the utmost value, is still surprisingly meager in its fruits. So long as we confine ourselves to the most immediate aspects of our experiences—to the way the tooth feels, or the rose smells *to us,* it would be absurd to talk of making a mistake. But we are seldom content to make statements so narrowly circumscribed. We claim to know by experience that the girl we can see in the distance is Mary, that the air is very humid this afternoon, that it is time to go home for supper; and all these beliefs involve a considerable element of *interpretation*. The core of our experience is the sight of something moving in the distance, and about this there is no question of a mistake; but the assertion that we see Mary may be debatable and subject to error; we may very well "see what we see" and yet be deceived in the interpretation. Similarly, when we say that the air is very humid this afternoon, the core of our experience is a certain complex of feelings—a dry tautness of the skin, a characteristic feeling of oppression and heaviness. It would be nonsensical to "doubt" that we have the feelings; that these feelings are a sign of the physical phenomenon known as "excessive humidity" is another matter. Our statement might be refuted by application to a humidity-meter—or by reference to the feelings of other people. Nor is the situation any different with respect to memory; we may "remember" that we mailed a certain letter, *i.e.*, have a certain kind of experience—as of "seeing" ourselves mailing the letter; and yet the letter may not have been mailed. Experience in the wide sense, not confined to the "core" of sensation or memory, but including elements of interpretation, is far from being infallible.

We need hardly insist on the *value* of appeal to experience: Basic beliefs arising from experience have a vividness and directness of appeal that needs no assistance from the critic of thinking. It is his part, rather, to insist on the ease with which appeal to experience can be abused. As in the case of appeal to authority, it is necessary to discriminate the critical from the dogmatic appeal to experience. Appeal to experience will be critical or undogmatic in proportion as full account is taken of lurking possibilities of error, and precautions are taken to establish the general reliability of the procedures used.

When use of experience leads to beliefs extending far beyond the "core" of immediate sensation or memory, the methods used become correspondingly complex. For the moment, we simply record the verdict that appeal to experience must be controlled and disciplined in order to be fully reliable.

Appeal to self-evidence. "We hold these truths to be *self-evident,* that all men are created equal, that they are endowed by their Creator with certain unalienable rights. . . ." These words may remind us that men have often regarded certain beliefs as being self-evidently true, and in no need of other support, whether by experience, authority, or otherwise. Among such truths, or alleged truths, have been principles of the greatest importance to the human race.

To say that a principle is "self-evident" is to say that it does not need the evidence of any *other* proposition. The principle, then, is perceived to be true as soon as it is "fully understood." However, these two words, "fully understood," may refer to mental processes of varying degrees of complexity.

Let us consider, first, the trivial proposition "A may be B's brother without B being A's brother." Some people may claim to "see" by inspection that the proposition is true. In one person's experience, however, the mental process took the following form: "I thought at first they must both be men. Then I said to myself 'perhaps there's a catch in it.' I'll see what happens when B is a *woman.* A is B's brother. . . . Of course. She's his sister. *I saw the answer in a flash."* In this case, the experience of mental illumination indicated by the words italicized came about *as a result* of certain preliminary steps. Some *argument* may have been involved. There *was,* nevertheless, a momentary experience which it is natural to describe in terms drawn from vision. It is clear, of course, that there is no *seeing* involved, in the literal sense in which flowers or rainbows can be seen; in claiming that the truth of a principle is "seen," we are employing a metaphor. What really occurs in such momentary experience of illumination or "intellectual insight" is a puzzling question.

For a second illustration of the appeal to self-evidence, we take the proposition that two straight lines cannot meet at more than one point. In this case the process required to make us "see" the "self-evidence" of the assertion is still more complex. We may draw or imagine a pair of straight lines crossing; we notice that they diverge, become progressively more separated after crossing, and finally "see" (again in this peculiar sense of the word) that it is "impossible" for them to cross twice. What we seem to be doing in such cases is reviewing an indefinite number of possible experiences and, in some way, "noticing" a common feature of all these experiences.

When we claim that there are no circumstances in which it is right to enjoy wanton infliction of pain, we may base our claim on a similar process. We may try to present to our imagination in as vivid a form as possible the spectacle of somebody hurting a person "for the fun of it"; and this "mental experiment" may convince us immediately that the practice in question is morally wrong.

If we were to make a full examination of the types of vivid imaginative experience on which the claims that some propositions are self-evident have been founded, we should have to find some place for revelation, mysticism, the promptings of feeling, and the weaker but still potent suggestions of "hunches." Many men, of varying degrees of saintliness, have claimed to have had the will of God revealed to them by direct communication; still more have had extraordinary experiences of a so-called "mystical" character, in the course of which they had access to otherwise unknowable truths concerning the universe. At a much humbler level, most of us have had the experience of "feeling" that a certain action is wrong, or a certain man unworthy of trust. In cases like these, or in those still more familiar instances in which we have a "hunch" that something will happen, we may be in no position to give coherent and intelligible reasons for our beliefs. Yet we may insist that our belief is trustworthy.

Enough has been said to call attention to the variety of grounds that may be invoked in an appeal to "self-evidence." These diverse processes are alike in producing beliefs held with great conviction. So great is the power of "self-evidence," indeed, that the term in common use often means roughly the same as absolute certainty.

It is all the more striking, therefore, that hardly a belief that has been held self-evident by some people has not been held false by others. At various times, men have believed that it was self-evident that the earth was flat, that some women were witches, that infants dying without baptism were doomed to eternal damnation, and that all animals belonged to divinely created and eternally unchangeable kinds. (If you believe in none of these, it would be useful to consider whether you believe that a whole must be greater than its parts, or that space is not infinite. For both of these, like our proposition concerning the crossing of straight lines, are not accepted by modern scientists as true without qualification.) In short, belief that a proposition is self-evident, however strong that belief may be, is no infallible guarantee that the belief is true.

Those who believe in the infallibility of revelation, or mental experiment, or intuition, or some other method of discovering self-evident truths, have a simple answer to the charge that their favorite method sometimes fails. They say that in cases where the alleged revelation proved later to be false, the man who claimed to have had the revelation must have deluded himself. Not all of those who believe they have heard the voice of God have in fact done so—but when the voice of God *is* heard, and *true* revelation occurs, the belief revealed is proof against all criticism.

What this means in practice is that it is possible to make a mistake about the character of the process by which allegedly "self-evident" propositions are generated: the experience of "apparent" revelation cannot be distinguished from the experience of "true" revelation, except by applying *tests not included in the experience itself*. The way of self-evidence has therefore the same weakness as the method of authority. Just as the plausible but unreliable authority may sound as convincing as the trustworthy expert, so also the unreliable experience of mock revelation may carry as much conviction as the genuine communication of God's will. The way of self-evidence, no less than the way of authority, must accordingly be subjected to critical scrutiny (though not on *every* occasion).

Yet, after all these reservations have been made, we should add, as we have done in the case of the other methods, that "self-evidence" may be a very valuable source for the discovery of truth. To condemn recourse to self-evidence because it sometimes produces mistaken results would be unreasonable, for exactly the same objection could be levelled against any and every method for supporting beliefs.

Ungrounded beliefs. A man under hypnosis can be made to suppose he is a dog: He runs on all fours, barks, and eats raw meat with relish. His actions prove that he *believes* he is a dog. Now we can hardly say that he has *established* his belief: Suggestions of the hypnotist, probably not consciously heard, have *caused* his belief, but that belief has no grounds. Such phenomena are not exceptional, though the resulting beliefs are seldom so ridiculous. All human beings are more or less suggestible, and are therefore prone to believe assertions constantly reiterated or taken for granted by the society to which they belong. Many of our basic notions concerning morality, the good life, economics, education, and other important matters are probably acquired in this way, by contagion and infection. Among the most potent of the factors that are known to be conducive to the acceptance of such beliefs, beside their general popularity, is the agreeableness of the belief. It is not without good reason that the term "wishful thinking" has become so popular—at any rate as a description for the beliefs of others.

Most striking of all such cases of ungrounded belief are those in which the belief persists in the face of good contrary evidence. In the celebrated Martian scare in which thousands of radio listeners were frightened by a broadcast into flying from the planetary invaders, not even the authoritative denials of the radio stations concerned were able to stem the wave of panicky belief.

It is worth repeating that such beliefs are not to be condemned just because they are *basic,* for we saw at the beginning of this chapter that some *basic* beliefs must be trustworthy if *any* beliefs are to be justified. When we condemn a basic belief as *unreasonable,* we claim that controls should have been applied to show that the belief (in its context) was unworthy of trust.

Basic beliefs need such controls, for practice shows that basic beliefs are often unreasonable. The fact that an opinion is widely held, or is often asserted, or is agreeable to our hopes and fears, proves to be the shakiest assurance of its truth. An unestablished belief, in fact, too often proves to be an ungrounded prejudice. We can hardly hope to rid ourselves of all our prejudices; we can, however, be alert to detect them. If our beliefs are warranted, they should survive the critical scrutiny of experience, authority, or insight. Such criticism should be used in moderation. But reluctance ever to submit our beliefs to scrutiny is often an indication that the belief is prejudice.

4. *The hygiene of belief.*

The various ways that may be used to produce basic beliefs should not be regarded as competitors. Our examination may have strengthened the suspicion that no method is infallible: As a great American writer has said, in a remark of wide application, "There is no safety in numbers or in anything else." If *no* method can therefore be relied on in general to produce nothing but true beliefs, the practical problem of the reasonable formation of beliefs reduces to the skillful practice of the art of *combining* methods. For one of the most important morals of any critical survey of the grounds of belief is that the various methods are more likely to be successful when used together than when used separately. The undogmatic, critical use of beliefs grounded in authority or experience, beliefs self-evident or unreasoned, consists in using the full resources of each method as a check against the excessive claims of any of them. What matters indeed is not so much the *source* of any particular belief as the critical tests to which it is submitted before full acceptance. And the intelligent *criticism* of thought consists mainly of a well-developed skill in *testing* the claims of beliefs, however generated.

The advice to use all the methods as checks against one another does not take us very far. What we should like to know is how to do this *in concrete cases,* but the full answer can be supplied only by learning the special sciences and disciplines. Part of the qualifications of a well-educated chemist, for instance, is his knowledge of the situations in which he ought to rely on authority rather than his own experiences, and similar observations apply to other methods and in other subjects.

In our own times, the critical appeal to *experience* (in conjunction with other methods) has become increasingly important. This method, in one elaborated form, is *scientific method,* to whose study the remainder of this book is largely devoted.

Summary

Deductive logic is concerned with the validity or *relative* truth of propositions; "criticism of thought" requires attention to be given also to methods of determining the *unconditional* truth of propositions. The practical problem, with which this chapter is concerned, is that of *justifying belief* in the truth of propositions. When a man's belief is derived from other beliefs that he would honestly offer in its defense, his belief has *reasons.* Not all beliefs have reasons, but all beliefs probably have *causes.* A belief having reason is a *derived belief;* one having no reasons is a *basic belief*. Deduction alone is unable to justify the unconditional truth of beliefs, and the attempt to do so results in circular arguments or an *infinite regress.*

Basic beliefs may be reasonable or unreasonable. All methods used to generate *basic* beliefs are subject to the test of *general reliability,* and are acceptable only if they yield beliefs that in most cases prove to be true.

Basic beliefs are classified as beliefs arising from *testimony, experience,* or *self-evidence.*

Testimony is defined as any assertion about a given topic made by another person. Reliance on testimony is a necessary condition for comprehensive individual knowledge and social continuity. A testifier who is *qualified to give testimony* or alleged to be so is called an *authority*. Among the qualifications of an authority are: recognition by and accord with other authorities, special competence, and established credibility. Authorities willing to submit to scrutiny of their qualifications are *undogmatic.* (Dogmatic authorities usually claim to be undogmatic, and often bolster their prestige by non-rational devices.)

Appeal to *experience* includes reliance on sensation and memory and also the elaboration of experience referred to as *"learning* from experience." There may be an infallible "core" to sensation and memory, but basic beliefs grounded in experience normally involve an element of *interpretation.*

Propositions believed as *self-evident* are thought to require *no* evidence; yet for them to be "seen," mental processes of varying degrees of complexity are required. "Intuition," "revelation," and the other means used to yield intellectual insight into self-evident propositions have proved far from infallible. Appeal to self-evidence is one of the weakest of all ways of grounding basic beliefs.

Many beliefs have *no* basis, and these may be called *unestablished.* Since unestablished beliefs prove often to be unfounded prejudices, the critic of thought will treat them with suspicion.

Intelligent criticism of beliefs calls for well-developed skill in *testing* the claims of beliefs (however generated) by the combined use of several of the methods enumerated.

Comprehension test

(For instructions, see page 10.)

1. A man is never justified in believing a false proposition to be true. (*true* *false*)
2. A basic belief need have no reasons. (*true* *false*)
3. Since basic beliefs have no reasons, a careful thinker will reject them. (*true* *false*)
4. Appeal to experience is infallible. (*true* *false*)
5. Learning by experience requires more than the simple registration of sensations and memories. (*true* *false*)
6. "Derived belief" and "basic belief" are polar terms. (*true* *false*)
7. A reason for a belief may also be a cause of that belief. (*true* *false*)
8. A dogmatic authority is an authority who is very positive in his statements. (*true* *false*)

9. The term "self-evidence" refers to several kinds of mental processes. (*true false*)
10. An infinite regress is not always objectionable. (*true false*)

Exercises

A

1. Explain the meanings of the following terms, then consult a good dictionary to discover improvements in your definitions:
   agnostic, sceptic, infallible, dogma, article of faith, catechism, intuition, axiom, self-evidence, prejudice, bias, revelation.
2. Explain the meanings of the italicized words and phrases in the following sentences:
   a. It is *obvious* that two and two make four.
   b. Dr. Jones is *no authority* on smallpox.
   c. *In my experience,* Mexicans cannot be trusted.
   d. In this Court of Law, what the witness thought is not *evidence.*
   e. What is your *reason* for disliking him?
   f. There is no use in my arguing with you: You will have to *see* that killing is wrong.
   g. It is *axiomatic* that prices increase in times of scarcity.
3. Identify the beliefs formulated in the following passage and the methods used in their justification:
   "Is it possible that men can be so absurd as to believe that there are crops and trees on the other side of the earth that hang downward and that men have their feet higher than their heads? If you ask them how they defend these monstrosities? how things do not fall away from the earth on that side? they reply that the nature of things is such that heavy bodies tend toward the center like spokes of a wheel, while light bodies, as clouds, smoke, fire, tend from the center to the heavens on all sides. Now I am really at a loss what to say of those who, when they have once gone wrong, steadily persevere in their folly, and defend one absurd opinion by another." (Lactantius, *On the heretical doctrine of the globular form of the earth,* 4th C. A.D.)
4. Give your own reasons for believing that the earth is round. Identify the method to which appeal is made in each case.
5. Examine a newspaper report of some recent event. Apply the test for beliefs based on testimony discussed in the text. (This will require the examination of other newspapers' accounts of the same events, etc.)
6. Explain carefully the meaning of "self-evidence." Get some of your friends to co-operate with you in an experiment to discover which of

the following are self-evident beliefs (for the persons concerned). (What methods could be used to determine this?)

a. That men and women should receive equal pay for equal work.
b. That all adult citizens ought to be entitled to vote.
c. That murder is never justified.
d. That every circle has an inside and an outside.
e. That nobody can remember the future.
f. That the time between 1 o'clock and 2 o'clock is just as long as that between 2 o'clock and 3 o'clock.
g. That everybody has a right to earn his living.
h. That all men must die.

(*Warning:* Remember what was said in earlier chapters about the need for defining terms if verbal issues are to be avoided.)

7. Make an outline for an essay on the value of basic beliefs. (A suitable title might be "In defense of having no reasons.")

B

1. How far are a man's beliefs under his own control? What is the bearing of your answer on the topics discussed in this chapter?
2. Explain, with illustrations, the differences in meaning between *reason, cause,* and *premise.*
3. Give your reasons for agreeing or disagreeing with the following statements:
   a. "Seeing is believing."
   b. Medicine is based on faith; every doctor accepts 99 per cent of the principles he uses because he was told as a student that they were true.
   c. If something is self-evidently true only a fool would doubt it.
   d. Whenever there is insufficient evidence either for or against some proposition, the wisest thing is neither to believe nor to disbelieve it, and to postpone action until more evidence is available.
   e. "To take on authority our notions of right and wrong, of what is just or expedient in politics, of what is true in religion or religious history, would be to become contemptible, or at least intellectually null." (J. M. Robertson, *Letters on Reasoning,* p. 49. London: Watts & Co., 1902.)
4. Why is an "infinite regress" in argument objectionable? Show that the attempt to *prove* the truth of logical principles without appeal to logical "insight" leads to an infinite regress.
5. Discuss the following argument in detail:
   "To judge the appearance we receive of things, we should need a

judicatory instrument; to verify this instrument, we should need demonstration; to rectify this demonstration, we should need an instrument: so here we are arguing in a circle!

"Seeing that the Senses cannot decide our dispute, being themselves full of uncertainty, we must have recourse to Reason; there is no reason but must be built upon another reason: so here we are retreating backwards to all eternity!" (*The Essays of Montaigne,* translated by E. J. Trechmann, vol. 2, p. 49. New York: Oxford University Press, 1927.)

6. How far is the view expressed in the following passage in agreement with the text?

   "Believe, certainly; we cannot help believing; but believe rationally, holding what seems certain for certain, what seems probable for probable, what seems desirable for desirable, and what seems false for false." (G. Santayana, *Character and Opinions in the United States,* p. 87. New York: C. Scribner's Sons, 1920.)

14

INQUIRY AT THE COMMON-SENSE LEVEL

The conception by which facts are bound together are suggested by the sagacity of discoverers. This sagacity cannot be taught. It commonly succeeds by guessing; and this success seems to consist in framing several tentative hypotheses *and selecting the right one. But a supply of appropriate hypotheses cannot be constructed by rule, nor without inventive talent.*—William Whewell.

1. Plan of the chapter.

IN the last chapter, in discussing the advantages and defects of various methods by which beliefs might be supported, we paid no attention to *the search for beliefs*. Taking for granted that some person already *had* the belief in question, we confined ourselves to criticism of the grounds offered in its defense. In many practical situations, however, it is important to know *what belief to adopt* concerning some topic. Our interest accordingly shifts to criticism of the methods appropriate to *answering questions* that are approached without previous commitment.

When the question presented is of some familiar and recognized type, there is often a known procedure leading to an answer. To learn the latest football scores, one may telephone the local newspaper; a visit to the bedroom will determine whether the baby has fallen asleep; "thinking about the matter" may be enough for a decision involving choice between two alternatives. In these instances, use is made of appeals to authority, experience, and deduction, respectively, of the types discussed in the last chapter. Once the appropriate procedure has been followed, there will result a belief that can be criticized according to the criteria already formulated.

There are other, and more puzzling, cases where no procedure is known to guarantee an answer to a question. A man who wonders why his car is not running smoothly, whether he is getting enough exercise, or what should be done to improve the efficiency of Congress, is seeking answers without knowing where the answers are to be found. A situation in which an answer is required to a question, in the absence of reliable information concerning the appropriate procedures to be adopted, will be called a **problem-solving situation.** This is in good agreement with the everyday meaning of "problem"; for what makes a question a "problem" or a "puzzle" is precisely the lack of any *obvious* way of settling it. We shall use the more inclusive term **inquiry** to refer to any proceedings directed toward obtaining reliable belief. This use of the term also agrees well with common usage. We see that a problem-solving process is an inquiry, but an inquiry need not call for the solution of any *problem,* though it will necessarily be directed toward the answer of some *question.*

A problem may arise at the *technical* or the *common-sense* level. A technical problem is one whose formulation calls for the understanding of complex notions and the possession of special information that is not usually at the disposal of an ordinary person; common-sense problems are those whose understanding and resolution call for no exceptional training, skill, or background of knowledge. We shall hope to find that the solutions of both technical and common-sense problems show certain common features. In this chapter we examine some relatively simple, "common-sense" examples; in later chapters we examine the special features of those technical modes of inquiry known as "scientific method."

We shall examine the features presented in cases where the problem-solver relies as much as possible *on his own resources* without invoking the help of outside authority. For the resort to authority, however legitimate as a shortcut to finding answers

ence of these various substances in the skin of the patient constitute the "B-", "C-", "D-",... factors.

When the process is successful, it proves possible to *eliminate* all the factors except one (say ragweed), and to confirm positively, by a sufficient number of confirmatory instances, that ragweed is the agent responsible for the sufferer's discomfort.

In spite of the usefulness of the method of agreement, it has grave weaknesses. The type of mistake that may result from its uncritical application is well illustrated by the Case of the Sophistical Drunkard.

A certain habitual drunkard, it is said, was urged by his friends to save his health and reputation by abandoning the practice of drinking generous high-balls each night. Being a student of logic, however, the reprobate insisted on performing a systematic experiment. On successive nights he was able to make himself insensible on whiskey and soda, brandy and soda, rum and soda, gin and soda, etc. Whereupon, appealing to the method of agreement and yielding to the entreaties of his friends, he took a solemn oath to abstain from the use of soda for the rest of his life!

In general, correct use of the method of agreement depends on *the accuracy of the classification of possibly relevant factors.* So long as the tippler insisted on analyzing his drink into soda-and-the-remainder, he was quite unable to obtain *positive* results of value. (The negative eliminations performed were quite sound, however.) No general rules can be given for suitable classification of the factors in a given situation. Here, once again, we have to rely on "good judgment," previous knowledge, and the imagination of the investigator.

A second possible source of error in the use of the method of agreement is illustrated by the recent (fallacious) claim that allergic children had been found to have better than average intelligence. (The claim was not supported by more searching inquiry.) The mistake committed did not arise from inappropriate analysis. It was due to overlooking the possibility that the children sent to doctors for testing might be *children of parents of more than average intelligence.* Here the A factor (presence of allergy) and the B factor (having above-average intelligence), which were found to be associated, were in fact accompanied by an *unnoticed* or "masked" C factor (being children of parents of above-average intelligence).

The danger of the presence in all the observed instances of unnoticed common factors (*i.e.*, of *biased sampling*) is always present in the use of the method of agreement. For it is very hard to be sure that *all* the possibly relevant factors have been considered in the preparation of the confirmation-table, and so to be sure that the instances agree *only* in the presence of A and B.

In view of this possible source of error in using the method, a practical maxim is *to vary the conditions as much as possible.* By examining children of all ages and both sexes, of different social positions, etc., etc., we have a better chance of fairly testing the allergy-high-intelligence hypothesis. In the light of this, we can understand why the *number* of confirmatory instances is so often stressed in supporting generalizations by confirmatory instances. For while the number of favorable instances is important only as it increases variation of the discarded factors, increase in the number of observations taken does generally, though not always, tend to ensure such variation.

The method of difference. Evidence has been accumulating in recent years to the effect that cattle (and other animals) are able to make fine discriminations between foods having different nutritive values. More especially, it has been shown that cattle will prefer to eat hay that has a high content of nitrogenous matter. The generalization involved may be formulated, according to the plan we have adopted, as: "Every case of there being available highly nitrogenous hay (A) is also a case of cattle preferring that hay (B)." How is this to be proved?

If the method of *agreement* were to be employed, it would be necessary to conduct a long series of observations with different kinds of food, different breeds of cattle, and so forth, in the attempt to show that *all* the observations agreed *only* in the presence of the factors A and B. This would be both tedious and expensive.

In one of the most striking experiments on this subject, the following, somewhat different, procedure was used. The cattle were allowed to feed off a haystack made up of two kinds of hay, *alike in all respects,* except that some of it had been grown on soil specially treated with nitrogen fertilizers. The result was spectacular. "The cattle cut this stack in two at the juncture of the two stackings by consuming first that part which included hay from the five acres formerly treated, and by leaving unconsumed the end made up wholly of untreated hay" (*Scientific Monthly,* Vol. 60, page 349). Since the two halves of the haystack were alike in all respects except the difference in nitrogen content, it was concluded that the difference in response of the cattle was due to the difference in food value.

This is an instance of the **method of difference.** We shall say that a generalization is supported by the method of difference when the following conditions are satisfied: (1) The generalization has the form *every case of A is also a case of B;* (2) one confirmatory instance takes the form of a report that in addition to A and B other factors, C, D, E, etc., occurred; (3) a second confirmatory instance takes the form of a report that in the presence of the *same* factors, C, D, E, etc., and in the absence of B, A was also absent.

This definition clearly applies to the case of the fastidious cattle. Here A will be the presence of highly nitrogenous hay and B the preferential choice by the cattle of that hay. The other factors, C, D, E, etc., will include such things as ease of access of the hay, its scent, its moisture content, and other factors assumed relevant in determining the feeding habits of cattle.

The confirmation table in this and other instances of the use of the method of difference takes the following form:

$$A_1 \rightarrow B_1 \;\&\; C_1 \;\&\; D_1 \;\&\; E_1 \;\&\; \ldots$$
$$B'_2 \rightarrow A'_2 \;\&\; C_2 \;\&\; D_2 \;\&\; E_2 \;\&\; \ldots$$

every case of A is also a case of B

in which the placing of a stroke alongside 'A_2' and 'B_2' respectively indicates the absence of those factors in the second confirmatory instance.

Careful note should be taken of the reason for interchanging the positions of the 'A' and 'B' symbols in the second line. The generalization "every case of A is also a case of B" can also be written in the "contrapositive" form "every case of not-B is also a case of not-A." (Compare the discussion of contraposition on page 81.) Thus if a confirmatory instance of the first form of the generalization is $A_i \rightarrow B_i$ (in which we *first* establish that A occurs and *then* find that B also occurs), a confirmatory instance for the contrapositive form should be $B_j' \rightarrow A_j'$ (in which we *first* establish that B does not occur and *then* find that A does not occur).

We must now try to understand how the method of difference supports a generalization. Let us consider what is shown with respect to the discarded factors in the example of the fastidious cattle. Suppose C is the scent of the hay. If B depended on the scent of the hay, it would follow that where B was absent the scent must be different. But the scent was supposed to have been kept constant in both parts of the haystack. Thus, the scent was *not* responsible for the preference. Similar arguments apply to the other discarded factors, D, E, etc. In general, the method of difference, in its negative aspect, is a way of *eliminating* all the factors considered relevant except one.

How much direct, positive, evidence does the method yield in support of the A-B connection? In the confirmation table on this page, above, we have just *two* confirmatory instances of the original generalization. This is, in general, not very strong evidence; it is usual, and desirable, therefore, to use both the method of agreement and the method of difference in conjunction, wherever possible.

Dangers in the use of the method of difference. The method of difference is illustrated by most planned scientific experiments. In the experiments on the influence of nicotine content of tobacco on the desire to smoke (already mentioned on page 294) special cigarettes were prepared having low nicotine content but, as far as possible, *the same appearance, taste, and aroma* as the regular cigarettes to which the smoker was accustomed. (*Science,* Vol. 102, p. 95, July 27, 1945.) The denicotinized cigarettes were, moreover, substituted for the regular type *at a time unknown to the subject of the experiment.* These precautions (and others that we shall not describe here) are clearly attempts to *vary one factor at a time,* as required by the method of difference.

Nevertheless, the method, in spite of its great usefulness, is subject to grave dangers. Suppose a person watching a conjuring performance were to argue in this way: "The magician has just said 'Abracadabra,' whereupon a live rabbit appeared. A minute ago he had not uttered the magic formula, and there was no rabbit to be seen. *Since nothing has changed* except that the spell was pronounced, the appearance of the rabbit must have been *due* to the utterance of the word Abracadabra." This is a mistaken use of the method of difference. And the mistake is obviously due to the assumption expressed by the words "nothing else has changed." (In fact, our guess is that the magician had "something up his sleeve" and performed some unseen act *in addition* to pronouncing the spell.)

This example illustrates one of the general weaknesses of the method, constituted by *uncertainty that all factors except one have been held constant.* Another way of describing this weakness is by saying that *it is difficult to be sure that all relevant factors have been recorded in the confirmation table.* In fact, the method of difference is now seen to be subject to one of the objections that was levelled against the method of agreement. The reader should check that the method of difference, like the method of agreement, is also subject to the fallacy of *erro-*

neous classification of factors (compare the discussion on page 297).

These dangers in the use of the method of difference can be neutralized, to some extent, by painstaking repetition of confirmatory observations.

3. *The process of induction.*

The pattern by which examination of confirmatory instances leads to the acceptance of a generalization deserves very special attention since it is the basis of all knowledge about matters of fact, whether in everyday life or in the most advanced sciences.

Let us vary our illustrations by considering the example of the generalization *Poison ivy stings.* The 'A' state of affairs is that which occurs when we have a case of *contact with* poison ivy; and the 'B' state of affairs is a certain inflammation of the skin. Each confirmatory instance takes the positive form *This particular piece of poison ivy in contact with human skin is in fact accompanied by inflammation of the skin* ($A_n \rightarrow B_n$), or the negative form *This particular case of absence of skin inflammation was in fact accompanied by absence of poison ivy* ($B_n' \rightarrow A_n'$). Each such confirmatory instance, positive or negative, will normally be accompanied by information tending to eliminate factors other than A and B.

If the generalization is true, there must be indefinitely many confirmatory instances—*anybody* whose skin were to come in contact with poison ivy would suffer the corresponding inflammation of the skin. Nobody, however, could hope to observe *all* of these confirmatory instances; it would be impracticable even to try to observe all the *positive* cases in which poison ivy came into contact with the skin. *In establishing the truth of the generalization we examine a sample of the relevant confirmatory instances.*

The poison ivy generalization is a rather weak one, subject to all kinds of exceptions that would have to be made explicit if we wanted to talk about the subject with scientific accuracy.

But even the most firmly established scientific generalization is no exception to the rule that a generalization is established by examining a *selection* of the cases (confirmatory instances) to which it applies. The student who begins to learn chemistry very soon finds out that the liquid known as hydrochloric acid turns blue litmus solution red, and this generalization, unlike that about poison ivy, holds without exception. Nevertheless, neither the student, nor his professors, nor the scattered hosts of practising chemists, have ever tested *all* specimens of hydrochloric acid with respect to its affect on blue litmus solution. The generalization about the acid is based on *sampling*.

The process by which we pass from evidence concerning *some* members of a certain class of objects to an assertion concerning *all* members of that class, is known as **induction.** To speak more precisely, we shall mean by an induction a process of reasoning in which a proposition of the form *all P are Q* is asserted on the basis of a number of propositions having the form *this P is Q* and *that P is Q* and *that other P is Q,* etc. (From this point onward, for the sake of brevity we prefer the formula *all P are Q* in preference to *every case of P is also a case of Q.*) By the usual "process-product ambiguity," it is customary to refer to the conclusion *all P are Q* as itself *an induction* from the evidence.

We shall find it often convenient to present the pattern of induction in the following shorter form:

$$\frac{P_1 \,\&\, P_2 \,\&\, \ldots \,\&\, P_n \text{ are } Q}{\text{all P are Q}}$$

in which the evidence for the inductive conclusion has been telescoped into a single statement.

Differences between induction and deduction. Induction and deduction are both processes of reasoning, *i.e.,* methods by which we pass from premises to a proposition that is "based on" those premises. The resemblance ends here. Let us consider some of the differences between the two processes:

1. In a deductive argument, the premises constitute *all* the evidence that is relevant to the soundness of the conclusion. The validity of the conclusion is determined by considering the premises, and the truth or falsity of other propositions has no bearing upon the result. In an inductive argument, likewise, the truth of the conclusion is determined by considering the premises, but the truth of *other* propositions *is* relevant. The truth of *all P are Q* requires that every confirmatory instance that shall later come to our attention shall accord with the conclusion, and a single case of a P that is not a Q will destroy the generalization. However firmly the conclusion of an inductive argument is established, it is always liable to possible rejection in the light of further evidence.

2. In a deductive argument, the test of the validity of the conclusion is consistency with the premises. More precisely, if we try to assert both the premises and also the *denial* of any proposition that is a valid conclusion from those premises, we shall be contradicting ourselves.

Contrast this with the case of induction. Supposing I were to maintain that the very next specimen of hydrochloric acid I tested would *not* turn the testing fluid red. I should then be running counter to the accumulated evidence of thousands of experiments, many times repeated by a great many chemists. *Nevertheless, there would be no logical contradiction involved in my denial of the inductive conclusion.* If a man says "I have seen you turn the litmus solution red a thousand times by adding the acid, but I still believe that the solution will turn green the next time," he is not contradicting himself. There is a *logical possibility* that he is right in supposing a miracle will occur. For the general evidence against the happening of miracles is *inductive;* and if our sceptic refuses to trust in *such* evidence, the utmost we can say in reply is "wait and see." The soundness of an inductive conclusion is *a matter of fact,* not merely a question of the logical relations between the premises and the conclusion of the inductive argument.

We can understand the implications of this last point more

clearly by considering what is needed in order to present an inductive argument in deductive form. Suppose we are testing the ripeness of a watermelon by the familiar procedure of cutting out a small wedge. The inductive argument takes the form:

this wedge of melon is ripe
~~~~~~~~~~~~~~~~~~~~~~~~~~
the whole melon is ripe

(We notice here the typical process from a sample to an entire class containing the sample. The example is particularly interesting because we seem to have here a *single* confirmatory instance as sufficient evidence for the generalization.)

Somebody who is impressed by the decisive character, the "finality," of deductive argument might try to convert our reasoning about the watermelon into a deduction. In order to do this, it is of course necessary to add an assumption, as follows:

this wedge of melon is ripe
[this wedge of melon is a fair sample of the whole melon]
---
the whole melon is ripe

To check that this argument is valid, we need a definition of the crucial phrase "fair sample." We might suppose that to call the wedge a fair sample of the whole melon is to assert that the properties of the wedge are a safe guide to the properties of the whole melon. We are, however, not concerned with *all* the properties of the wedge (*e.g.*, with the number of pips it contains) but only with its ripeness. Thus, all we need is a definition of *being a fair sample with respect to ripeness.* What this means is clear enough: To say that the wedge is a fair sample with respect to ripeness is to say that *if the wedge is ripe the whole melon will be ripe*. Thus the deductive argument proposed becomes:

this wedge is ripe
[if this wedge is ripe the whole melon is ripe]
---
the whole melon is ripe
~~~~~~~~~~~~~~~~~~~~~~~~~~

The argument is valid—but it is quite useless to us *if we are interested in knowing whether the melon really is ripe.* For we have been forced to make an assumption which is the very question that we are trying to settle. Naturally, if we assume that knowledge of the ripeness of the wedge is enough to ensure the ripeness of the whole melon, we can *prove* deductively that the whole melon is ripe. But the proof is useless. Our purpose is to pass from knowledge about the wedge alone to knowledge about the whole melon. And this we can do only by applying an inductive procedure, *i.e.,* by concluding in a manner *that has worked in the past* that the whole melon will have the desired property.

Induction is not an inferior kind of deduction. In the light of our discussion, the reader should now be on guard against the temptation to regard induction as a kind of inconclusive or otherwise inferior form of deduction. The point to emphasize is that induction and deduction are processes directed toward different ends. In deduction we discover what is logically involved in given propositions: it supplies us with a valuable means of organizing and re-organizing our assumptions and our beliefs. By means of *induction* we try to discover those generalizations that are true of the world in which we actually live.

No success in piling up the amount of *inductive* evidence for a conclusion will ever bring us "nearer" to turning the induction into a deduction. If everybody alive in the world spent 24 hours a day for a whole year turning blue litmus red by the addition of hydrochloric acid, without in that time finding a single exception—the prediction that the test would succeed the next time it was tried would still be supported by *induction.* The step from *ten billion cases of P have been Q* to *all cases of P are Q* is not justifiable on deductive grounds alone. That we are, in certain cases, nevertheless justified in making the transition is something we have to learn, inductively, through knowledge of the kind of world we live in.

Induction and deduction have their different and equally proper functions. A reasonable man is one who uses the method appropriate to the problem before him. It would be as unreasonable to try to prove *deductively* exactly how much rain will fall next month, as it would be to establish inductively the solution to a mathematical problem by taking a poll of mathematicians. The reader will have realized by now, of course, that in most inquiries it is reasonable to use deductive and inductive methods in combination.

(The all-important difference between induction and deduction is comparable to the difference between walking and swimming. Both walking and swimming are forms of locomotion, as deduction and induction are forms of reasoning. But swimming is not an inferior *kind* of walking in water—and induction is not an inferior kind of deduction suitable for use in cases where the premises are too weak to support the conclusion.)

Summary

When a generalization having the form "Every case of A is also a case of B" is supported by collecting confirmatory instances having the form "This thing that is A is also B" the method employed is said to be that of *simple enumeration.* In attempting to circumvent the weaknesses of this method (discussed in Chapter 14) recourse is sometimes taken to "scientific demonstration" of the generalization. The latter process is found to consist in part of replacing the original generalization by a chain of new and better supported generalizations. But this procedure does not show how generalizations can be established by *inductive* evidence.

One improvement on the method of simple enumeration is *the method of agreement.* In order to confirm by this method a generalization "Every case of A is also a case of B" (*now supposed fully explicit*), we need to list other factors C, D, E, . . . thought to be possibly relevant. Each confirmatory instance takes the form '$A_1 \rightarrow B_1 \& C_1 \& K_1 \& L_1 \& \ldots$,' *i.e.,* lists the occurrence of other factors than A and B. The method supports the generalization when and only when (i) all the lines of the confirmation table agree *only* in the joint presence of the A and B factors and (ii) no contrary instances are encountered. This procedure has the advantage over the method of simple enumeration of eliminating the discarded factors C, D, E, etc. Dangers in its use arise from the possibility of erroneous classification of the factors and inattention to possibly relevant but unnoticed factors. These can be guarded against by varying the nature of the confirmatory instances as much as possible.

In the *method of difference* the "discarded factors" (C, D, E, . . .) are held *constant,* while a second instance is produced in which the *absence of B* is accompanied by the *absence of A.* This procedure, like the method of agreement, succeeds in eliminating the discarded factors, C, D, E, etc., but its positive evidence for the A-B connection is weak unless supplemented by the method of agreement. The method is subject to dangers similar to those mentioned in connection with the method of agreement.

Both methods are special varieties of the process of reasoning known as *induction.* The generalization "all P are Q" is said to be based on induction when the evidence consists of a number of propositions of form "this P is Q." Induction differs from deduction in that (i) the truth of propositions other than those making up the evidence is *relevant* to the truth of the conclusion, (ii) the test of the conclusion is not deductive validity. The conclusion of an inductive argument is not (and is not intended to be) a deductively valid conclusion. Whether the conclusion is justified is a matter of *fact,* not of deductive logic. Induction aims at establishing true generalizations and so has a purpose different from, though in no way "inferior to," that of deduction.

Comprehension test

(For instructions, see page 10.)

1. The method of simple enumeration consists in counting the number of confirmatory instances. (*true* *false*)

2. The generalization "Every case of P, no matter what else is the case, is also a case of Q" is a "fully explicit" generalization. (*true* *false*)
3. The method of agreement is so called because all the cases examined agree in being confirmatory instances. (*true* *false*)
4. The method of agreement cannot be used unless all the factors that might be relevant have been listed. (*true* *false*)
5. The method of difference is liable to the fallacy of erroneous classification of factors. (*true* *false*)
6. In a sound inductive argument there is no contradiction involved in supposing the evidence true but the conclusion false. (*true* *false*)
7. However large *n* may be, the step from *n cases of P have been Q* to *all P are Q* is not justifiable on deductive grounds alone. (*true* *false*)
8. An inductive argument can be converted into a deductive one if suitable premises are added. (*true* *false*)
9. The truth of the conclusion of a sound inductive argument can never be upset by the discovery of further evidence consistent with the original evidence. (*true* *false*)
10. Deductive argument has a degree of perfection never attained by induction. (*true* *false*)

Exercises

A

1. Explain what mistakes are committed in each of the following inductive arguments.
   a. "The last three times I walked under a ladder, some bad luck came my way. I am going around that ladder even if it means getting off the sidewalk."
   b. Hunters and fishermen never "catch cold" even in the iciest weather. Exposure to low temperatures is not responsible for "colds."
   c. "Frenchmen are very unfriendly! Whenever I start a conversation with one of them, he makes an obvious effort to escape."
   d. "The heaviest attendances at cinemas occur on Sundays. And the largest attendances at Church occur on Sundays. Therefore whenever you have many people seeing films you also have many people going to Church. Support the Film Industry!"
   e. "I can't believe that the English are in favor of socialism. It is true that they voted for a Socialist government, but I have talked to

hundreds of people, and none of them were believers in socialism."

f. An infallible way to get a larger income is to grow old. For thousands of sample incomes drawn from many occupations and professions show that the average incomes of those above forty are higher than the average incomes of those below forty.

2. Which of the arguments used in the previous question make use of "simple enumeration"? Which use the "method of agreement"?

3. Analyze the inductive procedures used in the following investigations. Wherever possible, construct appropriate confirmation-tables. (Introduce appropriate symbols in each case, after having explained the meaning of each of them.)

a. "My Experiment was this. I took a number of little square Pieces of Broad Cloth from a Taylor's Pattern-Card, of various Colours. There were Black, deep Blue, lighter Blue, Green, Purple, Red, Yellow, White, and other Colours, or Shades of Colours. I laid them all out upon the Snow in a bright Sunshiny Morning. In a few Hours (I cannot now be exact as to the Time), the Black, being warm'd most by the Sun, was sunk so low as to be below the Stroke of the Sun's Rays; the dark Blue almost as low, the lighter Blue not quite so much as the dark, the other Colours less as they were lighter; and the quite White remain'd on the Surface of the Snow, not having entered it at all.

"What signifies Philosophy that does not apply to some Use? May we not learn from hence, that black Clothes are not so fit to wear in a hot Sunny Climate or Season, as white ones; because in such Cloaths the body is more heated by the Sun when we walk abroad, and are at the same time heated by the Exercise, which double Heat is apt to bring on putrid dangerous Fevers?" (Benjamin Franklin, Letter to Mary Stevenson, 1761. Quoted in J. G. Crowther, *Famous American Men of Science,* p. 28. New York: W. W. Norton & Co., Inc., 1937.)

b. "K. Frisch trained an Asiatic species of honeybee to come to a given color for food and to pick out that color from among others when no food was present. He used a series of pieces of paper of 15 shades, from white through various grays to black. The bees were then conditioned to some color, as blue, by associating that color with a sugar solution in a watch glass that was placed over the color. After conditioning of the bees was completed the blue paper, without food, was placed in various positions among the grays, and in every trial the bees gathered over the blue in search of food." (H. B. Weiss, "Insect Response to Colors," in *Scientific Monthly,* July 1945, page 51.)

c. In testing the theory that cancer is hereditary, post-mortems were made on over 40,000 mice (by Maud Slye, in Chicago). It was found that in some families every mouse living over 18 months developed cancer; while in others, kept under similar conditions, no members of the family had cancer.

d. After Pasteur had found a vaccine against anthrax, 24 sheep, one goat, and five cattle received the preventive inoculations. An equal number of sheep, goats, and cattle were added to the herd, and all 60 animals were infected with anthrax microbes. Two days later, all the unprotected animals were dead or dying, while the vaccinated animals were still in good health.

e. Newton's experiments to prove the equal gravitation of all substances: "The pendulums of which the oscillations were compared consisted of equal boxes of wood, hanging by equal threads, and filled with different substances, so that the total weights should be equal and the centres of oscillation at the same distance from the points of suspension.

"Hence the resistance of the air became approximately a matter of indifference; for the outward size and shape of the pendulums being the same, the absolute force of resistance would be the same, so long as the pendulums vibrated with equal velocity. Hence if any inequality were observed in the vibrations of the two pendulums, it must arise from the only circumstance which was different, namely, the chemical nature of the matter within the boxes. No inequality being observed, the chemical nature of substances can have no appreciable influence upon the force of gravitation." (W. S. Jevons, *Principles of Science,* 2nd ed., p. 443. London: Macmillan & Co., 1879.)

4. At what points in the inquiries described in the preceding question are judgments of the *relevance* of factors important?

5. Make a list of the respects in which the methods of agreement and difference (a) resemble, (b) differ from one another.

6. Outline the steps you would undertake to solve the following problems:
   a. You want to find out why the family car refuses to start on some days.
   b. You wish to determine whether going to bed earlier improves your work on the following day.
   c. It is claimed that your house will feel warmer if the humidity of the air is increased: it is desired to test this.
   d. Is it true that you sleep more comfortably if your bed lies north and south?

7. Explain how the inquiries mentioned in the last question illustrate the following points:
   a. The need to define the central terms used in the formulation of the inquiry.
   b. The importance of rendering generalizations "explicit."
   c. Pitfalls of the method of simple enumeration.
   d. Use of previous knowledge (about true generalizations) in selecting factors relevant to the inductive inquiry.
8. Which of the following arguments are *deductive* and which *inductive?*
   a. Whales are mammals, *therefore* whales suckle their young.
   b. Christmas has always been a national holiday, *therefore* Christmas will be a national holiday this year.
   c. Every time I have smoked "Unluckies" I have had a headache. They must have some ingredient that disagrees with me.
   d. He can't be an American citizen because he is an Oriental by birth.
   e. A was accompanied by B on this occasion, and it is known that no other factor but A is relevant to the occurrence of B. Hence whenever A occurs, B will occur.
9. "In a deductive argument, the *meaning* of the premises is sufficient to determine the validity of the conclusion; in an inductive argument, the soundness of the argument rests on an appeal to facts." Explain what this statement means, and illustrate its truth by reference to the arguments given in the previous question.

B

1. Explain the meanings of the following terms occurring in the text of this chapter:
   variation (of factors), *relevance, elimination, sampling, classification* (of relevant factors).

   (*Note:* What is asked for is the exact meaning of these terms *in the context in which they are used.*)
2. The name "method of simple enumeration" suggests that the most important aspect of the method is the *counting* of cases. Is this suggestion correct or not?
3. It is sometimes said that the inductive methods are best used "negatively," *i.e.,* as ways of *disproving* generalizations. *Discuss.*
4. A generalization to be tested by inductive methods can be regarded as a *hypothesis.* How far do the inductive methods conform to the rules for testing hypotheses discussed in Chapter 14?
5. [Both methods] "are formally vitiated by an extraordinary omission which also renders them scientifically nugatory. Both have forgotten

the scientific observer, who is surely an indispensable 'antecedent' to every experiment. His effect on the Method of Agreement is either that the two 'cases' always have *two* antecedents in common, viz. 'A' and the observer, or that the observer is himself the sole persistent antecedent. Now in the former case the Method is formally vicious, while in the latter it will conduct to the inference that he is himself the cause of the phenomenon and the author of the uniformity of nature. Nor can the identity of the observer be given up, for if he did not remain 'the same' throughout, the resulting change in his personality would probably vitiate his observations still more seriously. In an argument by the Method of Difference, on the other hand, the observer forms part of the rest of the universe which is supposed to undergo no change as the experiment progresses. But is not this to demand that the experiment shall make no difference to him, *i.e.*, that he is to be at the end as he was at the beginning? And does not this mean that he is to have no understanding of what he is doing? So soon as he understands what his experiment means, *two* circumstances have changed and his inference becomes formally invalid!" (F. C. S. Schiller, *Formal Logic*, 2nd ed., p. 267. London: Macmillan & Co., 1931.)
Write a detailed answer to this argument.

6. Examine critically the analogy with which the chapter concludes.

16

INDUCTIVE PROCEDURES II

In deduction we are engaged in developing the consequences of a law. We learn the meaning, content, results or inferences which attach to any given proposition. Induction is the exactly inverse process. Given certain results or consequences, we are required to discover the general law from which they flow.—W. S. Jevons.

1. Purpose of this chapter.

OUR examination of inductive procedures has made use of a number of simplifying assumptions. Throughout the last chapter, for instance, we took as a standard case generalizations having the form "Every case of A is also a case of B." We assumed, for the most part, that the generalizations, being "fully explicit," were intended to hold as stated *without exception;* and we supposed that there was no choice but unconditional "acceptance" or "rejection" of the generalizations examined.

These assumptions helped us to see the main outlines of the procedures by which generalizations are supported by observations of instances. Yet real life has an awkward habit of being more complex than the textbook, and in many important inquiries into matters of fact the assumptions we have listed will not be accurate.

Consider an inquiry directed toward the cure and prevention of unemployment. The following aspects of such an investigation will show the respects in which our examination is incomplete: (1) A major difficulty will be the discovery of hypothetical generalizations that are *worth testing:* the problem is not presented in the ready-made form of a significant generalization ripe for confirmation; (2) the generalizations actually tested may take the form "A is a cause of B" and other forms differing from those so far considered by us; (3) it is exceptional for any generalization to be found holding *without exception;* (4) it may thus be necessary to be content with "statistical generalizations" having the form "most cases, or such and such a percentage of cases, of A are also cases of B"; (5) and even such approximations to the more absolute laws we should like to establish may prove to be "probable" rather than certain.

Fuller consideration of the procedures appropriate to such complex inquiries would take us out of the context of "common sense" into that of scientific method, and is reserved for later chapters. Nevertheless, notions such as those of approximate or statistical connection, and causation, are also commonly used in non-technical inquiries. So it seems desirable to say something about them before proceeding to examine fully developed scientific method.

2. *The method of concomitant variation.*

Very often, it is hopeless to expect to find connections between the "presence" or "absence" of two factors, A and B. Suppose we are interested in finding a connection between *the calcium content of children's diet* (A) and *the growth of their teeth* (B). It would be futile to try to show that the "presence" of A is either sufficient or necessary for the "presence" of B: It is common knowledge that children's teeth will grow even if there is no calcium in their diet; and again, the presence of calcium alone will not be *enough* to make their teeth grow. Yet there is an interesting question concerning the *degree* to which the growth of the teeth is helped or hindered by *increase in the quantity* of the calcium in the diet. We are led then to consider how *variations in A* are connected with *variations in B.* This is an instance of a case where there is no simple connection between presence and absence of A and B.

In other cases, it may be *impossible to observe* "absence" of A, B, or other accompanying factors. We believe that the tides are "due to the moon," yet we cannot "remove" the gravitational influence of the earth (as required in the method of agreement) nor can we "remove" the tides or the influence of the moon (as required in the method of difference). But we *are* able to observe variations in the strength of these factors, and to notice how such variations or changes go together; our evidence for the connection between tides and the moon is based on knowledge of connected *variations* in the factors.

Concern with variations in related factors (rather than with their joint presence or absence) is quite characteristic of common-sense inquiries. A farmer's belief that "Fosteregg" is good for his chickens may well be based on his knowledge that *increase* in the amount of Fosteregg fed to the birds *increases* the number of eggs they lay. The confidence of a manufacturer in the value of his advertising will probably be based on evidence that *increased* expenditure on advertising is repaid in increased sales of his product.

In such cases as these, the method employed is said to be that of **concomitant variations.** We shall say this method has been successfully used when the following conditions have been met:

(1) The generalization to be tested has the form *A is a condition for B;* (2) the confirmatory instances take the form *this increase in A is also a case of increase in B,* or *this increase in A is also a case of decrease in B,* or *this decrease in A is also a case of decrease in B,* or *this decrease in A is also a case of increase in B;* (3) all other listed factors are meanwhile kept constant; (4) no contrary instances (of corresponding forms) are encountered.

We have used the vague form *A is a condition for B* in order to emphasize that the generalization established by successful use of the method is not of the form *Every case of A alone is also a case of B* (as in our previous discussions). It is true that in order to show that *increases* in A are accompanied by *increases* in B it is necessary for A and B to occur together. But in the cases where the method is most useful *it is not possible to eliminate other factors.* (Returning for a moment to the examples used above, increase in the amount of Fosteregg fed to hens will not lead to increased egg production *no matter what else happens;* similarly, increased expenditure on advertising is not *by itself* sufficient to produce larger sales of the product.)

What the method does establish is the generalization *Cases of increase (or decrease) in A are also cases of increase (or decrease) in B, other things being equal.* In such cases we say B is a **function** of A.

More precisely, we want to say *B is a function of A* when the following conditions are fulfilled: (1) A and B admit of degrees (*i.e.,* it makes sense to speak of "*more* A" or "*less* B"); (2) when all other factors remain unchanged, each case of a *change* in A is also a case of a *change* in B. Thus, we may say a child's height is a *function* of his age, or the volume of a gas is a *function* of its pressure.

We can now see that the method of concomitant variations is a refinement of the method of difference. In the latter we had to show that, "other things being equal," the presence (or absence) of A and B occurred together; in the new method we show that, "other things being equal," *changes* in A and B occur together.

The precautions necessary in using the method of difference (as explained in the last chapter) are also necessary in using the method of concomitant variations. Especially must we take care that in producing a variation of A we are not also making some other factor vary. Thus, a drugstore may discover that when the number of cigars on display is increased the sales of cigars go up. But to argue from this that the sales are a function of the number of cigars on display would probably be a mistake. For, very likely, *new brands* of cigars have been added in the process of increasing the stock of cigars. To make the generalization fairly secure, it would be necessary first to show that the change in brands was irrelevant.

In general (as in the case of all inductive methods) the method of concomitant variation is more powerful as a means of elimination (*i.e.,* of proving that B is *not* a function of C) than of positive demonstration.

Making a functional connection explicit and precise. When B is a function of A, the connection between changes in the two factors does not hold for *all* changes, without exception. Increasing the amount of food one eats will normally increase one's weight, but a surfeit of food may kill; increasing the pressure on a gas will reduce its volume, but too much pressure will convert it into a liquid. There is, therefore, a certain *range* in which the functional connection holds, and one way to make a functional connection explicit is to *state the range* in which it holds.

To learn that B is a function of A is to acquire knowledge, but it may be too vague to be useful. Suppose a manufacturer is told that an increase in his advertising expenditures will lead to increased sales. He would surely want to know *how much* increase in profits might be expected from a given increase in expenditure. (He would hardly spend the money if he received less in increased profits than he spent on increased advertising.) Similarly, when we are told that eating more vitamins will improve our health, we should like to know *how much* improvement will result, before deciding that it is worth our while to bother about the matter.

Asking the question "*How much* increase in B results from a given increase in A" marks the attempt to make the functional connection between A and B more precise. In order to answer it, we need to have some way of assigning numbers to, or *measuring* increases in A and B. Thus, the use of functional connections naturally leads to the search for *numerical laws.* When it is possible to measure A and B, it is possible, in favorable cases, to state the exact nature of the connection between the two. To take a very simple instance, the exact connection between the area and length of side of a square is expressed by the formula $A = I^2$ (when A is the area in square inches and I the length of the side in inches). The formula tells us not merely that the area is a function of the length of side; it also informs us exactly what changes in area will result from any given change in the length of the side. It is the aim of scientific method to replace the crude "hit-or-miss" generalizations of common sense (every case of A is also a case of B), first by statements of functional connection (B is a function of A) and eventually by an exact numerical law. (The measured values of B are related to the measured values of A by such and such an algebraic equation.)

3. *Some other notions used in common-sense inductive procedures.*

By this time it should be clear that inductive procedures can take many different forms and are capable of indefinite refinement. Even at the common-sense level, we could find examples of inductive inquiry that would not fit comfortably into the types we have selected for special attention. And we shall not even try to catalog the many transformations which inductive inquiries undergo in scientific investigations. We must therefore be prepared to meet inductive procedures in disguise, as it were: Whenever an inquiry involves the attempt to establish generalizations by examining instances of those generalizations, we may expect to find inductive procedures involved. This point will now be illustrated by considering the familiar notions of "analogy" and "cause," both of which will be found to involve reference to induction.

Argument from analogy. In one of the most persuasive forms of reasoning, we use resemblances between two objects as a ground for believing that they will have other properties in common. "The herring we ate last week was improved in flavor by being cooked in vinegar: The same can be expected from treating this mackerel in the same way." Here it is taken for granted that herring and mackerel resemble one another, and the property that *both* of them are expected to have is that of *being improved by cooking in vinegar*. The form of the reasoning can be shown diagramatically as follows:

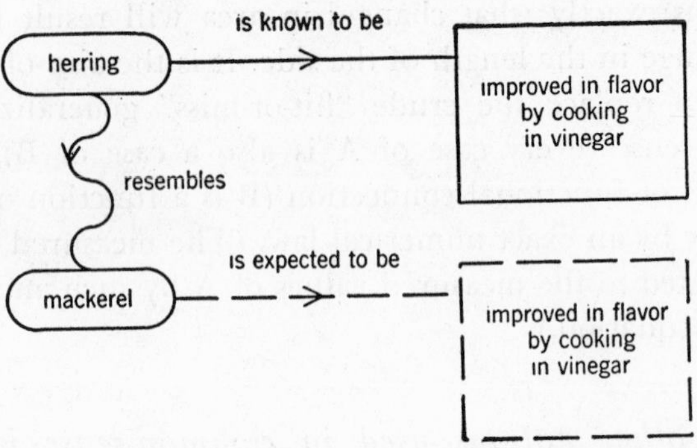

Another simple example will help to establish the pattern used in argument from analogy: "Ice is a solid, which, on heating, becomes liquid and, at a still higher temperature, turns into a gas. By analogy, we may expect carbon to liquefy and evaporate at higher temperatures." In this case, the common property assigned to both ice and carbon, is that of *becoming first a liquid and then a gas at higher temperatures.*

The general pattern of argument by analogy will be:

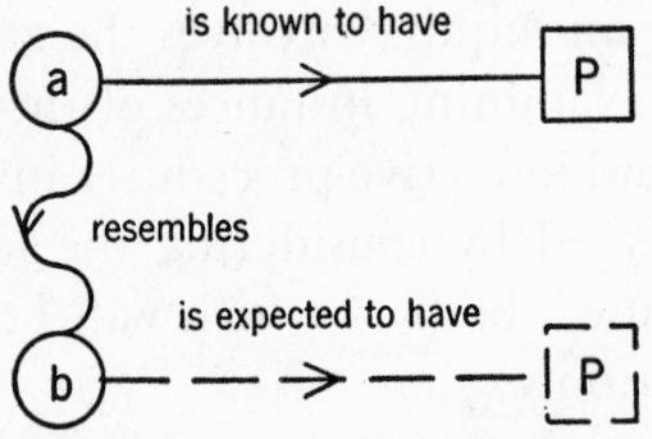

In any argument from analogy, there has to be some degree of resemblance between the things compared. By the **basis of resemblance** between *a* and *b* we shall mean the properties which *a* and *b* are *known* to have in common. Thus the basis of resemblance between a herring and a mackerel is that both are known to be salt-water fish; the basis of resemblance between a piece of ice and a piece of carbon is that both are known to be portions of matter. The soundness of an argument from analogy will therefore depend on whether the basis of resemblance is actually *connected* with the property *P* that is assigned to both *a* and *b*. The prediction that carbon becomes a gas at high temperatures is a sound one, since we know (on other grounds) that all matter can take the gaseous form. On the other hand, the prediction that two eggs that look exactly alike will taste exactly alike is a bad one, for we know by experience that the outward appearance of eggs is an unreliable guide to their inward condition.

If we represent by 'R', the properties that together make up the basis of resemblance, our typical diagram for argument by analogy becomes:

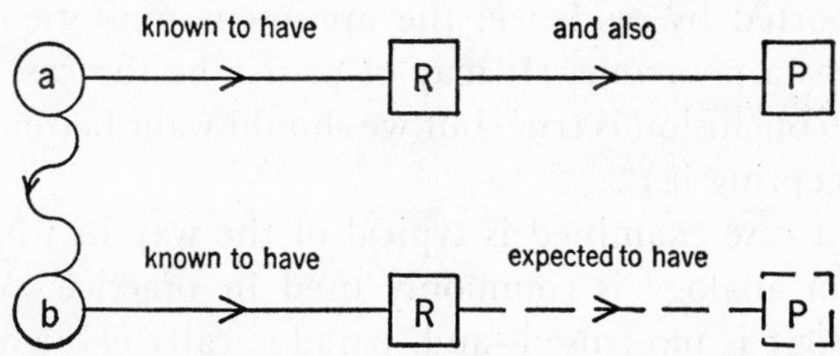

This shows that argument by analogy is a more or less explicit form of inductive argument. For it consists essentially in applying the generalization *whenever R occurs P also occurs* to the special case of *b*. Its strength therefore depends on the reliability with which the generalization *whenever R occurs P also occurs* has been established.

When the **linking generalization** (*all R are P*) is firmly established, argument from analogy can be used with confidence. Thus we need not hesitate to say "This egg, like the last, will have a yolk"; for the generalization that sustains this analogy, viz., that all eggs have yolks, has been firmly established by previous investigations.

Consider, however, the following argument from analogy: "In the application of fertilizer to increase the productivity of soil, there comes a point when the improvement produced by further treatment is so small that it is not worth the expense and energy involved. We may expect a similar law of 'diminishing returns' in education. Beyond a certain point, the attempt to teach a child more than he has already learned is not worth the expense and effort involved." In this instance, the basis of resemblance is slender, for the fertilization of soil and the education of young children are in most respects unlike. We might say, perhaps, that both are *processes of increasing productivity*—bearing in mind, however, that "productivity" means different things in the two cases. The linking generalization on which the analogy rests is, therefore, that *in all processes directed toward increasing productivity there is a law of diminishing returns at work.* This is a very wide generalization, not well supported by evidence; the argument must therefore be regarded as a poor one. (It may of course be the case that the suggested conclusion is true, but we should want better evidence before accepting it.)

The last case examined is typical of the way in which argument from analogy is commonly used in practice. Argument from analogy is most used—and, paradoxically enough, is most useful—in cases where the linking generalization is *not* well established. In such cases, the analogy ought to be regarded as *suggesting an hypothesis* to be confirmed by separate investigation.

Some of the most striking scientific discoveries have been made in this way. Thus it was found that the laws of propagation of light in many ways resembled those of the formation of waves in fluids. This analogy *suggested* the existence of other optical phenomena that were later confirmed by independent experiment.

Our discussion suggests the following practical rules for testing arguments from analogy:

1. *Make sure that the analogy is being used as a basis for argument and not merely as a way of making a more vivid assertion.* (For quite often the analogy is used merely as a decorative device.)
2. *State explicitly the properties constituting the "basis of resemblance."*
3. *State explicitly some of the respects in which the objects compared do*

NOT resemble each other (*i.e.,* the basis of *un*likeness, or the "*dis*analogy" between the objects).

4. *State the "linking generalization" from which the argument gets such force as it has.*
5. *Consider the nature of the INDEPENDENT evidence for the linking generalization.* (It is especially important to check that the disanalogy between the objects compared does not upset the generalization.)

These rules have already been illustrated in our discussion of arguments from analogy.

The common-sense notion of cause and effect. In discussing common-sense ways of establishing generalizations, we have tried to avoid using the words "cause and effect" as much as possible. One reason for doing this was that the general patterns by which generalizations are established (the methods of agreement, difference, etc.) are the same whether or not the generalization involves reference to causes. (It is important to know the generalization that swamps and mosquitoes occur together, even though it is not true that one is the *cause* of the other.)

Yet very often, in everyday life, we are interested not merely in showing that A is accompanied by B; we would like to know the *cause* of B. It is not much help to know, for instance, that a typhoid epidemic is usually accompanied by a sharp increase in the death rate of the community in which it occurs; it may be a matter of great practical urgency to know instead the *cause* of the epidemic. What do we mean when we ask for the cause of a toothache, an epidemic, or an outbreak of war?

A plausible answer is that we are, in all these cases, looking for something by means of which we could *control* the effect. Suppose tainted water is the cause of the typhoid epidemic—then removal of the infection in the water will stop the epidemic: If the building of armaments is the cause of outbreak of war, prevention of armament construction ought to prevent the outbreak of war; if the decay in a molar is the cause of our toothache, removal of that decay should stop the toothache.

Let us formulate the general pattern shown in these examples. Suppose E to be the effect we are investigating; then our discussion suggests that when we call something the cause, C, of E, *the removal of C leads to the removal of E, i.e.,* E does not happen unless C happens. Another way of saying this is that, *in these instances,* to say that C is the cause of E implies that *when C does not happen E does not happen.*

In all such statements to the effect that something is a cause, there is involved a generalization. When we say that the decay in our molar is the cause of the toothache, we imply that *if these conditions were repeated* (the same state of decay in the tooth, the same condition of our nerves, and so on for all the other factors concerned)—toothache would result. (In order to see this, consider what your reaction would be if the dentist were able to show you that exactly the same state of decay sometimes did, and sometimes did not, produce toothache—*the other factors being the same in all cases.* You would then surely not "blame" the toothache on the dental decay.) When we say that C is the cause of E, therefore, we are not only making a statement about two particular happenings, we are also implying a generalization about *any* happenings of the same kind.

So far we have considered only effects that are unpleasant, in which cases "control" of the effect naturally means the same as its *prevention.* But we also ask sometimes for the cause of desired effects: a good harvest, an increase in general prosperity, or an improvement in literacy.

A factor by which the effect could be "controlled" in such cases means something by which the effect could be *produced.* If the dry weather was the cause of a good harvest, a similar spell of dry weather—*other conditions remaining the same*—should produce another good harvest; if higher wages caused the increase in economic prosperity, increasing wages *in the same conditions* should again produce higher prosperity; if listening to the radio is the "true cause" of people learning to speak more effectively, the same factor should in similar conditions produce the same results.

The general pattern shown by this second batch of examples is this: When C is said to be the cause of E, the occurrence of C leads to the occurrence of E, *i.e.,* it is implied that *when C happens E also happens.*

It will be noticed that the analysis of what we mean by "cause" leads to *different* results according to whether the effect, E, is desired or not. We could avoid this ambiguity by speaking, in a way ordinary people seldom do, of "necessary" causes and "sufficient" causes. We might then say that "control" of an *unwanted* effect consists of knowledge of a *necessary* condition of that effect, while "control" of a wanted effect consists of knowledge of a *sufficient* condition of the effect.

To say that a factor can be "controlled" is to say that *we* could have done something about it. An insurance company's report that a fire was "caused" by a lighted cigarette end picks out a factor that human beings could have changed. But we also say that the cause of a house being blown down was a typhoon—and here we choose as *"the"* cause something over which human beings have no control. Thus "cause" sometimes means a condition (necessary or sufficient) that human beings can manipulate, while at other times it means a condition that for some reason is regarded as particularly interesting and important.

We are not yet finished with the ambiguities of this common but surprisingly elusive notion. One man may say that the cause of the strange sounds he is hearing is certain vibrations originating in his radio; another may say that the true cause is the curious vocal performance of some comedian hundreds of miles away in New York; a third may say that the "true cause" is the failure of the comedian's parents to strangle him at birth. Which of them is right? The best answer is that they *all* are, for "cause" sometimes means a condition near to the effect in space and time, and sometimes a remote condition.

This hunting down of the ambiguities of "cause" can continue almost indefinitely. We can say that the butter melted because the temperature increased (picking out a *change* in the environment) or because it has a low melting point (emphasizing a *permanent property* of the butter). And so on.

By this time the reader will understand why we have tried to avoid talking of "causes" and "effects" in our discussion. The common core of meaning in all the shifts of meaning of these slippery words is this: When C is said to be a cause of E, there is involved the notion of the occurrence of C being a necessary or sufficient condition (in the senses explained above) for the occurrence of E. This requires C and E to be connected by a law. The generalizations indicated by the common-sense use of words such as "cause" and "effect" are inaccurate and inexplicit. They hold only within ranges whose limits are not stated, and require other factors that often are not even mentioned to be held constant. In attempting to overcome these shortcomings, scientists tend to discard the common-sense notion of causality, with all its ambiguities, in favor of the more sophisticated notion of *functional connection.*

4. Statistical generalizations.

All the examples of generalizations so far considered have concerned *exact* connections between factors or variations in factors. In many important cases, however, it is possible to establish only a partial or approximate connection between factors. A fisherman visits a certain stream because he *usually* finds trout there; a doctor prescribes sulfa drugs because they have brought relief *in a majority* of cases of the infection; an animal breeder knows that *three-quarters* of the offspring of interbred black hybrid guinea pigs will be black. In such cases as these we commonly say "there will *probably* be fish in the stream" or "the drugs will *probably* give relief" or "there is a *probability* of three-quarters that a child of interbred black hybrid guinea pigs is black." One use of the terms "probable" and "probability" therefore is in connection with a prediction that a case of A will also be a case of B in circumstances where the connection between the A and B factors is approximate but not exact. Statements in which reference is made to (this kind of) probability do not give as dependable and precise information as predictions that *every* case of A will be a case of B; they are nevertheless of great value, both in everyday affairs and in technology or science. In a great many situations where decisions have to be made concerning matters of fact, the evidence is insufficient to warrant the assertion of uniform connection between factors, and reasonable action requires an accurate assessment of "the probabilities." (For further details see Appendix 3.)

From here on, we shall refer to a generalization having the form *Every case of A is also a case of B* as a **uniform generalization.** A generalization having the form *Most (or such and such a proportion of) cases of A are also cases of B* will be called a **statistical generalization.**

In order to understand how statistical generalizations are supported, let us consider a simple example. Suppose we were required to show that *Half of the cats in Middletown are males.* Then the procedure to be adopted would be the sufficiently obvious one of determining the proportion of males in *sample collections* of Middletown cats. In a very favorable case we might find that of the first 100 cats for which we had data, 48 per cent were males, and the corresponding figures for the first 200, 300, 400, and 500 cats might be 48.5 per cent, 49 per cent, 49.95 per cent, and 49.8 per cent. If we had reason to believe that these sample collections were selected *at random,* we might have considerable confidence in our generalization. (In any actual statistical investigation, the figures would not support the conclusion so unambiguously: The correct interpretation of data obtained by sampling calls for statistical theory too complex to be considered here.)

This deliberately simplified illustration shows some features characteristic of all processes of supporting statistical generalizations:

1. As in the case of all inductive procedures, support of the hypothesis considered requires the collection of confirmatory instances. This is most

easily seen by recasting the illustrative generalization into the form *Every case of a-collection-of-Middletown-cats, (C) will also be a case of a-collection-of-cats-of-which-half-are-male(D)*. Each *collection* of cats examined is "a case of C" and each such collection exhibiting approximately equal numbers of males and females is a "confirmatory instance" of the C-D connection.

2. As usual in inductive procedures, there is a risk that the confirmatory instances examined will have been selected in some special way and so fail to be representative of *all* the instances. (If male cats were relatively hard to catch our data might be very misleading!)

3. None of the "sample collections" examined showed *exactly* the ratio of males to females asserted in the generalization under test. Our reason for claiming that 50 per cent of Middletown cats (rather than some other proportion) are males is that the ratios for the sample collections *show a tendency*. Our prediction is, accordingly, that as the groups of cats (selected at random) become larger, the ratio of males to the total will get (and will stay) indefinitely close to 50 per cent. Such a prediction is bound to be somewhat uncertain. Most statistical generalizations are subject to correction as further data accumulate.

We have mentioned only the simplest case of partial connection between factors. Equally important but more complex cases arise in practice, and will be found treated in textbooks of statistics under the title of "correlation." But this and the other technicalities of statistics are too advanced for consideration here.

Summary

The chapter is especially concerned with generalizations having a form other than *Every case of A is also a case of B*. In the *method of concomitant variations* a connection is established between *changes* in two factors. When changes of A are accompanied by changes in B, other factors being held unchanged, B is said to be a *function* of A. The method of concomitant variation can be regarded as a refinement of the method of difference. It is subject to the risks of the other inductive methods studied, especially that of overlooking variations in neglected factors.

A functional connection between two factors is made more explicit by indicating the range in which it holds; it is made more precise by assigning numbers to the various degrees of A and B and discovering exact numerical laws relating these two sets of numbers.

In *argument from analogy* two things having some properties in common are claimed to have further common properties. There is involved a *basis of resemblance* between the things compared (the sum-total of the known common properties) and a *linking generalization* (a presumed general connection between the observed and the inferred common properties). The strength of an argument from analogy depends on the strength of the *independent* evidence available for the linking generalization.

The term "cause" (and its correlate "effect") is ambiguous in common usage, meaning according to circumstances either a necessary or sufficient condition, near or remote in space and time, sometimes but not always subject to human control. References to the causes of phenomena involve generalizations and can be tested inductively.

Generalizations having the form *Most (or such and such a proportion of) cases of A are also cases of B* are called *statistical generalizations.* When a statistical generalization connects A and B, it is said to be *probable* that a given case of A is also a case of B. Statistical generalizations are supported, in part, by examining sample collections. Each sample collection is, in favorable circumstances, a confirmatory instance of the statistical generalization when the ratio of A's to the total in the sample *approximates* to that asserted as holding by the generalization. The generalization is said to be established if the ratios exhibited in the samples "show a tendency" to approach the value asserted in the generalization. Since confirmation of a tendency is approximate at best, statistical generalizations are subject to correction as further data accumulate. In testing statistical generalizations special care is required to avoid biased sampling.

Comprehension test

(For instructions, see page 10.)

1. The method of concomitant variations is especially suitable for cases where the irrelevant factors cannot be entirely removed. (*true* *false*)
2. The method of concomitant variations is used for finding functional connections. (*true* *false*)
3. If A remains constant when B varies (while other factors are held constant) A is not a function of B. (*true* *false*)
4. An argument from analogy is sound only when the objects compared are alike in all respects. (*true* *false*)
5. The "basis of resemblance" can include *unknown* common properties. (*true* *false*)
6. When A is a necessary cause of B, B cannot occur unless A occurs. (*true* *false*)
7. If A is a sufficient condition for B, B must be a sufficient condition for A. (*true* *false*)
8. A single case of B following A is never enough to prove that A is a cause of B. (*true* *false*)
9. Assertions about causes are supported by induction. (*true* *false*)
10. A uniform generalization is a special case of a statistical generalization. (*true* *false*)

Exercises

A

1. Pick out pairs of factors in the following list that are "functionally connected":
   color, weight, height above sea-level, density, temperature, volume, chemical composition, shape.
2. If B is a function of A, changes in A will produce changes in B provided other factors are held constant. In each case of functional connection mentioned by you in answer to the previous question, name some of the "other factors" that must be "held constant."
3. There follows a list of possible connections between factors that might be tested inductively. To which of these inquiries would the method of concomitant variations be appropriate? (*Give reasons.*)
   a. Incidence of cancer and smoking habits.

b. Presence of "Northern Lights" in the sky and simultaneous occurrence of low temperatures.
c. Foreign origin and unemployment.
d. High incomes and low birth rate.
e. Length of life and dwelling-place (*i.e.,* rural or urban).
f. Sex and weight.

4. State generalizations to be tested in the inquiries listed in the previous question in a form that is as "explicit" and "precise" as you can achieve.
5. In each of the following arguments from analogy, state the "basis of resemblance" and the "linking generalization."
   a. "A country can no more live without foreign trade than a dog can live by eating his own tail."
   b. "Reasoning, like breathing, is something all men do well."
   c. "Like all previous democracies, this nation is headed for tyranny and dictatorship."
   d. "If you saw a clock you would infer the existence of a clockmaker. The human body is a machine even more intricate than the best watch ever made. It must have been designed by some Master Craftsman."
   e. "We know that our own movements are always accompanied by consciousness. It is hard to believe that some degree of consciousness does not accompany the movements of animals."
   f. "These two cars came off the assembly line the same day. They were made to the same specifications. I guarantee that their performances will be identical."
   g. "You wouldn't trust someone else to choose what milk you shall drink. Yet you allow the federal government to determine what food shall be available in the stores."
   h. "Everybody knows that the post office is inefficient. There is every reason, therefore, to expect the same of a federal medical service."
   i. "Look at your fingers and think of your throat!" (From an advertisement for cigarettes.)
   j. "After the First World War we got Hitler. After the Second World War we got Stalin. What can we hope from another war, except disaster?"
   k. "Since men are unequal in weight, height, intelligence, health, strength, and everything else, they certainly cannot deserve equality of economic opportunity."
   l. "Hit the ball with a one-string tennis racket? Might as well try to make truly great beer from just a single brewing" (from an advertisement).
6. Criticize the arguments just quoted.

7. Collect examples of fallacious analogies from advertisements.
8. Show some of the differences in meaning in the words and phrases italicized in the following:

   (Use the terms *necessary, sufficient, near, remote, permanent,* and *differentiating cause.*)

   a. Poverty *causes* war.
   b. Wars are *caused* by some act of aggression.
   c. The existence of armaments is a *cause* of war.
   d. One *cause* of war is the willingness of soldiers to obey orders.
   e. The attack on Pearl Harbor was *the cause* of our war against Japan.
   f. "No war really happens until the fighting begins. The *real cause* of war is the fighting."
   g. "Human nature is the *final cause* of war. If men had more intelligence they would not go to war."
9. Is it possible that all seven statements listed in the last question should be true? What light does your answer throw on the procedures that ought to be adopted in determining the causes of war?

B

1. People who believe that "black cats are lucky" are making a mistake about the causes of certain events. Describe two other superstitions with which you are familiar. How would you show that mistakes about causes were involved? How well does your account agree with what was said about causes in the chapter?
2. Use the definition of "function" to decide the truth of the following assertions:
   a. If two factors, A and B, are given, either A is a function of B or B is a function of A.
   b. If B is a function of A, and C is a function of A, B is a function of C.
   c. If B is a function of A, A is a function of B.
   d. If A is a function of B, and B is a function of C, A is a function of C.
3. Compare the discussion of metaphor in Chapter 10 with the discussion of analogy in the present chapter. Point out the respects in which the two discussions agree and differ.
4. Find five instances where arguments by analogy have been used (other than as illustrations) in the course of this book. Were these arguments sound?
5. How far does the discussion of analogy in this chapter apply also to "logical analogies" (page 43)?

6. It has been proposed by some writers to forego the use of the word "cause" altogether (on the ground of its vagueness and ambiguity). Would this proposal be feasible? (Consider some of its consequences in detail.)
7. "What is the use of knowing that four out of five people are cured by taking this drug? *I* want to be cured—I don't care about other people." *Discuss.*
8. Outline an essay to be entitled "Probability is the Guide of Life."

17

SCIENTIFIC METHOD

"There is no more difference, but there is just the same kind of difference, between the mental operations of a man of science and those of an ordinary person, as there is between the operations and methods of a baker or a butcher weighing out his goods in common scales, and the operations of a chemist in performing a difficult and complex analysis by means of his balance and finely-graduated weights. It is not that the action of the scales in the one case, and the balance in the other, differ in the principles of their construction or manner of working; but the beam of the one is set on an infinitely finer axis than the other, and of course turns by the addition of a much smaller weight."—T. H. Huxley.

1. Introduction.

THOUGHTFUL men have long realized that the decisive respect in which contemporary societies differ from earlier civilizations is in changes due to mastery and application of science. Men alive today are not noticeably more gifted in intelligence, moral insight, or artistic imagination, than the Athenians. Yet hardly more than a hundred years of intense scientific activity has given modern man almost godlike powers to remake the very stuff of the universe itself. The invention of the atomic bomb was hardly needed to demonstrate that understanding and control of science are cardinal conditions for survival of civilization, and understanding is a necessary preliminary to control.

Hundreds of books and many thousands of pages have been written about scientific method, and it might be supposed that the nature of the scientific activity would by this time be generally agreed upon. Yet, in spite of renewed efforts at clarification (often brilliant in their insight) on the part of distinguished scientists and philosophers, universal agreement concerning the nature of scientific method is still lacking. In some important respects, the subject on which we are now embarking remains controversial.

There are several reasons for this lack of agreement concerning the nature of scientific method.

(1) The ever-increasing complexity of science makes it hard to perceive clearly the *general* features of the entire scientific enterprise. This is the ancient and proverbial difficulty of "seeing the wood for the trees." The practicing scientist, who is a specialist in some subdivision of the enormous range of collective human knowledge, is often too absorbed in his specialty to be a safe guide to questions concerning the *general* features of scientific investigation. The man who has exceptionally detailed information concerning entomology, organic chemistry, or topology, is not necessarily aware of any pattern of investigation common to all scientific subjects.

(2) In the last paragraphs we have talked of "scientific method" in the singular, as if it could be safely assumed that all scientific inquiry shows a *single* pattern of investigation. The assumption is partly justified, and scientific inquiries, as we shall see, do show many interesting and uniform common features. Yet sciences also *differ* significantly among each other, and the variety of scientific methods is no less important than the unity of scientific method as a whole.

(3) It is a matter of historical record that the sophisticated scientific techniques in use today have evolved from simpler procedures at the "common-sense level." Physics and chemistry arose from the practical concerns of mining, pottery, medicine, and other crafts, and are still largely directed to the improvement of technology. This would hardly concern us here, but for the fact that the earlier and cruder methods of "common sense" are still in everyday use, side by side with other methods showing scarcely a trace of their humble origins.

Only a small part of science requires the manipulation of machines as elaborate as the cyclotron (or "atom-smasher"). The spectacular "miracles" of scientific experimentation are made possible by an enormous mass of prosaic, even routine, observations.

This continuity of scientific method with common-sense procedures makes all accurate description of scientific method necessarily an affair of differences of degree. We should not expect to find scientists constantly using some entirely new and "revolutionary" methods; there will be sufficient cause for wonder and admiration in noting the remarkable results emerging from the elaboration of methods already used in rough form at the familiar common-sense level.

Plan to be followed. Studies of scientific method are usually presented deductively, so that the writer states conclusions concerning the general features of scientific inquiry before deducing consequences that are supported by illustrations from actual scientific investigations. We have chosen instead to *begin* with examples of genuine scientific method, in the hope that the reader will try to determine inductively some of the significant features manifested. (There is no good substitute for such intelligent criticism of specimens of scientific method.) In succeeding chapters, we proceed to a more formal analysis of the main features of scientific method displayed.

The examples have been carefully chosen to conform to the following specifications: (1) They are genuine reports of the scientists, expressed in their own words; (2) they are sufficiently non-technical to be intelligible with a minimum of explanatory comment; (3) they are arranged to show a rough progression from "common sense" to more technical procedures.

2. *Specimens of scientific method.*

Suggestions for the reader. Before reading the comment supplied, the reader is advised to adopt the following procedure:

1. Read the account several times, using the "glossary of terms" supplied at the end of each harder passage as an aid to understanding any unfamiliar technical terms.
2. Determine the *data* of the investigation.
3. List any hypothesis and subsidiary assumptions you can detect.
4. Determine what use is made of methods previously studied (*e.g.*, the method of difference).
5. Describe the character of any *new* methods noticed.
6. Make a note of any features of the investigation that appeal to you as having especial significance.

Anybody with the patience to follow these suggestions should be in an excellent position to profit from the comments supplied in this and the later chapters.

The specimens.

A. *The formation of moss peat beneath translucent pebbles in semi-arid regions of the great plains.* "On a field trip . . . in the semi-arid Northern Great Plains, in western South Dakota, in May 1941, it was observed that a growth of moss and algae and an accumulation of moss peat, varying from a thin film to about one-fourth inch in thickness occur beneath translucent quartz and chalcedony pebbles and small stones which are embedded in the surface of well-drained soils. Such an accumulation was not found beneath opaque pebbles and stones. The discovery provides further evidence that stone fragments on the surface of the soil help to conserve moisture by checking evaporation.

"We made a general study of the area in the vicinity where the peat phenomenon was first observed in order to confirm my first impression that the peat occurs only beneath pebbles that freely transmit light. . . . During the past year observations of the phenomenon have been extended, by the writer and others, to much of the Northern Great Plains.

"The first requisite for the growth of moss and the formation of peat, as already indicated, is the presence of translucent pebbles. These must be in firm contact with, and slightly embedded in, the soil and their surfaces must be exposed to sunlight. Short-grass cover of thin stands of grass in semi-arid regions apparently furnish the most favorable habitat for the growth of mosses and the development of peat. The phenomena gradually become less noticeable, under natural conditions, in passing into arid regions on the one hand and into subhumid and humid regions on the other. In arid regions, because of the lack of sufficient moisture to support peat-producing plants, algae replace mosses. . . . Further study of the occurrence and the distribution of peat beneath pebbles and the plants contributing to its formation is indicated. Specific names for the plants have not yet been determined.

"The term 'pebble peat' is suggested for the phenomenon described. As yet no mention of the phenomenon has been found in the literature." (B. H. Williams in *Science,* Vol. 97, pp. 441-2, 1943.)

Comment: This is a good illustration of conclusions reached by reasoning from direct observations, performed at a level very close to "common sense." Most of the features emphasized in Chapters 14 and 15 are illustrated in this extract.

There is first the recognition of an unusual or unexpected circumstance (the presence of moss underneath pebbles in a very dry area) as constituting a problem. The problem thereby arising for solution is not technical, for the previous knowledge in the light of which the problem is first perceived (that moss does not grow in semi-arid regions) is such as any ordinary person might be expected to have picked up without special training. If the quoted report of the problematic situation differs at all from that which might be made by any casual tourist, it is in the care taken to describe the circumstances with precision. (We note, for instance, careful mention of both moss and algae, the reference to "well-drained" soil, and the indications given of the thickness of the layer of moss.)

The problematic situation (occurrence of peat) suggests the hypothesis that the peat occurs "only beneath pebbles that freely transmit light." This hypothesis fits the standard form adopted for a generalization ("Every case of A is also a case of B"—see p. 281) with *occurrence of peat,* and *occurrence of pebbles that freely transmit light* as the A- and B- factors respectively. The evidence consisted of instances in which cases of peat formation were invariably found to be cases of *translucent* pebbles, and of instances showing that opaque pebbles did not have the moss formation. Thus, typical instances had the form '$A_1 \rightarrow B_1$ & C_1 & D_1 & . . . ' or '$B'_2 \rightarrow A'_2$ & K_2 & L_2 & . . . ' The generalization is supported by the method of agreement.

Where common sense might be content to rest at this stage of the inquiry, it is interesting to notice how the scientist proceeds to *further analysis* of the factors involved. Repeated observations, first in the neighborhood of the original discovery and later in an ever-expanding area, show that other factors beside translucence are involved. The pebbles must be "in firm contact with the soil," "slightly embedded in it," and "exposed to sunlight." Thus, more careful analysis (presumably using the method of difference) shows that the first hypothesis should be replaced by a more exact one.

Finally, we notice, in the last part of the extract, indications of the use of the method of concomitant variation and a gradual transition, quite typical of scientific investigation, toward a quantitative law. (The object of later investigation might properly be to determine *how much* peat is produced in various conditions of humidity or aridity.)

In summary, we can say that this specimen of scientific investigation illustrates very well what we have described as the "pattern of common-sense investigation"—the main differences observable being the care taken to obtain exact descriptions of the phenomena investigated and to push the inductive inquiries in support of the explanatory hypothesis to a point where the first crude impressions are replaced by a more accurate hypothesis.

B. *The Red and Green Lights of the "Railroad Worm."* "A few luminous animals are known which emit light of two different colors. One of the most striking of these is the South American railroad worm or 'ferrocarril,' of the genus Phryxothrix. . . . The adult female, nearly two inches long, is larviform, with eleven pairs of brilliant, greenish-yellow luminescent spots on the sides of the body and a red luminous area in the head. The larvae of both male and female also possess similar luminescent spots. . . .

"I have recently received from Uruguay several living specimens of Phryxothrix in excellent condition. One was an adult female and the others probably larvae. They showed no light when at rest but if disturbed very slightly, by knocking the table gently or blowing air over them, they responded by shining the red light. When the disturbance was greater, the rows of greenish lights also appeared and the animal explored its environment with a brilliant display of pyrotechnics. The red light on the head resembled the tip of a glowing cigarette. Sometimes all and sometimes only certain of the greenish lights would be turned on. Later the greenish lights went out while the red remained on for some time, finally to disappear as the animal became quiet again.

"With these specimens it has been possible to determine the nature of the red luminescence. There are three ways in which a red light might be produced: (1) By emission of red wave-lengths, a red chemi-luminescence; (2) by the presence of a red color screen transmitting red but absorbing other wave lengths; (3) by red fluorescence of a compound, excited by shorter wave lengths emitted by some chemiluminescent reaction. The first method is the one used in producing the red light, as indicated by the following experiments.

"If the red luminescent material is dissected out of the head of Phryxothrix and examined on a slide in daylight, no red pigment can be detected. The tissue appears colorless and the easily visible (in the dark) red luminescence could not be due to a red color screen or to absorption by the chitin of the head which is a light brown in color. When hydrogen or nitrogen gas is passed over the excised red luminescent tissue in the dark, the red light disappears, and if the potentially luminous substance is now exposed to near ultra-violet light without the visible (from a mercury arc filtered through Wood's nickel glass), no red fluorescence can be detected. Since this near ultra-violet light is especially active in exciting fluorescence of a wide variety of organic compounds, we can conclude that the red luminescence is not a fluorescence.

"When oxygen is re-admitted to the luminous organ, the red luminescence re-appears, indicating that the red light is a red oxidative chemiluminescence comparable to that resulting from oxidation of Mg and Zn complexes of certain porphyrins, phthalocyanines and chlorophyll derivatives, as described by a number of investigators.... It is futile to speculate concerning the nature of the luminous substance responsible for the red and green luminescences in the same animal. Indeed, the mechanism of luminescence in the fireflies and related insects needs further investigation." (E. Newton Harvey in *Science,* Vol. 99, pages 283-4, 1944.)

Explanation of some of the terms used in the above: "larva"—the first form of an insect (as grub, maggot, or caterpillar); *"luminescence"*—sending forth of light; *"pyrotechnics"*—fireworks; *"chemiluminescence"*—luminescence due to chemical action between substances; *"fluorescence"*—luminescence produced in certain substances when they are exposed to invisible radiations such as ultra-violet rays or X rays; *"chitin"*—the chief constitutent in the outer covering of an insect: *"ultra-violet light"*—invisible radiation having wave length lower than that of just-visible violet light;

"oxidative"—involving combination with oxygen; *"Mg and Zn complexes of certain porphyrins, phthalocyanines and chlorophyll derivatives"*—certain complex pigments containing magnesium or zinc.

Comment: The first observations on the beetle's reactions to slight disturbances are at the same level of common-sense obviousness as in the previous example. Nor does the formulation of three hypotheses and the elimination of two of them by subsequent experiment offer any new features. What makes us feel that this specimen is more "scientific" than the last is the more technical character of the hypotheses advanced and the experiments used in testing them. The use of such words as "chemiluminescence," "fluorescence," and others not belonging to the vocabulary of common sense indicates greater reliance on *specialized* previous knowledge. The choice of the three hypotheses considered is sound only in the light of much knowledge already obtained by other scientists concerning the absorption and emission of light. A similar use of elaborate knowledge concerning physical and chemical phenomena is shown in the test used to eliminate the hypothesis of fluorescence, and in the final reference to the known behavior of certain zinc and magnesium pigments.

In summary, this specimen shows the now-familiar pattern of the use and elimination of explanatory hypotheses, modified by extensive reliance on previously established generalizations, of which one sign is the increased use of technical vocabulary.

C. *Rotation of Electrolyte Between Insulated Poles of Magnet.* "F. Ehrenhaft has described an experiment in which a drop of $FeCl_3$ rotates between the poles of a permanent magnet from which it is electrically and chemically insulated by a coat of Picein Wax.... By reproducing exactly F. Ehrenhaft's experimental set-up, the rotations were obtained at the Sloane Physics Laboratory. The waxed pole faces were 1.5 mm. apart. Light from a carbon arc was sharply focused on the center of a drop of $FeCl_3$ with the help of two lenses, the second of which was a microscope of objective focal length less than 2 cm. The drop was observed with a microscope. The insulation was checked electrically.

"By observing the drop with the naked eye it was found that the motion was not a true rotation. The liquid moves both to the right and to the left in a horizontal plane, and definite up and down motions also take place in the drop. The experiment was repeated with thin glass plates insulating the drop from contact with the metal of the pole pieces, and $CuSO_4$ and $CuNO_3$ were used, as well as $FeCl_3$. The same type of motion was observed in each case. When the magnet was turned upside down, thus changing the direction of the magnetic field, the motion was observed in the same direction. To test decisively the role of the magnetic field, the magnet was replaced by a replica constructed out of brass. Drops of $FeCl_3$, $CuSO_4$, and $CuNO_3$ were found to "rotate" to the same extent as before, both between layers of Picein Wax and between glass plates.

"Further experiments with the Picein-covered permanent magnet showed that there was a very definite acceleration as the light beam was first put on. Progressively dimming the illumination considerably slowed down the motion of the drop. Illuminating the drop from the opposite side definitely changed the direction of motion. The red and infra-red radiation was then filtered out by a 2 cm. layer of a solution known to pass about 25 per cent of the visible light. The motion stopped completely within 40 seconds and started again as soon as the filter was removed. When the total intensity of the beam was reduced to 25 per cent, by halving the diameter of a variable diaphragm, the motion slowed down, but did not stop.

"From the above results, we can conclude (a) that a magnetic field is not necessary for the production of this particular "rotation," (b) that this effect is due to the heat radiation of the illuminating light which causes convection currents in the drop (the center being maintained at a higher temperature than the lateral surface, at which evaporation takes place). No inferences should be drawn from these conclusions as to any other kind of rotation, either in liquids or gases. Further experimental work on these will be published later." (Thomas A. Perls in *Science,* Vol. 102, pages 45-6, 1945.)

Explanation of terms: electrolyte—a chemical compound that can be decomposed by an electric current; *"$FeCl_3$"*—Ferric chloride, a compound of iron and chlorine; *"Picein Wax"*—an adhesive substance used in physical experimentation for combining pieces of apparatus, also neutral to most chemical and electrical reactions; *"$CuSO_4$"*—copper sulphate, a compound of copper, sulphur and oxygen; *"$CuNO_3$"*—copper nitrate, a compound of copper, nitrogen and oxygen; *"infra-red radiation"*—invisible radiation having wave length longer than that of just visible red light; *"convection currents"*—motion of a fluid from the hotter to the colder part of the space in which it is confined.

Comment: The layman can appreciate that the experiment here reported is a beautiful example of scientific method, but he can hardly be expected to know its full significance. The exiled Austrian physicist, Felix Ehrenhaft (formerly of the University of Vienna), claimed to have discovered a number of phenomena supporting the generalization that "not only electric currents but also magnetic currents flow through the universe." It has long been known that an electrical current creates magnetic forces (the principle used in the electro-magnet and the electric motor). Professor Ehrenhaft's theory was that magnetism, no less than electricity, can act as a current and thereby exert a force on a droplet of a solution of ferric chloride (or other small portions of liquids that normally carry a charge of electricity). This theory, however, runs counter to some of the most fundamental and well-established of physical principles (the so-called *Maxwell's equations*). The claim therefore is of the utmost importance, since it would, if sustained, lead to a revolution in the basic notions and theories of physics.

Returning now to our scientific report, we notice first, but quite briefly, the familiar use of inductive methods. Particularly noteworthy in this connection is the substitution of a brass replica for the magnet (a striking instance of the use of the method of difference) and the series of observations showing concomitant variations between the application of light, which produces heat radiation, and the "rotation" of the droplet.

With this example, we have definitely passed out of the ken of "common sense" into a realm where the observations and methods of solution all call for a high degree of specialized knowledge. The "problematic situation" is itself a highly artificial one: The phenomenon of the rotating droplet is not observable except to a scientist who takes very exact measures to ensure its occurrence (and note in this connection the minute instructions to ensure that other scientists can repeat the experiment), and also its correct interpretation involves the use of a mass of knowledge previously required. A partial list of the well-attested generalizations to which appeal is made in the course of the experiment described would include those referring to the electrical properties of ferric chloride ($FeCl_3$), copper sulphate ($CuSO_4$), and copper nitrate ($CuNO_3$), the known electrical properties of many substances (especially those of the insulating wax used), the heat effects of light (and the differences in heat radiation between light of high and low frequency), and the phenomena connected with the "convection" of fluids.

D. *The Sun's Radiation and the Weather.* "Weather changes on earth may be indirectly controlled by changes in the sun's radiation, through variations in the thickness of the radio-wave-reflecting E layer of the earth's outer atmosphere. A close correlation between thickness changes in this layer and shifts in the weather has been found by Dr. Charles G. Abbot, research associate of the Smithsonian Institution, in a study of records extending over seven years.

"Dr. Abbot has for many years followed the apparent connection between the weather and the solar constant, or total radiant energy received from the sun, as recorded daily at Smithsonian observatories in California, New Mexico and Chile. Changes in the solar constant are small and difficult to measure at best—impossible under bad weather conditions. 'E' layer thickness variations, on the other hand, are easier to measure and observations are not affected by weather. These thickness variations are also measured daily, by observers of the Carnegie Institution of Washington; the best records are those kept by the Carnegie stations in Huancayo, Peru, and Watheroo, Australia.

" 'It is clear,' according to Dr. Abbot, 'that the sun's variations are a major factor in weather. The effects produced are large. In Washington temperatures it makes nearly 20 degrees Fahrenheit of difference in some months whether the solar constant rose or fell by three-fourths of one per cent a week or more previously. The effects are long continuing. They appear to begin three days before measurable changes in radiation occur, and to last at least until fourteen days after, making an important sequence of at least 17 days in weather, attending each change of solar radiation.'

" 'It appears that approximate predictions a week in advance could be made of dates of peaks and troughs of Washington temperature if daily reports of the E layer were obtained from a sufficient number of ionization stations, and if means could be found to anticipate by a few days closely the date of the next approaching solar change. Its sign would always be known to be opposite to that last observed. From present records we should expect solar changes of the same sign to follow each other at intervals of about nine days, with changes of opposite sign intervening. There is, I think, a fair hope that such important dates as heavy frosts may become predictable a week in advance from solar observations by this method.'" (*Science*, Vol. 102, page 112, November 16, 1945.)

Comment: The extract provides a good illustration of the method of "concomitant variations." Fluctuations in the thickness of the "E-layer" are found to be connected with marked weather changes. We notice the importance of attaching numerical estimates to the time intervals involved in order to make accurate prediction possible. This may be regarded as a very simple type of *measurement*.

E. *Experimental Research on Cancer.* The control of cancer is one of the great unsolved problems of contemporary science. The report on work in progress chosen for analysis here shows well the manner in which the general problem becomes broken down into precise and specific questions capable of scientific investigation.

"When cells become cancerous they undergo a transformation, said to be malignant, because thereafter they and their descendants behave like criminals unrestrained by the controls which shape the behavior of their normal neighbors. We know that a great many agents, called carcinogens, can produce this change and further that there is a long interval, usually amounting to several years, between their initial action and their final transformation.... Long before the actual expression of malignant behavior by the cells, it is often possible to demonstrate that these have changed and are, therefore, far from normal.

"The designation 'precancerous lesion' is applied to a type of structural change in a tissue in which clinical experience shows that the cells are more likely to become malignant than in other kinds of lesions."

There follows a description of different types of such lesions and reference to the difficulty of localizing cells particularly subject to malignant transformations.

"When clinicians are confronted with lesions of a precancerous type, they seldom know what caused them and they can not evaluate all the possibly modifying factors which have participated through the years in their development and persistence. It is high time that the problem be brought into the laboratory, where the precancerous type of lesion can be produced at will by a standardized technique in experimental animals and its evolution can be followed in a few weeks time. Indeed the main research project in the Barnard Hospital is analysis of the biological equation:

Chemically pure carcinogen (methylcholanthrene) + epidermis (an avascular tissue composed of cells of a single type) of closely inbred strain of mice = squamous cell carcinoma in a very high percentage of animals.

"This analysis is limited to the properties of epidermis that can be quantitatively determined. Our purpose is integrative, to discover whether the properties increase, decrease, or remain constant; and, when there is a change in a property, whether it is paralleled by alterations in other properties. It is, of course, not feasible to investigate many properties in one and the same group of mice. Nevertheless, by standardizing the equation through elimination of the principal variables, the observations made on properties in different lots of mice can in a sense be superimposed....

"By fluorescence microscopy and spectrography the carcinogen has been followed into the skin, where it soon disappears as such. Other fluorescent compounds make their appearance. To unravel them is quite a task. But a glimpse has been obtained of the conditions, somehow established in the epidermis by the carcinogen, which antedate the expression of malignant behavior by the altered cells. These include a new chemical equilibrium, the discovery of which was made possible by devising a method for the removal of epidermis from dermis in a state suitable for chemical analysis and by adapting polarographic and other techniques to epidermis. As has been reported in various papers, this equilibrium is characterized by marked decreases from the normal in calcium, iron, and lipid; while sodium, potassium, magnesium, and ascorbic acid show no noteworthy changes."

There follows a description of other quantitative changes produced, and a summary of some of the numerical relations discovered.

"But *where* and *when* the transformation occurs eludes us ... experience has shown that to obtain worthwhile data the analyses must be limited to very small young tumors in which necrotic material is not a complicating factor.... In our experimental material we set the stage by arranging for the same carcinogen to act to the same degree on the same tissue of mice of the same closely inbred strain for selected lengths of time."

Suggestions are added for limited applications of related techniques to cancerous tissue found in man. "These measurements ... may be considered as work on the first or lowest level in this project, for we are building constructively. Obviously such studies are limited merely by the number of properties that can be investigated quantitatively, and the more included the more valuable their integration becomes. Work on the second level ... is intended not to discover more facts, but, on the basis of the facts observed on the first level, to organize and carry out experiments designed to prevent the malignant change from taking place in tissue sufficiently exposed to the carcinogen otherwise to produce cancer.... While the first level obviously is fact-finding, the second is therefore one of purposeful control.

"On the third level comes more fact-finding investigation now of the chemical equilibrium of the resulting cancer and of all other possibly significant properties. . . . And on the fourth or highest level, are purposeful efforts based on knowledge of the equilibrium in the cancer to disturb it and cure the cancer, and also to determine the specific vulnerability of the cancer cells by bringing to bear on them influences of wide variety, for again an unexpected agent may prove to be the most effective. To concentrate on the first and third levels requires restraint bolstered by the belief that so doing will pay in the long run." (E. V. Cowdray in *Science,* Vol. 102, pp. 165-8, 1945.)

Explanation of terms: "lesion"—wound, injury, diseased area or area of local degeneration; *"epidermis"*—the outer skin; *"carcinogen"*—cancer-producing agent; *"avascular tissue"*—non-vascular tissue, *i.e.,* tissue not contained in blood, lymph, and related body fluids; *"inbred strain"*—a group of animals produced by mating closely related individuals; *"squamous"*—scaly (applied to epidermis); *"carcinoma"*—cancer; *"spectrography"*—photography of spectra (colored bands of light produced by passing light through a prism or other dispersing agency); *"dermis"*—a layer of skin; *"polarographic"*—relating to photography using polarized light; *"lipid"*—any of a group of substances including fats and other substances of analogous properties; *"necrotic material"*—dead tissue.

Comment: The chief points to be noticed here, in addition to those made previously in discussing the other specimens of scientific method are these:

(a) Still further progress has been made in analyzing an initial problem into a form favorable to experimental investigation. The general problem toward which the research is directed is understanding and control of the phenomenon known as cancer. The actual program of research here described is actually directed toward a more highly definite and even, to the lay mind, somewhat "theoretical" problem, viz., the study of the biological and chemical properties of an artificially induced condition similar to that encountered in humans before the onset of cancer. And this study is not made in human beings, or in animals closely related to humans, but rather in a specially bred strain of mice. The *indirectness* of this approach is characteristic. (The last part of the extract should be read with special care for the light it throws upon the relation between "pure research" and practical applications.)

(b) This example shows more clearly what was already implicit in the other specimens—the *co-operative* character of scientific method. Our extract from the original article has omitted the detailed references to the many investigators (22 mentioned by name) to whose joint labors the results described are due. In any case, the reader will have noticed the significance of the reference to "standardizing the equation through elimination of the principal variables" so that "the observations made on properties in different lots of mice can in a sense be superimposed." What this means is that the great care taken to render uniform the breed of mice used, the kind of skin to which the irritating agent was applied, and the nature of that agent itself —in short "standardizing" the conditions in which various experiments were performed—made it possible for the investigators to work independently and yet to produce results that were directly relevant to the work of the others in the research team. The kind of co-operation here illustrated is important positively in enabling a group of men working together to achieve results that would be beyond the reach of any of them as isolated individuals. It has also a great negative importance in that it permits any suitably qualified and trained observer to repeat the results, and so to check their accuracy. This *availability of results for verification by other scientists* is one of the most important aspects of scientific method. A glance at almost any scientific journal will show the care taken by scientists to see that their results are made publicly available in this way.

F. *The White Dwarfs.* We choose, as our final and most complex specimen of scientific method, a recent report on some of the most spectacular work that has ever been achieved in astronomy. This lengthy extract (from an article by Professor W. J. Luyten) is harder to follow than those already used, but it will repay the effort of attention:

"The discovery by Adams in 1915 that the faint companion to Sirius, the brightest star in the sky, was *white* caused a minor revolution in astronomical and physical thinking. In a sense this faint star had been discovered before it had been seen, for its existence had been proved by Auwers from the gravitational effect it produced in the motion of Sirius itself. By 1915 the orbits in which Sirius and this faint companion revolved around their center of mass were accurately known; likewise we knew the distance of the system from us, and thus from the apparent brightness could calculate the real, intrinsic luminosity. In this way it was found that the companion had a mass only slightly less than that of the sun, but a luminosity 400 times smaller. Taken by themselves neither of these figures appeared out of ordinary, but when Adams found that the star was much whiter than the sun, with a surface temperature of some 8,000° K, the situation took on an entirely different aspect. From the temperature we could calculate the surface brightness and found that the star gave out about three times as much light as the sun does per square inch and since the total luminosity is 400 times smaller than that of the sun, it follows that the surface of this faint companion must be 1,200 times smaller than that of the sun, and hence its volume 42,000 times smaller, or smaller than that of the planet Uranus. Yet in this space is concentrated virtually as much matter as there is in the sun, leading to a density 50,000 times that of water.

"At first sight it was unbelievable, and it appeared that an impasse had been reached.... The answer to the riddle came a few years later when Eddington showed that these stars are largely composed of or contain central cores of "degenerate matter" raised to such a high temperature that not merely the outer shells of electrons have been removed by ionization, but that in many cases all electrons have been stripped off and the atoms are reduced to their bare nuclei. In the words of Oliver Lodge, under ordinary circumstances when the atomic nuclei are surrounded by shell after shell of fast-moving electrons, matter can be compared to flies buzzing in a cathedral. But when the temperature is raised to several hundred million degrees the electrons become ionized away—the cathedral walls collapse and all there is left are the flies. And, naturally, one can pack a good many more flies than cathedrals in a cubic mile....

"Right at the beginning came Eddington's startling prediction that, because of the high density and the consequent high value of surface gravity of these stars, the light rays leaving their surface should, if Einstein's relativity is correct, be slowed down in their vibrations. Thus spectral lines produced by any given chemical element should be shifted toward the red as compared to the same lines produced by sources on the earth. The verification of this prediction at Mt. Wilson by observations on the companion of Sirius killed two birds with one stone, since it not only proved that Eddington's picture of the structure of the white dwarfs was correct but also that Einstein was right....

"In the course of this survey," [further experimental work undertaken by the scientist reporting] "some 30 million stars were examined, and from among them some 100,000 were selected because of a conspicuous displacement across the sky, a 'proper motion.' This, of course, is an angular displacement, and, other things being equal, a swift angular displacement must mean that the star in question is comparatively near, and a star which is both near and very faint in appearance must be a star of low luminosity. After this first screening test, the search was narrowed down still further by selecting from among the 100,000 stars with appreciable motion, the 3,000 stars of *largest* angular motion. These 3,000 stars constitute the most likely selection of really intrinsically faint stars from among the entire 30,000,000. Finally, it is evident also that since white dwarfs are to be found among stars of low luminosity this final list of 3,000 faint stars with large proper motion constituted by far the richest potential sources of white dwarfs.

"It was to be expected that the vast majority of them would be ordinary red dwarfs with a surface temperature around 3,000° K and the problem was to find those that were not red but white. To distinguish between the two kinds, it would be necessary only to compare two photographs, one taken in blue light, the other through a red filter: as compared with the average of the other stars shown on the plates the red dwarfs would be much brighter on the red plates, the white dwarfs much brighter on the blue plates." [The writer goes on to mention other methods which have been elaborated for the discovery of white dwarfs, and describes some of the properties of the 70 white dwarfs known to exist at the time the report was made.] (W. J. Luyten in *Science,* Vol. 101, pp. 79-81, January 26, 1945.)

Comment: In this specimen we see scientific method in its most highly developed form. The following points deserve special notice: (a) the use of prediction as a test of theory, (b) the use of theory to explain puzzling observations, (c) the use of observation *directed* by theory.

3. Omissions from the survey of scientific method.

Six specimens of scientific method can hardly be expected to give comprehensive and accurate insight into the nature of scientific method.

We therefore record here certain features of scientific method which have been omitted or underplayed in our specimens:

1. Our accounts give little indication of what is involved in scientific *discovery:* the emphasis is, as usual in technical papers, on the clear description of the *results* of inquiry. We should, however, be interested in knowing also how the scientists whose work we have been examining discovered their fruitful ideas.

2. There is too little in these accounts of the "feel and smell of the laboratory"—of the attitudes and practices that a young scientist learns by imitation and contact.

3. Little has been said about the principles of scientific measurement.

4. No examples have been given in which statistical methods are used.

5. And in general, little evidence has been given of the increasingly important part played in the sciences by theories capable of mathematical formulation.

6. No specimens have been supplied of research in the so-called "social sciences," of economics, psychology, sociology, etc.

Summary

The importance of science in contemporary society makes understanding of scientific method imperative. Among the obstacles to such understanding are: the complexity of contemporary science, the variety of procedures used by science, the continuity between scientific and "common-sense" procedures. Six specimens of scientific method arranged in order of roughly increasing complexity are presented in the chapter.

The inquiry into *the formation of peat on pebbles in semi-arid regions* was found to differ from "common-sense inquiry" chiefly in the particular care taken to make exact observations; the central generalization required little imaginative effort and was confirmed by routine use of the method of agreement. In the case of *the "rail-road worm,"* by contrast, extensive use was made of authoritative theory concerning the various ways in which luminescence could be produced. Simple experiments, in conjunction with relatively superficial observations, succeeded in eliminating all but a single explanation of the phenomenon investigated. The test of Ehrenhaft's *theory of magnetic current* showed more sophisticated experimental techniques in use (providing striking incidental illustration of the method of difference). The report on *the sun's radiation and the weather* showed a simple scientific generalization in the making, still far from achieving the precision of a numerical law. The elaborate report on *experimental research on cancer* illustrated analysis of a large-scale problem into components suitable for scientific investigation, the use of highly developed experimental techniques, standardization of experimental conditions, and the importance of scientific co-operation. The research on *white dwarfs* illustrated the complex ways in which observation and theory react on each other.

The specimens studied were not fully representative of scientific method, for they insufficiently emphasized a scientific discovery, the "scientific attitude," the use of measurement and other mathematical techniques.

Comprehension test

(For instructions, see page 10.)

1. The assertion that science is continuous with "common sense" implies that all differences between the two are differences of degree. (*true* *false*)
2. A scientific investigation may make no use of experiments. (*true* *false*)
3. The method of agreement is too crude to be used by scientists. (*true* *false*)
4. A scientist never speculates concerning the possible causes of a phenomenon. (*true* *false*)
5. The chief reason for rejecting Ehrenhaft's hypothesis is its inconsistency with basic principles of physics. (*true* *false*)
6. One reason for preferring numerical laws in science is the desire to make precise predictions. (*true* *false*)
7. To "standardize" the conditions of an experiment means to arrange that they can be reproduced without important fluctuations. (*true* *false*)
8. The experimental research on cancer discussed in the text is directed in the first instance toward the prevention of cancer. (*true* *false*)
9. In view of Adams' prediction in 1915, the discovery of white dwarfs came as no surprise to scientists. (*true* *false*)

10. The types of observation made in looking for white dwarfs was largely determined by theoretical considerations. (*true* *false*)

Exercises

A

1. Find specific illustrations from the specimens of scientific method in the text of each of the following points:
   a. The use of previous knowledge to determine what kind of observations shall be made.
   b. Prediction used as a test of the correctness of a generalization.
   c. Search for *causes* of phenomena.
   d. Search for *non-causal* connections between factors.
   e. Attempts to render a generalization more "explicit."
   f. Use of crude observations ("looking and seeing").
   g. Appeal to scientific authority.
   h. Use of instruments.
   i. Presence of terms whose use presupposes acceptance of a scientific theory.
2. Answer the following questions about the specimens:
   a. What was the point of extending observations of "pebble peat" to "much of the Northern Great Plains"?
   b. Why was the explanation that the luminescence of the railroad worm was due to its being *disturbed* unacceptable?
   c. Why were hydrogen and nitrogen passed over the excised red luminescent tissue?
   d. What assumption was made in experimenting on the *excised* tissue?
   e. Explain the purpose of turning the magnet upside down (in specimen C).
   f. Would you have covered the "brass replica" with Picein Wax if you had been conducting the experiment? (Give reasons.)
   g. Why would observations of the E-layer be preferred to determinations of the "solar constant"? (Specimen D.)
   h. What assumptions would limit the applicability of the cancer research (specimen E) to the prevention of cancer in humans?
   i. What other motives than disinterested curiosity might impel research into the properties of "white dwarfs"?
3. Analyze three further specimens of scientific method.
4. Make a list of respects in which scientific method as illustrated in the specimens (a) agrees with, (b) differs from "common-sense" procedures.

18

SCIENTIFIC DATA

The first step in beginning the scientific study of a problem is to collect the data, which are or ought to be "facts."—J. A. Thomson.

Nobody ever reaches truly illuminating and fruitful generalizations concerning vital phenomena who has not himself experimented and tilled, in hospital, operating theater and laboratory, the fetid and palpitating soil of life.—Claude Bernard.

1. The importance of experience.

IF one trait, more than any other, is characteristic of the scientific attitude, it is *reliance on the data of experience.* As musical aptitude requires exceptional sensitivity to tones and rhythms, so scientific aptitude demands an exceptional flair for the *objective aspect* of experience—the stubborn capacity of objects to reveal themselves as they are, independent of human desires, hopes, and expectations. In the lives and labors of the great scientists (say Faraday, Newton, Darwin, or Pasteur) it is plain to see an exceptional capacity to put speculation to the test of observation and experiment.

The history of science should disabuse us of any notion that respect for experience comes naturally to men, or is achieved without persistent struggle and self-discipline. It is easy to smile today at the "glorious folly" of those opponents of Galileo who preferred to rely on Aristotle's authority rather than look through the newly invented telescope, and labored "with logical arguments, as if with magical incantations, to charm the new planets out of the sky." Since astronomy, no longer thought relevant to controversial questions of theology, has ceased to be literally a burning subject, it is easier to be objective about it. But where the testimony of observation still impinges on jingoism or sectarian prejudice, the investigator must still tread delicately or bury his results in the obscurity of learned journals. Economists are sometimes treated like witches in otherwise civilized communities, and there are parts of the world where inquiry into racial differences ranks among the dangerous occupations.

The position of those who resist an appeal to experience in controversial subjects would be weaker than it is but for two circumstances: The unwarranted claims often made in behalf of science in fields of inquiry where science is still a hope rather than an achievement; and the difficulties that arise in determining what exactly *is* "shown by experience." It is easy to advise "recourse to the facts"; often enough it proves difficult to determine what kind of evidence shall be recognized as a "fact."

If we are to get a reasonable understanding of the aims and values of science (avoiding the philistinism of those who ignore its importance and the dogmatism of those who use it as a prop for unexamined prejudices) we need familiarity with the procedures employed in the *scientific* use of experience. The implied distinction between "scientific" and non-scientific appeal to experience is intended to emphasize the point, now sufficiently obvious, that a scientist does not accept experience *uncritically* or *passively*. He exercises the privilege of *discriminating* between experiences, carefully preserving one result but promptly rejecting another, recorded when he was "too tired to notice what he was doing." In arranging an experiment, as our examples have shown, the scientist takes elaborate steps to *ensure* that "things will happen." We shall therefore pay special attention to the principles used by scientists in the sifting and manipulation of experience, with particular reference to the possible influence such intervention might have on the resulting data. Since critical and active scientific recourse to experience tends to take the form of an *experiment,* we shall be particularly concerned with establishing the difference between experiment and "mere" observation.

2. *The nature of scientific observation.*

The use of the senses. The simplest conceivable use of experience consists in noticing something seen, heard, felt, or smelled. Not all such experiences are of equal value to science, yet without them no knowledge could be reached through experience. In modern scientific procedure, elaborate use is often made of cameras and other instruments for the automatic recording of observations. But those recordings must, in their turn, be *seen* by the human observer if they are to be of any use. Steps are often taken to eliminate the use of the senses of hearing, touch, and smell; and vision may be confined to the observation of a number on a dial; yet the scientist must still use his eyes if any observations are to be made. Scientific observation begins with use of the senses, though it does not end there.

Choice of significant material. Some important scientific observations have been made accidentally. Thus, Becquerel's famous discovery of the radio-activity of uranium compounds arose through leaving a photographic plate in the neighborhood of the radio-active material. It has even been said that "a great science has *in many cases* risen from an accidental observation."*

Such cases are, however, exceptional, and have always been followed by long series of deliberate, intentional, and directed observations. Very seldom does haphazard garnering of observations have much contribution to make to the discovery of the generalizations, theories and principles sought by scientists. And it is only in the light of accepted generalization that the scientist knows where to look for *significant* data.

The examples of scientific method discussed in the last chapter contain reference to many hundreds of individual observations—observations of the presence of moss or pebbles, of the color of light emitted by fluorescent stuffs, readings of rulers, thermometers, spectroscopes, and other instruments, and many more. The vast majority of them were undertaken deliberately

* Jevons, *Principles of Science,* 2nd ed., p. 399. He gives several illustrations.

in order to test, support, or modify some tentatively adopted hypothesis; very few observations made by scientists have any other origin. As Darwin said, "all observation must be *for or against some view,* if it is to be of any service."

Selection of significant features. This is closely related to the last point. Some occurrence impresses us as "significant." The rainbow has been so regarded, for instance, throughout recorded history. To what aspect of the rainbow shall we turn our attention? To the colors, the shape, the position in the sky, the accompanying clouds or other conditions of the sky—or even to our own state of health and the moral shortcomings of our society? In the absence of previous knowledge, all of these suggestions, and an indefinite number of others, are *equally plausible.* When the scientist decides to concentrate on one aspect of the phenomenon rather than another, it is because his previously acquired knowledge gives some intimation of *what to look for.*

There is one further and most important consequence: The selection made partly determines what shall be seen. To a casual observer all canaries look alike; it is only to the investigator who has determined to record minute differences in appearance that each bird comes to have a look as distinctive and individual as that of any human. There is in short an *increase in discrimination determined by selectivity of attention.*

Observation of the sort required in fruitful scientific study is, accordingly, an art that has to be acquired by deliberate and prolonged training. Especially is this the case in the use of instruments. To be able to "read" an instrument means to have been trained to notice the relevant and to discard the accidental or unimportant. The various special sciences demand different types of observation and call for appropriately differentiated types of training.

Neglect of "illusory" experiences. A particularly important case of the selection of significant features of experiences occurs when, as frequently happens, certain aspects of an experience (or even the entire experience) are rejected as "illusory."

The distinction between "illusion" and "reality," or between "correct" and "mistaken" experiences is a familiar one. Spots seen to rise and fall against a clear sky are attributed to defects in vision; a stick "seen" to be bent when immersed in water is not believed to have changed its shape. The scientist similarly discards certain aspects of his experiences as illusory. The colored fringes of an object seen through a microscope are neglected, and in all readings of measuring instruments the variations that result when successive attempts at determination are made are treated as "errors." Such picking and choosing among the data of experience is a universal rule in scientific observation; the well-trained scientist must know what observations *not* to notice.

What right, it may be said, has the scientist to legislate for nature? And what becomes of his vaunted objectivity and respect for fact if he exercises the right to neglect features genuinely present in his experiences? If the scientist were a mere recorder of phenomena there would be no answer to this accusation, for the bent stick *does* look bent, the mosquito leg is *seen* to have colored fringes, the *recorded* weight of an object does vary from reading to reading. But such observations, as we have said, are made "for or against some view"—that is, in the light of hypotheses and generalizations of which they are instances. A scientist is not interested (as a painter might be) in how the bent stick *looks* merely; he wishes to discover laws *connecting* the various appearances of the stick. He is, therefore, entitled to neglect such features of the actual experience as he pleases, *provided the neglected features do not contradict the laws he proclaims*. In establishing the measurable length of a stick he may properly neglect its "bent look"; in counting the number of bristles on an insect's foot, he is justified in paying no attention to the color.

The case of the deviations in the observed weight of an object is a little more complicated. Here the scientist is looking for some **constant,** a property that will be a permanent feature of observations made by himself and other observers on other occasions. Now it is a matter of experience that by taking the average of the numbers furnished by a balance (or using some more complicated procedure to obtain a *calculated weight*) such a constant *can* be found. The calculated weight proves to be a feature of the individual experience that agrees with experiences of other qualified observers in a wide range of similar conditions.

It will be noted that the "illusory" features of the experience are not permanently *rejected*. The distinction between "illusion" and "reality" in a scientific observation is a *provisional* one between features usable in generalizations and features temporarily not so usable. It is the ultimate (and probably unattainable) aim of science to account for *all* observed features of phenomena. Thus the phenomena of the bent stick and the colored microscopic image are explained in optics; variations in the reading of a balance can be elucidated by study of the rigidity and elasticity of instruments; and so forth. At any given time, however, even the most advanced sciences have a multitude of unexplained phenomena labelled "for future attention."

Public verification and the elimination of bias. The criteria that determine the selection of acceptable features of scientific observation now begin to be clear. In order to be acceptable, a feature of an observation must be: (a) capable of being presented again *in similar conditions;* (b) if possible, connected with other *constants* by means of generalizations.

How dissimilar may conditions be, before they cease to count as "similar"? To a color-blind man, blood may always have the same color as coffee, yet such identity of color would not be acceptable as a scientific constant. It is required that any individual observation must be capable of confirmation by *any* qualified observer—that is, anybody who is in a position, through training, to understand the conditions of the alleged experience, manipulate the tools and instruments required to produce it, and respond to tests certifying him as a "normal" observer.

A central aim of scientific investigation is to submit the first crude experiences of the individual to the continuing control of confirmatory investigation by the whole body of scientists. Science rests on the fidelity and integrity of the individual scientist, and the day when individual researchers began to report what some authority decreed is the day that would mark the beginning of the end of genuine science. (This is one reason why the so-called "experiments" conducted by elementary students of the sciences bear so little resemblance to the real thing; the student knows or can guess what is expected of him, and therefore more or less consciously "cooks" the answer.) Yet the report of the individual scientist gets no more credit than it can win through the critical repetition of the observations by other scientists. This availability of scientific observation to the inspection of any suitably qualified scientist is commonly referred to by use of the term **public verifiability.**

An individual observation is said to be publicly verif*iable* when it *could* be confirmed by any suitably qualified scientist; it is said to be publicly verif*ied* when it *has* been so confirmed by a sufficient number of other observers. (It should be noted that observations that have not been publicly verif*ied* are sometimes accepted. The photographic record of a new star made by a reputable astronomer is not rejected on the ground that he alone made the observation, but it would be required that *other* astronomers should be *able* to make corroborating observations. Astronomy has no dealings with any stars that can *in principle* be seen only by a single, favored, individual.)

The requirement of public verification has been sometimes abused by being enlisted to discredit startling innovations and deviations from current scientific orthodoxies. Yet it is the best instrument we have against personal bias and prejudice. The history of science has shown again and again the importance of this test (and the corresponding test for scientific generalizations); and all pessimistic commonplaces concerning the diversity of human opinions must take account of the historical demonstration that men *can* reach universal agreement—at least about scientific topics.

Search for abstract structures. Stress on public verification has important consequences on the practice of scientific observation. It leads first to emphasis on features of experience concerning which agreement can in practice be reached. Since sensations of touch, smell, and hearing are both vague and variable, modern science relies almost exclusively on *vision.* What needs to be seen tends to be increasingly narrowed down to the position of a pointer on a numbered scale (the so-called "pointer-readings" or "coincidence observations"). All scientists, of course, continue to use the vaguer, more variable, and richer experiences with which life abounds—if only to recognize each other and their instruments, and careful analysis of *all* that is involved in performing a typical scientific observation would show how much reliance is still placed upon such vague observation. At the crucial moments, however, when all finally depends on "getting the observation right" (timing the eclipse, counting the particles, and so forth) the scientist will be found characteristically intent on the position of some line (a pointer, the surface of a mercury column, or the like) relative to the numbered gradations of a scale.

This particularly important example of "pointer-readings" illustrates the tendency for the objects of scientific discourse to become increasingly abstract. What the scientist sees is *not* what "any man" would see: The situation to be observed is defined in the light of increasingly more complex theory, and what is recorded becomes increasingly something selected, abstracted, or calculated from the direct observation. The "felt warmth" of an object is replaced in turn by the readings of a mercury thermometer, a "calculated value" that is "corrected for errors," and later by a still more complex structure. It is for this reason the reports of scientific investigation become increasingly hard for the layman to follow. It is not merely that the scientist has come gradually to discover unusual and hidden phenomena; the cause of the obscurity is still more to be found in the transformation imposed on common-sense concepts by the criterion of public verifiability.

3. *The nature of scientific experiment.*

The distinction between observation and experiment. We have seen that the term "observation" may refer to a whole series of more or less sophisticated procedures. The simplest (and least useful) type of observation consists in the uncritical report by a casual observer of something seen (or otherwise learned through the senses). This is a long remove from the procedure used by a skilled scientist, highly trained in the choice of significant features of an experience, using delicate instruments, and applying calculation to obtain the results of observation in a form amenable to public verification.

Yet even the most sophisticated and elaborate observation is not an *experiment*—though every experiment requires the taking of observations. In order to understand the nature of the difference we may consider, as a very simple illustration, the experiment (which Galileo is said to have performed), of dropping a heavy and a light body simultaneously from a high tower. An attempt of this kind, to show that the time of flight is independent of the mass of the body concerned, would unhesitatingly be described as an *experiment*. Yet if Galileo had *happened* to notice the time taken by different objects to fall the same height he would, just as unhesitatingly, be said to have performed a series of *observations*.

The difference between the two cases seems to consist in the following points: (a) The experiment was *deliberately undertaken;* (b) involved the setting up of an *artificial situation* contrived by the scientist; (c) was arranged to answer a *definite* question; (d) involved systematic *variation of factors* in the situation observed. (Only the last of these calls for further explanation. By the "variation of factors" we mean the attempt to reproduce the situation with change in only one factor at a time, a procedure with which we became familiar in our study of the method of difference. Thus Galileo supposedly dropped two bodies, identical in *all* respects except for the difference in their mass.)

Of the four differences between experiment and observation listed in the last paragraph, the first and third are differences of degree alone. We have already seen that scientific observation, in its most highly developed forms, tends to be undertaken deliberately as a test of a definite hypothesis, or in order to answer a definite question. We shall therefore concentrate on the artificiality and induced variability that seem especially characteristic of scientific experiment. But before going further we shall do well to check our tentative conclusions by examining some *example* of scientific experimentation. We choose for this purpose Newton's famous work on the spectrum, as reported in his own original communication to the Royal Society (1671).

An example of experimentation.

"*Sir,*

To perform my late promise to you, I shall without further ceremony acquaint you, that in the beginning of the year 1666 (at which time I applied myself to the grinding of Optic glasses of other figures than *Spherical*) I procured me a triangular glass-prisme, to try therewith the celebrated *Phaenomena* of *Colours*. And in order thereto having darkened my chamber, and made a small hole in my windowshuts, to let in a convenient quantity of the Suns light, I placed my prisme at his entrance, that it might be thereby refracted to the opposite wall. It was at first a very pleasing divertisement, to view the vivid and intense colours produced thereby; but after a while applying myself to consider them more circumspectly, I became surprised to see them in an *oblong* form; which, according to the received laws of Refraction, I expected should have been *circular*. They were terminated at the sides with *streight* lines, but at the ends, the decay of light was so gradual, that it was difficult to determine justly, what was their figure; yet they seemed *semicircular*.

Comparing the length of this coloured *Spectrum* with its breadth, I found it about five times greater; a disproportion so extravagant, that it excited me to a more than ordinary curiosity of examining, from whence it might proceed. I could scarce think, that the various *Thickness* of the glass, or the termination with shadow or darkness, could have any Influence on light to produce such an effect; yet I thought it not amiss, first to examine those circumstances, and so *tryed* what would happen by transmitting light through parts of the glass of diverse thicknesses or through holes in the window of divers bignesses or by setting the Prisme without so that the light might pass through it, and be refracted before it was terminated by the hole: but I found none of those circumstances material. The fashion of the colours was in all these cases the same.

Then I suspected, whether by any *unevenness* in the glass, or other contingent irregularity, these colours might thus be dilated. And to try this, I took another Prisme like the former, and so placed it, that the light, passing through them both, might be refracted in contrary ways, and so by the latter returned into that course, from which the former had diverted it. For, by this means I thought, the *regular* effects of the first Prisme would be destroyed by the second Prisme, but the irregular ones more augmented, by the multiplicity of refraction. . . ." (*Philosophical Transactions,* Number 80, Feb. 19, 1671.)

A series of further experiments finally led Newton to conclude "that Light consists of rays differently refrangible," *i.e.,* is composed of different kinds of light having varying refractive powers.

We notice a number of points of interest in this account. The first observations in the series seem to have been made out of curiosity and with little intention of performing a deliberate experiment. The stimulus to serious investigation is provided by recognition of a significant conflict between observation and the theoretical prediction ("I became surprised to see them in an *oblong* form; which, according to the received laws of refraction, I expected should have been circular"). The subsequent experiments are directed toward *explaining* the observed phenomenon (the oblong shape of the spectrum), and consist in *systematic variation* of the factors in the experimental situation. Thus the hypothesis that the spread of the light is due to the thickness of a prism is tested by passing the light through various thicknesses of the prism, *while keeping all else unchanged.* Next the hypothesis that the shape of the aperture by which the light is admitted is responsible is eliminated in a similar fashion. And so forth.

This example, then, confirms our view of the importance of systematic variation of conditions in an experiment.

Artificiality of experiments. The experiences that come to people in the surroundings of everyday living occur within a relatively small range of climatic and other physical conditions. Early scientists took every opportunity to obtain observations made in *unusual* circumstances (as by climbing mountains, descending under water, or, after the invention of efficient pumps, observing phenomena in a vacuum). Today an important aspect of experimental technique consists in producing exceptionally high or low temperatures, artificially intensified electrical charges, or other exceptional circumstances not otherwise encountered. The method of "going to extremes" has proved especially valuable: "When the scientist studies extremes he is often as not rewarded by both knowledge of abnormal facts and also by a new viewpoint on the normal."*

In calling the conditions of an experiment "artificial," we must not be misled by the word into supposing that the scientist somehow makes or creates the phenomena investigated. Liquid helium at a temperature close to absolute zero is still a "natural" substance; what is "artificial" in the experiments in which it is used is the creation of conditions in which its "natural properties" can be observed.

The kind of artificiality most fruitful in experimentation consists in the creation of conditions in which one factor at a time can be varied in independence of the others. Sometimes this can be done by *isolating* factors from other interfering factors (as in the electrical insulation of apparatus for experimental research in electricity, the preparation of "chemically pure" substances for chemical research, and so forth). The "shielding" or "isolation" of relevant factors in an experiment is often the hardest part of the undertaking, and may call for the highest kind of ingenuity and resourcefulness.

Systematic variation of factors. This is the crux of scientific experimentation. Any random observation will be an instance

* W. H. George, *The Scientist in Action,* page 290. New York: Emerson Books, Inc., 1938.

of indefinitely many factors that may contribute to the phenomenon attracting attention. If a group of children suddenly make exceptional progress in their studies, the result might plausibly be attributed to the personality of the teacher, the quality of the textbook used, the competitive atmosphere of the school, exceptional endowment of the children, or a host of other factors. On general grounds we might expect the result to be due to a *combination* of factors not detectable by superficial observation. Scientific investigation of such a question requires conditions to be created in which each suspected factor can be varied independently of the others.

A powerful means of effecting this is the use of so-called *control experiments*. Thus, if the question studied is the effect of adding iron to the diet of fish, *two* groups of fish will be used, chosen to be as alike as possible in species, average weight and length, and so on. One group will then be fed small quantities of iron, while the other *control group* will be treated similarly in all other respects. Increased growth in the iron-eating group may, in such conditions, be held to be reasonably significant. (It is much harder to design similar conditions for educational experiments. If it were possible to establish two schools whose students and teachers were all identical twins, we might begin to approximate to the best conditions.)

4. *The use of instruments.*

Establishing the conditions for a scientific experiment will normally call for extensive use of instruments.

Some of the instruments used will be accessories, *i.e.,* means to make the phenomena more available to the observer. Before an observation or an experiment can be made, there is usually a considerable amount of preliminary work to be done in order to make the material ready for inspection: The rare butterfly must be caught, the diseased liver set in wax, stained and sliced, the gas chamber exhausted of air, the child induced to answer questions. Among accessory instruments we should include all the tools, appliances, and machines used in transporting or arranging the material of investigation into a condition in which it can be inspected—the knives, collecting nets, microtomes, vacuum pumps, rat-mazes, questionnaires, of current scientific practice.

Among the accessory instruments deserving special attention are those used as extensions of human sense organs. Thus the camera is like an artificial eye supplied with a device for fixing the image in a durable form, and a sound-recording ribbon bears a similar relation to the human ear.

The justification for the use of such instruments can easily be seen by examining the relatively simple case of the microscope. We place a small drop of water under the eye-piece and immediately see a number of objects in rapid motion. When similar appearances are seen with the naked eye, it is usually possible to touch and otherwise examine the object seen. Now experience shows that the things seen in a microscope are also related, though in a more complex way, to other observable properties. After seeing the drop of water, we may be able to predict that the water will increase in weight, grow a mould, be poisonous to cattle, and so on. Our success in making such predictions leads us to claim, rightly, that what we see in the microscope is "real"—*i.e.*, a sound guide to further experience. The pattern exhibited here is shown in all uses of instruments as extensions of sense organs; all yield appearances (things seen in a lens, or heard from a loud-speaker) that experience shows to be correlated in a dependable manner with other experiences.

The discovery that it is possible to extend sense experience in this way—to "see" the invisible, "hear" the inaudible, to have cameras and other recording instruments making "observations" in the absence of human agency—has been of the greatest importance in furthering scientific progress. Such instruments multiply by many times the accuracy, persistence, and range of human observation.

Instruments of *measurement* are needed to render the results of observation (made available by the use of accessory instruments) sufficiently precise for the purpose of formulating numerical laws. Our discussion of inductive procedure showed how progressively more attentive examination of phenomena led to the substitution of functional correlations for "hit-and-miss" generalizations. Some of the principles on which the scientific practice of measurement are based are explained in the next chapter.

5. *Obstacles to observation and experiment.*

We can place the results of our discussion in a different perspective by considering the conditions that limit the possibility and effectiveness of scientific observation and experiment. This will also serve as a preparation for our later discussion of the relation of scientific method to other modes of interpretation of experience.

The difficulty of correcting personal bias. In order for scientific investigation to be possible, it is necessary, as we have seen, to develop some systematic method of counteracting the interference produced by the observer's idiosyncrasies and prejudices. The intention on the part of the observer to be impartial, and to "observe the facts as they really are" is essential. *But good intentions are not enough.* For in advance of detailed knowledge of a particular subject, it is impossible to determine what is "objective fact" and what "illusion" or "error." (We saw that the "objective" was distinguished from the "illusory" or "subjective" as that which leads to dependable knowledge, *i.e.*, that which can be brought within the scope of sound *generalizations.)* From the heights of our superior knowledge, it is tempting to say that the early alchemists who expected to find "spirits" in chemical substances were victims of a characteristically human bias in favor of finding *human* traits in nature. Yet the expectation that iron has a "spirit" or "soul" is *antecedently* as reasonable as any other; if chemists waste no time today in looking for the "temperament" or "characters" of different kinds of matter (in the sense of those terms applicable to human beings) it is because the accumulation of scientific knowledge has shown such inquiries to be fruitless.

In comparatively undeveloped fields of inquiry, where the elimination of bias has most importance, objectivity is hardest to achieve. It is easy to say that the unbiased observation is that which will ultimately win the credence of all "qualified observers"; the practical difficulty is that of deciding who shall *count* as a "qualified observer." We meet here a circularity very characteristic of scientific procedure: Elimination of bias waits on the acquisition of reliable information; acquisition of reliable information waits on elimination of bias.

Subjects such as history, which deal with fragmentary and ambiguous data from the vanished past, are in a particularly difficult position. For whatever data are used are bound to be a minute selection from the total, and bias enters into decisions of relative significance.

Inaccessibility of data. Events that are very remote in space or time, and those involving extremely large or extremely small magnitudes and velocities, are obviously hard to observe even by the unbiased observer. Though the generation of living matter may be a purely chemical phenomenon, it is conceivable that we shall never have enough time to reproduce the proper condition; it has been supposed that space is full of dark stars, which we have no way of observing, or even of many too remote for light signals from them to have reached us. But the difficulties created by the restricted range of our sense organs are being constantly overcome through the creation of appropriate instruments of observation.

The difficulty of perceiving significant data. This is closely related to the difficulty of recognizing bias. If a scientist from Mars (where there is no music) were to listen to a human violinist, he might perceive nothing more significant than the scraping of horse hair over catgut, yet the composer's musical ideas are truly present in the musical performance *for those who are prepared to find them.* Scientific observation, we have seen, is an *active* process, in which the observer *interrogates* nature. The difficulty in psychology or economics or other young sciences is to know *what questions to ask.* "The problem of science is not to discover examples of laws when we know what kinds of law to look for; it is to know for what kind of law to look." (N. R. Campbell, *What is Science?* p. 76.) Once again we take note of the circularity of scientific procedure: Without knowledge of generalizations, no significant observations; without significant observations, no generalizations.

The difficulty of creating experimental situations. In trying to answer some questions of urgent human interest, it may be impossible to arrange for the variation of conditions, and the use of control situations, as required in scientific experiment. Many people would like to know how far Hitler was responsible for the Second World War. A god who could make the history of the world "repeat itself" with the *sole* exception that the infant Hitler *died at birth* might have a "scientific" answer to the question; mere mortals must rely on weaker procedures of analogy, comparison with similar historical conditions, and so forth. Even where experiment is theoretically possible, it may be restrained by humanitarian considerations. We hesitate to infect *humans* with lethal diseases or deliberately create socially maladjusted communities.

When no other difficulties arise, it may be practically impossible to insure isolation of one factor from others. This is typically the case in the social sciences, where any factor of interest (say juvenile delinquency) tends to be highly complex and related to an unmanageable variety of other factors.

One special difficulty of this general type is due to *interference by instruments.* Introduction of *any* instrument produces some change, no matter how small, in the situation observed. In certain important cases, such disturbances are not trivial and cannot safely be neglected as irrelevant. The study of ultramicroscopic phenomena in physics is particularly embarrassed by this difficulty. Trying to learn the properties of electrons (or other infinitesimal particles) by bombarding them with other electrons is like trying to discover the properties of rocks by shooting cannon balls at them. Similar difficulties arise in other sciences; the conclusions of the biologist are likely to be mistaken to the extent that he is compelled to study the properties of tissue *removed from the living animal;* a society in which Gallup pollsters and other social investigators are active often shows characteristics not found in undisturbed societies.

The moral of these difficulties. A catalogue of the obstacles to scientific observation and experiment can be made to appear very impressive. To draw pessimistic conclusions concerning the value of scientific method on this account would be unreasonable, nevertheless. The triumphs of scientific method in the most complex fields of inquiry are sufficient demonstration that the obstacles to observation and experiment can be overcome. Only a very rash or a very foolish critic would chart the boundaries of possible scientific investigation; the cure for lack of scientific knowledge of a subject is more and better scientific study.

An understanding of the obstacles to scientific method, and the consequent limitations of its present accomplishments, ought, however, to be a safeguard against the prevailing idolatry of science. Scientific observation and experiment are excellent and admirable avenues to knowledge *when they can be used.* But to ban other methods in cases where science has yet no aid to offer would be highly unreasonable. *Scientific* observation and experiment themselves are not achieved by following a single uniform prescription guaranteed to produce results. The scientific observer is a tactician, using one maneuver or another as his own ingenuity and the nature of his subject matter suggest. No doubt he would be happiest if all science could approximate the condition of physics. Failing this, the procedure deserving the praise usually implicit in the label "*scientific* method" is whatever is *appropriate* to the actual material. We may learn from the scientist's own willingness to *experiment with methods* the value of a similar flexibility of approach to the confused problems of the world surrounding the scientific laboratory. And we may well bear in mind the ancient and wise dictum of Aristotle that "precision is not to be sought for alike in all discussions, any more than in all the products of the crafts."

Summary

Science is marked by reliance on experience, but the approach to experience is critical and discriminating, and calls for special training of the scientist. All scientific use of experience begins with something seen, heard, felt, or smelt, and this simplest "use of the senses" cannot be avoided. Very few observations are, however, made accidentally. The vast majority are made in the service of some hypothesis to be tested. Observation requires the selection of significant features, but what is significant is determinable only in the light of acquired knowledge. The selectivity of attention required in scientific observation leads to increased powers of discrimination. An important type of insignificant feature of experience is the so-called "error" or "illusion." An "illusion" is a feature of experience not related, by generalization, to other data in the field of investigation. "Errors" may be neglected provided their presence is indifferent to the truth of the scientific laws proclaimed. "Errors" or other neglected features of experience are to be explained by later theories and are discarded only provisionally. The use of *calculated weights* (or similar quantities in other measurement) illustrates the search for *scientific constants,* features observable on indefinitely many occasions by any qualified observer. All scientific observation must be *publicly verifiable,* subject to the possibility of general inspection. Stress on public verifiability leads to a search for abstract features of experience and thereby contributes to the high technicality of science. Scientific experiment is distinguished from scientific observation by deliberate design, artificiality, relation to definite questions, systematic variation of factors. The first and third of these are differences of degree. Artificiality of an experiment consists in the arrangement of conditions seldom or never found in nature. "Going to extremes" is a useful procedure in the sciences: More important is the contrivance of conditions in which one factor, by being shielded or isolated from others, can be caused to vary independently. One way of effecting systematic variation of factors is the use of control experiments, agreeing with the parallel experiment in all except the factor to be varied. Most experiments use instruments either as *accessory instruments* (for rendering the material ready for observation) or as *instruments of measurement.* A special kind of accessory instruments consist in *extensions of human sense-organs,* contrivances to extend the range in which observations can be taken. Among the obstacles to scientific observation and experiment are *the difficulty of correcting personal bias* (especially in fields where insufficient knowledge is available for the recognition of bias), *inaccessibility of data,* and *the difficulties of perceiving significant data and creating experimental situations.* These difficulties are most acute in the so-called "social sciences," where significant factors are complex and not easily isolated. The moral of such limitations to the collection of scientific data is the need to press for "more and better science" while being ready meanwhile to use other less precise methods whenever appropriate.

Comprehension test

(For instructions, see page 10.)

1. In "criticizing" experience, a scientist is led to neglect some things that are "actually seen." (*true* *false*)
2. Knowledge of generalizations is required in order to determine which features of an observation are significant. (*true* *false*)
3. What a scientist can see, "any man" could see. (*true* *false*)
4. The only features of an observation a scientist is entitled to neglect are those that do not contradict the laws he wishes to affirm. (*true* *false*)
5. Every accepted observation in science must be publicly verifiable, but not necessarily publicly verified. (*true* *false*)

6. A "random observation" may show "systematic variation of factors." (*true* *false*)
7. No situation that is artificially arranged can be used for scientific observation. (*true* *false*)
8. An experiment need not involve the setting up of artificial conditions. (*true* *false*)
9. An instrument that is an "extension of human sense organs" is an "accessory" instrument. (*true* *false*)
10. The "circularity of scientific procedure" is a case of "arguing in a circle." (*true* *false*)

Exercises

A

1. Determine how far the aspects of scientific experimentation discussed in this chapter are illustrated in the discussion entitled "Rotation of electrolyte, etc." in Chapter 17 (page 341).
2. How would you show the illusory character of the following experiences?
   a. Small organisms are seen under the microscope to be moving with extraordinarily high velocities.
   b. In the evening, when lamps have already been lighted, the sky looks remarkably blue.
   c. The full moon seems to be larger when near to the horizon.
   d. A cavity in a tooth always seems very large to the tongue.
   e. Seen from the window of a train, the landscape appears to be rotating.
   f. A polished floor feels colder to the touch than a carpet in contact with it.

   How far do these examples illustrate the following points: (i) an "illusion" is a genuine experience, (ii) an "illusory" feature of an experience is one that is not correlated in a simple fashion to other experiences?
3. Which of the following (alleged) data ought, in your opinion to be acceptable to scientists (give detailed reasons)?
   a. A medium undertakes to materialize the spirits of people who are dead, but insists that this cannot be done in the presence of cameras or other signs of "scepticism."
   b. Professor X discovers a new element that nobody succeeds in isolating except his own students.
   c. A man claims to be able to "see" future events in dreams.
   d. An explorer brings back from an expedition an account of a new

tribe, never seen by any other visitor before, who were completely obliterated by an earthquake before his return.

Relate your account to the discussion of "public verification" in the text.

4. What is the opposite of "scientific *constant*"? Mention five scientific constants known to you. Do they conform to the description of "constant" given in the text?
5. Is it possible to perform experiments (a) in astronomy, (b) in history, (c) in logic? How does the answer bear on the question of whether these subjects are "scientific"?
6. Define "instrument." Make a list of some instruments used in the *social* sciences and classify them as "accessory" or "measuring" instruments.
7. Make a critical study of some of the evidence for the occurrence of either "spirit messages," "telepathy," or "crystal gazing." (Consult a good encyclopedia for references.) In so doing, indicate with illustrations what tests of "scientific respectability" are applied to the alleged phenomena.

B

1. Find out (from an encyclopedia or handbook of statistics) something of the procedures by which "errors of measurement" are "corrected."
2. "Strictly speaking, there are no 'errors' in measurement, and therefore nothing to be 'corrected.' " Explain and defend this statement. If somebody objects that there *are* errors of measurement, is he raising a merely verbal issue?
3. Would it be possible for a race of completely blind men to be "scientific"?
4. "You say science takes account only of the observations of *normal* persons. But who is to say what constitutes normality? To the scientist, those who agree with him are normal, but to the lunatic the so-called sane are distinctly abnormal." *Discuss.*
5. The acceleration due to gravity is usually regarded as a scientific constant, yet its magnitude is not the same at all points on the earth. Is this fact consistent with the definition of "constant" in the text?
6. Explain the point of stressing "*systematic* variation" in scientific experimentation.
7. "You admit that experiments are 'artificial,' *i.e.,* that the scientist *makes* the conditions he observes. How can you maintain in the same breath that science yields *objective* knowledge?" *Discuss.*
8. Discuss the views presented in the following quotations:
   a. "The sceptic often takes refuge in the statement that he is prepared to accept these phenomena when they can be reproduced at will.

He believes in wireless because he can turn on his wireless set with the certainty that it will function. He will believe in ectoplasm when ectoplasm can be reproduced at will.... We cannot reproduce at will Shakespeare's Sonnets or the dodo, yet we do not deny that the Sonnets were written by Shakespeare or that the dodo existed. There is, indeed, no a priori reason to suppose that mediumship must be either fraudulent or as consistent in its efficiency as a wireless set. Physical mediumship may be as rare as genius. We do not yet understand its laws, but it is perverse and irrational to insist that no facts shall be recognized as occurring until science can discover the laws responsible for their occurrence." (Arnold Lunn, *The Flight from Reason,* p. 278. New York: The Dial Press, 1931.)

b. "Scientific method, although in its more refined forms it may seem complicated, is in essence remarkably simple. It consists in observing such facts as will enable the observer to discover general laws governing facts of the kind in question." (Bertrand Russell, *The Scientific Outlook,* p. 15. New York: W. W. Norton and Co., Inc., 1931.)

c. "The method of experiment cannot be freely applied where we are dealing with the events and processes that constitute the unreturning stream of history.... One revolution follows another, one nation after another rises to power and declines. But we cannot with scientific assurance eliminate the differences between pre-revolutionary situation so as to establish one specific causal series culminating in revolution.... Whatever comparable situations we may find we cannot control them. Each situation passes, merges into a new one. It does not abide for our renewed questioning." (R. M. MacIver, *Social Causation,* p. 256. New York: Ginn & Co., 1942.)

d. "... the scientific method ... is not the sole perquisite of workers in laboratories, but is in fact applied at least as rigidly and honestly in their proper fields by historians and even theologians....

"Particular events, even if they are what is commonly called miraculous or supernatural, can be scientifically studied by investigation of the evidence for them and of their supposed effects, by comparison with similar or analogous phenomena, and by relation to the general body of knowledge so far as this is appropriate to them." (C. E. Raven, *Science, Religion, and the Future,* pp. 86, 90. New York: Macmillan, 1943.)

e. "The fact that science is confined to a knowledge of structure is obviously of great 'humanistic' importance. For it means that the problem of the nature of reality is not prejudged. We are no longer required to believe that our response to beauty, or the mystic's sense of communion with God, have no objective counterpart. It is perfectly possible that they are, what they have so often been taken to be, clues to the nature of reality. Thus our various experiences are put on a more equal footing, as it were. Our religious aspirations, our perceptions of beauty, may not be the essentially illusory phenomena they were supposed to be. In this new scientific universe even mystics have a right to exist." (J. W. N. Sullivan, *Limitations of Science,* pp. 186-7. London: Penguin Books Ltd., 1938.)

19

SCIENTIFIC THEORY

The recording of facts is one of the tasks of science, one of the steps toward truth; but it is not the whole of science. There are one-story intellects, two-story intellects, and three-story intellects with sky lights. All fact collectors, who have no aims beyond their facts, are one-story men. Two-story men compare, reason, and generalize, using the labors of the fact collectors as well as their own. Three-story men idealize, imagine and predict. Their best illumination comes from above, through the sky light.—Justice O. W. Holmes.

1. The importance of theory.

IN the last chapter we stressed the concern of science with getting *facts,* through the patient and faithful record of individual experiences. It soon appeared that fact collecting calls for the use of general principles (especially those dictating the choice of materials, and the design of instruments and experiments) and is constantly submitted to the critical control of other general principles. A "hard-headed practical man," interested only in getting hold of particular facts, and having "no patience with theorizing," would soon find himself forced to theorize *in order to "get the facts."* And if he wanted to *use* his facts, to "learn from experience" whether a bridge would bear his weight, or some grain were fit for his pigs to eat, he would necessarily have to generalize.

Without the connecting link of generalization, each particular experience is an isolated happening, without relevance to anything else in the universe. A man who refused or was unable to generalize might perhaps be able to remember what had already happened to him, but he would never know what to expect, or how to prepare for the future.

These remarks apply also to the kind of common-sense "understanding" and "control" with which we are satisfied in everyday situations. Even the mere *description* of an object of experience as a piece of wood, or a tree, or a storm implies the acceptance of some generalizations: Wood is the *kind* of stuff that floats in water, burns, has a grain, and so on. And when we rely on a chair to bear our weight, or a friend to behave honestly, we are again obviously making use of generalization. Indeed all knowledge that rises above the mere recognition of an undifferentiated "something-or-other" is knowledge of *general* characteristics.

We should therefore expect to find "common-sense" generalizations shading off into scientific theorizing by hardly perceptible gradations. Only when we proceed a long way along the continuous line that unites science to common sense do we meet striking differences. We found a similar situation, it will be remembered, in discussing the relations of scientific observation to the methods employed in common-sense collection of facts. Just as we found that *sufficiently sophisticated* scientific observation showed distinctive features of its own (*e.g.*, the emphasis on pointer-readings and public verification), we may expect to find similarly striking features in sufficiently sophisticated processes of scientific generalization.

A note on terminology. In talking about the theoretical aspects of scientific activity, it is customary to make a rough distinction between *generalizations, laws,* and *principles.* All three of these terms mean statements referring to whole classes of instances (or else the "things-mentioned" by such statements), and thus having the form *Every case of A is also a case of B.* The three kinds of statements are distinguished by their relative generality and explanatory power. A comparatively "superficial" general statement, such as *Water causes rust,* or *Milk is a liquid,* or *Magnets attract iron,* is a generalization. Generalizations can be "explained" or "accounted for" by more precise and comprehensive general statements concerning the chemical and physical properties of bodies. These are called *laws* (or "laws of nature"). Laws, in their turn, can be brought within the scope of very wide general statements applying, without exception, to a very large range of instances. These most extensive general statements are usually called *principles*. The basis for these distinctions will become clearer after we have discussed the nature of explanation. We shall use the terms "theory" and "theorizing" to cover general statements of *all* levels of generality.

2. *The uses of scientific theory.*

The process of theorizing enters into scientific work in three ways: in the *description* of data, the *prediction* of data as yet unobserved, and in *explanation*. The first of these was discussed in Chapter 18.

How prediction depends on theory. The prediction of previously unobserved phenomena is always a spectacular scientific achievement, and the use of prediction as a test of theory is a particularly important aspect of scientific method. When a scientist tries to generalize about *known* phenomena, he is always liable to the temptation of making the facts square with his theory: The need to select among the available data by discriminating significant from insignificant details leaves considerable latitude for interpretation. But when the scientist makes a definite prediction, he stakes the fate of his hypothesis or theory on the outcome. Conversely, a successful prediction gives relatively strong support to any hypothesis on which its success depended.

Predictions may require complicated calculation and great powers of imaginative insight, yet they display a very simple logical pattern. Let us examine a typical instance. When astronomy had developed sufficiently for the average distance of the planets from the sun to be calculated, it was found that the ratios of the numbers obtained could be expressed by a simple formula known as "Bode's Law." We write down the series 0, 3, 6, 12, . . . doubling as we go; then we add 4 to each number, obtaining the series 4, 7, 10, 16, 28, 52, 100, 196. Of these eight numbers all except the fifth (28) and last (196) agreed well at the time of the law's formulation with the relative distances of the known planets from the sun. Thus, taking the Earth's distance as 10, the actual figures for Mercury, Venus, Mars, Jupiter, and Saturn are 3.9, 7.2, 15.2, 52.0, and 95.4. After the discovery of Uranus, its average distance (191.9) was also found to agree approximately with the last number in the series (196). But the fact that no planet was known to correspond to the number 28 in Bode's series led to the systematic search for a new planet and the eventual discovery (by accident, however) of the planet Ceres.

This simple instance of scientific prediction clearly involves the use of *known data* (the actual distances of the planets) and a *generalization based on them* (Bode's Law). The process of prediction consisted in *deducing* the existence of a hitherto unobserved instance conforming to the generalization. Such use of generalizations for inferring the character of the unknown from the known will be found in all cases of prediction. When a lump of sugar is put in a cup of coffee one can predict the outcome because the subsequent happening (the sugar dissolving) can be *deduced* from the known data (the fact that sugar was placed in the hot coffee) and an accepted generalization (that sugar dissolves in coffee of that temperature). An astronomer, predicting with admirable accuracy that "the sun will rise totally eclipsed at 6:14 A.M. MWT, about 10 miles southeasterly from Cascade, Idaho, on July 9, 1945" is using the same procedure. He, too, is using known data concerning the longitude of Cascade, the positions of the moon and sun in the heavens, and a host of other detailed facts. And he is using generalizations, in large number, concerning the path of the moon and the sun, the properties of light, and so on. His prediction *follows from* his data in conjunction with his accepted generalizations or other theories.

How explanation uses theory. To understand anything is to have an explanation of it. Insofar as science is dedicated to the advancement of understanding, it is, therefore, a search for *explanations* of phenomena.

What is an explanation? In ordinary life we are constantly seeking for explanations, yet we demand explanations only of *some* events. The office boy is asked to explain his late arrival at work, but he is not asked to explain *punctual* attendance *unless this should be an exceptional occurrence;* that butter should taste like butter is normally taken for granted, but if it should on one occasion reek of whiskey we should then certainly "demand an explanation." These are illustrations of the fact that explanations are demanded for unusual or exceptional or puzzling events, *i.e.,* events that do not conform to expectations: *The occasion of explanation is a deviation from an expected routine of events.*

What form does an explanation take? Let us see what might be offered in explanation of the exceptional events cited in the last paragraph. The tardy office boy might say the streetcar in which he had been coming to work had been involved in an accident, so that no transportation was available for half an hour. If this were true, his late arrival could be *inferred.* The alcoholic taste of the butter could be explained by the report that the maid had spilled some whiskey on it. If this were true, the strange taste of the butter could be *inferred.* These suggestions illustrate the point that explanations consist of additional data and generalizations from which the event to be explained could be inferred or *deduced*: Explanations take the form of additional data and principles of which the event to be explained is a consequence.

In science, as in other inquiries after knowledge, we seek *true* explanations; thus, a set of additional data and generalizations from which an unusual event can be deduced will not be acceptable as an explanation unless independent confirmation of the alleged explanatory circumstances is forthcoming. Kepler "explained" the absence of a planet, which should have existed if he was right in believing a certain generalization, by supposing that God must have destroyed it at some time. In the absence of independent evidence of God's alleged behavior in this regard, the explanation was singularly unconvincing. It is always easy to find explanations, for very little skill is needed to state circumstances and generalizations from which an unusual event *could be deduced*; but *true* explanations may be very elusive. The process of explanation often requires appeal to hypothetical entities that are supposed to exist, and is not complete until the suppositions are shown to be justified.

An example of scientific explanation. Since the examples we have used for illustration are trivial, we shall add an instance from an actual scientific research. Organic chemists engaged in the analysis of whale oil (a valuable commercial source of vitamin A) had some evidence (derived from the examination of light transmitted by the oil) to suspect that the vitamin A was accompanied by some unidentified substance. They accordingly distilled the mixture at a temperature that should have removed all vitamin A, leaving only the additional substance D, behind. Yet, on inspection, "to their consternation (they) found that they were dealing with a strong solution of vitamin A without any of the spectral material C showing." (*Science in Progress,* 4th series, page 244. New Haven: Yale University Press, 1945.)

The occasion for explanation is the failure of an event to accord with expectation: If the distillate had contained no vitamin A, but some other substance instead, this would have been in agreement with the prediction; no surprise would have been felt, and no explanation sought. The *tentative explanation* offered was that the unknown substance, C (since christened "kitol") *decomposed into vitamin A at the temperatures used.* This had the *form* of an explanation, for if it were true the puzzling phenomenon could be inferred. It remained to be shown, by other investigations (which we shall not describe) that such a substance *was* present in the oil, and *did* have the properties hypothetically ascribed to it.

The relativity of explanation. Whether a phenomenon seems sufficiently "puzzling," "exceptional," "unusual," or "unfamiliar" to demand explanation will depend on our own notions of the routine and the familiar. What one man will accept as natural will puzzle a man who is more inquisitive. Most people would have a ready explanation for the fact that a piece of string holds a parcel together, and would be satisfied to point to the knots; but it might be asked why a knot should prevent string from slipping. And if an explanation were produced in terms of known laws concerning the friction of bent strings, we might perhaps be interested to know why strings *have* friction; and so on indefinitely. Any event might conceivably be explained, and, to the sufficiently curious, any explanation might call for further explanation.

The value of explanation is not merely the negative one of dispelling puzzlement concerning an unexpected phenomenon; it has also the great positive virtue of promoting insight by exhibiting, in the form of theory, the connections between phenomena previously unrelated. In science the ideal of satisfying curiosity concerning the unusual gradually becomes transformed into the ideal of *universal* explanation. Science is committed to explaining all things, the familiar no less than the unfamiliar, by constructing theories of utmost comprehensiveness and range.

Whether an explanation will satisfy an inquirer in ordinary life does not depend merely on its truth and the possibility of deducing from it the phenomenon to be explained. If an economist offers the existence of the business cycle as an explanation of a certain tendency for prices to increase, the explanation may well be true and adequate, without being convincing to a lay hearer. For the business cycle may be as puzzling a phenomenon as any rise in prices. It has been said that natives seeing a steam locomotive for the first time were much perplexed until they hit on the explanation that horses must be concealed in its iron belly!

This tendency to explain in terms of factors whose *familiarity* renders them convincing is characteristic of common-sense theorizing. The early history of science shows repeated attempts to make use of explanatory notions drawn from familiar experience. But as the ideal of universal explanation becomes accepted, it proves increasingly hard to satisfy this early desire for explanation in terms of the well-known. Scientists' notions of a "convincing" explanation change, and a theory is held to be "acceptable" in proportion to its comprehensiveness, no matter how remote from everyday affairs the notions that it uses. Thus gravitation, the mutual attraction of massive bodies for each other, is not a notion exemplified in everyday affairs; yet a theory of gravitation is one of the supreme examples of scientific explanation, on account of the vast range of phenomena it brings into mutual relation.

The explanation of generalizations and laws. Explanations may appeal to puzzling phenomena, which in turn raise a demand for explanation. Since an explanation consists, in part, of a provided generalization, it may prove necessary to explain *generalizations,* as well as particular phenomena.

It may seem somewhat paradoxical that a generalization, which is a *regularity,* should itself be puzzling and so in need of explanation, yet a little thought will show this to be truly the case.

It is known that the inhabitants of one or two small towns in the United States never suffer from dental decay. We are in possession, therefore, of a true *generalization—All those who have lived in X-ville a sufficient length of time have undecayed teeth.* Though this is a *generalization,* it is at least as puzzling as the case of a single man with perfect teeth would be. Indeed, if the existence of a single person with perfect teeth provoked a demand for explanation (as it reasonably might), the fact of *so many* similar individuals seems even more remarkable. If all human beings had perfect teeth, we should not feel the need for explanation so urgently: It is the *lack of connection* between what is known about the inhabitants of X-ville and what is known about human beings in general that attracts attention.

Generalizations then, no less than particular phenomena, may seem remarkable or unusual, and so in need of explanation. What form will the explanation take? Suppose we were able to discover that the water in X-ville contained fluorine, and were able to prove independently that anybody drinking such water in sufficient amounts never suffered from dental decay. Then, no doubt, we should be satisfied that we had found an explanation. Here the new data and generalizations (about the presence of fluorine in X-ville water and its beneficial effect on teeth) have the generalization to be explained as a consequence. In the same way Kepler's laws about the motions of the planets and the shapes of their orbits were *explained* by being deduced from Newton's theory of gravitation, and many chemical laws are today being explained by deduction from very general physical theories of atomic structure.

The pattern of explanation of generalization is similar, therefore, to that of the explanation of phenomena; in both cases the things to be explained (whether particular fact or generalization) are *deduced* from known data and generalizations with the help of additional explanatory data and generalizations. The scientific search for *universal explanation,* therefore, requires comprehensive system of principles by which generalizations as well as particular phenomena may be related to one another.

The unification of scientific principles. We have seen how pursuit of the ideal of explanation leads to the search, in science, for principles of the highest generality, of which a great number of known laws and generalizations may be consequences. Principles of this sort—of which those of the conservation of energy and matter are among the best-known examples—are great triumphs of scientific method.

Let us examine a famous case of such *unification* of principles. Many people have heard of the legend that the fall of an apple on Newton's head suggested to him his theory of gravitation, but not so many understand why the apple should have been so important. Before Newton formulated his theory of gravitation, laws were known concerning the free fall of apples and other heavy bodies in the direction of the earth, and another set of laws (those of Kepler) were known concerning the motion of the planets. Scientists had, therefore, *one* explanation, in the form of a generalization (G_1) for terrestrial motion; and another explanation, in the form of a second generalization (G_2), for celestial motions. Newton's achievement was the formulation of a *wider* generalization, a theory (T_1) applying to *all* massive bodies, whether apples or planets. In the special cases to which G_1 applied, he could show that G_1 followed from T; and in the special cases in which G_2 applied, that G_2 followed from the *same* theory. We may say, then, that Newton's single theory T *did the same work* as G_1 and G_2 together. And since both generalizations could be deduced from T (in the circumstances in which they applied), we may also say that Newton's theory *explained* the generalizations that it replaced.

In the unification of a number of generalizations, then, they are replaced by a single generalization, from which they are deducible. We may say that laws unify particular facts, by bringing them into the scope of a formula from which they can be deduced; and theories unify laws by means of a more general formula from which they in turn can be deduced.

One may well wonder what need there is for the unification of generalizations: If we already have laws applying to all the known facts, is there anything to be gained except economy in expression by replacing these laws by a fewer number of generalizations? If the unifying theory did *exactly* the same work as the generalizations it replaces, there would be no important gain. But the theory does the same work of explanation or description *only* in the fields to which the old generalizations originally applied. Just because the theory is sufficiently general to embrace *all* these fields, it also has application to a range of phenomena that would have been unintelligible or even unknown but for its help. Newton's theory, for instance, led to a series of discoveries (*e.g.*, concerning the tides and the interior of the earth) that had been previously unsuspected. In this way the comprehensiveness of a unifying theory leads to a great extension in predictive power. A scientific theory is not a mere shorthand statement of laws already known but less concisely expressed: it is also a signpost to new knowledge.

Are there ultimate explanations? If facts are explained by being brought within the scope of generalizations and those in turn by laws that are themselves explained in terms of more comprehensive principles—where does the process end? It is natural to wonder whether we shall ever arrive at a *final* or "ultimate" explanation of the universe.

There are two ways in which a scientific explanation can be "final." It may *satisfy* us, so that we no longer *seek* for further explanation. Such complacent abstention from further inquiry is foreign to the spirit of science; it may be necessary to rest satisfied with unexplained laws or principles for the time being, for lack of more powerful principles by which they might be explained or unified. But such a situation will always be regarded in science as a challenge, not a victory.

In a second sense of the term, a principle might be regarded as "final" if it were *impossible* to deduce it from more comprehensive principles. If the universe were finite, it is conceivable that eventually *one* grand formula would explain everything in it; the scientific ideal of unification would then have been achieved, and there would be no sense in asking for *further* explanation. There is no danger of such a nightmare, for the known universe continually expands its boundaries to the inquirer, and each fundamental new discovery opens up a vista of hitherto unsuspected phenomena. Indeed, there is some reason to suppose that scientists will never possess a final explanation, in either sense of the term "final." They will never in fact be satisfied with the knowledge achieved, and they will never be in a position in which further theoretical knowledge could *in principle* be known to be impossible.

The complaint is sometimes made that science becomes increasingly unintelligible, through the increased remoteness from the context of everyday life of the concepts used in scientific theorizing. And those who hope for final explanations of the universe sometimes yearn wistfully for a finally *intelligible* account of phenomena. Scientists, it is said, succeed in finding wider and wider descriptions of *how* things happen, but they give no reason *why* things should happen as they do, *why* the universe should have the character it has. To such requests for explanations transcending what can be observed or inferred from experience, the scientist has no better answer than to quote the anecdote concerning Margaret Fuller and Carlyle. The lady was reported as having ecstatically pronounced "I accept the universe!" "Gad, sir," said Carlyle, "she'd better!"

3. Measurement and the use of mathematics.

The value of mathematical formulations. Scientific theories increasingly tend to be expressed in the form of numerical equations. And scientific observation increasingly tends to take the form of measurements yielding *numbers* to serve as the raw material for *numerical* laws and principles. So important to science is this reliance on mathematics that some people actually *identify* scientific theorizing with the use of mathematical methods. Why should mathematics play so decisive a part in science? The question is complex, but the outlines of a correct answer are not hard to understand.

Mathematics is, from one standpoint, a system of symbols that may be used in communication. It has been called "the language of science." Considered as a language, mathematics has the great advantages of universal intelligibility and extreme precision. A Venezuelan and a Bulgarian might come to blows in any discussion of each other's wives, ancestors, political affilations or personal habits; but doubt concerning their heights could be quickly resolved by a process of measurement leading to agreement on some *number*. As a "language of science," mathematics excellently serves the ideal of public verification.

More important still is the relation between the use of mathematics and the practice of logical deduction. When we use mathematics for *calculation* we are engaged in *telescoped deduction*. A simple example may serve to make the meaning of this clearer. In paying for a purchase of 75¢ in value by a dollar bill, we do not *explicitly argue* that the change ought to be 25¢, we simply remember that 25 plus 75 makes 100. But in case of dispute we *could* give an explicit argument, *e.g.,* by saying "There are four quarters in a dollar, and three in 75¢; three from four leaves one, so the change is a quarter." To convince a child, we might have to enter into more detail still, and to expose the grounds of our arithmetical belief in sufficient detail to satisfy a philosophical logician might require hundreds of pages of tricky deduction. But we are not usually called on for such elaborations. A memorized arithmetical formula allows us to *dispense* with a long process of stepwise deductive argument. When we have learned the formula, we no longer need to remember the arguments: The formula is a kind of primitive machine for giving us the right answer each time. This is true of all mathematics, no matter how complicated; mathematics as a whole is *a contrivance of astonishing ingenuity for rendering deductive arguments automatic.*

The second and more important value of mathematics to science, therefore, arises from the ease with which its use allows us to perform the most complicated trains of deduction. By looking at the form of a mathematical equation expressing a discovered generalization concerning some subject, the mathematically trained scientist is able to see in a surprisingly short time a large number of deductive consequences and analogies with other laws and theories.

In view of the important part played by deduction in the process of explanation (as our previous discussion has shown), even this brief sketch of the place of mathematics in scientific method should help to account for the tendency for science to become increasingly mathematical in form. Respect and admiration for mathematics should, however, always be tempered by the obvious reflection that scientists using mathematics must have *something to count.* However important, mathematics is but an instrument of science, and without the measurement of the products of *experience,* the mathematical quantities occurring in scientific theory would have no link with the real world.

Some aspects of measurement. "Measurement," in the widest sense of the word, refers to any process by which numbers are assigned to the results of observation and experiment. The practice of scientific measurement is interesting and complex: We shall confine ourselves to mentioning some of its more obvious features.

Perhaps the simplest way in which numbers and observations can be correlated is by the use of numbers as labels or *tags.* It is often convenient to use numbers as ways of identifying objects. Thus, soldiers receive individual identification numbers, the volumes in a library may be referred to by number, and scientists sometimes use numbers in preference to verbal names for the objects of discussion. But such use of numbers is comparatively unimportant and would hardly be thought to constitute "measurement."

A more interesting case arises when numbers are used to indicate the *order* of occurrence of a set of objects. A simple illustration is provided by recent work on the *pecking behavior* of hens and other animals kept in confinement. Observation of a group of hens reveals the truth of the following generalizations: Given any two hens, A and B, either A always pecks B or B always pecks A; and if A always pecks B and B always pecks C, then A always pecks C. It is easily seen that these generalizations permit the hens to be arranged in order. At the head of the order comes an "unpecked pecker," A, who is attacked by no other hen; next comes a hen, B, who is pecked by A but by no others; and so on, until at the end of the order we reach some sufferer who is pecked by *all* the others without offering reprisal.

When a situation of this character arises (as it frequently does in scientific practice) numbers may be assigned to indicate the relative order of the objects concerned. Thus, the hens might be numbered from 1 to 20, according to their mutual pecking relations. When we know the basis for such measurement, the assignment of a number to an object gives much information in a condensed form; to know that hen D has a pecking number 15, say, is to know that the two generalizations stated in the last paragraph hold, and also that D pecks all hens with larger numbers and is pecked by all hens having smaller numbers. In such a case as this, the *addition* of the numbers assigned has no significance. That hens K, L, M, have pecking number 6, 4, 2, does not mean that K's pecking is somehow the "sum" of the pecking of L and M. This type of measurement, in which only the order of the numbers is significant, is sometimes called **intensive measurement.**

In a still more complex form of measurements, the sums and ratios of the number used *also* have significance. Thus, if three *masses* K, L, M, have weights represented by the numbers 6, 4, 2, we do know that the mass produced by combining L and M will have the same weight as K. This type of assignment of numbers in known as **extensive measurement.** We saw that intensive measurement is possible only when certain generalizations are true of the field to be measured; in order for *extensive* measurement to be possible still more generalizations must hold (whose detailed character we shall not discuss). Thus, to have the extensive measure of some object is to be in possession of a good deal of general information about the relations of that object to other objects and about the kind of relations that hold in the field investigated.

Scientific measurement is a device for assigning numbers to the results of observation in such a way that the mathematical relations between the numbers will reflect observed regularities in the things measured. For this reason, laws and theories using measurements have great predictive, explanatory, and unifying power. For a numerical law or principle refers compendiously to the large range of observations and generalizations on which the possibility of the measurements depended. Mathematically formulated statements have a high concentration of observable consequences.

4. Scientific theories as approximations.

We have now mentioned some of the most significant aspects of scientific theorizing: The deductive relation of theory to observations and laws, the function of theory in prediction, explanation and unification, the pursuit of the ideal of universal explanation, reliance on recondite notions and the use of mathematical methods. In completing our survey we want to stress particularly the fact that *all scientific generalizations, laws,* and *principles are approximations.*

The word "approximation" suggests something that is *"near to"* the truth. If we say a man's height is *approximately* six feet, we mean that while his height is not *exactly* six feet, it is in the neighborhood of that figure. Another way of putting the matter would be to say that six feet is a *provisional estimate* of the man's height, later to be *corrected*. We might say 6′1″ was a *better* approximation, 6′1.3″ a still better approximation, and so on.

What we have just said is misleading in a certain important respect. It suggests that there *is* an "exact truth" to which the various estimates approach more and more closely as the approximations improve. In scientific practice, however, we do not find such "exactness." The height of an object, to return to our illustration, is determined by an *unending* series of successive approximations; where we shall stop is determined only by the accuracy of the instruments we use, and further improvements in the instruments always lead, sooner or later, to the "correction" of our data.

The first reason for the provisional or approximatory character of scientific theory is the possibility of indefinite increase in precision of the data. So long as we are content to notice that grass is green, we do not need any complicated generalization to describe our observations; but as soon as we make our observations more precise by paying attention to the different shades of green, we have to search for correspondingly more complex generalizations to take account of the new distinctions revealed in the data. Throughout science, increase in precision of observation leads to the replacement of accepted generalizations by more complex but more adequate substitutes.

Closely related to the last point is the tendency to make explicit the limitations of range of any generalization (or law or principle). A scientist discovers, for example, the generalization, *Liquids expand on heating*. Closer examination reveals that this holds only within certain ranges of temperature. So the original generalization takes the *corrected* form *Liquids expand when heated within such and such a range of temperature*. This does not end the process of inquiry: More careful and searching examination shows that the ranges of temperature vary for different liquids, that pressure and other conditions are relevant, and so on. The second approximation is accordingly replaced by a third, that by a fourth, and so on indefinitely.

One reason for this endless revision of scientific theory is *the possibility of finding an indefinite number of generalizations to accord with any given set of observations*. A simple illustration will make this clear. Suppose an astronomer observes on successive nights a number of red spots on the surface of the moon. After five spots had appeared, their positions might be roughly as follows:

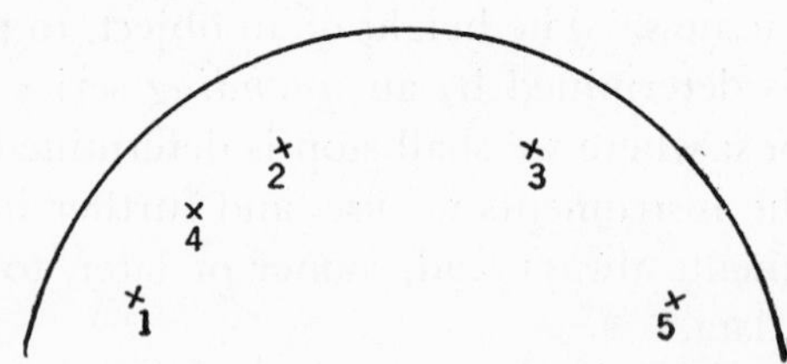

We suppose now that the astronomer wishes to generalize, *i.e.*, to provide a formula or general description applying to *all* the spots—those yet to be observed as well as those already noticed. The simplest way of doing this is to draw a curve showing where the later spots may be expected. For this purpose *any* of the solutions shown in the next figure may be chosen, for all of these are consistent with the data already obtained.

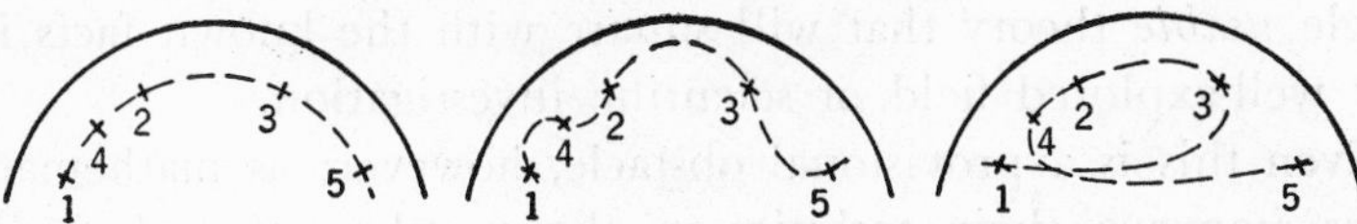

And it is obvious that an indefinite number of other solutions would "square with the known facts." (For all that the astronomer needs to do is to draw *some* line passing through the five spots already observed.)

After the sixth spot had been observed, many of these proposed solutions would have to be rejected (because the curve did not pass through the observed *sixth* position); but there would still be indefinitely many other remaining solutions for the problem of generalization.

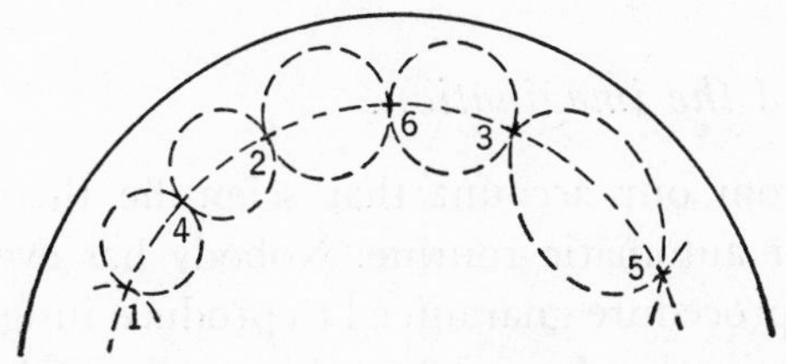

And this would be true no matter how many spots were observed.

However many observations are taken, the scientist always has at his disposal a *finite* number of established facts (though the number may be very large). In generalizing, therefore, he must always choose between indefinitely many generalizations (laws and theories), all of which would be consistent with the data.

In practice, however, his choice is very restricted by the practical need to adopt a theory sufficiently simple to permit of its deductive elaboration with the help of mathematics. Too complicated a theory is useless in practice, because it cannot be used for making further predictions, the mathematical problems being out of the power of mathematicians to solve. Usually, therefore, great ingenuity has to be exercised to find even a single *usable* theory that will square with the known facts in any well-explored field of scientific investigation.

Even this is a provisional obstacle, however; as mathematicians improve their techniques, the number of technically adequate theories to be tried becomes correspondingly larger, and the prospects of obtaining better approximations improve. Scientists can never hope to be in a position to know *the* truth, nor would they have any means of recognizing it if it came into their possession.

We must be careful not to regard this as an indication that all scientific theories are mistaken. A map of a region is not regarded as erroneous because it is later replaced by another showing more detail; scientific theory is a provisional map of the universe, constantly revised as new knowledge accumulates.

5. *The use of the imagination.*

It is clear from our account that scientific theorizing is no mechanical or automatic routine. Nobody has ever been able to discover a procedure guaranteed to produce insight, and even the greatest scientists have been able to do little more than marvel at the apparently miraculous source of their most fruitful notions. Here is a typical statement: "Finally, I succeeded, not on account of my painful efforts, but the grace of God. Like a sudden flash of lightning, the riddle happened to be solved. *I myself cannot say what was the conducting thread which connected what I previously knew with what made my success possible.*" (Gauss, quoted in J. Hadamard, *The Psychology of Invention in the Mathematical Field,* page 15, Princeton University Press, 1945.)

Most of us have had humbler experiences of the same sort in trying to solve crossword or other puzzles, when with an almost audible "click" of the mind, the elusive but obviously right solution appears before us. In applying the analogy of the solution of a puzzle to clarify the position of a scientist searching for a scientific generalization, we must bear in mind one essential difference between the two cases. In the crossword puzzle there is a uniquely correct solution *waiting to be discovered*: In scientific research there are no unique answers.

The language we use about scientific thought tends to mislead us: We talk about the scientist "looking for," and eventually "finding" or "discovering" the scientific theory—as if it had been awaiting its discoverer from the beginning of time. This way of speaking correctly emphasizes the *objective* side of scientific theorizing—the need to make theory square with the facts—but it minimizes the creative and inventive side of scientific theorizing. The theorist has to *choose* the terms in which his theory will be formulated, and he must *decide* how his basic terms are to be combined and related. The activity involved in such choice is very similar to the activity of the musical composer, the painter, or any other creative worker.

In science, as elsewhere, creative ideas come to those who have deserved them by the hard work required for thorough mastery of relevant data. But scientific theorizing also requires a flair for the notions worth pursuing, and calls in its higher reaches for rare qualities of intellectual imagination.

Summary

Scientific theorizing is continuous with common-sense generalization, and no sharp line can be drawn between the two. Generalizations, laws, and principles are understood to be of gradually increasing generality. Each of them has the form *Every case of A is also a case of B*. The term "theory" is used to cover *any* kind of general statement.

Scientific theory is used for prediction and explanation, and it plays a part (previously discussed) in description of phenomena. In successful prediction, some hitherto unobserved event is shown to be a consequence of known data and accepted generalizations. The need for explanation is felt when some unexpected event occurs; an explanation takes the form of additional data and generalizations which, in conjunction with known data and theory, have the event to be explained as a consequence. To be accepted, independent evidence must be forthcoming for the "additional" data and generalizations involved in the explanations. Generalizations (or other generalities) may call for explanation, as being unrelated to known regularities, and the explanation takes the same form as that just mentioned. The type of situation needing explanation, and the type of explanation acceptable, vary with the individual; science sets up the idea of *universal* explanation, and accordingly searches for the *most comprehensive* theories. The explanation of generalizations and laws leads to the formulation of unifying principles. A principle that unifies two generalizations (*i.e.*, from which they can be deduced in the circumstances in which they apply) has novel consequences and so leads to increase in predictive power. Science cannot provide explanations that are "final" in the sense of being incapable of further explanation, and the spirit of science is hostile to theories that are "final" because they arouse no further curiosity.

Scientific theory makes extensive use of mathematics and measurement. Mathematics is a highly precise and universally understood language, well fitted to serve the ideal of public verification. And, as an instrument of *calculation*, is an ingenious means for rendering deduction automatic.

Measurement consists in the assignment of numbers to phenomena. Numbers may be used as substitutes for names or, less trivially, to indicate *order* in phenomena *(intensive measurement)*. In *extensive measurement* the sums and ratios of the numbers, as well as their order, have objective significance. Statements using the results of measurement imply a number of generalizations concerning the field measured, and have a "high concentration of observable consequences."

All scientific theory is *approximate,* taking the form of *provisional* formulations, liable to later correction. Theories are corrected to take account of greater precision in the statement of data, and in order to make the range of their application more explicit. Since an indefinite number of generalizations can be made to accord with any given set of data, the scientist must *select* his theory. This requires use of imagination, comparable to that occurring in the creative activity of the fine arts.

Comprehension test

(For instructions, see page 10.)

1. The chief value of explanation is that it removes "puzzlement." (*true* *false*)
2. In prediction, a phenomenon not yet observed is deduced from known data and accepted theory. (*true* *false*)
3. Science cannot hope to explain the principles of *highest* generality used by it. (*true* *false*)
4. An explanation always uses data and principles that are more familiar than the thing to be explained. (*true* *false*)
5. All scientific principles are "approximations." (*true* *false*)
6. Since "pecking numbers" cannot be significantly added, they cannot be derived from extensive measurement. (*true* *false*)
7. Mathematical calculation is a way of performing complicated deductions semi-automatically. (*true* *false*)
8. Unification of generalizations leads to increase of predictive power. (*true* *false*)
9. If enough data are available, there must be a unique law connecting them. (*true* *false*)
10. Since scientific laws are found by the use of the imagination, they cannot be said to be true. (*true* *false*)

Exercises

A

1. A "letter to the editor" says "we need more practical men and fewer theorists to guide this country in international affairs." Compose a reply, in the form of a letter which might be printed by the newspaper.
2. Is there any shade of meaning associated with the word "theory" that is neglected in the text? (Consult a dictionary.)
3. Explain in detail some of the *general* statements involved in the assertion "I saw the sun at 12 noon on July 1st."
4. Criticize the following explanations:
   (a) Eskimos have perfect teeth because they eat so much meat.

(b) The reason for America's entry into the war was the attack on Pearl Harbor.

(c) Since the Bible tells us that many animals were created in their present form, fossils must have been placed in the earth by God.

(d) "Somebody must be at the bottom of the class—that's why I'm there."

(e) Birds return to the same nest year after year because they have a sense of direction.

(f) The presence of life on this planet must be explained by spontaneous generation.

5. Explain the relations in meaning of the following words: "reason," "cause," "explanation," "understanding."

6. Use the following account to illustrate the various points made in the discussion of the nature of explanation in the text:

"In the sea round Tierra del Fuego, and at no great distance from the land, I have seen narrow lines of water of a bright red colour, from the number of crustacea, which somewhat resemble in form large prawns.... At a distance of several leagues from the Archipelago of the Galapagos, the ship sailed through three strips of a dark yellowish, or mud-like water... separated from the surrounding water by a sinuous yet distinct margin. The colour was caused by little gelatinous balls, about the fifth of an inch in diameter, in which numerous minute spherical ovules were imbedded.... There are two circumstances in the above accounts which appear remarkable: first, how do the various bodies which form the band with defined edges keep together? In the case of the prawn-like crabs, their movements were as coinstantaneous as in a regiment of soldiers; but this cannot happen from anything like voluntary action with the ovules.... Secondly, what causes the length and narrowness of the bands? The appearance so much resembles that which may be seen in every torrent, where the stream uncoils into long streaks the froth collected in the eddies, that I must attribute the effect to a similar action either of the currents of the air or sea... on no other hypothesis can I understand their linear grouping." (Darwin, *A Naturalist's Voyage Around the World,* entry of March 18th, 1832.)

7. Expand the statement "mathematics is *telescoped* deduction" in such a way as to eliminate the metaphor used.

8. Which of the following can be measured *intensively* and which *extensively?* (Explain your reasons.)

   Volume, age (of a person), hardness, intelligence, temperature, income, happiness, loudness (of a sound), beauty.

9. In a football league containing five teams, the results at the end

of the season were as follows: A tied with B and beat C, D, E; B beat C and D, but lost to E; C defeated D and E. Is it possible to arrange the teams "in order" in the sense explained in the text? (Explain the assumptions you are using.)

10. Are the following three statements consistent: (a) The temperature was between 40 F. and 41 F.; (b) the temperature was between 40.4 F. and 40.5 F.; (c) the temperature was between 40.47 F. and 40.48 F.? What features of scientific theory does your answer illustrate?

B

1. Read some report on the present status of the Theory of Evolution and use it to illustrate the features of scientific explanation discussed in the text.
2. Show the relation of the views expressed in the following quotations to the discussion in the text and give your reasons for agreeing or disagreeing with them.
   a. "The progress of science lies in the continual discovery of more and more comprehensive formulae, by aid of which we can classify the relationships and sequences of more and more extensive groups of phenomena. The earlier formulae are not necessarily wrong, they are merely replaced by others which in briefer language describe more facts." (Karl Pearson, *Grammar of Science,* p. 85. Everyman Library Ed.)
   b. "I regard all explanation as a patterning process ... The scientific patterning is found in practice to give a more usable policy of action, but this tells nothing about the 'correctness' or 'truth' of the explanation." (W. H. George, *The Scientist in Action,* p. 213. New York: Emerson Books, Inc., 1938.)
   c. "It is a test of true theories not only to account for, but to predict, phenomena." (William Whewell, *Novum Organum Renovatum,* aphorism 12.)
   d. "The part played by measurement and quantity in science is very great, but is, I think, sometimes overestimated. Mathematical technique is powerful, and men of science are naturally anxious to be able to apply it whenever possible; but a law may be quite scientific without being quantitative." (Bertrand Russell, *The Scientific Outlook,* p. 67. New York: W. W. Norton & Co., Inc., 1931.)
3. Examine the following definitions of science (quoted in C. J. Keyser, *The Pastures of Wonder*. New York: Columbia University Press, 1929). How far are they consistent (a) with one another, (b) with the conception of scientific method presented in the text?

a. "Science is knowledge gained by systematic observation, experiment, and reasoning." (Pasteur.)
b. "Science is knowledge, not of things, but of their relations." (Poincaré.)
c. "Science is organized common sense." (Thomas Huxley.)
d. "Science is the process which makes knowledge." (Charles Singer.)
e. "Science is an attempt to systematize our knowledge of the circumstances in which recognitions occur." (Whitehead.)

Formulate your own definition of science.

Appendices

Appendix 1

GENERAL THEORY OF THE SYLLOGISM

1. Preliminaries.

THE methods explained in Chapters 7 and 8 are sufficient to determine the validity of every type of syllogism that can be constructed. When presented with any syllogism, we can either prepare the appropriate Venn diagram in order to "see" whether the conclusion is valid, or we can choose instead to determine whether any of the rules of the valid syllogism (page 139) have been broken. The second of these methods is not so different from the first as might initially appear, for in order to convince ourselves that the rules were correct when they were first proposed we had to "see" their truth. Yet, having once "seen" that the rules *are* true, we can apply them mechanically and so with less fear of making mistakes than is the case with the Venn diagrams.

In establishing the eight rules of the valid syllogism we convinced ourselves that they were *necessary, i.e.,* that no syllogism could be valid *unless* it conformed to them. But we did not show that these rules were *sufficient, i.e.,* that any syllogism conforming to them *would* be valid. (The rules resemble other groups of fundamental principles in this respect. Rules of morality, legal procedure, or musical composition are usually presented as *necessary* conditions.)

It is, however, the case that the rules of the valid syllogism are sufficient as well as necessary. When we shall have established the truth of this assertion, as we propose to do in this appendix, we shall be in a position to use the eight rules *alone* to determine questions concerning the validity of syllogisms. In the course of establishing the sufficiency of the rules, we shall incidentally discover all the valid types of syllogism. Apart from the intrinsic interest of the results so obtained, the arguments we shall need to employ will provide good exercise in deductive thinking.

2. *Classification of the various types of syllogism.*

How many different types of syllogism are there? Let us remind ourselves of the definition of the terms of a syllogism and their location in it. The major term, p, is by definition the predicate of the conclusion, and must occur, together with the middle term, m, in the major premise. For the major premise, therefore, we have the following possibilities: p is either the subject or the predicate, and the proposition is A, E, I, or O. There are accordingly *eight* possible forms that the major premise can take:

$$\left\{\begin{matrix}\text{All}\\ \text{Some}\end{matrix}\right\} p \left\{\begin{matrix}<\\ \not<\end{matrix}\right\} m \qquad \left\{\begin{matrix}\text{All}\\ \text{Some}\end{matrix}\right\} m \left\{\begin{matrix}<\\ \not<\end{matrix}\right\} p$$

Similar argument shows that the minor premise can take one of eight forms. Since *any* form of the major premise can be associated with *any* form of the minor premise, we have $8 \times 8 = 64$ possible forms for the premises.

Finally the conclusion must take one of the *four* forms:

$$\left\{\begin{matrix}\text{All}\\ \text{Some}\end{matrix}\right\} s \left\{\begin{matrix}<\\ \not<\end{matrix}\right\} p$$

Since any of these four kinds of conclusions could be associated with any combination of premises, there must be $64 \times 4 = 256$ different forms of syllogism. Our task is to show that of these 256, all that conform to the rules previously given are in fact valid.

The different kinds of syllogism are classified *first* by showing the location of the middle term. If we continue to write the major premise first, the location of the middle term automatically determines the location of the major and minor terms.

Thus, suppose we are given the following locations of the middle term:

(1)

(2)

(3) (4)

(where the numbers are added for convenience in referring to the various positions).

Then (3) is occupied by *s*, and (4) by *p* (definitions of the minor and major terms); (1) is occupied by *p* (definition of the major premise); and (2) is occupied by *s* (definition of the minor premise).

The arrangement of the terms must therefore be:

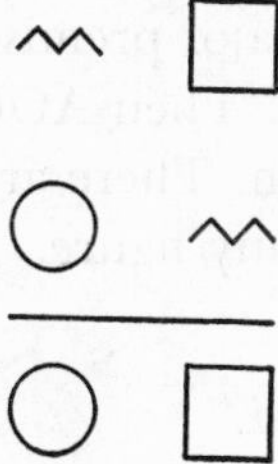

i.e., the major term is the *predicate* of the major premise, and the minor term is the *subject* of the minor premise.

The arrangement of the terms in the syllogism is known as a **figure.** There are four figures possible:

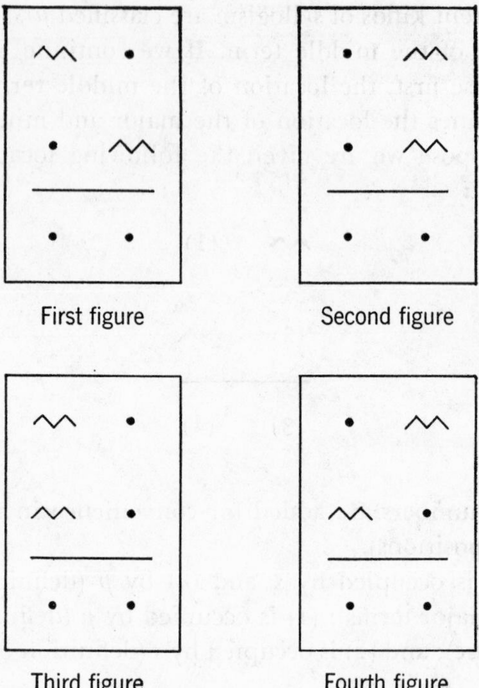

The second way of classifying the various types of syllogism is by specifying the kind of propositions of which they are composed. Thus suppose the major premise is A, the minor premise is O and the conclusion O. Then AOO is said to be the **mood** of the syllogism in question. There are 64 possible moods, and each mood may occur in any figure.

3. *Illustrations of method.*

We shall now show how the rules of the valid syllogism can be used systematically to eliminate invalid types of syllogism. It will be found that we make much use of distribution patterns, which help to simplify our discussions.

Exercise 1: To prove that the mood IE is never valid

We exhibit the data in a distribution analysis as follows:

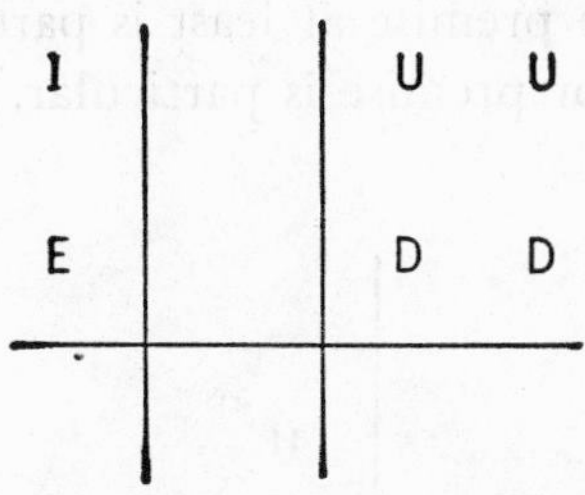

Notice that we are not given any information about the character of the conclusion or the figure of the syllogism. Next we insert four obvious deductions, *numbering them* as we go to permit of easy checking afterwards.

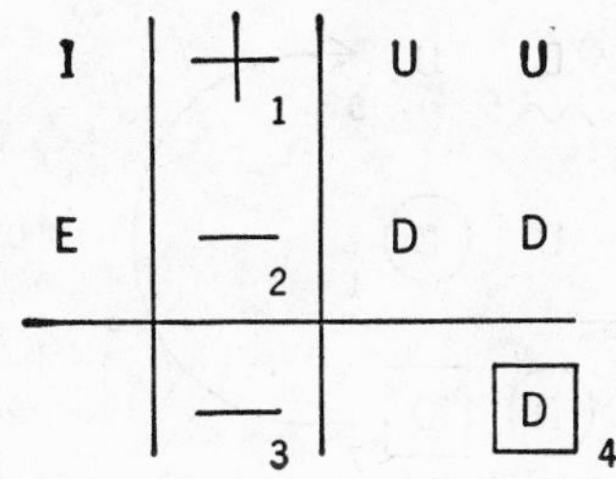

Explanation: The I proposition is positive, the E proposition negative; hence the conclusion is negative. A negative proposition has a distributed predicate, and this must be the major term, by definition.

Finally the diagram now reached shows the syllogism cannot be valid. For the major term must be U in the major premise, and hence cannot be D in the conclusion without producing the fallacy of illicit process.

Exercise 2: To prove that if the conclusion is universal both premises must be universal

Let us try an *indirect* proof. We suppose that the conclusion is universal but one premise at least is particular.

Case a: The minor premise is particular. The data are:

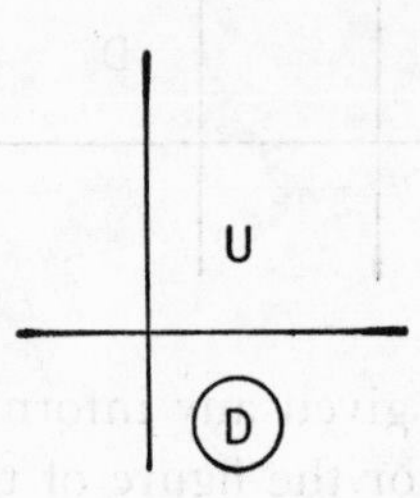

This time we shall insert all the deductions on a single diagram, thus:

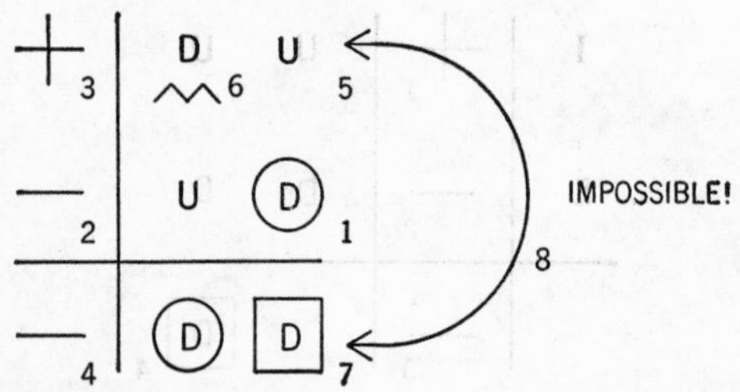

Explanation: (1) The D minor term must be associated with a D minor term in its premise; (2), a proposition with a D predicate is negative; (3) and (4), the remaining premise must be positive and the conclusion negative; (5), a positive proposition has a U predicate; (6), the middle term must be D at least once; (7), a negative proposition has a D predicate; (8) the fallacy of illicit process of the major is committed.

We have shown *the minor premise cannot be particular.*

Case b: The major premise is particular and the minor premise universal. (We have already shown that the minor premise cannot be particular.) The data are:

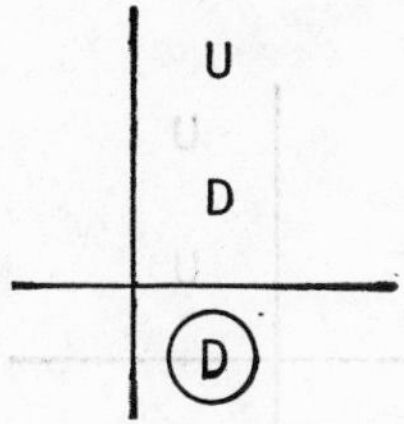

Case b1: The conclusion is positive. We show the argument without comment now:

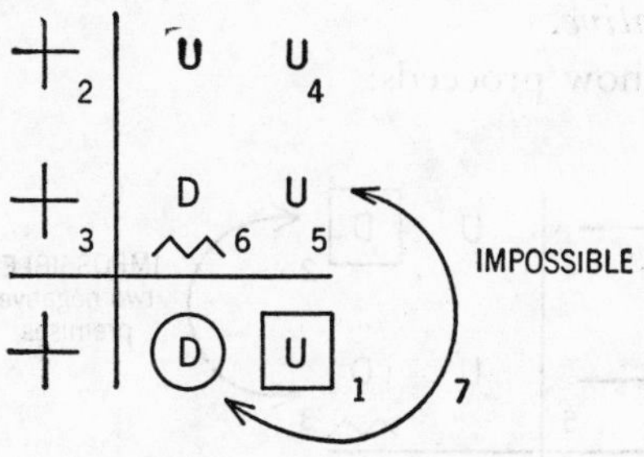

Case b2: The conclusion is negative. The argument is:

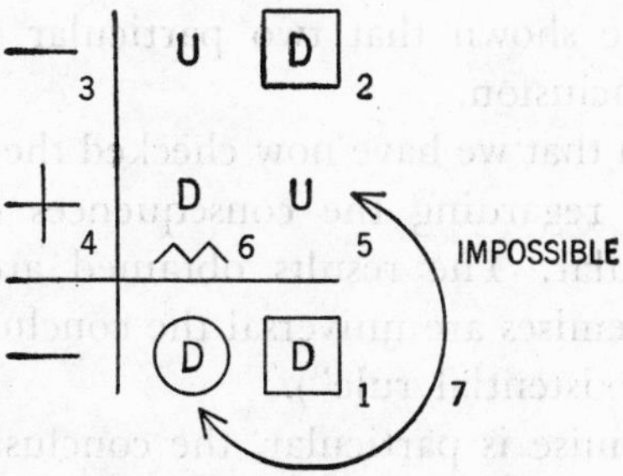

Having now examined all the cases, we have succeeded in proving our original assertion:

Exercise 3: To prove that two particular premises cannot give valid conclusion

The data are:

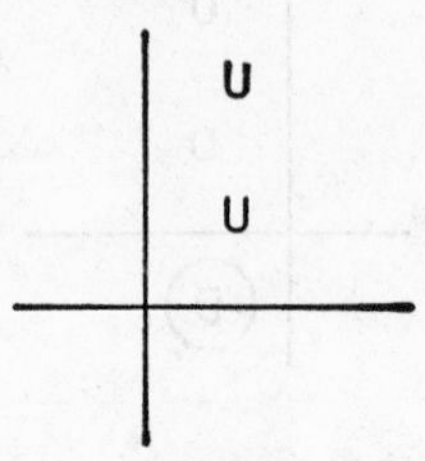

Since the middle term must be D at least once, it is the predicate of one premise, making that premise negative and *the conclusion negative.*

The argument now proceeds:

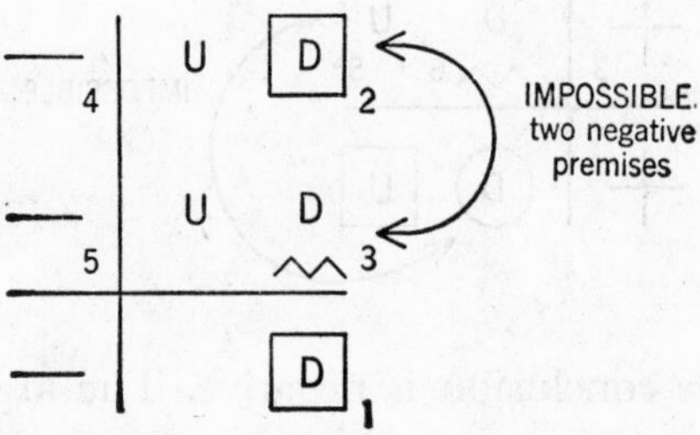

Thus we have shown that two particular premises cannot yield a valid conclusion.

It will be seen that we have now checked the statement made earlier (p. 142) regarding the consequences of having some premises particular. The results obtained are:

1. If both premises are universal the conclusion is universal (by the "existential rule").
2. If one premise is particular, the conclusion is particular (by exercise 2 above).
3. If both premises are particular, there is no valid conclusion (exercise 3).

4. Elimination of the invalid moods.

We can use the following table:

Minor premise \ Major premise	A	E	I	O
A		(2)		
E			(3)	
I	(1)			
O				

to show what happens when any of the 16 possible combinations of types of premises is given. Thus, in compartment (1) we would insert data for the syllogism having mood AIX, and compartments (2) and (3) respectively would serve similarly for the moods EAX and IEX.

We know that there can be no valid conclusion in the following cases:

1. Both premises negative (rule 2a of the valid syllogism).
2. Both premises particular (exercise 3 of the last section).
3. The mood is IEX (exercise 1 of the last section).

Insertion of these data in our diagram gives:

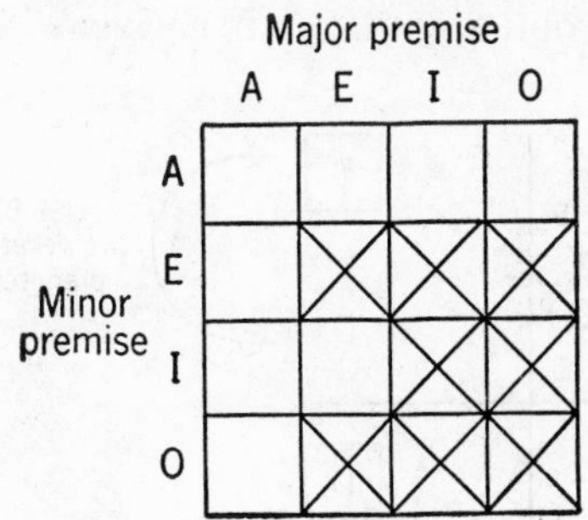

which we can conveniently show as follows:

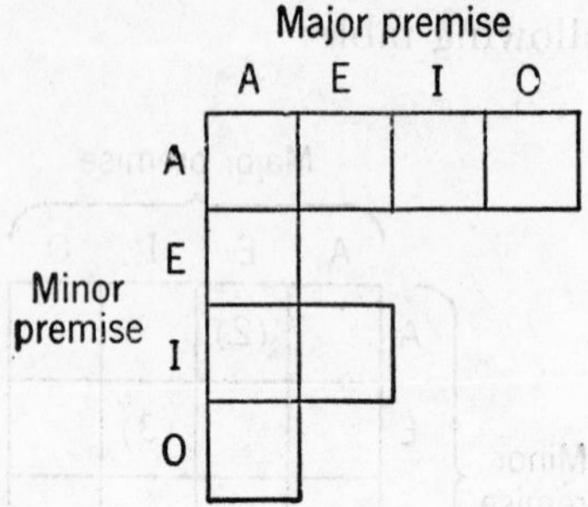

It will be found that each of the eight possibilities remaining is valid in *some* figure.

5. *The valid moods of the first figure.*

We turn our attention now to the *first* figure, so that we can assume:

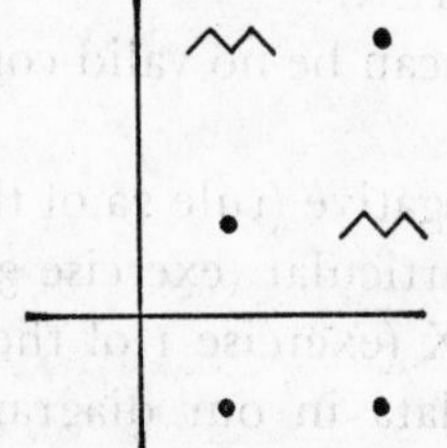

Case a: The second premise is negative:

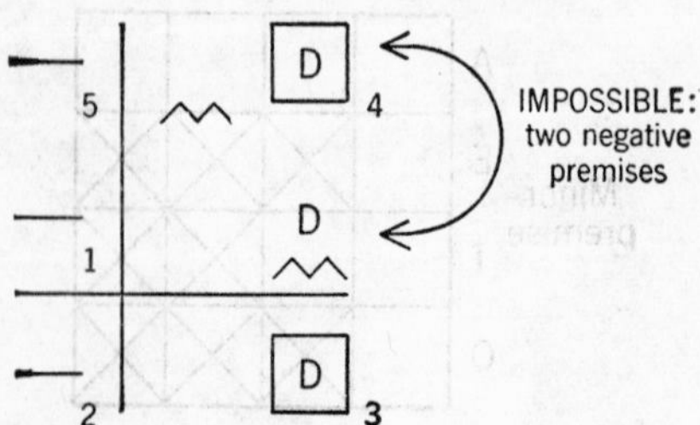

Hence, *the second premise must be positive:*

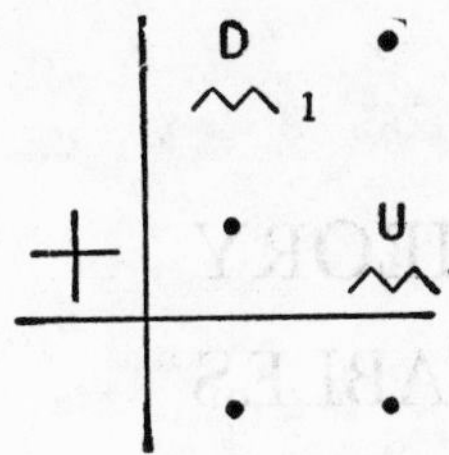

and *the major premise must be universal.*

The diagram obtained at the end of the last section accordingly becomes:

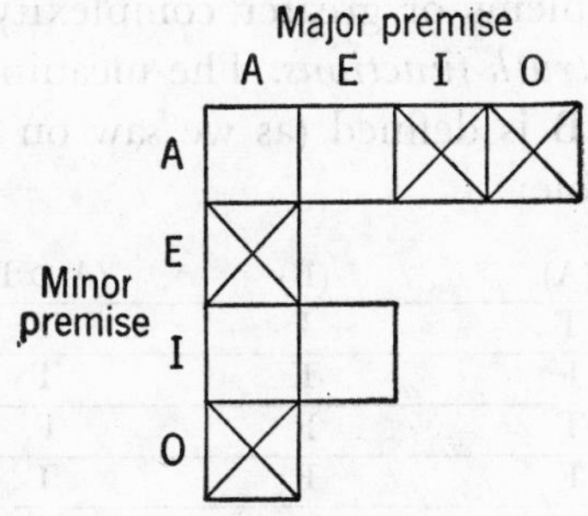

The only permissible moods must accordingly be: AAA, EAE, AII, EIO. It is easily verified, with the aid of Venn diagrams if necessary, that all four of these are in fact valid.

We shall leave the examination of the remaining three figures to the reader. The results obtained are: 2nd figure, AEE, EAE, AOO, EIO; 3rd figure, AII, IAI, EIO, OAO; 4th figure, EIO, AEE, IAI.

Of the 256 possibilities which we recognized at the beginning of this chapter, exactly fifteen are valid.

Appendix 2

GENERAL THEORY OF TRUTH-TABLES

WE have used truth-tables (in Chapters 5 and 6) to settle questions about arguments of relatively simple forms. In this appendix we shall show in outline how truth-tables can be used to solve problems of greater complexity and generality.

The totality of truth-functions. The meaning of the complex proposition $A \supset B$ is defined (as we saw on page 85), by the following truth-table:

(A)	(B)	$(A \supset B)$
T	T	T
F	T	T
T	F	F
F	F	T
(1)	(2)	(3)

The table shows us the truth-value (truth or falsity) of $A \supset B$ for each combination of truth-values of A and B. $A \supset B$ is called a **truth-function** of A and B, because its truth-value depends solely on the truth-value of its components, A and B.

Given two propositions, A and B, how many distinct truth-functions of them can be found? If we start with the following diagram:

(A)	(B)	
T	T	
F	T	
T	F	
F	F	
(1)	(2)	(3)

we shall get different truth-functions by filling column (3) with T's and F's in different ways. (For instance, if we write TTTF, we get the truth-function (A ∨ B.) It is easy to see that there are 16 different ways of completing column (3); accordingly, there are exactly 16 different truth-functions of A and B. (Similarly there are 256 truth-functions of A, B, and C. Generally, if *n* components are taken, the number of distinct truth-functions resulting is 2^{2^n}.)

An interesting exercise consists in writing out all 16 of these truth-tables and proceeding to identify each truth-function by using symbols explained in the text. (For instance, the truth-function defined by writing TFFT in column 3 is A≡B.)

The use of truth-functions to determine validity. We shall illustrate this by means of an example. Suppose we have to determine whether the following argument is valid:

$$\begin{array}{c}(A \vee B) \supset C \\ (A \vee C) \supset B' \\ \hline B \supset A\end{array}$$

What we do is build up, step by step, truth-tables for all three propositions concerned. The calculation would look as follows:

			D		E			
A	B	C	A ∨ B	D ⊃ C	A ∨ C	B′	E ⊃ B′	B ⊃ A
T	T	T	T	T	T	F	F	T
F	T	T	T	T	T	F	F	F
T	F	T	T	T	T	T	T	T
F	F	T	F	T	T	T	T	T
T	T	F	T	F	T	F	F	T
F	T	F	T	F	F	F	T	F
T	F	F	T	F	T	T	T	T
F	F	F	F	T	F	T	T	T
(1)	(2)	(3)	(4)	(5) *	(6)	(7)	(8) *	(9) *

In this table, the columns we finally need are (5), (8), and (9), which show the truth-value of the three propositions in our argument for *all* combinations of truth-values of the components,

A, B, and C. (The other columns are simply intermediate steps in the calculation.)

To determine whether the argument is valid, we need to know what happens when both $(A \vee B) \supset C$ and $(A \vee C) \supset B'$ are true. Comparison of columns (5) and (8) shows that this case corresponds to lines 3 and 8 of our table. Finally, examination of lines 3 and 8 of column (9) shows that in each case the conclusion $B \supset A$ is also true. The argument is, accordingly, *valid.*

The procedure is rather laborious (though we could easily invent short cuts if we had much occasion to use it). Its theoretical importance consists in its showing us that *any* question about the validity of conditional arguments *could* be settled, no matter how complex the argument might be.

The method can easily be modified to provide answers to many other questions concerning the logical relations of propositions—notably, to the question whether a given set of propositions are *consistent* with each other.

Appendix 3

ARGUMENTS INVOLVING PROBABILITIES

1. The nature of the problem.

IN the course of our examination of reasoning, we have tried to answer two types of question: (1) *Certain propositions having been supplied, what other propositions rigorously follow?* (Or, more simply, *If given premises were to be true, what conclusions would therefore have to be true?*) (2) *What conditions must the evidence for a generalization satisfy in order that the generalization shall be established as true?*

The first of these questions formulates the central problem of *deductive* logic; the second draws our attention to the need for criticizing and clarifying *inductive* procedures. Very often, however, we are faced with problems of reasoning calling for attention to further considerations.

Consider the following example. A man who is about to go on a camping trip to Colorado is advised to inoculate himself against "Rocky Mountain spotted fever." Let us suppose he knows the disease to be prevalent in the region he is to visit and its consequences to be, at best, disagreeable and, at worst, fatal; on the other hand, the inoculation itself is expensive, painful, and somewhat dangerous. He would very likely find it hard to make a wise decision. One source of the difficulty is that only *partial information* is available. If the camper knew *for sure* that he would be infected, he would not hesitate to take precautions; while if he knew *for sure* that he would not be attacked, he would not waste time and money to defend himself. As it is, the best he can do is to weigh the degree of risk, that is to say *the chance* or *the probability* that he will be infected.

Now this type of case constantly arises in ordinary life. We are constantly required to make decisions (sometimes of the greatest importance) on the basis of a "balance of probabilities." To refuse to act because the deductive and inductive evidence at our disposal does not categorically establish the conclusion that interests us, would be folly. Suppose I have the choice of going to New York by automobile, train, or plane. In each case there is *some* risk of accident, but I do not know for certain either that I shall or that I shall not be involved in an accident. It would be most unreasonable to conclude that therefore I have *no* evidence favoring one alternative against the others. (Suppose nine out of ten planes crashed, but only one train in a million!) My decision is determined here, as in other cases where I *must* choose between alternative courses of action, by a *comparison of probabilities.* (Other considerations, such as the relative convenience of the alternatives, are also relevant —but we shall not discuss them here, as they hardly belong to a study of logic.)

The *meaning* of probability assertions is not obvious to inspection—and is, indeed, matter for high controversy among experts. "Critical thinking," here as elsewhere, demands more explicit awareness of the standards and principles involved. More specifically, we need to understand more clearly what it is we are claiming when we say "There is such-and-such a chance that so-and-so will happen." And we need to become clearer about how such claims can be supported and justified by appropriate evidence.

2. *The meaning of probability assertions.*

The simplest assertions. The simplest (and weakest) type of assertion involving reference to chance or probability takes the form *"There is a chance that* (such-and-such will happen)," or some equivalent form. For example, "There is a chance that the Republicans will win the next election," or "There is some chance that I will catch a cold before the end of this month," or "There is some probability that I will be dealt a singleton in a game of bridge." (Notice the alternative idioms.)

The meaning of such assertions is as follows: To say that there is a chance that the Republicans will win is to say that *it is not certain that they will* win *and not certain that they will not* win. In general, "There is a chance that *P*" means the same as "It is not certain that *P* and not certain that not-*P*" (in other words, *P may* be the case). Again "There is *no* chance that *P*" means the same as "It *is* certain that not-*P*."

The sense of certainty that is relevant here is *factual,* not *logical,* certainty. "There is no chance that an ordinary man can run a mile in ten seconds." This is true; yet there is no *logical* absurdity or contradiction in an ordinary man being supposed to run the distance so swiftly; we simply mean that an ordinary man cannot *in fact* do this.

The last example illustrates a most important point, that in the simplest probability assertions we are claiming that there is a *relation* between *two* propositions (or facts, or situations, or possibilities). *Given* that we have in mind an "ordinary man," running naturally, without the aid of a motor, etc.—given all this, there is no chance of his running a mile in ten seconds. But if we had in mind a different set of data, we might well say there *was* a chance. I may say, correctly, "Rocket has a chance to win the Derby"; but his jockey, who knows Rocket has gone lame, may say "Rocket has *no* chance." The two assertions do not contradict one another, for they are based on different bodies of information. The question "Is there a chance that *P*?" is incomplete, and the full form is "Given that *Q*, is there a chance that *P*?" We shall call the proposition *Q* the **basis** of the probability assertion, and *P* the **outcome** of the assertion. (Other names that have been suggested are "proposal" and "supposal," respectively.) Thus every probability assertion claims that there is a relation between a given basis and a given outcome.

What is the relation? A probability assertion of the kind so far considered (Given *Q*, there is a chance that *P*) asserts that its basis *does not determine* its outcome. To test the truth of such an assertion, we must find out whether, in similar cases, the truth of the basis *sometimes* goes with the truth of the outcome. For instance, to test the probability assertion "There is a chance that this penny, when tossed, will come down heads," I must toss the penny, in circumstances *similar to those I am describing*, and see whether it does sometimes come down heads. Should the penny sometimes come down heads and sometimes not, I was right in my original assertion; otherwise not.

Comparison of probabilities. A comparison of probabilities takes the form "There is less (more, at least as much, just as much) chance that *R* than that *S*." As is customary in ordinary, non-technical talk about probabilities or chances, we have not indicated explicitly what basis or bases are supposed to be understood. A comparison of the chances of *R* and *S* is easiest when both *R* and *S* are being considered with respect to the *same* basis, say *Q*. In some still more special cases, we can decide the truth of such a comparison by exclusive appeal to *logical* considerations. The following, indeed, is a statement that is necessarily true: Suppose *S* logically follows from *R*; then the chance that *S*, given *Q*, is *at least as great* as the chance that *R*, given *Q*. (In other words, for a given basis, weakening the outcome may improve, and cannot worsen, the chance.)

This and similar cases are somewhat special, however. Very often we need to compare chances or probabilities defined in terms of *different* bases. Our only recourse then is to form some *numerical estimate* of each of the chances. This is commonly known as "estimating the odds."

Numerical estimates of probability. When a man says "The chances are one in six that this die will fall with the two uppermost," he is giving a numerical estimate of *the degree to which the "basis" determines the "outcome."* There is no direct way of calculating the extent of leeway that the basis leaves to the outcome. We must rely on the indirect evidence of *what happens in repeated trials.* When we find that *many* cases of the basis being true are cases of the outcome being true, we say the basis closely determines that outcome ("there is a high chance . . ."); when we find relatively *few* cases of the outcome and the basis being true together, we regard the basis as only loosely determining that outcome ("there is a low chance . . ."). More generally, we measure the chance by determining *the proportion of cases of a true basis in which the outcome specified is also true.*

Three important points should be noticed concerning the verification of such numerical estimates of probability. (1) The proportion, or "relative frequency," as it is sometimes called, that we have to determine, is the proportion *in the long run.* So we need inductive procedures to arrive at such results. (*E.g.,* we perform an induction when, after tossing a penny a great many times we conclude that it *would* come down heads about as often as it came down tails.) (2) Statements about what would happen in the long run are of the nature of approximations (compare the discussion in Chapter 19, pages 393-396). The evidence for the truth of the assertion "The chance that this penny will fall heads is one-half" is that in the long run *approximately* half the cases in which the penny is tossed are cases of "heads." (3) If the evidence for the probability assertion is to be fair, the factors *not* mentioned in the basis must all be "treated alike." Suppose I ask "What is the chance that a Republican will be a woman?" Because chance, not certainty, is in question, we know that other factors besides membership of the Republican party will determine whether a given individual is a Republican *woman.* It would be fallacious to collect statistics exclusively from those engaged as cooks, say, for we know that a majority of such persons will be women, anyway. We need, in fact, a sample so chosen as not to prejudice the answer for or against the outcome. In other words, we need a "random sample" of cases of the basis being true. This important but difficult topic cannot be discussed further in this outline.

3. The mathematics of probability.

Since the days when mathematicians became interested in games of chance, enormous strides have been made in the mathematics of probability, and today this subject has wide importance and a multitude of applications to many branches of science. These successes have been achieved, in part, by a kind of simplification of the subject-matter that is quite characteristic of mathematical procedure. The mathematician does not, in general, ask how probability assertions are shown to be true; he takes for granted, most of the time, that there is *some* way in which probabilities can be measured. All he postulates is that such measures will confirm to a few principles that he lays down as "axioms" at the outset of his mathematical inquiries. (Among the most important of such axioms are the so-called "addition" and "multiplication" principles. They give rules for calculating *the chance that R ∨ S, given Q* and *the chance that R & S, given Q.* Rules for more complex cases can easily be deduced.)

Where it does prove necessary to consider *applications* of these somewhat abstract principles, the mathematical text books usually adopt the further simplification of determining the measures of probability by simply counting the proportion of favorable cases among those taken to be "equi-probable." (Thus the chance of a die falling with an even number showing is said to be one-half, because there are six faces, of which three are "favorable" to the outcome in question.)

Such inquiries, though their value to scientists can hardly be exaggerated, are not often directly relevant to the daily problems of ordinary people. The mathematics of probability may help a poker player calculate his odds, but it is questionable whether this is altogether conducive to success in that intricate pastime.

4. Critical thinking about probability.

What, then, *would* help the ordinary man make probability judgments with greater finesse and less liability to error? He might find the following suggestions helpful:

1. Hold firmly to a few simple truths about probability that follow from the meanings of probability assertions. Among the more important of these are (a) that probability is relative (to what we have called the "basis"), (b) that high probability of *P* is compatible with the falsity of *P,* (c) that what is highly probable is *not* "bound to happen if we wait long enough," (the fallacy of the so-called "Law of Averages").

2. Remember that in practical affairs we need *as wide a basis as possible* for probability assertions, and so cultivate habits of searching for as much relevant evidence as can be obtained *before* commitment to judgments of probability.

3. Try systematically to attach numerical estimates of the chances to any probability assertions that are likely to be important. (*E.g.,* by asking "What odds would I be prepared to accept that such-and-such is the case?")

4. Try to improve one's estimates of probabilities by noticing how often, and *for what reasons* they prove to be mistaken.

The full elaboration of such exhortation to "good judgment" would call for a separate book as long as this one.

Appendix 4

ANALYSIS OF EXTENDED ARGUMENT

THE analysis of extended arguments, expressed informally (see pages 66-73, 144-150), is of such great practical importance that it seems advisable to add a few further illustrations of the problems that may arise.

Example 1: "Up and down the world, wherever you go, you will find that proverbial wisdom prescribes the wine of the country as the best drink of all. And what could be more logical than to assume that men will thrive best upon the fruits of the self-same land that bore them. Here in Britain our native wine is beer."

Comment: As in many advertisements, the logical structure of the arguments used is quite simple. We can disentangle at least two syllogisms:

> Whatever proverbial wisdom prescribes is true.
> That the "native wine" is best is prescribed by proverbial wisdom.
> ———
> It is true that the native wine is best.

> The things that men thrive best on are fruits of their native soil.
> The native wine is a fruit of the native soil.
> ———
> The native wine is a thing that men thrive best upon.

The first of these syllogisms is valid, the second invalid. However, it would be a mistake to make too much of this—or even of the charming semantical trick by which beer appears as a "wine." It is more to the point to notice how skillful choice of language produces a kind of idyllic, traditional, almost biblical setting for the prosaic drink advertised. The advertisement aims at producing a favorable set of associations (as a colored illustration might). The "argument," such as it is, is of subordinate importance.

Example 2: "As to style, what would you say to a young writer about symbolism?" "I don't understand symbolism in fiction. It is only a fashion of the day, so far as I can judge, and it will disappear. What is a symbol? You say one thing and you mean another. Why the hell shouldn't you say it right out?" (From an interview with Somerset Maugham, reported in *The New York Times Magazine,* January 23, 1949.)

Comment: While this hardly deserves classification as serious argument, it seems worth citing, lest any reader think that the modes of discussion illustrated in our imaginary dialogue (pages 239-242) are too far-fetched. Maugham's remarks, as reported, illustrate also the importance of making assumptions explicit (see page 27). It is far from obvious that what is said by means of symbolism *can* be said "right out." In fact, most literary critics would emphatically deny it. (The reader is left to make the "argument" explicit.)

Example 3: "If matter is supposed to exist necessarily, then in that necessary existence there is either included the power of gravitation, or not. If not, then in a world merely material, and in which no intelligent being presides, there never could have been any motion; because motion, as has been already shown, and is now granted in the question, is not necessary of itself. But if the power of gravitation be included in the pretended necessary existence of matter: then, it following necessarily that there must be a vacuum (as the incomparable Sir Isaac Newton has abundantly demonstrated that there must, if gravitation be an universal quality or affection of matter), it follows likewise, that matter is not a necessary being. For if a vacuum actually be, then it is plainly more than possible for matter not to be." (From Samuel Clarke, *Demonstration of the Being and Attributes of God,* 1705.)

Comment: This difficult passage is offered, by way of contrast, to illustrate what needs to be done in full analysis of a piece of intricate reasoning.

The main premises of the argument are:

1. If matter is a necessary being, either the power of gravitation necessarily exists or not.
2. If the power of gravitation does not necessarily exist and the world is merely material and is not presided over by an intelligent being, motion does not exist.
3. Motion does not necessarily exist of itself.
4. [If motion does not necessarily exist of itself, then in a "merely material" world in which the power of gravitation does not necessarily exist, motion does not exist.]
5. [Motion exists.]
6. If the power of gravitation necessarily exists, a vacuum must exist.
7. If a vacuum exists, matter is not a necessary being.
8. [If matter is a necessary being, the world is not presided over by an intelligent being.]

These may be symbolized as:

1. $A \supset (B \vee B')$
2. $(B' \& C') \supset D'$
3. E'
4. $[(E' \& B' \& C') \supset D']$
5. $[D]$
6. $B \supset F$
7. $F \supset A'$
8. $[A \supset C']$

The conclusion *Matter is not a necessary being* (A′) follows validly from these premises.

Finally, the reader may enjoy analyzing for himself the following amusing specimen of informal argumentation. It is taken from Livingstone's *Missionary Travels* (1st edition, pages 22-25).

Example 4: "As for the rain-makers, they carried the sympathies of the people along with them, and not without reason. With the following arguments they were all acquainted, and in order to understand their force we must place ourselves in their position, and believe, as they do, that all medicines act by a mysterious charm. The term for cure may be translated 'charm.'

Medical Doctor: Hail, friend! How very many medicines you have about you this morning! Why, you have every medicine in the country here.

Rain Doctor: Very true, my friend; and I ought; for the whole country needs the rain which I am making.

M.D.: So you really believe that you can command the clouds? I think that can be done by God alone.

R.D.: We both believe the very same thing. It is God that makes the rain, but I pray to him by means of these medicines, and, the rain coming, of course it is then mine. It was I who made it for the Bakwains for many years, when they were at Shokuane; through my wisdom, too, their women became fat and shining. Ask them; they will tell you the same as I do.

M.D.: But we are distinctly told in the parting words of our Saviour that we can pray to God acceptably in His name alone, and not by means of medicines.

R.D.: Truly! But God told *us* differently. He made black men first, and did not love us, as he did the white men. He made you beautiful, and gave you clothing, and guns, and gun-powder, and horses, and wagons, and many other things about which we know nothing. But toward us he had no heart. He gave us nothing, except the assegai, and cattle, and rain-making; and he did not give us hearts like yours. We never love each other. Other tribes place medicines about our country to prevent the rain, so that we may be dispersed by hunger, and go to them, and augment their power. We must dissolve their charms by our medicines. God has given us one little thing, which you know nothing of. He has given us the knowledge of certain medicines by which we can make rain. *We* do not despise those things which you possess, though we are ignorant of them. We don't understand your book, but we don't despise it. *You* ought not to despise our little knowledge, though you are ignorant of it.

M.D.: I don't despise what I am ignorant of; I only think you are mistaken in saying that you have medicines which can influence the rain at all.

R.D.: That's just the way people speak when they talk on a subject of which they have no knowledge. When we first opened our eyes, we found our forefathers making rain, and we follow in their footsteps. You, who send to Kuruman for corn, and irrigate your garden, may do without rain; *we* cannot manage in that way. If we had no rain, the cattle would have no pasture, the cows give no milk, our children become lean and die, our wives run away to other tribes who do make rain, and have corn, and the whole tribe dispersed and lost; our fire would go out.

M.D.: I quite agree with you as to the value of the rain; but you cannot charm the clouds by medicines. You wait till you see the clouds come, then you use your medicines, and take the credit which belongs to God only.

R.D.: I use my medicines, and you employ yours; we are both doctors, and doctors are not deceivers. You give a patient medicine. Sometimes God is pleased to heal him by means of your medicine: sometimes not—he dies. When he is cured, you take the credit of what God does. I do the same. Sometimes God grants us rain, sometimes not. When he does, we take the credit of the charm. When a patient dies, you don't give up trust in your medicine, neither do I when rains fails. If you wish me to leave off my medicines, why continue your own?

M.D.: I give medicines to living creatures within my reach, and can see the effects though no cure follows; you pretend to charm the clouds, which are so far above us that your medicines never reach them. The clouds usually lie in our direction, and your smoke goes in another. God alone can command the clouds. Only try and wait patiently; God will give us rain without your medicines.

R.D.: Mahala-ma-kapa-a-a!! Well, I always thought white men were wise till this morning. Who ever thought of making trial of starvation? Is death pleasant then?

M.D.: Could you make it rain on one spot and not on another?

R.D.: I wouldn't think of trying. I like to see the whole country green, and all the people glad; the women clapping their hands and giving me their ornaments for thankfulness, and lulli-looing for joy.

M.D.: I think you deceive both them and yourself.

R.D.: Well, then, there is a pair of us (meaning both are rogues).

The above is only a specimen of their way of reasoning, in which, when the language is well understood, they are perceived to be remarkably acute. These arguments are generally known, and I never succeeded in convincing a single individual of their fallacy, though I tried to do so in every way I could think of. Their faith in charms as medicine is unbounded. The general effect of argument is to produce the impression that you are not anxious for rain at all; and it is very undesirable to allow the idea to spread that you do not take a generous interest in their welfare."

Appendix 5

HINTS FOR SOLUTION OF EXERCISES IN REASONING

FIRST SERIES, P. 10

1. Where were the natives when they made the remark quoted?
2. What, exactly, is the nation "giving away?"
3. Try the following variant: "In a city of at least 366,000 inhabitants, at least 1,000 must have their birthdays on the same day of the year." Why?
4. Calculate the number of colored persons, then the number of colored women.
5. Are we told what percentage of nonsmokers have bad teeth?
6. Would a brave man and a coward differ in their answer to the question, "Are you brave?"
7. Use the data concerning heights to find out who is the man whose height is *nearest* to that of the violinist. Then use the number of phonograph records to show that this man is not the pianist's son.
8. What must the first player do in order to be in a position after the first move always to *imitate* what the other player does?
9. What is the shortest distance the basket must be carried? Would carrying it further than this conceivably involve less total work?
10. After the switch is turned at A, how much information shall we have?
11. Argue from the standpoint of the winner. First assume that you have a *blue* mark, and see how much you can infer.
12. Try treating two of the three children as *one party* to the transaction, thus reducing the problem to the case of two children dividing the cake.
13. Use capital letters for the men, and small letters for the owners of the cars. Then write down the information given in the form of a series of inequalities, e.g., $B \neq f$.

Appendix 5 (continued)

HINTS FOR SOLUTION OF EXERCISES IN REASONING

SECOND SERIES, P. 156

1. Suppose the quiz is not given by the Friday after the announcement. Will the date of the quiz then be known? What, then, is known at the time of the announcement of the quiz?

2. Consider the product of b by b (line 2) for information about the possible values of b. Next consider the product of ab by b (line 2) for further information about b. Look at line 4 to determine the value of h, and so on.

3. Would the argument apply equally well to seeing the moon, a lamp, a person's face?

4. What does "fall" mean here? Is the term used in the same sense each time?

5. What are the colors of the squares that the domino covers when placed on the chessboard?

6. Could Annabel get no money at all under the conditions of the will?

7. Imagine that the officer leaves New York on the 8th of the month. Which west-bound ships of the line are at sea?

8. Use small letters to designate ladies, capital letters for the men. Then tabulate all the information supplied.

9. Assume there is at least one train in each direction. Represent the stations by dots, and each train by a line going through the dots representing the stations at which the train stops.

10. Similar to Question 8.

11. If the barber shaves himself, he is shaved by the barber. If he does not shave himself, he must be shaved by the barber.

12. Imagine the maze to be carved out of a surrounding mass of rock. Is there a continuous boundary between the rock and the interior of the maze?

13. Argue from the standpoint of one of the players. Then let him consider what the *other* player will be arguing meanwhile.

14. Consider first the possibility that the first player, or A, has at least one move such that no matter how B plays, A can (with best play) always win. Then consider the remaining possibility.

Appendix 6

ANSWERS TO COMPREHENSION TESTS

1. (page 10)	TFFTT	FTTFT
2. (pages 28-29)	TFFTF	TFFTF
3. (page 51)	FTTFF	FTFTT
4. (page 75)	TFFFF	TTFTT
5. (page 93)	TTTFT	TFTTF
6. (page 109)	FFFTT	FTFFT
7. (page 129)	TTFTF	TTTFF
8. (pages 151-152)	FFFFF	TTFFT
9. (page 178)	FFTFF	TTFFT
10. (page 199)	FFTTT	FTFTT
11. (page 224)	TFFFF	FFTTF
12. (pages 242-243)	FTFTF	FFTTF
13. (pages 267-268)	FTFFT	TTFTF
14. (pages 286-287)	TTFFF	TFTTF
15. (pages 308-309)	FTFFT	TTTFF
16. (page 330)	TTTFF	TFTTF
17. (pages 352-353)	FTFFF	TTFFT
18. (pages 373-374)	TTFTT	FFFTF
19. (page 399)	FTFFT	TTTFF

GLOSSARY

This glossary contains most of the technical terms and expressions used in this book. An asterisk shows that the term in question was invented, or used in some special sense. Italicized words occur elsewhere in the glossary.

A. Used as an abbreviation for a positive *universal* proposition.

Accident, fallacy of. A fallacy involving the application of a rule or *generalization* to cases to which it is not intended to apply.

Ad hominem, argument. An argument that attempts to disprove an opponent's position by using propositions asserted or accepted by him. (More generally: any appeal to the opponent's convictions or prejudices.)

Agreement, method of. A method of *induction,* in which the evidence for a generalization *Every case of a is also a case of b* consists of a number of instances agreeing only in the presence of both *a* and *b*. For a more exact account, see page 296.

Alternation. The *operation* by means of which the *compound* proposition, *Either A or B* is obtained from the original propositions, *A, B*. If the resulting proposition is *Either A or B or both,* the case is one of **inclusive** or **weak*** alternation; if the proposition is *either A or B but not both,* **exclusive** or **strong*** alternation. (Some writers prefer the name "disjunction.")

Ambiguity. A word (or other sign) is ambiguous in a certain usage when the reader or hearer is unable to decide between alternative and apparently equally appropriate meanings of the word.

Ambiguity, fallacy of. A fallacy depending upon a shift of meaning in a word occurring more than once in an argument. See also: *Equivocation, fallacy of.*

Analogy. *1.* Similarity (of two things). 2. An argument based on such similarity (*i.e.,* an *argument from analogy*).

Analogy, argument from. An argument in which the known similarity of two things in certain respects is used as a reason for expecting them to be similar in other respects. See also: *Basis of resemblance, linking generalization.*

Antecedent. In a *conditional proposition,* having the form *If A then B,* the proposition *A* is the antecedent. See also: *Consequent.*

Argument. A process of reasoning in which the truth of some proposition (the conclusion) is shown, or is alleged to be shown, to depend on the truth of others (the premises).

Argumentative leap, fallacy of.* The fallacy committed in an argument whose conclusion is consistent with, but does not follow from the premises. (Commonly known as "non sequitur"–literally, "it does not follow.")

Asserting the consequent, fallacy of. An argument having the form: *If A then B,* also *B;* therefore *A.*

Assumption. *1.* A proposition treated as true without examination. *2.* A proposition needed in an argument but not part of the explicit *statement* of the argument.

Authority. A person alleged to be qualified to give an opinion on a subject is an authority on that subject. For a discussion of the meaning of "qualified," see page 255. See also: *Dogmatic authority.*

Basic belief.* A belief having no *reasons.* Contrasted with: *derived belief.*

Basis of resemblance.* In *analogy,* the set of properties that the things compared are known to have in common.

Begging the question, fallacy of. See: *Circle, arguing in a.*

Blanks.* Spaces left in the symbolization of the *form* of propositions or arguments. They serve the same purpose as *variables.*

Chain argument.* An argument whose premises consist of a set of *conditional propositions,* the consequent of each premise being identical with the *antecedent* of the next. (More commonly known as "hypothetical syllogism.")

Circle, arguing in a. The fallacy of assuming what is to be proved, either by using as a premise the conclusion itself or a proposition that could not be established except by assuming the truth of the conclusion.

Circular definition. A definition in which the *definiendum,* or a part of it, occurs in the *definiens.* Also applied to a definition whose *definiens* contains a term *polar* to a term occurring in the *definiendum.*

Class. A set of things labelled by the same name or having some common property. Each of the set or collection of things is said to be a member of the class.

Classification. *1.* The process of arranging things in classes. *2.* The set of names and definitions resulting.

Code letter.* One of the symbols, *A, E, I,* or *O,* used to indicate the four types of *subject-predicate* propositions.

Complex proposition. See: *Compound proposition.*

Composition, fallacy of. A fallacy in which what is true of a part is, on that account alone, alleged to be also true of the whole. See also: *Division, fallacy of.*

Compound proposition. A proposition constructed out of other propositions (its components or constituents). Also called a complex proposition. Contrasted with: *Simple proposition.*

Conclusion. See: *Argument.*

Concomitant variations, method of. A method of *induction* in which the evidence for *Every case of a is also a case of b* consists in showing that cases of change in *a* are also cases of change in *b*. For fuller discussion, see page 316.

Conditional argument. An argument containing one or more *conditional propositions* as premises.

Conditional proposition. A proposition having the form *If A then B,* where both *A* and *B* are propositions. (Sometimes called a "hypothetical" proposition.) See also: *Antecedent, consequent.*

Confirmation table.* A device for displaying the inductive evidence for a generalization in a standard symbolic form. For further details, see page 284.

Confirmatory instance.* A confirmatory instance of the generalization *Every case of a is also a case of b* is a true proposition having the form *This thing which is a is also b* (symbolized $a \rightarrow b$). Opposed to: *Disconfirmatory instance.*

Conjunction. The operation by means of which the compound proposition *Both A and B* is derived from the two propositions *A, B.*

Connotation. The connotation of a term is the sum total of properties that anything must have in order that the term will apply to it. See also: *Denotation.*

Consequent. In a *conditional proposition,* having the form *If A then B,* the proposition *B* is the consequent. See also: *Antecedent.*

Constant, scientific. *1.* A property that is a permanent feature of some series of observations made by scientists. **2.** The measure of such a property.

Context. The circumstances accompanying an utterance. That part of the setting consisting only of the other words uttered at the time makes up the **verbal context.**

Contextual meaning. The meaning a word (or other *sign*) has in a particular *context.* Opposed to: *Dictionary meaning.*

Contradiction. The operation by which a proposition is converted into its contradictory.

Contradictory. The contradictory of a proposition *A* is the proposition *B* which is true when *A* is false and false when *A* is true. Distinguished from: *Contrary.*

Contrapositive.* The contrapositive of the *conditional proposition, If A then B,* is the proposition *If not-B then not-A.* (This word is more commonly used in the theory of the syllogism.)

Contrary. Two propositions are said to be contraries if they cannot simultaneously be true.

Converse. The converse of *If A then B* is *If B then A.* (Also used by some writers on the theory of the syllogism in such a way that the converse of *All a are b* is *All b are a.*)

Copula. *1.* The relation (of inclusion or exclusion) connecting the subject and predicate of a proposition having *subject-predicate form.* *2.* The word or symbol for this relation.

D. Used in a *distribution-pattern* to show that a term is *distributed.*

Deduction. *1.* Reasoning that aims at *valid* conclusions. *2.* A specimen of such reasoning (*i.e.,* a deductive argument).

Definiendum. The word, or other *sign,* to be explained in a *definition.*

Definiens. The phrase or sentence that explains the *definiendum's* meaning.

Definition. *1.* The process of explaining the meaning of a word, phrase, or other *sign.* *2.* The words used in this process. See also: *Definiendum, definiens.*

Denotation. The denotation of a term is the sum total of things to which that term applies. See also: *Connotation.*

Denying the antecedent, fallacy of. An argument having the form: *If A then B,* also *not-A;* therefore *not-B.*

Derived belief.* A belief having *reasons.* Contrasted with: *Basic belief.*

Dictionary meaning. The meaning that a word, or other *sign,* has according to the conventions of the language to which it belongs. Also called "standard meaning." Opposed to: *Contextual meaning.*

Difference, method of. A method of *induction,* in which the evidence for a generalization *Every case of a is also a case of b* consists of two instances alike in all respects except that in one the presence of *a* is accompanied by the presenec of *b,* while in the other the absence of *b* is accompanied by the absence of *a.* For a more exact account, see page 299.

Differentia. The characteristic or property used in dividing a *genus* into its *species* in the process of *division* or *classification.*

Dilemma. An argument having the form ($A \vee B, A \supset C, B \supset D$; therefore $C \vee D$) or special cases of this form.

Disconfirmatory instance. A disconfirmatory instance of the generalization *Every case of a is also a case of b* is a true proposition having the form *This thing is a but is also not b* (symbolized $a \rightarrow b'$). Opposed to: *Confirmatory instance.*

Distributed. See: *Distribution of terms.*

Distribution of terms. A term (*subject* or *predicate*) is distributed in a proposition when the proposition refers to every member of the class concerned. (Thus the subjects of *universal* propositions are distributed.) Opposed to: *Undistributed term.*

Distribution-pattern.* The representation in diagrammatic form of the distribution of the terms of a proposition or syllogism. (Thus the proposition *some men are not happy* has the distribution-pattern "UD".) When an entire syllogism is analysed, certain additional symbols are needed in order to show the location of the terms. For fuller details see page 141.

Division. The progressive decomposition of an inclusive class into smaller classes and sub-classes contained within it.

Division, definition by. Explaining the *connotation* of a term by showing its position in a scheme of *division.*

Division, fallacy of. A fallacy in which what is true of a whole is, on that account alone, alleged to be true also of a part. See also: *Composition, fallacy of.*

Dogmatic authority. An *authority* whose opinions are not to be challenged, either by other authorities or by appeal to methods other than that of authority.

E. Used as an abbreviation for a *negative universal* proposition.

Elimination, proof by. An argument in which at least one of a number of propositions is known to be true, and all except one are then shown to be false (usually by *indirect argument*).

Emotive language. Words particularly adapted to the expression and communication of feelings, especially by *suggestion.* Contrasted with: *Neutral language.*

Enumeration, simple. A method of *induction* in which the evidence for *Every case of a is also a case of b* consists of a number of instances in which the presence of *a* is accompanied by the presence of *b*. For a more exact account, see page 291.

Equivocation. Deliberate shift in the meaning of words used.

Equivocation, fallacy of. A fallacy depending on equivocation.

Existential proposition.* A proposition asserting that some object or objects exist.

Existential rule of the syllogism.* The rule that in a valid syllogism the conclusion cannot be particular unless one premise is particular. (It is understood that *universal* propositions are taken in a non-existential sense.)

Explicit generalization.* A generalization becomes explicit in the degree that the understood but unstated conditions are formally presented. A fully explicit generalization has the form *Every case of a, no matter what else happens, is also a case of b.*

Extensive measurement. A type of *measurement* in which the ratios and sums of the numbers assigned have objective significance. Contrasted with: *Intensive measurement.*

Form. Shape, pattern, arrangement of parts. See also: *Material, structure.* For illustrations, see page 45.

Form, logical. The form of propositions and arguments.

Four terms, fallacy of. The fallacy committed in a syllogism that mentions four classes while apparently referring only to three.

Function. *B* is said to be a function of *A* when: (1) *A* and *B* admit of degrees; and also (2) if all other factors are held unchanged, each case of a change in *A* is also a case of a change in *B.*

Generalization. A proposition concerning all or some members of a class. A **uniform generalization** has the form *Every case of a is also a case of b;* a **statistical generalization,** the form *Most (or such and such a proportion) of a are also b.*

Genus. A class *a* is a genus of the class *b* when *a* contains *b,* so that every *member* of *b* is also a member of *a.*

Hypothesis. *1.* A proposition not known to be definitely true or false, examined for the sake of determining the consequences that would follow from its truth. 2. a tentative solution of a problem.

Hypothetical syllogism. See: *Chain argument.*

I Used as an abbreviation for a *positive particular* proposition.

Ignoratio elenchi. See: *Irrelevant conclusion.*

Illicit process, fallacy of. The fallacy committed in a syllogism containing a term distributed in the conclusion but undistributed in the premise in which the term occurs.

Impersonal aspect of utterance.* Those features of the utterance that do not give information about the speaker. Opposed to: *Personal aspect of utterance.*

Implication. The operation by means of which the proposition $A \supset B$ is derived from the propositions *A, B.* (Commonly used also as equivalent to *suggestion.*)

Indefiniteness. A proposition is indefinite in the degree that it omits more detailed information that could be supplied concerning the situation to which it refers.

Indirect argument. An argument in which a proposition *P* is proved by showing that if not-*P* were true, *P* must be true.

Induction. A process of using evidence concerning some members of a class of objects as a basis for an assertion about all or more members of that class.

Inference. See: *Deduction.*

Infinite regress. An argument in which the premises are made to depend on other premises, which in turn depend on others, and so on without end.

Inquiry.* Proceedings directed toward obtaining reliable beliefs about some topic or subject.

Intensive measurement. A type of *measurement* in which only the relative orders of the numbers assigned is significant. Contrasted with: *Extensive measurement.*

Irrelevant conclusion, fallacy of. The fallacy committed when an argument has a conclusion other than the one it set out to establish. (Sometimes called: "ignoratio elenchi.")

Joint method of agreement and difference. A method of induction in which the generalization *Every case of a is also a case of b* is supported by instances agreeing only in the presence of *a* and *b* and instances agreeing only in the absence of both *b* and *a.*

Linking generalization.* In *argument from analogy,* the generalization needed to justify the passage from the known to the predicted similarities in the things compared. See also: *Basis of resemblance.*

Major premise. In a *syllogism,* the premise containing the *major term.* See also: *Minor premise.*

Major term. In a *syllogism,* the predicate of the conclusion. See also: *Minor term.*

Material. Whatever has *form.* See also: *Structure.*

Measurement. Assignment of numbers, in accordance with some regular procedure, to the results of observations. (The term is commonly used in somewhat more restricted senses.)

Member. See: *Class.*

Metaphor. A word occurs metaphorically in a certain *context* if it is there used to indicate a *referent* similar to but different from that to which it normally refers.

Middle term. In a *syllogism,* the term occurring in both premises. See also: *Major term, minor term.*

Minor premise. In a *syllogism,* the premise containing the minor term. See also: *Major premise.*

Minor term. In a *syllogism,* the subject of the conclusion. See also: *Major term.*

Negation, logical. See: *Contradiction.*

Negative proposition. A proposition of *subject-predicate form* whose *copula* is the relation of exclusion, *i.e.,* a proposition of form *Some (or all) a are excluded from b.*

Neutral language. Language that is not *emotive.*

Non-sequitur, fallacy of. See: *Argumentative leap.*

O. Used as an abbreviation for a *negative particular proposition.*

Operation. A word used to refer to the way in which complex entities are related to the simpler ones of which they are composed. Thus the number 7 + 5 is said to be derived from the numbers 7, 5 by the operation of addition. A **logical operation** is an operation on propositions (such as *implication, alternation,* etc.).

Particular proposition. A proposition of *subject-predicate form* having the *quantifier* "some." Contrasted with: *universal proposition.*

Personal aspect of utterance.* Those features of an utterance that convey information about the speaker, especially about feelings, attitudes and wishes of his that caused the utterance.

Place-holder.* See: *Variable.*

Polar words.* A and B are polar words if it is impossible for an instance of A to exist unless some corresponding instance of B also exists. (Thus "husband" and "wife" are polar words.)

Positive proposition. A proposition of *subject-predicate form* whose *copula* is the relation of inclusion, *i.e.,* a proposition of form *Some (or all) a are included in b.*

Predicate, logical. The second class mentioned in the expression of a proposition in *subject-predicate form.* See also: *Subject, logical.*

Premise. See: *Argument.*

Problem-solving situation. A situation in which an answer is required to a question, in the absence of specific information concerning the appropriate procedures to be used in seeking the answer.

Process:product shift of meaning.* The use of a word to refer sometimes to the doing of something (a process) and at other times to a result of such doing (a product).

Proposition. A term used to refer to what there is in common in a number of acts of knowing, asserting, believing, doubting, etc. A proposition is expressed by a sentence, and must be either true or false. See the fuller account on page 19.

Quality. The negative or positive character of a *subject-predicate* proposition.

Quality, rule of. One of the three rules of the valid syllogism, concerned with determining the circumstances in which the conclusion is positive or negative. For further details, see page 140.

Quantifier. The word "some" or "all" indicating the *distribution* of the subject in a proposition having *subject-predicate form.* (Words such as "many," "a few," etc., are also sometimes called quantifiers.)

Quantity, rule of. One of the three rules of the valid syllogism, concerned with the distribution of the major, minor, and middle terms. For further details see page 140.

Reason * (for a belief). A proposition that the owner of the belief could honestly offer in its defense. For discussion, see page 251.

Rebuttal of a dilemma. A method of countering the dilemma ($A \vee B$, $A \supset C, B \supset D$; therefore $C \vee D$) by a new dilemma ($A \vee B, A \supset D'$, $B \supset C'$; therefore $C' \vee D'$).

Reductio ad absurdum. An argument in which a proposition *P* is proved by showing that if not-*P* were true, two mutually contradictory propositions could be deduced.

Referent.* Whatever is mentioned or referred to by a *sign.* (Some writers apply the word only to the *denotation* of a sign.)

Relativity of definition, principle of.* The principle that a *definition* ought to be formulated in a manner intelligible and useful to the particular person addressed.

Reported definition.* A *definition* claiming to describe how the *definiendum* is actually used. Includes *dictionary* and *contextual* definitions. Contrasted with: *Stipulated definition.*

Semantics. The study of the theory of symbolism, especially the theory of the relation of symbols to the objects they represent.

Shift in meaning.* Used to refer to the capacity of a word (or other sign) to change its meaning according to the *context* of its occurrence. (Some writers use "ambiguity" for this.) See also: *Process:product, sign:referent.*

Sign.* An object that leads the observer to attend to something other than the object itself. Anything having meaning. For a better description and examples see page 162. (Some writers prefer to say "symbol".)

Sign:referent shift of meaning.* The use of a sign to mean sometimes the thing-mentioned by the sign (its *referent*) and at other times the sign itself.

Signal.* The simplest kind of *sign.* For examples, see page 163.

Simple proposition. A proposition having no parts that are themselves propositions. Contrasted with: *Compound proposition.*

Slipping between the horns (of a dilemma). A method of rejecting a *dilemma* by denying the truth of the alternative premise (usually by claiming to find a third proposition representing a position midway between the alternatives offered).

Sound argument. An argument whose conclusion is reached by a reliable method. In the case of a deductive argument, an argument having true premises and a valid conclusion.

Species. If class *a* contains class *b,* so that every *member* of *b* is a member of *a, b* is a species of *a.* See also: *Genus.*

Statement.* An explicitly formulated assertion, command, desire, judgment, etc. Opposed to: *Suggestion.* (It would be more usual to confine this to the formulation of propositions alone.)

Stipulated definition. An explanation of how some word or other will be used. A proposal or resolution concerning the meaning of a term. Opposed to: *Reported definition.*

Structure.* An object consisting of *material* having some *form.*

Subject, logical. The first class mentioned in the expression of a proposition in *subject-predicate form.*

Subject-predicate form. The form of any proposition capable of being symbolized as *Some* (*or all*) *s are included in* (*excluded from*) *p* (where *s* and *p* are classes).

Suggestion.* Whatever is conveyed, though not explicitly formulated, by an utterance. Opposed to: *Statement.*

Syllogism. An argument consisting of two premises and a conclusion, purporting to be all of *subject-predicate form* and to involve three classes altogether.

Symbol.* An artificial, non-verbal *sign* (such as '⊃,' '∨,' etc.).

Tabloid formula, fallacy of.* A fallacy in which some slogan, catchword, or over-simplified statement is accepted without critical examination.

Taking a dilemma by the horns. A method of rejecting a *dilemma* by denying the truth of one of the conditional premises.

Term. *1.* A word, phrase, or other *sign.* *2.* In the theory of the syllogism, the classes mentioned by propositions of subject-predicate form.

Testimony.* Any assertion, or set of assertions, made by another person. (The word is commonly restricted to a narrower class of such assertions, *e.g.,* to the report of personal experience.) See also: *Authority.*

Truth-table. A diagram in which the *truth-value* of a compound proposition is shown for each combination of truth-values of its constituents.

Truth-value. The truth-value of a proposition is truth or falsity (as the case may be).

U. Used in a *distribution-pattern* to show that a term is undistributed.

Undistributed term. A term (*subject* or *predicate*) is undistributed in a proposition when the proposition does not refer to every member of the class concerned. (Thus the subjects of *particular propositions* are undistributed.) See also: *Distribution of terms.*

Undistributed middle, fallacy of. The fallacy committed by a syllogism in which the middle term is undistributed in each premise.

Universal proposition. A proposition of *subject-predicate form* having the *quantifier* "all." Contrasted with: *Particular proposition.*

Utterance. A statement; words or other signs actually pronounced by a speaker, writer or other user of signs.

Vagueness. A word (or other *sign*) is vague in a certain situation when it is impossible to discover from the word's definition whether it does or does not apply in that situation.

Valid. An *argument* (or its conclusion) is valid when it is impossible for all the premises to be true while the conclusion is false.

Variable. A *symbol* (usually a letter from the end of the alphabet) inserted into the symbolization of a proposition or argument to assist in displaying the *form* of the letter. (Also used by writers to refer to the alleged referents of such symbols.)

Venn diagram. Geometrical diagrams (usually circles) used to show the information given by *subject-predicate* propositions or the premises of a syllogism. See page 122.

Verification, public. Confirmation of one scientist's findings by other qualified observers. (**Public verifiability** is the possibility of such testing.)

$\supset$ "A $\supset$ B" means "Either A is false or B is true or both" (or "If A then B"). Used in symbolizing *conditional* propositions.

$'$ A$'$ is the *contradictory* of A.

& The sign of *conjunction.*

$\vee$ "either . . . or . . . or both"; the sign of *inclusive alternation.*

$\veebar$ "either . . . or . . . but not both"; the sign of *exclusive alternation.*

$\equiv$ "if and only if." (Sometimes referred to as the sign of "logical equivalence.")

$<$ "is included in." See: *Copula.*

$\nless$ "is excluded from." See: *Copula.*

$\rightarrow$ "$A_1 \rightarrow B_1$" means "this particular case of A also a case of B." Used in *confirmation-tables* to represent *confirmatory-instances.*

SUGGESTIONS FOR FURTHER READING

(*Note:* I have tried to make this list quite short, including only books certain to be useful to a beginner in logic. The bibliographies contained in several of the books are a sufficient guide to wider reading. E = "elementary." A = "advanced.")

General works

Eaton, Ralph M., *General Logic.* New York: Charles Scribner's Sons, 1931.

Cohen, Morris R., and Nagel, Ernest, *Introduction to Logic and Scientific Method.* New York: Harcourt, Brace and Co., Inc., 1942.

Stebbing, L. S., *Modern Introduction to Logic.* London: Methuen & Co., Ltd., 2nd. ed., 1933.

All three are "intermediate" textbooks, considerably harder than the present book.

Conditional argument

Ambrose, Alice and Lazerowitz, Morris, *Fundamentals of Symbolic Logic.* New York: Rinehart & Co., Inc., 1948. A good introduction to the vast field of symbolic or mathematical logic.

The syllogism

Sinclair, W. A., *Traditional Formal Logic.* London: Methuen & Co., Ltd., 2nd. ed., 1945. E

Joseph, H. W. B., *Introduction to Logic.* New York: Oxford University Press, 1916. A

See also the first three books in this list.

Language and related topics

Bloomfield, Leonard, *Language.* New York: Henry Holt & Co., Inc., 1933. A Very useful for general reference.

Langer, Susanne K., *Philosophy in a New Key*. New York: The New American Library, 1948. The title is misleading: largely concerned with semantics.

Miller, George A., *Language and Communication*. New York: McGraw-Hill Book Co., Inc., 1951. A useful guide to the psychology of language.

Richards, I. A., *How To Read a Page*. New York: W. W. Norton & Co., Inc., 1942. Stimulating discussion of ambiguity, with illustrative examples.

Walpole, Hugh R., *Semantics*. New York: W. W. Norton & Co., Inc., 1941. **E** The best of the elementary books on this subject.

Fallacies

Schopenhauer, Arthur, *The Art of Controversy*. (translated by T. Bailey Saunders) London: Allen & Unwin, Ltd., 1896. **E** Also contained in most collected editions of Schopenhauer's writings.

Sidgwick, Alfred, *Fallacies*. New York: D. Appleton-Century Co., Inc., 1884. Well worth reading on most of the relevant topics.

Stebbing, L. S., *Thinking To Some Purpose*. New York: Penguin Books, 1939. **E**

Thouless, R. H., *Straight and Crooked Thinking*. London: Hodder and Stoughton, Ltd., 1930. **E**

The two last books are more entertaining than most novels. Warmly recommended.

Inductive Methods

Mill, John Stuart, *System of Logic*. London, 1843. Worthier of reading than most later accounts. See the second book in this list for criticism of Mill's doctrines.

Scientific Method

Bacon, Francis, *Novum Organum*. 1620. A great classic, beautifully written. Not to be missed.

Campbell, Norman, *What Is Science?* London: Methuen & Co., Ltd., 1921. **E** The best elementary account.

Jevons, W. Stanley, *Principles of Science*. New York: The Macmillan Co., 1874. Only Books III to V are recommended. Slow-moving, in the Victorian fashion, but very illuminating on most topics.

Ritchie, A. D., *Scientific Method*. New York: Harcourt, Brace and Co., Inc., 1923. A good discussion at the "intermediate" level of difficulty.

Margenau, Henry, *The Nature of Physical Reality*. New York: McGraw-Hill Book Co., Inc., 1950. **A** Full of interesting materials for the advanced student.

Meyerson, Emile, *Identity and Reality*. (translated by Kate Loewenberg) New York: The Macmillan Co., 1930. **A** One of the outstanding modern books on philosophy of science.

Examples of scientific method

Leonard, Jonathan Norton, *Enjoyment of Science*. New York: Doubleday, Doran & Co., Inc., 1942. **E** A good guide to the relatively "popular" literature of scientific research.

Cambridge Readings in the Literature of Science. New York: The Macmillan Co., 1928. Short extracts from original papers, with useful explanatory comment.

The *Everyman Library*. New York: E. P. Dutton & Co., Inc., contains reprints of several classical works by earlier scientists.

For contemporary examples see the magazines *Science* and *The Scientific Monthly* (both published by the American Association for the Advancement of Science) and *The Scientific American*.

Index

INDEX